Roads to Wisdom,
Conversations with Ten Nobel Laureates
in Economics

I dedicate this book to the memory of my parents, Jürgen Horn and Ilse Ritter, born way back in the twenties, both economists, endowed with endless sympathy and a great appetite for the world of ideas.

Roads to Wisdom, Conversations with Ten Nobel Laureates in Economics

Karen Ilse Horn

Head of Berlin Office,
Institut der deutschen Wirtschaft Köln, Germany

Edward Elgar
Cheltenham, UK • Northampton, MA, USA

Published by
Edward Elgar Publishing Limited
The Lypiatts
15 Lansdown Road
Cheltenham
Glos GL50 2JA
UK

Edward Elgar Publishing, Inc.
William Pratt House
9 Dewey Court
Northampton
Massachusetts 01060
USA

A catalogue record for this book
is available from the British Library

Library of Congress Control Number: 2009928616

PEFC
PEFC/16-33-111
CATG-PEFC-052
www.pefc.org

ISBN 978 1 84844 670 0 (cased)

Printed and bound by MPG Books Group, UK

Contents

PART III   ALL THOSE ROADS TO WISDOM: ANSWERS

Acknowledgements

I would like to thank some people without whose support this book might not have seen the light:

Johannes Ritter, my soul mate, for his loving care, his unfailing encouragement, thoughtful advice, patience and understanding, for sharing the fun and also the burden.

Michael Wohlgemuth, a true friend, for his invaluable support in discussing my concept and method, in drawing my attention to some relevant literature and even providing it, and of course in shouldering the tedious task of first proofreading.

Ulrike Hotopp for her example as much in faithful friendship as in work ethic, for her enthusiasm, support, and intelligent comments, as ever.

Wolfgang Schürer, Chairman of the Board of the Foundation Lindau Nobelprizewinners Meetings at Lake Constance, and his wife Monika, who encouraged me substantially and insistently enough to get me started.

Edward Elgar and his entire staff, for their friendly enthusiasm, promptness and absolutely outstanding professional work.

And of course the ten Nobel laureates who so kindly agreed to share many hours with me talking about their path. Those conversations often made my day and much more.

PART I

All those roads to wisdom: questions

Purpose and theory

'All roads lead to Rome'. Everybody has heard this phrase plenty of times. Maybe a little less if one belongs to a religious group other than Catholicism. One of the current etymological explanations of this saying is that in the Middle Ages, that city, with the Vatican in its center, was viewed as the (spiritual) center of the Christian world. The saying itself is derived from the 'Liber Parabolarum' written by Alanus de Insulis in the twelfth century, where he says: 'Mille viae ducunt hominem per saecula Romam' (a thousand roads lead mankind always to Rome). While this was of course meant in a positive sense, the phrase was later also used pejoratively, denouncing Rome's overarching imperial control and intrusion. A more secular explanation just refers to the road system in ancient Rome, where all the empire's roads radiated out from the capital city. The metaphorical meaning stays the same: if one has a goal, the essential thing is to get there – and one will get there. It doesn't matter which way. There is not 'the' one right road. Everything depends on where one is and when, what means one disposes of, what one's preferences are and what one thinks one should and shouldn't do.

The same can be said about academic progress, which is the core topic of this book. For scholars making their individual contributions, the essential thing is probably just to get there – provided that once you get there, you aren't confronted with the bad surprise that 'there is no there there', as Gertrude Stein famously quipped in her book *Everybody's Autobiography*[1]. . . and there may in fact be multiple instances of bitter disillusionment. But all these caveats put aside, for any scientist, it is progress as such that is important. As George J. Stigler has it, 'the great fascination of scientific endeavor . . . is precisely in the speculative pursuit of new ideas that will widen the horizon of our understanding of the world'.[2] After the fact, it doesn't matter how he or she got prepared for making a contribution to progress in the field. As long as it was efficient, it was good. The goal is the goal. Contrary to the popular Chinese saying, after the fact, the specific individual itinerary doesn't matter so much. The essential thing is to have this one decisive idea, to make these one or more original contributions that qualify as a move in the right direction, or progress, however one chooses to define it exactly. Or *wisdom*, if I am allowed to use an even more encompassing, elevated notion. Wisdom is more than knowledge, it is a state of mind. It is love of learning, and it is this knowledge judiciously applied in order to solve problems. As Confucius said, wisdom comes from reflection, imitation and experience. Adam Smith speaks of 'prudence' here.[3]

I have chosen the notion of 'wisdom' as part of the title of this book not solely because I happen to take delight in puns,[4] but much more so for the sake of clearly indicating that I have drawn some of my inspiration from the remarkable work of the great Austrian economist and social philosopher Friedrich August von Hayek (1899–1992). Hayek's research has provided us with an important defense of classical liberalism and free-market capitalism against socialist and collectivist thought in the mid-twentieth century. He taught at the London School of Economics, in Chicago, in Freiburg (Germany) and in Salzburg (Austria). He shared the 1974 Nobel Prize in Economics with his ideological rival Gunnar Myrdal, which is one irony. The other, more bitter irony is that he received the prize for his 'pioneering work in the theory of money and economic fluctuations and for their penetrating analysis of the interdependence of economic, social and institutional phenomena' – and not exactly for his outstanding social philosophy.

Summing up his own contributions, Hayek always liked to say that, throughout his academic career, he had made one discovery and two inventions. The discovery was the knowledge-assembling and knowledge-generating features of the price system in decentralized, competitive markets. The inventions were the denationalization of money and a specific system of government with two chambers. Hayek's discovery clearly was more fundamental than the two inventions.

I have to stress that, other than the pun, meant as reverence only, there is no substantial analogy intended with Hayek's famous book. *The Road to Serfdom* was an alarming outcry voiced in 1944, grown out of Hayek's impression that collectivist and totalitarian forces were winning the upper hand again everywhere. More than sixty years later, his concern hasn't lost any of its acuteness and his warning none of its importance; quite the contrary.[5] However, my book is just about the determinants of individual itineraries that contribute to the advancement of economic theory, not about the general state of the world, or the ideological undercurrents directing it. And even here, in my much more limited field, my purpose is not to warn the profession that it is moving in a fatally wrong direction – or else I would have had to call my book 'The Road to Random' or 'The Road to Boredom' instead, for example. While it is indeed true that I view the development of the economic sciences with a substantial dose of skepticism, especially after the recent financial crisis that exploded in the autumn of 2008, this is not the major thrust of my book.

The inspiration that I have taken from Hayek and which serves as my starting block here is his one major philosophical discovery, namely his insight about the '*division of knowledge*' in markets through which evolution and – perhaps – progress take place, in an analogy to Adam Smith's division of labor.[6] Both 'divisions' are aspects of those processes of social interaction in which no central body has or even needs oversight over everything that is going on. There is no super mind directing it all. The spontaneous processes of anonymous social self-coordination through markets are 'marvels', as Hayek puts it.[7] Here, in this book, the focus will be on the division of knowledge in the process of social self-coordination not with respect to the provision and allocation of goods and services in general, but with respect to the generation of knowledge itself – that is, within science.

Hayek's theory is based on Adam Smith's broad perspective on self-regulating or self-organizing systems in which individual interests are harmoniously aligned.[8] The market is the prime example of such a self-regulating system; it serves as a platform for social interaction and exchange, and as such it is a manifestation of the *spontaneous order* that evolves through social interaction.[9] It is a *cosmos*, an order that pursues no given hierarchy of ends, unlike the fixed plan of the consciously and intentionally arranged *taxis*, reflecting a particular hierarchy of ends that individuals manage to balance within their own selves, their families, or any other small group they belong to.[10] For the market order, Hayek also suggests the term 'catallactics', derived from Greek verb *katallattein*, which means not only 'to exchange', but also 'to admit into the community' and 'to change from enemy into friend'.[11] This spontaneous order arises from human action but is not specifically planned by men. Hayek's famous phrase, borrowed from Adam Ferguson, is: 'the results of human action but not of human design'.[12] A classic and often-quoted example for an outcome of such a spontaneous process is money:[13] as individuals sought to exchange goods more efficiently than by means of barter trade, at some point they started using coins made from precious metals. This money found mutual recognition and thus spread out to become an economic institution, very much as an unintended consequence of rational individual action. This is Hayek's underlying crucial point: no one actively made it. Norms, values and standards often evolve exactly in this same way.

Social interaction in the market place is not only recommended because it is free of coercion,[14] but also because it allows people to use their knowledge in the most productive, creative and innovative way. There are several essays of Hayek that, especially when taken together, make this point: 'Economics and knowledge' (1937/1980), 'The use of knowledge in society' (1945), and 'Competition as a discovery procedure' (1968). In his 1945 paper, Hayek describes that

the economic problem of society is thus not merely a problem of how to allocate given resources – if given is taken to mean given to a single mind which
deliberately solves the problem set by these data. It is rather a problem of how
to secure the best use of resources known to any of the members of society,
for ends whose relative importance only these individuals know. Or, to put
it briefly, it is a problem of the utilization of knowledge which is not given to
anyone in its totality.[15]

Given the 'unavoidable imperfection of man's knowledge', there is a
need for 'a process by which knowledge is constantly communicated and
acquired'.[16] The verb still missing here is 'generated' – but this follows
from his 1968 paper where he presents competition as 'a procedure for
the discovery of such facts as, without resort to it, would not be known
to anyone'[17] and the results of which are 'unpredictable and on the whole
different from those which anyone has, or could have, deliberately aimed
at'.[18]

In these three important papers, Hayek refers to knowledge not as the
sum, or aggregate stock of academic knowledge, but to the more humble,
individual 'knowledge of the particular circumstances of time and place',[19]
that is special or local knowledge that is necessarily distributed unevenly
throughout society. He argues that 'we need decentralization because only
thus can we insure that the knowledge of the particular circumstances of
time and place will be promptly used'.[20] In a competitive market, this task
is being performed by the price system. 'We must look at the price system
as such a mechanism for communicating information.'[21] As mentioned
earlier, this mechanism has been brought about in the course of cultural
evolution. 'The price system is just one of those formations which man
has learned to use . . . after he had stumbled on it without understanding
it. Through it not only a division of labour but also a coordinated utilization of resources based on an equally divided knowledge has become
possible.'[22]

This shall suffice for now to roughly sketch the framework of analysis
here, as it is inspired by Hayek. The science-as-market analogy will reappear later, in Part III of this book.

A CLOSER LOOK AT TIME AND PLACE

While Hayek, in his endeavor to explain social processes, didn't have
to bother himself with the particular characteristics of those individual,
dispersed bits and pieces of 'local knowledge' that are being accumulated,
spread and expanded through the process of social interaction, just like
it doesn't matter whether one starts from Berlin, Frankfurt, Blacksburg

VA, or Tucson AZ on one's way to Rome, it *is* however interesting to know what the particular individual ingredients are that have made existing scholars productive in this great social self-coordination process of science. This necessitates a switch from the macro to the micro level. In science viewed as a market, it is possible to picture the individual scholar as a producer/investor who offers his theories on the marketplace of ideas. At the same time, he is a customer/consumer who demands other people's scientific output as well. The focus here is now on why the producer produces what he produces, and why the customer seeks what he seeks.

Thus the aim is now to find out what the particular 'circumstances of time and place' – and character – have been in individual cases. This look at specific itineraries may help one to understand more generally what the prerequisites for scientific originality and overall academic excellence are and where it is that path-breaking ideas fundamentally tend to come from. As Paul A. Samuelson writes elsewhere, 'what is important in scholarship is an aesthetic sense for what is an important problem. Otherwise the facile mind can spend itself on patterns that are merely pretty.'[23] But what are the major sources of inspiration that makes us grasp which problems are important and which aren't? Beyond a given talent, does 'wisdom' come from within or from without? Does it help to be a lone wolf, working away on one's own, or is it systematically better to work as a team person, constantly interacting? Is it preferable to be a 'puzzler', as Hayek said, rather than to be a 'master of one's subject'?[24] What kind of approach does the modern market for ideas favor: is it rather that of the incremental 'puzzle-solver', as Robert M. Solow puts it,[25] or that of the 'system builder' who endeavors to build a 'theory of everything'?[26] And which of those is conducive to a true advance of knowledge in economics?

This volume is, however, not at all a handbook on how to make outstanding contributions and on how to become an academic celebrity.[27] First, because this is not really the goal. My aim here is ultimately to shed more light on the miraculous process of the generation of excellence and progress in science, both at a micro and a macro level. Second, because it would be an impossible task, too. There are way too many influences that one would have to control for. And yet, it will be rewarding to highlight a couple of them, at least tentatively. Third, as the title of this book already indicates, because there turn out to be many 'roads to wisdom'. The interviews will reveal just how breathtakingly varied these roads may be. And that, as such, may be enough of an encouragement for future scholars who might now grow up and later create different schools yet to be discovered.

It is thus not alone the spontaneous process of social self-coordination that must fill one with awe. One should marvel just as much at the courses of individual lives, at the amazing coincidences of the *right* circumstances of *right* time and *right* place. Some of this may be due to sheer luck. But luck cannot be everything. The purpose of this book is to investigate the more systematic conditions and influences that enable outstanding individuals to make substantial contributions to science. The scope of this book is limited to my own field, economic science, for obvious reasons.

In the approach taken here, the development of economics as expressed by the genesis and rise of new ideas, paradigms, approaches or methods can be described as a complex and dynamic process which, just like the changing tides of world views, is a compound product of many influences. I would like to give special emphasis to three simultaneous, evolving and of course intertwined undercurrents which I will abbreviate as 'history', 'theory' and 'personality'. In this context, 'history' means the particular economic background of a country or the world at a given time, that is the economic problems and policy challenges that leave their marks in daily life and to which politicians need answers, sometimes directly seeking academic advice. The economic background thus does set at least part of the agenda for economic research, and the political necessity to tackle certain real problems does have a link with the general awareness about specific questions that may not be a concern before or after. The historical–economic background at a certain point of time thus has an immediate impact and relevance, as such, but it is also interesting to look at its more complex derivative: at how the change of economic background affects the itinerary of science over time.

The label 'theory' refers to the evolving 'state of the art' in economics, with its changing toolkits, its ongoing paradigmatic disputes, its ramifications and varying ideological fashions. The state of the art in economics, with its varying approaches and underlying philosophies, determines the way in which policy challenges are looked at in economic theory, and theory usually does have an impact on political choices in reality, be it directly or indirectly. John Maynard Keynes so famously quipped in his *General Theory of Employment, Interest and Money*: 'Practical men, who believe themselves to be quite exempt from any intellectual influences, are usually the slaves of some defunct economist. Madmen in authority, who hear voices in the air, are distilling their frenzy from some academic scribbler of a few years back.'[28] Keynes views ideas as having much more power than vested interests, ascribing this mainly to the fact that people are inflexible in their profound beliefs: 'There are not many who are influenced by new theories after they are twenty-five or thirty years of age.'[29] He provides himself a terrific example: Keynes's legacy is paramount, in economic science itself as much as in economic policy. Keynes threw the doors wide open for government action, providing a rationale for intervention – and that seems to have created very much an irreversible 'ratchet effect'.[30] As Friedrich August von Hayek has explained, this process is based upon the intermediation of intellectuals, the 'second-hand dealers in ideas'.[31]

'Personality' finally takes account of the fact that personal character traits, living conditions and concrete experiences also tend to have an influence on scholars' research interests and specific working method, directing both their world views generally and the specific issues that they choose to address in their work. Even more interesting than the static correlations are, of course, the dynamic forward and backward linkages between all these three evolving undercurrents. The evolution of economic reality, the progress of economic theory, and the personal growth of scholars are simultaneous processes that draw on each other at all times.

Most of the time, these interactions between major influences come about by coincidence and behave in 'unruly', unpredictable ways. Nonetheless, it is instructive to analyze these influences and their interactions for some individual cases at least ad hoc, and to put them into the broader context. This is why I have chosen to have a closer look and to interview some Nobel Laureates in order to find out how these outstanding scholars relate to reality, or history, to theory, and to their own experiences in their personal lives. A host of related questions, each one of them worth long individual analyses for their own sake, could be simultaneously addressed this way; for example: why is it that certain tools in economic science – such as experiments – have taken so long to take off, why have some of them only survived for a while, without ever becoming the mainstream, and why have some – like Public Choice analysis – made almost for a revolution in academic life? What are the psychological backgrounds that make some people more prone to using Keynesian rather than neoclassical approaches, and vice versa? What is it that makes mathematical approaches so popular, as opposed to the more verbal philosophical analysis of complex phenomena? What is it that determines ideological slants, whether one tries to do value-free research or not? Do these biases ever change? And ultimately, the biggest question of all: Is economics making progress – or does the discipline just follow a random walk, that is a completely arbitrary path of unknown ending? How strong is path dependence? This list of questions is of course not exhaustive. There is much more one would like to know and understand. Anyway, some of these questions are addressed directly in the interviews, while the answers to others crystallize almost entirely on their own. Others remain to be answered. At any rate, as one asks these questions, one automatically grows aware of the extreme complexity of the long-winding process of 'division of knowledge' that gives birth to relevant new scientific findings or even paradigms.

The structure of the book is as follows. In the next (that is, the second) chapter of this first part of the book, I will explain my essential choices and my specific method in some detail. I will explain why I have focused on Nobel Laureates exclusively. I will go into some detail to introduce and evaluate the rules and some of the peculiarities of the Nobel Prize. I will briefly address the difficult question of defining excellence in the economic sciences – only briefly, because this will again be a topic in Part III – and see whether the Nobel Prize meets any of the relevant criteria. Furthermore, I will make the reader familiar with the idea and tool of 'oral history' in general and with my own, much less pretentious interview technique in particular.

The following second part will contain one interview with a Nobel Laureate in each of its first ten chapters. The order in which they appear strictly follows the chronological sequence of the awards. The affiliations that are indicated refer to the universities at which the scholars in question were teaching when they received the prize, even though they may be elsewhere now. Information about their current whereabouts and affiliations is provided in the introductions that precede the individual interviews. Those introductions have a quadruple purpose: they will give the reader an idea of the setting, time frame and atmosphere in which the interview was held; they provide short information about the individual career paths, major contributions, and general thinking, putting it all into as much context and perspective as possible without being too long; they will offer an evaluation of those achievements so that it becomes clear why they are important, interesting and outstanding, and in what respect; and finally, a short sum will be drawn concerning the major creativity-fostering influences as they have appeared in the interviews. The reader may notice that while I have tremendous admiration for each one of the Nobel Laureates that I have spoken with, this does not mean that I endorse everything they have done or said in their research or in the political arena. With due respect, some critical comments now and then may be in order. Another chapter will group the answers to a questionnaire that all the Nobel Laureates were asked to fill in, which half of the group graciously did; these provided striking insights as well as a considerable amount of fun.

In the third part of the book, I will then sum up the findings from the interviews, and I will analyze them together with observations and evidence from other sources. This will bring us back from the micro to the macro level, from the particular cases of some admirable individuals to the process of social coordination. And so I will turn back to the science-as-market analogy and to the Hayekian framework. I will look at social interaction in science, analyzing its potential to generate progress – a non-trivial notion, by the way. There will be a host of fascinating insights from both of these perspectives, at the micro and the macro level.

NOTES

1. Gertrude Stein tells the story of how she tried to visit her childhood home but couldn't find the house (Gertrude Stein, 1937).
2. George J. Stigler (1982/1983).
3. Especially in his *Theory of Moral Sentiments* (1759).
4. The pun refers to Friedrich August von Hayek (1944), *The Road to Serfdom*. Others have already made use of a pun in order to pay tribute to Hayek: Erich Streissler, Gottfried Haberler and Friedrich A. Lutz (1969), *Roads to Freedom: Essays in Honour of Friedrich A. von Hayek*.
5. As I am writing these lines, the world is being engulfed in a major financial crisis threatening to turn into a serious global depression, the worst since 1929. The 2008 global financial crisis was an outcome of the mortgage crisis originating in the United States. The American real estate bubble began to burst in 2006. Public opinion has turned heavily against capitalism and yearns for government *dirigisme*. Most commentators see in this crisis the 'bankruptcy' and 'demise' of global capitalism, the well-deserved breakdown of 'neoliberalism', and the long overdue and welcome end of deregulation and liberalization. 'The collapse of America's financial giants was brought about by excessive greed of banks, mindless deregulation, lax supervision, and a false belief represented by the bipartisan Washington Consensus that financial markets know best. Handed a gun and set minimal rules, the financial ultimately market [*sic*] shot itself in the foot' writes Yousuf Nazar on 11 October, 2008, in the online edition of Dawn News (www.dawn.com), reflecting very much the majority view. As is easy to see, Francis Fukuyama (1992) proclaimed the 'end of history' a little bit too early after the breakdown of socialism. Liberal democracy, based on free markets, is not achieved once and for all. Just like Sisyphus, Hayek's stone has to be rolled up the steep hill again.
6. Adam Smith (1776).
7. 'The marvel is that in a case like that of a scarcity of one raw material, without an order being issued, without more than perhaps a handful of people knowing the cause, tens of thousands of people whose identity could not be ascertained by months of investigation, are made to use the material or its products more sparingly; that is, they move in the right direction. This is enough of a marvel even if, in a constantly changing world, not all will hit it off so perfectly that their profit rates will always be maintained at the same even or "normal" level. I have deliberately used the word "marvel" to shock the reader out of the complacency with which we often take the working of this mechanism for granted. I am convinced that if it were the result of deliberate human design, and if the people guided by the price changes understood that their decisions have significance far beyond their immediate aim, this mechanism would have been acclaimed as one of the greatest triumphs of the human mind. Its misfortune is the double one that it is not the product of human design and that the people guided by it usually do not know why they are made to do what they do.' Friedrich August von Hayek (1945/1948, p. 87).
8. See Adam Smith (1776) and (1759). We will come back to this topic in more detail in Part III of this volume.
9. Hayek himself referred to evolution and spontaneous order as 'twin concepts'. In his epilogue piece to *Law, Legislation, and Liberty*, concentrating on the 'Three Sources of Human Values', Hayek explains that humankind lives under at least three layers of rules, some of which are transmitted genetically (natural evolution), others are inherited through tradition (cultural evolution), and still others are consciously designed on top (Friedrich August von Hayek (1982, Vol. III, p. 158).

10. Friedrich August von Hayek, (1973, Vol. I, p. 37).
11. Friedrich August von Hayek, 'The confusion of language in political thought' (1968/1978b p. 90).
12. Friedrich August von Hayek 'The results of human action but not of human design' (1978). In his *New Studies in Philosophy, Politics, Economics, and the History of Ideas*, pp. 96–105). The phrase was coined by the Scottish enlightenment philosopher and historian Adam Ferguson (1723–1815) talking about human institutions, or establishments: 'which are indeed the result of human action but not the execution of human design'. Adam Ferguson (1767, p. 187).
13. See Carl Menger *Principles of Economics* (1871/1981).
14. Friedrich August von Hayek (1945/1948/1980, pp. 89).
15. Friedrich August von Hayek (1945/1948/1980, pp. 77/78).
16. Friedrich August von Hayek (1945/1948/1980, pp. 91).
17. Friedrich August von Hayek 'Competition as a discovery procedure'. (1968/1978/1982, p. 179).
18. Friedrich August von Hayek (1968/1978/1982, p. 180).
19. Friedrich August von Hayek (1945/1948/1980, p. 81).
20. Friedrich August von Hayek (1945/1948/1980, p. 84).
21. Friedrich August von Hayek (1945/1948/1980, p. 86).
22. Friedrich August von Hayek (1945/1948/1980, p. 88).
23. Paul A. Samuelson (1992, p. 246).
24. Friedrich August von Hayek (1978, pp. 50–56). This point will come back in the introductions to individual interviews as well as in Part III of this volume.
25. See the interview with Robert M. Solow in this volume.
26. See the essay by Robert M. Solow in Michael Szenberg (1992, p. 273).
27. Jokingly, if not frivolously, Howard R. Vane and Chris Mulhearn give some advice to 'Nobel Memorial aspirants': They should 'be a US citizen (65 percent of the laureates are), be affiliated to an American University (75 percent of laureates are), more specifically be an affiliate of a member of an elite group of 12 universities with a track record of employing laureates at the time of their elevation (10 of the 12 are in the US), have doctoral training at one of 14 select universities with a track record of training laureates (of these 14, eight are in the US and have trained more than half of all the laureates; first win a prestigious award like the John Bates Clark Medal (39 percent have so far gone on to win a Nobel Memorial award), be affiliated to the University of Chicago or train there . . .; and be a man.' Howard R. Vane and Chris Mulhearn (2005 pp. 11–12).
28. John Maynard Keynes (1936, p. 383).
29. John Maynard Keynes (1936, pp. 383–4).
30. A ratchet effect, in economic theory, is simply a development that cannot be undone, in analogy with the mechanical ratchet that holds the spring tight as a clock is being wound up.
31. Friedrich August von Hayek (1949, p. 417).

Choices and method

When looking at concrete individual cases, how can one track down the major influences that have prepared the ground for academic excellence and lasting original contributions? I have chosen simply to rely on the reflections of some outstanding individuals. Interviews provide valuable insights in the form of 'a first-rate highbrow form of gossip',[1] as Ben Bernanke, the current Chairman of the Federal Reserve, would probably say. They are not only a very readable way to present someone's valuable recollections, as such; they also differ from purely unilaterally written autobiographies in that they can be directed to a certain extent.[2] An interviewer can ask follow-up questions that permit to highlight something, to explain some necessary background, to clarify some terminology, and to give context.

For this book, I have interviewed ten Nobel Laureates in economic science. Why only Nobel Laureates? A priori, I admit that there is no entirely conclusive reason for this. There are many other outstanding scholars out there. Excellence doesn't automatically translate into 'Nobelity'. In some cases not yet, in most other cases never. The main reason why I have nevertheless chosen to deal exclusively with Nobel Laureates is just that, on average, their excellence tends to be less disputed than that of other scholars.

NOBELITY AS A GOOD GUESS FOR EXCELLENCE

Everybody can think of one or more Nobel Laureates whose award-worthiness was controversial. But in statistical terms, that is just the standard error, and on the whole, Nobelity cannot be said to be the worst indicator for excellence. Of course, its range doesn't cover everybody, but on average, for those who have indeed received the Nobel Prize, there is little doubt as to the significance of their contributions. Nobelity is a good guess for excellence. That's enough for my purpose.

Another reason is that Nobel Laureates are relatively well known. This is an advantage, in that these interviews may also attract readers who would otherwise perhaps be scared away. I'm catering both to insiders and outsiders here, to people who have followed or even taken part in the academic debate as much as to more remote readers who just have a distinct interest in economics. People from both groups will join in their 'craving to share the lives of well-known individuals', as the economist Michael Szenberg says. 'We are boundlessly curious about their accomplishments, their motives, and the resources they bring to their tasks. We also attempt to probe the inner landscape of scientists' lives. Our interest is in the how and the why, which can lead us to discover the wellspring of the creative impulse.'[3] Even if this is not to absolutely everybody's liking,[4] he is right. That curiosity may have to do with the – imperfect – human means of perception. As Hayek states, 'our tendency to personify . . . the events we observe is probably the result of . . . an application of schemata which our own bodily movements provide.'[5]

There will be some academic insider-talk in the interviews, and a considerable amount of name-dropping as well, that is for sure. But I have provided explanatory notes, from the approximate dates of the Great Depression to the meaning and origin of 'Gresham's law'. So nobody should feel lost.

Odd as it may seem, an important reason for including only Nobel Laureates here is also that most of them are now senior citizens. All those that I have interviewed are now above the age of 67. As I will subsequently explain, this is, at least for me, a welcome selection bias. The average age at which the Nobel Laureates have received the prize is precisely 67 years. The youngest Nobel Laureate ever to receive the prize was Kenneth J. Arrow, at age 51, in 1972, followed by Robert C. Merton at age 53 in 1997 and preceded by Paul A. Samuelson, at age 55, in 1970. The oldest ever to receive the prize was Leonid Hurwicz, one of the three 2007 Laureates, at age 90, followed by Thomas Schelling, one of the two 2005 Laureates, at age 84.

THE ADVANTAGE OF OLD AGE

Old age is something to appreciate and value, especially in this context here. As these people look back, they remember and communicate things that are beyond younger people's own reach. And they have reflected upon them. They are now quite laid back and don't seek to impress others as much as they would probably have tried to in younger years. Age doesn't always necessarily square with wisdom, but in most cases that I know of, there is at least some grain of truth in the saying. And therefore, these extremely erudite senior economists will help others understand an era that is beyond their own memories. They will drive us back to a land which we have never seen with our own eyes, even though we have built our own intellectual homes on its ground. These reports from the eyewitnesses of another time bring their own insights, and they have their own, moving beauty.

For example, it is not difficult to imagine that the *General Theory of Employment, Interest, and Money* by a certain John Maynard Keynes[6] caused quite a stir when it came out in the late 1930s. But what did it really mean to those who were entering the field of economics at that moment? To those who grappled to make sense of the Great Depression, the general economic downturn that started in 1929 and dissipated so much affluence everywhere?[7] In which way, and by which aspects did it fill a void that most economists felt painfully? How much did the profession struggle to accept it? How much of it was a question of philosophy? How much had the Great Depression shaken up the confidence in self-coordinating markets, while skepticism towards government agencies (such as the Federal Reserve, for this specific case) might have been even more appropriate? All these questions are of acutely renewed relevance today. To get a feeling for the development of economics at this crucial crossroads, both in terms of the evolution of economic science and in terms of popular economic policy beliefs, there is nothing more instructive than the memories of those who were there and saw it – and made it – happen.

Paul A. Samuelson is a wonderful source here – and yes, I am fully aware that I am not the first one to notice that. Samuelson is a much-sought interview partner generally and not least for this reason. His perspective, stretching from his first publication in 1937 to the current days, is unparalleled in its length and width. He makes us understand just how desperate the profession was for new ways of thinking, and how badly they were looking out for tools that would allow economics to be almost as precise as the natural sciences. The impact of the Great Depression overshadowed everything else. It created the general sense that something had to be done.

For most contemporary economists, the shattering, horrendous experience with the abuse of government power in later years, especially in Germany, Italy and Japan, did not change their attitudes and persuasions much. Put simply, those had been and now were viewed as criminal governments – and criminal politics was not a topic that economists felt they had much to contribute to. Economics was there for enlightened, well-intentioned governments. Until this day, most scholars pride themselves in their ensuing attitude, which they call 'pragmatism'.[8]

This was where the rise of the Public Choice and the New Political Economy schools struck. In the evolution of economic science, this was a similarly remarkable experience. Nowadays, it is impossible to imagine the intellectual world of economics without it. Today, every student gets confronted with the recognition sooner or later that governments cannot necessarily be viewed as benevolent dictators, as once was heuristically assumed. At some point, their attention does get drawn to the fact that government action should be explicitly endogenized, in an analysis that is based on the same assumption of purposive, rational behavior that is made elsewhere in neoclassical theory. The idea that bureaucrats tend to maximize budgets and latitude, and that politicians maximize votes, doesn't come as a surprise any more today. It is true that, given the predominant Keynesian undercurrent in modern macroeconomics, questioning the legitimacy and aptitude of government intervention still only comes as a second step in the academic curriculum – but at least it does come. It seems almost inconceivable today that this was something entirely unheard of at some earlier point. But it was, and the Public Choice revolution came as a shock. What was meant as – and is – a realistic and systematic approach to the public sector and collective choice procedures, was at first widely interpreted as an ill-meaning, not very helpful, but rather destructive, and foremost ideological act of sabotage. This is understandable: while the mainstream proponents of macroeconomics and welfare economics worked hard to frame the world in a way that would allow government to take beneficial concrete policy steps, this school started out by thinking about how to limit the pervasive abuse of power in representative majoritarian democracy. This was shocking and definitely not welcome. James M. Buchanan, however, one of the key founders of this school, had enough of a backbone to survive the intellectual hostilities. His recollections provide an impressive sketch of those days, including the persistent animosities between American Southerners and the Yankees, with outright discrimination as a result. On a personal basis, Buchanan teaches us how important it is to have an independent, courageous, non-erring, and not overly peer-impressionable mind.

INTEREST IN HISTORY: A PERSONAL CONFESSION

To cherish this kind of experience, one needs to have an interest in history – in history *tout court*, and in the history of thought in economics. As Joseph Schumpeter explains, one needs to concern oneself with the history of thought in economics precisely due to the fact that economics is not a hard natural science. 'Much more than in, say, physics is it true in economics that modern problems, methods, and results cannot be fully understood without some knowledge of how economists have come to reason as they do.'[9] He goes on to write that our minds are apt to derive new inspiration from the study of the history of science. Some do so more than others, but there are probably few that do not derive from it any benefit at all. A man's mind must be indeed sluggish if, standing back from the work of his time and beholding the wide mountain ranges of past thought, he does not experience a widening of his own horizon.[10]

Personally, I have always had that interest. It all goes back to my parents. They were both enrolled in economics at the University of Freiburg, Germany, in the 1940s. My mother had been fortunate enough to start her studies during the war, spending a first semester at home in Königsberg, East Prussia. My father came to Freiburg in 1946. The towering figure in the economics department in those days was Walter Eucken (1891–1950), who also had a sympathetic and encouraging eye for the young couple.

Walter Eucken, son of the philosopher Rudolf Eucken (1846–1926),[11] and his wife Irene, an artist painter, was an interesting person in at least two respects: first, he had started out within the German Historical School, which admittedly is nowadays almost forgotten. It concentrated much on pure data-collecting and limited itself to inductive theory. Eucken then set out to try to bridge the gap between the Historical school and the Austrian marginalists around Carl Menger, whose aim it had been to explain the spontaneous rise of institutions, to analyze those institutions, and of course to derive real economic 'laws', and all of that in a deductive, truly theoretical way. The tensions between these two schools had culminated in the famous 'Methodenstreit' in the late nineteenth century.[12] Walter Eucken, with his research program focusing on the different styles of economic order, tried to overcome this, as he called it, 'Great Antinomy'.[13] Eucken was one of the key figures of German 'ordoliberalism'. He was in touch with Hayek and became one of the founding members of the Mont Pèlerin Society.[14]

Second, as a scientist with a pronounced taste for academic (as well as general) freedom and also as a committed Christian, he had played a role in the academic opposition resisting Adolf Hitler's regime. This fact, in addition to his general humanity and unusual personal stature, gave him considerable moral authority after the end of the war and the collapse of the Nazi system.[15] My parents admired Eucken greatly. They were not alone in this. Eucken's students all continued to gather in Freiburg for commemorative meetings once a year until the 1990s, many decades beyond Eucken's premature death in 1950. When I was a child, I found this unfailing veneration a little disturbing. As I grew up, however, I couldn't help being intrigued. I ended up wanting to learn more about the context – about the times, the challenges and the intellectual heritage.

Fortunately, my parents were able and eager to share with me what they knew and remembered. They were 'living history books' for me. They opened a window for me to this amazing, troubling, crucial era in German history. I found those conversations fascinating, and that's perhaps what has marked me for life: I still deeply treasure conversations with people who are, like them, more than forty years older than I am. The stories that they have to tell reach back beyond my own imagination and way beyond what constitutes the current collective preoccupation with recent history. In the concrete case of Walter Eucken, the aspect that mainly drew me at first, clearly, was his connection with the resistance, remote or not – and this topic then opened up a vast historical field before me, ranging from moral philosophy and Catholic social ethics to economics as such. All I can say is that those are incredibly interesting fields, and reflecting deeply along those lines can make one happy.

EXCELLENCE IN ECONOMICS

While this 'living history book' function is one that was clearly crucial in deciding me in favor of concentrating exclusively on Nobel Laureates in this book, this latter decision also helps me avoid fruitless debates about the definition of excellence, originality and progress in economics – at least for now. This issue will be picked up again in the third part of this book. Suffice it to say right now that nothing is trivial about defining and measuring excellence and originality as such. How could one possibly do so in such a way that anybody could agree? If one tries to do this objectively, what could meaningful operationalizations look like? Some attempts at this have been made, of course. Counting publications in refereed journals is one possibility. But that is too coarse a method. Even though they differ only by the middle consonants, quantity and quality are not necessarily related. They can even be contradictory. Often 'less is more', as the traditional saying has it. Everybody knows that the devise 'publish or perish' can lead to perishing through publishing.

Counting how much somebody's publications have been cited, in order to measure their impact, might be another possibility. The Social Science Citation Index (SSCI) lends itself perfectly to this kind of exercise. And yet this indicator is not very convincing. Quoting someone doesn't necessarily mean that one builds on their work. Another reason that makes the SSCI an imperfect indicator is that traditions differ on both sides of the Atlantic, with the North Americans facing the 'publish or perish' imperative more than the Europeans who, at least in some countries and to some point, have to go through the 'Habilitation' or 'Quatrième Cycle' thesis before they can apply for a chair at University – which of course makes them publish less in younger years. And afterwards, 'once a chair is gained, there is no need nor incentive to publish', as Frey and Pommerehne point out [16] This means that – for simple institutional and historical reasons numbers cannot be compared. Another argument against the SSCI as an indicator of academic excellence is that people have meanwhile adapted their behavior to it. Not only have citation cartels become fashionable. The focus on the SSCI has also increased the trend towards co-authored pieces instead of papers that individual scholars are alone responsible for. There are many other important advantages to co-authoring, originating especially in the economies of scale and scope following the increased interaction which is possible between highly-specialized scholars thanks to the improved communication technology – but this one has proved non-negligible as well.

Whether seriously or not, the American statistician Stephen M. Stigler – Nobel Laureate George J. Stigler's son – once suggested that one might instead look at the eponymous record of individual scholars, that is take it as an indicator of the quality and lasting impact of some scholarly work whether the name of the scholar in question has become a household name attached to some law, effect or paradox.[17] Examples are Say's law, Schumpeter's pioneer entrepreneur, the Keynes effect, the Arrow paradox, the Solow model, the Modigliani–Miller theorem, the Stolper–Samuelson theorem, and so on. But again, this is totally arbitrary. Many outstanding scholars have left their mark in economics without leaving their name together with it. In some cases, the name may just have been too complicated. In other cases, it just didn't happen, for whatever reason, and the invention became known under a name that says something about its meaning – which is not a bad idea. Examples are bounded rationality (Herbert Simon), competition as a discovery procedure (Friedrich August von Hayek), and the natural rate of unemployment (Milton Friedman and Edmund S. Phelps). So 'Stigler's law' even has it that inventions never get named after their inventors, but rather after those coming right after them who pick up the idea.

THE NOBEL PRIZE

The Nobel Prize avoids all the intricate questions about excellence and progress by relying on straightforward peer review. Prima facie, this is probably the best possible compromise. Still, it is also an imperfect method, since there is no guarantee that the majority knows best. How is this system being operated?

The Nobel Prize in Economics is not really a Nobel Prize. Its full correct name is 'Sveriges Riksbanks Prize in Economic Sciences in Memory of

Alfred Nobel'. It was instituted in 1968 on the occasion of the 300th anniversary of the Swedish central bank, who has funded it ever since with an endowment 'in perpetuity'. Responsibility for the decision was again given to the Royal Swedish Academy of Sciences. The prize was first awarded in 1969, and the recipients were Jan Tinbergen and Ragnar Frisch. The prize ceremony always takes place in Stockholm on 10 December, the anniversary of Alfred Nobel's death. Since 2001, the value of the award has been 10 million Swedish crowns; if there is more than one Laureate per year, the winners have to share the amount. The peculiarity here is that Alfred Nobel (1833–1896), the ingenious Swedish chemist and industrialist who invented dynamite, couldn't stand economics.

Thanks to his invention and the subsequent industrial manufacture of dynamite and other explosives, Alfred Nobel became a millionaire.[18] Alfred Nobel never married and had no children. He decided to bequeath the greatest part of his fortune to a foundation in his own name, which would regularly honor mostly scientific contributions that would be in the best interest of all humankind. The family at first fought his will, but ultimately, the first prizes were awarded in 1901. Nobel had designated three disciplines in the natural sciences, namely physiology (that is, medicine), chemistry, and physics, as well as two non-scientific fields, namely literature and peace, for the one directly political prize. Nobel even designated the institutions responsible for the prizes he wished to establish: The Royal Swedish Academy of Sciences, of which Nobel himself had been a member, for the Nobel Prize in Physics and Chemistry, the Karolinska Institute for the Nobel Prize in Physiology or Medicine, the Royal Swedish Academy for the Nobel Prize in Literature, and a Committee of five persons to be elected by the Norwegian Parliament (Storting) for the Nobel Peace Prize.

Economics was nothing Alfred Nobel appreciated as such, even though he was himself a pretty successful business man. Rather to the contrary: 'I have no training in economics myself and also hate it from the bottom of my heart', he wrote in a letter that was published only in 2001, as some members of the Nobel family tried to end the episode.[19] They did not succeed. And yet, apart from his visceral rejection, one can imagine why Nobel didn't want or even envisage awarding a prize to findings in economics. Economics is a social science. Some critics actually argue that economics is no science at all, simply because it doesn't allow for making any safe predictions. But if one takes Schumpeter's definition of science as 'any kind of knowledge that has been the object of conscious efforts to improve it',[20] economics of course qualifies as a science, but not a natural science. What distinguishes the social sciences from the natural sciences, which alone Nobel accepted, is that it is not a 'hard' science. In the natural sciences, right or wrong are easily tracked down. In any social science, things are not that simple. As Hayek said, economics is dealing with complex phenomena.[21]

THE CRITERIA AND PROCEDURE

The criteria for the prize are analogous to the statutes of the real Nobel Prize. As one can read on the Nobel Foundation website, the 'Statutes for the Sveriges Riksbank Prize in Economic Sciences in Memory of Alfred Nobel approved by the Crown on the 19th day of December 1968' declare that

> the Prize shall be awarded annually to *a person* who has written a work on economic sciences of the eminent significance expressed in the will of Alfred Nobel drawn up on November 27, 1895. . . The Prize shall be awarded by the Royal Academy of Sciences in accordance with the rules governing the award of the Nobel Prizes instituted through his will.[22]

In Nobel's will, then, which one can also find on the Nobel Foundation website, it is stipulated that the prize shall be awarded annually to a *single* living person 'who, *during the preceding* year, shall have conferred the greatest benefit on mankind'.[23] While it is by no means straightforward to determine who, in economic science, has 'conferred the greatest benefit on mankind', it must also be noted that the letters of two essential rules are permanently being violated: the cases in which the prize is awarded to individual persons have become rather rare over time. And, quite understandably, the prize is also not recognition for a work written in the very preceding year. It takes many years to find out whether some contribution in economics has been a major paradigm shift and whether it has triggered further fruitful research.

One striking example for the substantial time lag that can precede Nobelity is Ronald Coase. Coase was awarded the prize in 1991 for a lecture that he had given in 1932 in Dundee, titled 'The nature of the firm'. It was eventually published as a research paper in *Economica* in 1937.[24] The time lag was almost sixty years. Part of this time lag may have been due to some sort of backlog in the list of likely and worthy recipients, given that the prize was instituted only in 1968 – but the major reason is that contributions need time to sink in. The gist of Nobel's rule is nevertheless respected in that the prize rewards specific breakthroughs in economic science, whether they have been carried out by one or more (maximum three) scholars, rather than lifetime achievements of individuals.

Practically, the Economics Prize follows the rule that the academic contribution in question should be specific, original and important. As Assar Lindbeck, the long-time Chairman of the Economics Prize Committee, explains, the

> selection Committee has looked, in particular, at the originality of the contribution, its scientific and practical importance, and its impact on scientific work. To provide shoulders on which other scholars can stand, and thus climb higher, has been regarded as an important contribution. To some extent, the Committee has also considered the impact on society at large, including the impact on public policy.[25]

The procedure is a complex one. Its essential feature is that it relies heavily on peers. Each September, the Economics Prize Committee, attached to the Royal Swedish Academy of Sciences 'sends invitations to thousands of scientists, members of academies and university professors in numerous countries, asking them to nominate candidates for the Prize in Economics for the coming year. Members of the Academy and former laureates are also authorized to nominate candidates', we can read on the Nobel Foundation website. Usually, the Committee receives 200–300 nominations, covering 100 nominees. All these proposals must be received until the beginning of February and then get reviewed by the Prize Committee and some experts. The Committee is composed of five to nine Swedish economists who are appointed for three years,[26] one of them functioning as Chairman. This relatively large number of members, as compared to the other fields, is meant to reduce the risk of bias. The Committee narrows the selection and makes its choice – through a vote by majority rule – until September. This choice then has to be submitted as a recommendation to the Ninth class, that is the social sciences division, of the Royal Swedish Academy of Sciences who cast their final vote in mid-October. The protocols of these votes are kept secret for at least fifty years. Since the first Prize in Economics was awarded in 1969, the first year when the public will learn something about the internal procedures at the Royal Swedish Academy of Sciences will be 2019.

CRITICISMS

While the Nobel Prize is widely regarded as a hugely prestigious prize, and while the decisions for the Economics Prize have never raised any serious controversy (unlike in the case of the Peace Prize), some criticisms have been voiced. They all have a point. One problem has to do with the funding of the prize. Unlike the other Nobel Prizes, the Economics Prize is not privately funded. Since the money comes from the Swedish central bank, this implies that it is funded essentially by seignorage, that is the net revenue derived from issuing currency. Seignorage derived from coins arises from the difference between the face value of a coin and the cost of producing, distributing and ultimately withdrawing it from circulation; seignorage derived from notes is the difference between the interest earned on securities acquired in exchange for bank notes and the costs of producing and distributing those bank notes.[27] There have been endless debates about whose property seignorage really is or should be. In most countries, central banks transfer their seignorage gains to the government at the end of the year – which is an explicit acknowledgement of the fact that it is essentially taxpayer money. The Swedish taxpayer is made to renounce this money.

Rather recently, Paul A. Samuelson has also argued that the prize has unfortunate collateral effects in that not receiving it comes almost as a disgrace to scholars whose work has a quality equal to or only marginally inferior to those contributions that are awarded the prize. As he wrote in a piece for the 2nd Lindau Meeting of the Winners of the Bank of Sweden Prize in Economic Sciences in Memory of Alfred Nobel, he had already argued ten years before the inception of the prize that 'providing rewards to one elite would exclude from tribute a larger group of worthies whose body of research achievements is, if anything, only slightly different in quality and quantity.'[28] Apart from this, Samuelson is also a little uneasy with the peer-review process as such, having 'a dislike for creation of a self-perpetuating elite'.[29]

Another criticism that can sometimes be heard is that, with time lags as in Ronald Coase's case, the award comes much too late to encourage further research in this area. In a sense, the award really is an after the fact recognition and thereby loses out on the potential to effectively foster certain branches of research. On the other hand, that may be exactly desirable. Anything else would amount to interventionism in the free market of ideas – and that intervention would be sponsored with taxpayer money, to top it. This lack of direct influence also means that Friedrich August von Hayek's fear is unwarranted, namely that the prize would simply reinforce short-run flings and fashions in economics.[30] However, as Harriet Zuckerman points out in her great study, the prize seems to promote the so-called Matthew effect, according to the term coined by the sociologist Robert K. Merton: 'The Matthew Effect confers further authority and influence on those who are already influential and authoritative, and brings further honors to those who have already been honored.'[31] Hayek was also worried that the prize would confer to the Laureate(s) a degree of notoriety that would ultimately be harmful. In his view, 'Nobelity' would be felt as an entitlement to give comments even on fields that one knows nothing about. He probably has a point. Harriet Zuckerman writes that 'as the prestige of the prize has risen, this has led to conditions that tempt some laureates into claiming general wisdom and authority as well as demonstrated expertness of a high order. The social control system in science may work to curb some of these excesses, but it scarcely eliminates them.'[32] Mark Blaug, the famous scholar in history of thought, even asks whether 'perhaps economists would be a little less arrogant about other subjects without the Nobel Prize in Economics and, surely, that would be a good thing?'[33] Hayek suggested that all Nobel Laureates should swear an oath of humility.[34]

Yet another criticism is directed against the required specificity, that is against the fact that not the individual scholars, but their contribution must be prize-worthy. I have a lot of sympathy for the idea that it is rather an individual's ongoing struggle for knowledge and his or her incremental generation of new ideas along a coherent thread of thought and genius, within the span of an entire lifetime that should be recognized. This would endow the world of economic science with true – and visible – role models. Some of the earlier Nobel Prizes went in that direction, without admitting it: just think of Paul A. Samuelson and George J. Stigler, for example. As the interviews in this book will show, and as I have said earlier, it is not alone the spontaneous process of social self-coordination that must fill one with awe. One should marvel just as much at the course of those outstandingly productive individual lives.

Some argue that the Nobel Prize attracts too much attention and that it has sort of a monopoly in the field, which gives it too much influence. It is true that the Nobel Prize is the most important award in the field and enjoys the highest prestige. But it doesn't really have a monopoly. There are legions of other awards out there, even if most of them dole out smaller amounts of money. Let me just name the Erwin Plein Nemmers Prize for Economics from Northwestern University (150 000 dollars), the Bradley Prize from the Lynde and Harry Bradley Foundation (250 000 dollars), and the IZA Prize in Labor Economics (50 000 euros). Unfortunately, the American Economic Association gave up its renowned Francis A. Walker medal, instituted in 1947, in 1981. The John Bates Clark medal for scholars under 40 years of age however remains.

Finally, not all observers are happy with the fact that the Nobel Prize has been dominated by American recipients so far. Of the 61 economists who have received the prize until mid-2008, 39 have been US citizens. Instead of viewing this as some kind of arbitrary bias, it should however be recognized as demonstrating the leading role of economic research done in the United States. I will have a closer look at this in the last part of this book.

In conclusion, I like to think that the Sveriges Riksbanks Prize in Economic Sciences in Memory of Alfred Nobel is not only a highly respectable, but also a valuable institution. Nevertheless, all the criticism that I have just reported does contain a considerable grain of truth, or more. What worries me personally is what Paul A. Samuelson calls the 'self-perpetuating elite', and the dominance of the formal, mathematical, situational approach to economics instead of the broader vision of economic problems as complex phenomena, both tendencies being a consequence of the peer process; the funding by way of seignorage, which is not without causing opportunity costs to the Swedish public; and the quasi-monopoly position which perhaps gives the prize excessive weight in the perception of the public. But on the whole, the global picture is still positive. Most of the decisions made by the Royal Swedish Academy of Sciences have been acceptable, and some have been even laudable. It is good to draw the public's attention to the field in a pleasant sense from time to time anyway. It just needs to be hoped that Harriet Zuckerman is wrong with her fear that the prize 'tends to divert scientists from research on deep intractable problems to "prizable" ones', and that it only makes for 'more elbows in science'.[35] However, as the famous English journalist Samuel Brittan cautions, 'to abolish would simply increase the influence of the kind of anti-economics which embraces for instance rent controls, minimum wages and arms promotion "for the sake of jobs". The best way forward would be . . . to extend the Prize to the social sciences in general and really mean it.'[36] Also, as Mark Blaug says, 'it is good for economics to get a little jolt now and then from a partially-outside institution like the Nobel Prize Committee'. It would be even better if there was a competitor of comparable size out there. Ideally with private money.

THE INTERVIEWEES

From the 62 scholars who have been awarded the Nobel Prize ever since its inception in 1968, 37 are still alive today.[37] That number is too large for the purpose and scope of this book, however, and so I had to make a choice. I chose ten laureates – and I chose them in a partly objective and a partly subjective manner, as I must admit. Objectively speaking, I aimed at diversity. I hoped to persuade people from different ideological backgrounds (leftist Keynesians like Paul A. Samuelson, Robert M. Solow and George A. Akerlof on the one hand, classical liberals such as James M. Buchanan, Douglass C. North and Vernon L. Smith on the other hand, for example). I was looking for people with different methodologies, ranging from the more formal to the more verbal approaches. I was interested in people

who might know each other and who have had academic struggles to
fight out in the past, so that I would learn something about their interaction (James M. Buchanan and Kenneth J. Arrow, or Robert M. Solow
and Edmund S. Phelps). I was hoping for people of different generations
(Paul A. Samuelson in his nineties versus George A. Akerlof in his sixties).
Given my own national background, I approached the one German laureate, of course. And I tried to find laureates with whom it would be fun
and exciting and enriching to speak – that is my personal subjective part. I
hoped for people whom I knew a little or whom I could at least reasonably
expect to be willing to open up. While Amartya Sen was too overbooked,
and Ronald Coase physically not well enough to meet my request, I was
fortunate that the others all graciously agreed to take part in my project:
Paul A. Samuelson, Kenneth J. Arrow, James M. Buchanan, Robert M.
Solow, Gary S. Becker, Douglass C. North, Reinhard Selten, George A.
Akerlof, Vernon L. Smith and Edmund S. Phelps.[38] I asked all these Nobel
Laureates to engage in deep introspection before me, that is to cast a scru-
tinizing eye on their own paths in their careers and personal lives, and to
undertake an interpretation of what their most important driving forces
and sources of inspiration have been. I am aware that I have been asking a
lot. And I am grateful for the lot that I have got.

ORAL HISTORY

This project is one that has received much inspiration from the idea
and method of oral history, without being a work of historiography, of
course. Generally speaking, oral history just means that historical information based on the personal experiences and opinions of individuals
gets recorded, preserved and interpreted.[39] This technique has developed
into a whole field of historical research. Historians aspire to something
else, though, and perhaps to more than is my purpose here. As E. Roy
Weintraub formulates, 'for historians, context is everything, so they would
treat the conversations as partial source material of some limited use in
constructing a serious history'.[40] And that 'serious history' would then
not just be a 'history told by the research scientists themselves, but it is a
history of the import and impact of ideas'.[41] What I am doing in this book
probably fully falls into the category that he describes, rather drastically,
as follows:

> Most economists will see the development of economics as a sequence of prob-
> lems thrown up either by the world, called the economy, or by the development
> of tools, techniques, and theorizations. That is, most economists see economics

as a problem-solving activity and the history of economics as a sequence of problems posed, solved, re-described, and further re-posed and resolved. For them, the economist is a figure who is trained and socialized to recognize these economic problems and to operate in a world in which framing and solving such problems defines the profession of economics.

All of this then gives rise to

> a writing of the history of economics that historians have called OTSOG-ery, an acronym for 'On the Shoulders of Giants'. . . The historical narrative is not a succession of this, then that, then that, then that. Rather it is an inter-weaving of many stories in a tapestry involving the local, and contingent, in a contextualization of all the this-s and that-s.[42]

While it is indeed my explicit aim to view and to analyze such a 'sequence of problems posed, solved, re-described, and further re-posed and resolved', my perspective is not really a Hegelian one, where academic science, like any other activity of humankind, is a dialectic process inevitably leading upwards. Such an upwards process cannot even be assumed at the individual level: as people grow older, they may produce more clever papers, but this is not inevitably the case. It has been shown empirically that scholarly productivity follows a life-cycle trend, with a peak at young adulthood and a decline after forty.[43] Also, later publications may simply belong to different categories, so that a classification as being 'better' is not warranted.[44] The interviews confirm this. They show 'how messy and non-linear the search for new paradigms can be', as Ben Bernanke, the current Chairman of the Federal Reserve, has said in a similar context.[45]

Also, while it is true that it is precisely my aim to provide 'partial source material' which others may of course 'use in constructing a serious history' if they so wish, I must insist that history as such is not my focus here. I am interested precisely in the individual story, that is in the way in which the individual scholars view and explain their itinerary now, looking back. I expressly ask them for a 'succession of this, then that, then that, then that' – of course not in the cheap way that Weintraub seems to dread, however, but trying to dig deeper into the personal histories. As the reader will see, for example, a lot of time and words have been dedicated to finding out about eventual influences in childhood and youth. Now here one could argue, as Weintraub indeed does, that memories are systematically biased: as a psychological rule, one doesn't remember much from early childhood once one is 75 years of age, but a lot from early adulthood – and then the density of our recollections falls off again, to increase again only after age 50, which is simply due to the shorter time distance. This pattern, the 'recollection bump', he argues, is stable across all cultures and kinds of memories.[46] It implies that people tend to put disproportionate emphasis on what they have learnt at university: 'Don't trust anyone who's past our bump.'[47] This is a fact that must be acknowledged, of course, but that is not worrisome as such – that's just the way humans are.

The point with my kind of proto-oral history is precisely that, instead of relying on an account of prima facie necessarily unrelated objective facts, it accepts subjectivism up front. What this kind of oral history can deliver is not *the* truth, but individual truths. Each of them is interesting. When 'my' Nobel Laureates talk about the Keynesian revolution, when they remember how the different factions formed in the discipline and how they fought with or against each other, when they remember how some new paradigms added new levels of understanding while others failed, then what one gets is not *the* history of economics, of course, but a personal history of economics, and even a very personal account of a particular kind of economics. Everything is interpretation. And that is a valuable product in its own right. It is then up to the reader to construct his or her own interpretation on the basis of the various qualified viewpoints that are given as inputs.

It is well-known, for example, that Robert M. Solow is a Keynesian liberal. Keynesianism received a major blow in the 1960s, when Edmund S. Phelps and Milton Friedman demolished the Phillips curve, according to which there was a trade-off between unemployment and inflation that could be used for policy. And yet, while it is impossible to expect anything but discord, it will be fascinating to see in the interviews how Solow and Phelps talk about these years, how they lived the academic battle, which kind of memory they keep of it today and how it has affected them personally. Can you be friends if you fight each other so fiercely? To just give an appetizer here, Solow says:

> What replaced the initial Phillips curve was the Friedman–Phelps natural rate of unemployment long-run vertical Phillips curve. And I have never, from the very first day, thought that that was other than a flimsy theory supported by flimsy empirical analysis.[48]

Phelps, on the other hand, remembers:

> I was being attacked by the most senior and most admired figures in the profession. I was made fun of. Some of them still remained my friends at some gut level, but it was a very serious competition for academic status, and for the truth. It was a rivalry about who was to be regarded as the one who had understood this right.[49]

It is not so easy to say who has won the intellectual battle. The bone of contention is still there.

Another example is the theoretical debate about Social Choice theory that started in the 1950s, centering at first around Kenneth J. Arrow's piece.[30] While Arrow still proudly states that 'on its own terms, my theory has never been subverted',[51] James M. Buchanan fundamentally criticized and still criticizes today the 'notion of the social welfare function. It made no sense to me, and still makes no sense for me.' He reminds us that

> Black and Arrow had this notion that if we could generate a social ordering or welfare function, that would be good. To me, it was just the other way around. Their ideal was a structure of preferences that we wouldn't want to have. We need to avoid dominance, and so we actually want to have a cycle.[52]

This bone of contention is also still being gnawed on. It is surprising to see that, even half a century later, this is still the case.

These two examples demonstrate how subjective the views necessarily are that one gets in interviews. But that is not a flaw. It is something that one must be aware of, that's all. The subjectivity is what makes the interviews so utterly interesting. It is precisely this subjectivity that enables the reader to get a feeling for what these scholars' mindsets were when they engaged in their intellectual battles – what drove them. Subjectivity is also present on the side of the interviewer, some of it involuntarily, some of it very much on purpose. It has been my endeavor to walk the line between acute academic interest and more straightforward journalistic curiosity. In both departments, my own subjectivity has led me to ask certain questions and to drop others. It has led me to insist on some points, reiterating a difficult question if necessary, even offering my own, divergent viewpoints, and to rapidly jump over others.

Generally speaking, oral history faces the problem that interviewees often have a message to convey. Sometimes this may amount to conceit meeting conceit: 'After all, the reader's expectations in reading an auto-biographical memoir of an economist, when the reader is an economist, will be to find either a moral cautionary tale, or a shining path exemplar, to help reconstruct the narrative of the reader's own life.'[53] Hughes calls this the issue of 'contested interpretation', where a 'well-entrenched actor's history'[54] rather obscures the view on 'true' history. De Vorkin hints at a general tendency of interviewees not to tell the full truth, simply because they are 'on the record': 'In the mere act of . . . making the scientist aware that his or her opinions and recollections will be preserved . . ., scientists may be prompted to adopt a public image, even a mask, if you will, that reflects what they want to have remembered about themselves, their life and their accomplishments.'[55] Questions trigger certain kinds of answers, too. And as Weintraub indicates, 'misremembering is not uncommon'.[56]

Well, all these caveats are in order. And yet, these 'distortions' are either unavoidable or even welcome. While Weintraub quite understandably views autobiographical materials as outright problematic if they are supposed to construct a larger historical narrative, I don't even aim at such generality. It is precisely the individual subjectivity that I am after, that I find instructive. In some cases, one may indeed wonder whether things really have come about the way it is told. Maybe the interviewee is just trying to be funny, maybe he wants to impress one, or maybe he doesn't want to admit a weakness. But if one reads the interviews in the present volume with a little bit of sensitivity and humane sympathy, then these things will doubtless not go unnoticed. One will realize that Kenneth J. Arrow, for example, polite and warm as he is, is still also very eager to appear brilliant. It will be clear that Paul A. Samuelson still feels Milton Friedman's thorn in his flesh. It will be striking to see just how much Douglass C. North cultivates his unorthodox ways. There is nothing wrong with that. On the contrary, again, all this is interesting in its own right.

QUESTIONS

In all interviews, I have followed the same pattern. I first explained my project and my research interests, and then I asked all Nobel Laureates to tell me the story of their lives. All of them had received a detailed project draft beforehand; they knew what was coming up. My method then consisted of asking questions which shed light at the same time on the economic history background, the state of the art in economics, and the personal backgrounds of the thinkers in question. The question I always started out with is what it was that had originally drawn them to economics and whether there had been something in their youth, in their family background and upbringing, that had roused an interest in these matters. The next important steps to dwell on have been school, graduate studies, doctoral studies, first employments in research, and, where applicable, wartime occupation – all with a focus on important personal influences such as teachers, colleagues, teammates and friends, as well as on the economics and politics of the time. We then proceeded stepwise, from one path-breaking idea to the next, from one important paper to the next. This seemed a reasonable approach precisely because it is inspirations for excellence that I am trying to track down. Here, of course, I asked individually prepared questions, but all were following this same pattern. Of course, we sometimes couldn't resist the temptation and drifted away a little, discussing interesting topics related to the Nobel Laureate's field of expertise in some greater detail.

As for the level of the conversations, I have tried to keep it rather non-technical. With my double background as an economist and a journalist, I hope that I have been able to avoid the two notorious problems with interviews of this kind: they easily draw the reader either in too much gossip or in too much abstraction. As an academically trained economist, I aimed to touch the crucial theoretical fields and to ask conceptual follow-up questions wherever useful, while as a journalist, I kept in mind to add a human touch and to eschew too technical a conversation between economists that would be difficult to follow for 'outsiders'.

I have endeavoured to let the tone of my questions document the profound respect that I have for my interviewees. While I gave them impulses and tried to cover a certain ground, I have never tried to push them anywhere. In this, I have strayed from the quintessential journalistic pattern, which is not just a cliché, unfortunately. It is true; journalists often ask artificially aggressive questions because that makes for more vigorous and interesting answers. Personally, I do not appreciate this modern plump and noisy style. I don't like it when I read it, and I like it even less when I am supposed to apply it. I prefer a civilized conversation. In the present case, however, this is not just a matter of personal preferences. It is also simply a question of effectiveness. What I wanted to achieve in these interviews was to have the Nobel Laureates open up and tell me their story, to induce them to self-reflection and interpretation, to have them share their recollections with me. That requires confidence and comfort. Any pushing, aggressive tone would have been entirely inappropriate and counterproductive here. My more withdrawn, respectful attitude was rewarded by a beautiful set of interviews conducted in a relaxed, mostly humorous atmosphere with ten outstanding scholars of uncommon intellect and enormous wit. They shared their knowledge and introspection in an act of invaluable generosity. Especially in one case, the conversation was as enriching as it was demanding, not only intellectually, but also emotionally: you develop some ties when you dig so deep together with someone who could be your father. I have enjoyed these conversations like little else.

I also tried one unusual tool that I have inherited from journalism but adapted to academic economics, and that is a questionnaire along the lines of the classical Marcel Proust Q&A. *Frankfurter Allgemeine Zeitung*, Germany's leading serious daily newspaper (and my former employer), used to have this questionnaire in a weekly magazine supplement; unfortunately, the supplement had to be discontinued for financial reasons in the late 1990s. I remember relishing these questionnaires week after week. They consisted of a relatively long list of questions, all of which were answered by no more than one sentence. Ideally, a couple of words were enough.

This brevity is a quite challenge for those who give the answers. One really has to make up one's mind there – and quick. After all, there are two possible ways to deal with the challenge: either one reflects at length, and that may take forever, or one shoots out spontaneous answers, relying on one's instinct. Both methods have some merit. For the reader, these questionnaires were probably the speediest way imaginable to get an impression of a personality. Topics went from 'What are your favorite figures in history' to 'What are you most afraid of?' and 'How would you prefer to die?' Everything is telling in such a questionnaire – the answer itself, of course, but also the style, the length of a sentence, the sense of humor (or absences thereof). Thus I took the model of those Marcel Proust questionnaires and adapted it – or rather narrowed it – to the field of economics. My remodeled questions now range from 'What is the worst economic policy error that you can remember?' or 'What was the most important theoretical breakthrough?' to tough ones like 'If you had to choose between liberty and justice, which would you pick?' and 'What would you name as your most painful failure in professional life?' to complete trivia such as 'What is your favourite dish?' To this latter question, Paul A. Samuelson replies, rather stunningly, 'skim milk'.

I have not managed to convince everybody to do this exercise, however. While Paul A. Samuelson, Robert M. Solow, Kenneth J. Arrow, Vernon L. Smith and Edmund S. Phelps seem to have enjoyed the fun of this playful exercise, James M. Buchanan and Reinhard Selten indignantly rejected the very idea, considering it even a waste of time. Douglass C. North, George A. Akerlof and Gary S. Becker have dropped their promises without any further comment, even after numerous polite reiterations of the request on my part. Even though I wasn't happy with this at first, I didn't fail to realize at some point that these were reactions fully in line with their independent personalities and with their dislike of anything that could even remotely look like a lack of complexity. Even a rejection does shed some light on the underlying personality and mindset – and that is valuable. Therefore I did not insist. The remaining questionnaires serve as a kind of brief overview of some essential issues. They are not only informative, but also extremely fun to read. I shall reveal no more. Enjoy the fun.

NOTES

1. Ben Bernanke in Randall E. Parker (2002, pp. vii–viii).
2. All Nobel Laureates have been asked by the Nobel Foundation to provide autobiographies. These texts were then published in *Les Prix Nobel* and were also made available

online. Most of the Laureates have followed this request, even though in different forms. Especially in the earlier years, some 'dissidents' preferred to provide either very brief autobiographies or some rather non-autobiographical but nevertheless personal notes instead. In the later years, then, everybody has obeyed the rule. The Nobel auto-biographies have not only become increasingly long over the years, but there have even been 'Addenda' for later updates.

3. Michael Szenberg (1992, p. x). In his book, which assembles 22 strikingly different essays by some great economists, his aim is, just like mine, to 'probe how background and upbringing moulded their attitudes, ethics, religion, and how these, in turn, affected choice of occupation, political preference, selection of original research areas, and the related methodology – the theorizing matrix.' Michael Szenberg (1992, p. xi).

4. Robert M. Solow, for example, is 'put off by peeks into the hearts and minds of people who should in some important sense be anonymous.' He fears that knowledge about those inner landscapes might distort our reception of theories. There is undeniably such a risk. People who have a problem with homoerotic tendencies, for example, might transfer their unease to the novels of Thomas Mann as much as to the theories of John Maynard Keynes and reject them for that very reason. 'I do not suppose that anyone would be crass enough to say or believe that the personal characteristics of an author have any bearing on the truth or falsity or value of her or his written work', says Solow in Michael Szenberg (1992, p. 270). I'm afraid he is wrong here. At any rate, especially in arts and literature, it is a recurrent issue of debate whether a work of art or theory should be viewed in isolation or take the personal context of the author in account. Consensus is still far from being reached.

5. Friedrich August von Hayek (1962/1967, p. 52).

6. John Maynard Keynes (1936).

7. Understanding the Great Depression is the 'Holy Grail of macroeconomics', as Ben Bernanke once wrote. See Ben Bernanke (1995). Randall Parker, in his beautiful book filled with interviews with economists who have experienced the Great Depression per-sonally, sets out to find more hints as to what its causes really were. His book is 'about the most prominent economic explanations of the Great Depression and how the events of this period affected the lives, experiences, and subsequent thinking of the leading economists of the twentieth century who lived through that era'. In his introductory chapter, he also provides a state-of-the-art overview over the theoretical explanations that have so far been found. Randall E. Parker (2002, p. ix).

8. 'Being witness to the most extreme form of human bestiality in the history of human-kind, I know all too well the destruction that visionaries with their paradigms have wrought upon societies. In this light, Robert Solow's suggestion that economists should aspire to be competent technicians, "like dentists", as Keynes once remarked, appears very attractive.' Michael Szenberg (1992, p. 13).

9. Joseph A. Schumpeter (1954, p. 6).

10. Joseph A. Schumpeter (1954, pp. 4–5).

11. Rudolf Eucken was the winner of the Nobel Prize in Literature in 1908.

12. See Bruce Caldwell (2004 pp. 74–82).

13. Walter Eucken (1950, p. 41).

14. See Nils Goldschmidt and Michael Wohlgemuth (2008), especially pp. 119–51 and 191–220. The Mont Pèlerin Society is a discussion platform for classical liberal scholars and thinkers of various fields and nationalities, founded in 1947 on the initiative of Friedrich August von Hayek at Mont Pèlerin, Switzerland.

15. See Nils Goldschmidt (2005a). Eucken was a member of the three secret 'Freiburg circles' and formally even a co-author of the famous paper entitled 'Politische Gemeinschaftsordnung', which contains an outline of a post-war economic order. This paper was ultimately discovered by the Gestapo and landed the two main authors, Constantin von Dietze and Adolf Lampe, in deep trouble (meaning imprisonment and torture). See Helmut Thielicke et al. (1979).

16. Bruno S. Frey and Werner W. Pommerehne (1988, p. 106).

17. Stephen M. Stigler (1980).
18. At the time of his death, he owned more than 80 manufacturing plants and companies in twenty different countries, producing 66 000 tons of dynamite and plastic every year. Some of these companies are still in operation today. For one, there are the diverse leftovers of Dynamit Nobel in Germany, for example. The company was founded in 1865 by Alfred Nobel. In the 1930s, it became part of IG Farben and spun off again after the war. It was acquired by Flick, then taken over by Deutsche Bank who sold it off to MG technologies (now GEA), and was then split up in 2004 into various smaller entities which were, for the most part, taken over by Rockwood Inc. Another company was Nobel Enterprises, once part of the British ICI. Nobel Enterprises is now owned by Inabata & Company, a Japanese trading firm. Its original precursor Nobel Industries Limited was founded in 1870 by Alfred Nobel and merged with Brunner, Mond & Company, the United Alkali Company, and the British Dyestuffs Corporation in 1926, creating Imperial Chemical Industries (ICI), then one of Britain's largest firms. Nobel Industries continued as the ICI Nobel division of this company. Upon the sell-off to the Japanese, it was renamed Nobel Enterprises.
19. The main activist here is Peter Nobel, the great-grand-nephew. He has served as Sweden's first Ombudsman against Ethnic Discrimination (1986–91) and Secretary-General of the Swedish Red Cross (1991-94). 'Economy was never in Alfred Nobel's will and does not have the spirit of his prizes', declared Peter Nobel in the *Financial Times* (24 November 2001). See also Peter Nobel (2001).
20. Joseph Schumpeter (1954, p. 7).
21. Friedrich August von Hayek (1964/1967). See Part III.
22. www.nobel.se (emphasis added).
23. The text of his will runs as follows: 'the capital, invested in safe securities by my execu-tors, shall constitute a fund, the interest on which shall be annually distributed in the form of prizes to those who, during the preceding year, shall have conferred the greatest benefit on mankind. . . . It is my express wish that in awarding the prizes no consid-eration whatever shall be given to the nationality of the candidates, but that the most worthy shall receive the prize, whether he be a Scandinavian or not.' Nobel uses the singular and speaks expressly of 'the person who shall have made the most important chemical' or other discovery or improvement (www.nobel.se, emphasis added).
24. Ronald Coase (1937).
25. Assar Lindbeck (1999).
26. This rule is the result of a dispute about the 1994 prize. Before, there was no term limit. In 1994, there was a major controversy between the Economics Prize Committee and the Economics Class of the Royal Swedish Academy of Science concerning the ques-tion whether John F. Nash should receive the award along with John C. Harsanyi and Reinhard Selten. The bone of contention was not the quality of his contributions, which is beyond question. It was rather the fact that his relevant contributions were more than 40 years past; that he was a mathematician seeing his major contributions himself as not being in the field of economics, but in mathematics; the fact that his career had been overshadowed and interrupted by schizophrenia; and that it was not clear whether he would be able to participate in the traditional Nobel Award Ceremony. The vote was tight. Ultimately, Assar Lindbeck, the last member of the original Nobel Committee from 1969 and Chairman of the Committee still in 1994, was dismissed, and new, tighter rules were created for the Committee.
27. Other authors have a nastier, while not misguided description. According to Alex Cukierman, seignorage is 'the amount of real purchasing power that [a] government can extract from the public by printing money'. See Alex Cukierman et al. (1992).
28. Paul A. Samuelson (2006, p. 1).
29. Paul A. Samuelson (2006, p.3).
30. As he said in his Banquet Speech, Hayek was already a little reassured when he himself got the prize – simply because he considered his own work as not being fashionable at all. He was only half joking. 'I feared that such a prize, as I believe is true of the

activities of some of the great scientific foundations, would tend to accentuate the swings of scientific fashion. This apprehension the selection committee has brilliantly refuted by awarding the prize to one whose views are as unfashionable as mine are.' (www.nobel.se).

31. Harriet Zuckerman (1977, p. 251). See Robert K. Merton (1968).
32. Harriet Zuckerman (1977, p. 246).
33. Mark Blaug in the foreword to Howard R. Vane and Chris Mulhearn (2005, p. xi).
34. Hayek in his Banquet Speech, available at www.nobel.se.
35. Harriet Zuckerman (1977, pp. 246–7).
36. Samuel Brittan (2003).
37. As of November 2008.
38. For the sake of perfect information: I had met James M. Buchanan, Robert M. Solow, Gary S. Becker, Douglass C. North and Edmund S. Phelps several times before. The others were new personal discoveries.
39. See Ronald J. Grele et al. (1991).
40. E. Roy Weintraub (2007, p. 5).
41. E. Roy Weintraub (2007, p. 8).
42. E. Roy Weintraub (2007, pp. 4–5).
43. See Stephen Cole (1979).
44. John B. Davis makes such a point in his excellent monograph on John Maynard Keynes's philosophy: 'Ironically, though the principal interest of the recent literature on the subject of Keynes and philosophy is to explain the contribution of Keynes's philosophical thinking to his later economics, most scholars have begun their research with the Treatise on Probability, as if Keynes's chronological intellectual development betokened a parallel conceptual or logical development, that is, as if later ideas depend upon earlier ones just as they follow earlier ones.' John B. Davis (1994, p. 7). George Stigler argues along the same lines when he warns that 'biography distorts rather than illuminates the understanding of scientific work'. George J. Stigler (1970, p. 426).
45. Ben Bernanke in his foreword to Randall E. Parker (2002, p. viii).
46. E. Roy Weintraub (2005).
47. E. Roy Weintraub (2005, p. 10).
48. Robert M. Solow in an interview with 'The Region', recorded in September 2002. Available online at http://minneapolisfed.org/publs/region/02-09/solow.cfm.
49. See the interview with Edmund S. Phelps in this volume.
50. Kenneth J. Arrow (1951).
51. See the interview with Kenneth J. Arrow in this volume.
52. See the interview with James M. Buchanan in this volume.
53. E. Roy Weintraub (2005, p. 8).
54. Jeff Hughes (1997).
55. David H. De Vorkin (1990, p. 47).
56. E. Roy Weintraub (2005, p. 2). In particular, Weintraub highlights that everybody usually experiences two cognitively important moments at which he or she can choose: the first one when action has taken place and one picks – subconsciously – what to remember and what to forget; the second one when remembering and recounting what is left of one's story.

PART II

The interviews

Paul A. Samuelson

*Massachusetts Institute
of Technology (MIT),
Cambridge, MA, USA*

The Sveriges Riksbank Prize in Economic Sciences in Memory of Alfred Nobel 1970 'for the scientific work through which he has developed static and dynamic economic theory and actively contributed to raising the level of analysis in economic sciences'.

INTRODUCTION

MIT spreads out squarely along the northern shore of the Charles River, just opposite Boston. That's however about the only flattering thing one can say about the place. Most buildings have seen better days. The Sloan School of Business is no exception, even though many stars of economic science have their offices here, amongst them Paul A. Samuelson, sitting right next door to Robert M. Solow, his all-time sparring partner in macroeconomic theory. His cubicle is somewhat larger than the others, but the windows badly need cleaning, and the worn-out furniture seems to have remained unchanged ever since the 1970s, including the bulky grey telephone with its anachronistic bell tone. In the antechamber, where Janice Murray, the secretary, has her empire, a series of relatively recent sports photographs up on the wall signal what kind of personalities are assembled here: Janice Murray, boxing; Robert

M. Solow, sailing; and Paul A. Samuelson, playing tennis. Right now, however, the small, frail figure of 92-year-old Samuelson almost disappears behind his desk. He warmly welcomes the interviewer and starts talking right away.[1]

Paul Anthony Samuelson is certainly one of the most awe-inspiring Nobel Laureates, extremely sharp, witty, playfully humble, but always with a harsh judgment on others coming rapidly and easily. Born in Gary, Indiana, on 15 May 1915, as the son of a Jewish pharmacist, he studied at Hyde Park High School in Chicago and then, starting at age 16, at the University of Chicago before switching to Harvard in Cambridge, Massachusetts. At Harvard, he got his MA together with the rank of a 'junior fellow' and, in 1941, his Ph.D. He was strongly influenced by Wassily Leontief, Joseph Schumpeter, and especially Alvin Hansen, who popularized the works of John Maynard Keynes in the United States. In 1940, at age 25, he was offered an assistant professorship at MIT – which he accepted, given that Harvard didn't step up the bid, perhaps for anti-Semitic reasons as some suspect. During the war, Samuelson worked on the National Resources Planning Board, the War Production Board, and the Office of War Mobilization and Reconstruction. In 1947, he received tenure at MIT and started to create the department as we know it today. He also worked for the RAND Corporation, for the American Treasury, for NATO and for American Presidents Dwight D. Eisenhower, John F. Kennedy and Lyndon B. Johnson. He was an advisor to the Federal Reserve Board. A prolific writer in almost every field of economics, he has published some books, most importantly *Foundations of Economic Analysis*[2] and *Economics*,[3] which is now in its eighteenth edition, as well as hundreds of papers, averaging almost one per month in his fully active years. He received the David A. Wells Award at Harvard in 1941, the John Bates Clark Award from the American Economic Association in 1947, and the Albert Einstein Medal in 1971.

With his never idly resting mind, he has covered almost every imaginable field of economics to which he contributed fundamental concepts and theories. In trade theory, for example, he left his mark, amongst other things, by explaining the conditions for beneficial trade and by showing that protectionism tends to raise the real wages of a country's relatively scarce production factor, while opening up the borders benefits the relatively abundant production factor ('Stolper–Samuelson theorem'). In consumption theory, he derived demand curves from the 'revealed preferences' that people display as they buy things, instead of messing around with marginal utilities which are impossible to observe otherwise. In capital theory, he showed how to deal with heterogeneous capital goods. In growth theory, he worked out the 'turnpike theorem' describing conditions for maximum growth. For dynamic theory and stability analysis, he invented the 'correspondence principle' that provides the missing link between static and dynamic theory and which thereby helps to understand situations outside equilibrium. In business cycle theory, he created accelerator-multiplier models that permit the phenomenon of business cycles to be understood in a rather simple way. And in public finance, he showed what optimal taxation for public goods should look like. One may want to call Samuelson's approach eclectic, but that misses the point. It would be more appropriate to say – and he does it himself – that he is one of the last generalists. The breadth of his research agenda is due to his genius, for one, but also very much to the fact that when he started out, economic theory was not yet as diversified. He has been active in an era when economics only started to unfold and flourish – and he himself made that happen.

Interestingly, outside and inside observers are divided when it comes to the question of whether Samuelson has created a school of thought of his own. Given the generality of his approach and his non-dogmatic way of using every tool available, some people deny this. It is our view, however, that his impact has been tremendous, and this because in all the fields that he has covered, Samuelson has brought his one major general innovation to bear: formalization, mathematization, or, as the Nobel Committee has it, he 'actively contributed to raising the level of analysis in economic sciences'. In this, Samuelson has turned out to be not only one of the most brilliant, but also one of the most influential economists ever. By demonstrating that all economic behavior can be studied in the form of some maximization problem, he fundamentally changed economics. In a sense, it is fair to say that all modern economics is economics of the Samuelson school. What had once been a more verbal, or literary field with close ties to classical philosophy now became a relatively rigorous, mathematical discipline, and this development seems to be irreversible. While this may be deplorable for what has been lost, it must be acknowledged that formalized theory simply has won out in the market for ideas. The profession wasn't satisfied with the more withdrawn philosophical approach any more; something more concrete and precise allowing for state action was desired.

The desire to have such an almost 'natural' hard science that would lend itself more easily to political action has really come up in economics ever since the late 1920s. The existing tools of (then) orthodox economics didn't seem to provide satisfactory explanations and answers to the Great Depression.[4] As Samuelson himself points out, the Great Depression made a deep impact on him; he still views it as the 'most important economic catastrophe so far'.[5] What was needed in this serious situation was a theoretical body that would allow the understanding of disequilibrium, on the one hand, or, even better, equilibrium with persistent unemployment, on the other hand. For this reason, the profession not only gracefully picked up the new trend that originated in England, with John Maynard Keynes's *General Theory of Employment, Interest, and Money*,[6] but also started looking out for tools that would make analysis more precise. Given this desire, mathematization was a natural, straightforward choice. Paul A. Samuelson indeed quotes John Maynard Keynes as one of his major role models – even though, when the *General Theory* came out, he 'didn't take to it at once',[7] as he says elsewhere, precisely because it didn't square with neoclassical equilibrium theory. He instantly set out to do what seemed impossible – to incorporate Keynes's insights into equilibrium theory. This is what became known as the 'neoclassical synthesis'. In doing so, he created a new orthodoxy, a new mainstream in economics.

Paul A. Samuelson looks at the world in what one might want to call an American liberal way. His personal experience in life and work have triggered and confirmed the feeling that the optimal economic system is something like a 'third way', that is a mixture between free markets and active collective choice, avoiding both libertarian and socialist extremes. The Great Depression forever disenchanted him with 'unfettered' capitalism. He therefore admires President Franklin Delano Roosevelt, whose 'New Deal' supposedly helped to end the disastrous effects of the Great Depression and established a social safety net in the United States. In Samuelson's view, 'Laissez-faire' just means that the state doesn't live up to its responsibilities. Libertarianism, for him, is a misleading philosophy. Samuelson likes to warn that the market is never and can never be perfect – and so, in one of his more recent papers, he has managed to stir up the whole profession once more by showing mathematically that there are situations in which free trade is not welfare-enhancing for everybody.[8] His paper encountered a lot of criticism for not taking technical progress into account, but his warning nevertheless met with particular interest as some Americans were growing more and more suspicious of the strong competition coming from China. Samuelson showed that even though customers on average benefit from this competition, some groups inside the United States, especially those with low professional qualifications, may lose out. Unlike some lobbies, however, Samuelson doesn't imply that the pace of globalization should be slowed down through protectionism. Instead, he advocates some compensation: the winners should share their gains with the losers.

Paul A. Samuelson's path is a perfect example of how the economic challenges of changing times, the evolution of economics as a field of science, and personal biographies all act together in the progress of economic theory. All these three lines of development were relevant and interacted. Samuelson's approach grew out of the puzzling times of the Great Depression, which he lived through as a child and was eager to understand, even though his family background was not a genuinely intellectual one. At any rate, Paul Samuelson discovered that economics wasn't quite apt to give satisfactory answers. In leaving his own mark in economics, in showing the way towards mathematization, Samuelson then triggered new debates that kept the process of theoretical refinement going. This developed some dynamism of its own. As he acknowledges, much of what he has been working on just came up as a topic because somebody else had written something that he felt the urge to straighten out. One might say therefore that Samuelson provided the mathematical tools that set the profession on its modern track and then browsed through the upcoming ramifications in a more or less leisurely way. In the interview, we can see that in many and recurring instances, he simply reacted to Milton Friedman, a figure that constantly gave him both annoyance and inspiration, as it seems. The dialectics of intellectual progress obviously requires one to have somebody resisting and somebody to resist.

INTERVIEW

Professor Samuelson, please tell me what made you turn to economics in the first place. What role did your upbringing play, if any? Let's go back to your first years.
I started out as a bright kid, I skipped grades. As I look back, I realize that I had an enormous amount of self-confidence as a child, most of it unearned. Just because I counted the numbers faster than anybody in the classroom, I thought I could be a great radio announcer, for example. I thought I would succeed in anything that I'd put my hand to. That was of course absurd. Well, I had a supportive family, I had a bright older brother, and as an afterthought, I must say that I also had a bright younger brother. My cousins were not quite as smart. Actually, I have one unusual part in my autobiography in that from the age of 17 months until 5½ years old, I spent half of my time at what I now have to think of as a foster family, on a farm in Porter County next to Lake County, near Gary, Indiana, where I was born.

How did that come about?
That's something I have never understood. It could have been a disaster, but it wasn't at all. This whole adventure cost one dollar a day for food, lodging and love from someone who was not my DNA. I learnt this from my mother, when she was in her late eighties – I never had any curiosity

about this before, but at that time, we needed something to talk about. The setting was just like a late nineteenth century protestant American rural environment. No inside-the-house plumbing, chamber pots in the alcoves, no electricity. That means you have to use oil lamps when it's dark. But those oil lamps are no good to read by, and therefore you end up going to bed early. I can't think there was a great deal of mental stimulation from that environment. By contrast, my younger brother Robert, who was the father of the former president of Harvard University, Lawrence Summers,[9] he and his son spent a lot of time every day talking about economic and other problems. I think the same was true for David and Milton Friedman.[10] If you talk to David Friedman, he says he's never been influenced by Milton, but in reality, David Friedman is like Milton squared, and not less. In my case, that wasn't so at all.

What about your supportive parents?
My parents both came from the same little part of Poland between Lithuania and East Prussia. As I learnt later, my mother pursued my father, her first cousin, to America. My father came over, and after a brief stop in the New York area, he went to the Midwest, became a registered pharmacist, druggist, and had his own drugstore. This was a common pattern for relatively poor immigrants who might otherwise have gone to medical school. In 1912, my parents eloped from Chicago to Kenosha, Wisconsin.

Why would they do that?
They had to do that because they were first cousins, as I mentioned earlier. In those days, they were illegal in Illinois, but not in Wisconsin. That's why I have six fingers, you see (*chuckles at his joke*). My father was quite good at a couple of things, at algebra for example, which he did discuss with me. We didn't discuss the state of the world, though.

So some mathematical affinities were in your blood, so to speak?
Yes. And I did actually learn something about solving simultaneous equations while I was still down at grade school.

What about your mother?
Well, my mother's case must have been somewhat unusual because in her kind of environment, a female would not be expected to get much education. But she had some proficiency in French and Latin. I don't know exactly where that came from. I think that her family was a bit more prosperous than the others around her because her grandfather had come to the US around the time of the Civil War in the middle of the century. He probably started out as a peddler, left his family in the old country, sent and brought

money back. That, too, was a very common pattern. He became a wheat merchant. My mother was a person whose metric of what was important was very much conditioned by how well off they were. I also think she was a premature feminine activist. She didn't like home duties. That's perhaps one reason why I went to the farm as a child. Maybe I was a difficult eater, too. At any rate, she was a wretched cook. It's all understandable.

What did the economic environment look like, and how did that influence you?
I was born into the boom of World War I. Actually, I was born in a frontier town, a new town, Gary, with the biggest steel mill in the world, where ten years before my birth, it had been all sand dunes. Being a big company town, it had a really excellent school system. The same is true for Milton Friedman, by the way, by coincidence. He was born in Brooklyn but they lived in Raleigh, New Jersey, which is nothing of a town. They had a good school system there, too. When we moved to Chicago later, after an interlude in Florida, I went to good schools, too. The city was also very important for my macroeconomic background. Anyway, my point is that I could feel around me the boom that the breakout of the war in 1914 had created. We weren't into the war, but all the allied countries bought steel, and the steel mills operated every hour of the week, you could see the fire. Men worked a twelve-hour day seven days a week. They probably got a dollar an hour. The population was mainly from Eastern and Central Europe. We called them 'Slawish'. They really were Slovenes, Serbs, Croats, Czechs and Poles. And on the other hand, also as a kid, I had already experienced the prosperity of a hundred-acre farm. The war sent up the price of grain, and the Keynesian multiplier was operating. Of course, I later also experienced the opposite of that at the end of the war, when there was the rather sharp, short-run recession, prior to the next boom period. Another key was when my family, in 1925, moved to Miami Beach, Florida, because there was a great land bubble that we wanted to take advantage of. We didn't see it coming to the burst. You know how to make a small fortune in Florida real estate? You start out with a bigger one (*laughter*). So the relative degree of affluence that had been accumulated in the family from the World War I prosperity gradually was dissipated. That was something which I experienced. And it left a mark.

How did your schooling go?
After returning from Florida, I went to a good Chicago public school, Hyde Park high school. I had very good mathematics courses there. I had a great mathematics teacher, Ms Smith. She was a spinster, and she more or less wore the same dress every day. She later left 10 million dollars to the

University of Chicago, her Alma Mater. I was surprised to hear that, and when I inquired, I was told she probably just had a good broker. Anyway, even before I graduated from Hyde Park high school under a familiar arrangement, I could go already to Chicago University, which was only two miles away. It never occurred to me to go to Harvard, as would today be the pattern, or Princeton, or Yale, or Cornell, or whatever. I landed at the University of Chicago on 2 January 1932 and I walked into my first lecture class. I was still in my teens then. I can truly say that I was reborn that instant. The lecture that I heard which was actually given by a professor of sociology was on Malthus's theory of population.[11] It was very interesting. It seemed so simple, I thought I wasn't really understanding this, it must be more complicated. But it wasn't more complicated. Actually, I had come in one quarter late. The economics of the famous Chicago core curriculum had taken place during that first quarter. So to make up for my deficiency, I was put in an old-fashioned introductory course in economics. That worked out very well because the teacher was Aaron Director.[12] He was a person who has never published anything important, but he was very influential. He really was the one who converted the first Chicago School of Frank Knight, Jacob Viner and Paul Douglas, which was pretty eclectic, into the second one, with Milton Friedman and so forth. I guess with Gary Becker[13] et al. we're at the third right now. So there I was, completely by chance, and I discovered the subject that interested me and that I would be good at. Economics is a subject which is quite attractive to somebody who is both interested in statistics, analysis, metrics, but also in people and policies. And so I became a very good student there.

But with those interests, you could also have turned to political science or sociology. So economics was actually a coincidence?
To be sure, I came to Chicago only because of location. It was an accident that I liked the subject. I had not even thought about economics in my high school years. In my father's library, there was a copy of Adam Smith's *Wealth of Nations*[14] in the – abridged – Harvard Classics Series. I didn't even notice it was there. I only looked at two books of that famous series; one was a translation of Virgil that helped me cheat in Latin and the other one was some novel. It wasn't that with my mother's milk I was getting economics. But it was important – and it shows the importance of coincidence and chance – that Aaron Director assigned me a chapter in a famous advanced book by Gustav Cassel, the Swedish economist, on the arithmetic of the price system.[15] This was his plagiarism of Leon Walras's general equilibrium. It was exciting to see that the math that I knew could be used. And then I realized I didn't have enough math, so I spent the time at Chicago catching up on it.

So Chicago played an important role in giving you the necessary tools.
Oh yes, and it was also valuable that the Chicago I went to was the best place in the world at that time in neoclassical economics. But that does not mean it was the best place in the world to understand the Great Depression.[16] The Great Depression was not Euclidian geometry. I was very sensitive to this mismatch, that is to the fact that what I was learning in class could not rationalize for me that almost every bank in my neighborhoods in Northern Indiana and Illinois went broke and that almost all the money that my older brother had earned to go to college was lost. In a nutshell, about one third of the population had no jobs. And the two thirds who had jobs would not trade with them. The one third without jobs would gladly trade with them or gladly work for even less. But of course they couldn't do that. To try and handle this kind of disequilibrium system with the historic tools of economics that were in the textbooks I was being assigned was impossible. So you can understand why, then, by complete good luck, I happily got out of Chicago.

How did that happen?
The reason was that I had won an extraordinary new scholarship to pay all my graduate training but I couldn't stay where I had started out. All my mentors, all famous people like Frank Knight, Jacob Viner, Paul Douglas, Henry Simons, all of them said I should go to Columbia, not Harvard. At Columbia, there was better statistics, with Harold Hotelling, and there was also Wesley C. Mitchell, the institutionalist. But I didn't listen to my elders much. I picked Harvard mostly because I thought it would be like a nice small New England village with a white church and a good library and a lot of green there. I was pretty shocked then when I came on the streetcar across the river here and got to noisy Harvard Square. Every decision I have made in my life that has been at first the wrong one, I changed. But this one, by luck, was the right one. I didn't realize it then, but Harvard was in kind of a boom period because Adolf Hitler was so beastly and many refugees started out there. One effect of that was that I was by far the best prepared member of that entering class. I was kind of a brash youngster; I would correct my professors when they made mistakes. I was already publishing articles during my doctorate at Harvard.

When you started economics, was it clear to you from the very beginning that you were heading towards an academic career?
No, it wasn't clear to me. You see, I came from a family with a Jewish heritage, but not an observant family. One knew, for example, that you could be as bright as anything and do well in chemistry, but you

wouldn't get a job with DuPont or something. Different fields were different. There was anti-Semitism in some degree everywhere, but less in Chicago than at Harvard or Princeton. As a result, this gave Chicago a certain monopoly advantage; they could get talent that the others didn't think they wanted. So it would be wrong for me to think that in my freshman year at Chicago I had an academic life in mind. At that time, I would probably, like my older brother, have tried to become a lawyer. That was a more common path. However, once I got to be proficient with publications, I knew that I would get a good job, even though I didn't know where.

And when you were at Harvard?
I spent five wonderful years at Harvard, especially with the status of a fellow, which meant that I didn't have any duties. Most of what I got the Nobel Prize for, I did it at that time. I wasn't allowed to work for a degree, but I also didn't need to. And then, when I finished that stint, I was an instructor at Harvard, and I got a good offer here at MIT. In the meantime I was married. My wife was a small town banker's daughter, a WASP, that is, a white Anglo-Saxon protestant. We said, well, this will be a test, we will see whether Harvard can match this offer or do better. They didn't, and so we came three miles down the river. I have always been within three miles of Harvard yard, and I still live three miles off Harvard yard. At the time, the economics department at MIT, an engineering school, was a mediocre department. But I didn't need the stimulus of bright colleagues; I knew that I was a self-starter. Also, I still had all my Harvard friends and the great Harvard library which was important. I was very lucky in my marriage; she was bright and sensible.[17] Actually, she was Schumpeter's assistant at one time, and a protégée of Wassily Leontief.[18] So, summing up, I've always been overpaid and underworked. The reason why I'm underworked is because what I do is not work. And as you can see, at age 92, I'm still doing it.

How did you become a Keynesian?
I was dissatisfied with the analysis of economic fluctuations. By the way, the word macroeconomics was not yet coined then. But the alleged 'macroeconomics' of the orthodox neoclassical economists would have been that overall permanent unemployment is impossible, Say's law[19] prevails, and in the Walrasian general equilibrium system, there can be proved to always be a root.[20] But a disequilibrium system was no subject for them. In my very first year at Harvard, John Maynard Keynes' *General Theory*[21] came out, and we received books in advance of the publication. When I read it, I was not converted.

It is a difficult read

Yes, and actually, if you just have the words of the text, it's not completely coherent. But pragmatically, I said this is the best bicycle in town, you can't wait for that better bicycle. Maybe we don't know what its micro-foundations are, but it does explain why, in my sophomore year at the University of Chicago, Franklin D. Roosevelt came in to office and began to spend billions of dollars in his New Deal,[22] just as Hitler was beginning to do, too, and the same effects came. I understood this because I had experienced it in Gary, Indiana, in the World War I period. I had a certain amount of interest in the stock market. I had helped my freshman math teacher pick stocks, most of which ended up badly after the 1929 crash. I made a loop of faith. I really thank Darwin or whoever runs the universe that I wasn't stuck at Chicago. I would have missed out on the monopolistic competition revolution, which they didn't believe in. I would have missed out on the Keynesian revolution that they also didn't believe in. I would have missed out on mathematization of economics, although some of that did even take place at the University of Chicago. I was lucky. When I came here, to this mediocre department, with World War II just around the corner, some government money needed to be spent on computers, on radar, secretly on the atomic bomb, etc., so that MIT was 85 percent engineering. Now it is probably 15 percent engineering. Wherever the tide was rising, I was by good luck there.

What about your colleagues? Wasn't Milton Friedman one of your most important sparring partners?

Oh yes. Milton Friedman and I became known as two poles, early on, but we managed to stay on civil and fairly friendly terms. Milton Friedman never made a mistake in his whole life. That's remarkable, isn't it? He is as bright a guy as you would ever meet. But I don't think he realizes the tremendous number of mistakes he made in his life. I don't think anybody has read every item of Milton Friedman's work in the world except me. I always feel that I learn more from my enemy than I can learn from my friend, because my friend and I already are at the same point. Most of my jokes about Milton Friedman are actually deep truths. Sometimes I say he's got such a high IQ that he has no protection against himself. He looks at his work and is satisfied with it. However, I think that it is a tragedy when somebody really takes the wrong train in his life.

I'd rather talk a little bit more about you

This *is* about me. See, unlike Milton, I look at my work, I realize that my opinions are fallible opinions; they are always changing over time. That's not something I regard as a fault but rather as a virtue. I'm always self-conscious,[23] and I like to get not two viewpoints on every matter, but three!

After all, the great gift to be a skilled economist is to be eclectic. As I would tell my macro seminar: if you must forecast, forecast often. It sounds like a joke, but it's true. Also, I have changed my opinions in many ways, and in each case, that's no rejection of my earlier opinions. The earlier opinions were geared to a particular system.

Right. That sounds a bit like the Popperian position – the historical context matters. But let's turn to some of your own major contributions. First of all, and most importantly, what drew you so much towards mathematization, culminating in your dissertation, better known as your landmark 1947 book Foundations of Economic Analysis?[24] *It revolutionized economic theory.*
Mathematics has an evolution built into it, and that's what I like about it. You start out and it teaches you. You don't know what it teaches you until you've done it and you suddenly realize what it is. Fundamentally, all the different parts of the *Foundations of Economic Analysis* just grew out of actual lively topics that my teachers – a great generation – weren't able to handle adequately.

And what caused you to write your world-famous bestselling textbook?[25]
All that I just said had no bearing on my textbook. The textbook was actually written upon invitation by the head of the department here at MIT. Every MIT student in the third year had to take two full semesters of introductory economics, and they hated it. And so he said to me: 'Paul, would you take a few months off and write a text which they will like?' And I agreed: 'Sure, I'll do it.' What I didn't realize was that it would take me three years and more of beastly hard work. I had the choice: I could have made it a simple mathematical introduction, simple mathematics, but I decided not to do that, because MIT students like to do analytical problems. In the book, it's only diagrams and so forth. I spent a lot of time on expository virtues. I didn't do it for the money, although there was a lot of money to it, after the fact. But there was a different layer of fame that opened up for me this way: the book set a pattern for all textbooks ever after. Just this morning I was over at the medical department for some appointment, and a Chinese came up saying 'oh, Doctor Samuelson, you're still alive!? You're so well-named out there. . .' And I asked: 'Did you study my book in Mandarin or English?' In his case, he studied it in English, but you could do it in both. My book no longer has a monopoly on the field in America, but around the world, it still has an important role to play.

Did politics ever directly trigger the questions that you worked on?
Very uncharacteristic was the fact that for some time, I became the principal economic adviser to President John F. Kennedy. It is true that

this involved an internal dilemma, for a number of reasons, even though it was extremely interesting and pretty important for me. At the time, I was an Adlai Stevenson follower, so I had to warn Kennedy: 'I'm not even for you!' He said: 'I don't want your vote, see, that would be only one vote anyway. But I'm going to make a shot at the presidency and I may get it. And I think that your ideas are important for the country. Think about it.' And so I did think about it. And Kennedy ended up persuading me that this country is too important to have John Kenneth Galbraith and Walt Rostow act as the principal economic advisers. I could have gone to Washington in a high position, but I really preferred the academic life. I even had my doctor prepared to say that this wouldn't be good for my health. Fortunately, I never had to use that excuse. Anyway, it was a wonderful team that I helped to select: Walter Heller as the chairman of the Council of Economic Advisers, James Tobin,[26] etc. As a matter of fact, before the 1960 election, the American dollar had become an overvalued dollar. And so we proposed quietly that the first act of the President should be to depreciate the dollar, with the British. But Kennedy said: 'The last thing I want is to be known as a currency tinkerer.' What you learn when you are advising the prince is that the prince gets the kind of adviser that he wants. As a result, for a whole decade, we did everything possible to hide the fact that we were cheapening the dollar.

You've covered a vast area of topics throughout your career. What guided you there? For example, in Public Finance, the theory of taxation for public goods[27] – how did that very particular idea come about? Was it some kind of request from politics?

No. There is this much-cited article which, in a way, I regret because I should have gone to my friend Richard Musgrave[28] and said 'Let's make this a joint article'. Because everything I knew about the theory of voluntary taxation, I knew from Dick. I wrote the article because some fool out of the RAND Corporation[29] had written an article saying that mathematics was useless in social sciences, that nothing had ever been done by mathematics that was of any use. Seymour Harris who was the editor of the journal, made me lead a symposium on the topic. And so I thought I'd give this as an example that mathematics can be useful, since nobody had ever exactly clarified the Lindahl problem.[30] I wrote it probably in an afternoon or two. That's the genesis. This probably kept Musgrave from getting the Nobel Prize. Which is a shame. But that's the trouble with honors for one person. The people at the top tier who don't receive the prize are just as good. Science is a group activity.

As I can see, much of what you do seems to be a reaction to foolish papers of other people that needed correction. And also, a lot of your ideas seem to have come out of discussions with colleagues, e.g. Richard Musgrave and Wolfgang Stolper,[31] the latter in trade theory.

Yes, that's true. Talking of trade theory, there was a big fuss about an article a couple of years ago, a paper in the *Journal of Economic Perspectives*[32] in which I told a simple truth: if Toyota has innovations and takes away business from Ford and General Motors, then it is true that you get cheaper and better quality Toyotas for consumers, and therefore, a simple-minded answer would then be that all globalization and innovation anywhere is good for everywhere. But that's simply not true. But I had a new metric, a new way of measuring, just what the benefit of the cheapness of the import was against the drop in real wages produced in that country. And there was a clear case where it would be harmful. By and large, globalization has helped both China and the US. But the point is that the winners in the US are a very unbalanced group. In the old New Deal days, with Presidents Franklin D. Roosevelt, Harry Truman, John F. Kennedy, Lyndon Johnson, the government would have made the winners – with the use of the tax system and the expenditure system – share some of their winnings, so that potentially, everybody could be better off. However, there is a big change in my understanding: only to a limited degree can you take a market system and improve on it by government buy-out.

And why isn't state intervention a good remedy?

Mine is not the Hayekian argument that it would turn totalitarian.[33] To me, all of current history just shows that if you do that, as in Sweden, you kill the goose that lays the golden eggs. You can rectify distribution only to a very limited degree. The real trouble with the modern world from an ethical viewpoint is not an idiot like President George W. Bush or a mean guy like President Richard Nixon, it's the electorate. The more we get away from the Great Depression, when everybody felt we had the same problems and need of mutual reinsurance, and from the 'necessary war', World War II, the more the electorate no longer has altruism. But you can't just dispel the electorate, as the German playwright Bertolt Brecht noted sarcastically.[34] Yet, this emphasis upon the limited improvements that you can make within a modern democracy is a fundamental change in my thinking. The other thing that has changed is that because of Japan and Singapore and Hong Kong and Taiwan, the US economy in the ancient tradition of my textbook is a different one from the one of the current edition. In those old days, the Fortune 500 companies had a measure of oligopoly power which they were forced to share with the trade unions. Well, in the meantime, the trade unions are gone in America, except in a few localizations and in government. We have a coward labor force. The result is that we are much more like in a Say's law situation. All that conversion to the disequilibrium system, into Keynesianism, seems no longer useful to me.

Why is Keynesianism losing ground?
What dethroned plain vanilla Keynesianism was stagflation. If you have a supply shock like in the seventies, you knew what to do: cure either the 'stag' or the 'flation'. But one would hurt the other. However, even nowadays, you still have to worry about liquidity traps[35] and stuff like that. So my attempt is to stay eclectic. That's a major gift, I think, a gift that major scholars should buy into. It allows you to focus on what's relevant. But of course, one explanation for anything is always short of the other things.

How would you define progress in economic theory?
Oh well. I would say that something like the Taylor rule[36] is progress. What I was espousing at the Federal Reserve academic classes is that you don't look at one thing, but you look at many things, and you have two goals. One is, if you are tolerant towards inflation, it will stop being tolerable inflation, and so you have to have a penalty on too much stimulus. And the other thing is that you have to look whether the economy is creating enough jobs and purchasing power etc. From this viewpoint, the problem is not that jobs disappear because they go to China. The problem is that the jobs that reappear in America are 20 percent below in wage as compared to what your last job was. That's good sound neoclassical economics. But politics doesn't deal with that. By the way, it's a very hard message for the public to understand.

Well, that's the problem with economics generally, I guess, it's often times just counterintuitive. . . Are you happy with economics the way it is being taught right now?
There is one thing that I'm not very happy about, even though I understand it. It's that the profession has gone very much to the right ideologically. And guess who was the most important person responsible for that. . . it was Milton Friedman, not Friedrich Hayek. The libertarianism which puts all the emphasis on Pareto optimality[37] efficiency doesn't realize that even if you get 100 percent of the market return, and therefore you have a Pareto optimum, this outcome would still not satisfy any distributive justice criteria. I hope that my colleagues under 45 years of age in this wonderful department here at MIT understand that.

And otherwise? In terms of topics?

The deeper truth is that people go where the money is, even in research. I know lots of economists who are drawn to financial engineering, but also to judicial testifying. You tell me which side I'm to testify on. . . and then. . . It's an honorable thing to do for a lawyer, and I won't say it is dishonorable for economists. But there is a famous story about this that tells it all: when Willie Sutton, the bank-robber, went to jail, a reporter asked him: 'Why do you rob banks?!' And the answer was, sure enough: 'That's where the money is'.[38] If you had a son who would go into economics and you advise him on his career, you say: 'Try to find a justification for non-regulation.' That will pay off best. And also, your self-esteem depends on public esteem, that is, on the public's esteem. Well, summing up: the old gang of people was nicer people than the new gang. That's not to say that there are not nice people in both. At any interdisciplinary meeting, economists always stick out, and they are being viewed as being crazy and mean, but often they're just realistic, which the others aren't.

That certainly has to do with the underlying idea of the self-centered, super-rational homo oeconomicus. People from other fields often tend to think that we really believe in it.

Well, Gary Becker has indeed explained that a smoker who shortens his life is maximizing his hedonistic pleasure from smoking. That's not very acute psychology. Anyway, what I have always known is that a lot of people who don't come to the same conclusions as I do are smart and hard-working people. What they find will always be interesting. Even though their findings may shift a lot along the way.

What do you think are the most important challenges for economic theory in the future?

The biggest challenge is probably globalization. As a big country, you can bear a lot of inefficiency. But with globalization, that leeway vanishes. The increase of globalization is inevitably associated with an increase in inequality, and also with an increase in anxiety. It used to be that if you were a graduate of Harvard business school, you would get a job, you get promoted with age, and then you retire in honor. It's not like that any more. The length of time in one job has been seriously shortened. This is a source of a lot of corporate misgovernance. You can make a big killing and laugh all the way to the bank, even though you've left havoc behind you. Well, economists will never run out of work. And good analytical economics is always a good cure for incoherent economic policy.

Thank you, Professor.

NOTES

1. The inte; vi.w was held on 4 June 2007.
2. Paul A. Samuelson (1947). This book was also his dissertation, under the title 'The operational significance of economic theory'.
3. Paul A. Samuelson (1948a). The book has in recent years (after 1985) been co-authored by William Nordhaus. The book has been translated into 41 languages and has in total sold over 4 million copies.
4. 1929–1937. For a precise account of the Great Depression as such and how some major economists, including Paul A. Samuelson, experienced it, see Randall E. Parker (2002).
5. See questionnaire.
6. John Maynard Keynes (1936).
7. See Randall E. Parker (2002, p. 29).
8. Paul A. Samuelson (2004).
9. The Summers family changed their name in order to avoid anti-Semitic discrimination.
10. Milton Friedman (1912–2006) was awarded the Nobel Prize in 1976 'for his achievements in the fields of consumption analysis, monetary history and theory and for his demonstration of the complexity of stabilization policy'.
11. 'That day's lecture was on Malthus's theory that human populations would reproduce like rabbits until their density per acre of land reduced their wage to a bare subsistence level where an increased death rate came to equal the birth rate', explains Paul Samuelson in his 2003 paper 'How I became a economist', available at www.nobel.se. Thomas Malthus (1826).
12. Aaron Director (1901–2004), professor at the University of Chicago Law School and Rose Friedman's elder brother, played a central role in the development of the Chicago School of economics. He founded the *Journal of Law & Economics* in 1958, which he co-edited with Ronald Coase. Indeed, he didn't publish much, but as his colleague George Stigler once said, 'most of Aaron's articles have been published under the names of his colleagues'.
13. Gary S. Becker was awarded the Nobel Prize in 1992 'for having extended the domain of microeconomic analysis to a wide range of human behavior and interaction, including non-market behavior'.
14. Adam Smith (1776).
15. The book was Gustav Cassel's *Theory of Social Economy* (1923).
16. The Great Depression was a worldwide economic downturn starting in most places in 1929, following the stock market crash on 29 October 1929, and ending at different times in the 1930s or early 1940s. It was the largest and most important economic depression in modern history. It originated in the United States. The Great Depression had devastating effects in the whole world.
17. His first wife was Marion Crawford (1916–78), herself an economist, whom he had met in Boston. Since 1981, Samuelson has been married to Risha S. Eckaus, a former student of his.
18. Wassily Leontief (1906–1999) was awarded the Nobel Prize in 1973 'for the development of the input–output method and for its application to important economic problems'.
19. Say's law, named after the French economist Jean-Baptiste Say (1767–1832), states that supply always creates its own demand. The approach behind this 'law' focuses more on the conditions for supply, rather than concentrating on demand, as the Keynesians do (Jean-Baptiste Say, 1803).
20. This means simply that the system of equations mathematically depicting the economy can be solved, so that such an equilibrium does actually really exist.
21. John Maynard Keynes (1936).
22. Franklin D. Roosevelt became President of the US in 1933. The New Deal was a program of government interventions aiming at relaunching the economy, simultaneously

   providing relief for the poor and unemployed and creating new regulation for the banking system.

23. See, for a differing interpretation, the interview with Kenneth J. Arrow in this book.
24. Paul A. Samuelson (1947).
25. Paul A. Samuelson (1948a). Now in its eighteenth edition, the book has in recent years (after 1985) been co-authored by William Nordhaus. The book been translated into 41 languages and has in total sold over 4 million copies.
26. James Tobin was awarded the Nobel Prize in 1981, 'for his analysis of financial markets and their relations to expenditure decisions, employment, production and prices'.
27. In this paper, Samuelson establishes what later became dubbed the 'Samuelson Rule'. It says that the sum of the marginal rates of substitution between the public good and the private good for all members of the community should equal the marginal rate of transformation between the two goods (Paul A. Samuelson, 1954).
28. German-born Richard A. Musgrave (1910–2007) was an eminent scholar in public finance. He systematized his field by splitting it up into the three classical subdivisions of allocation, distribution and stabilization policy. He also invented the somewhat controversial idea of 'merit wants' that should be provided for by the state.
29. The RAND Corporation is a research institution created originally in 1946 by the United States Army Air Forces as Project RAND, under contract to the Douglas Aircraft Company. In 1946, they released the Preliminary Design of an Experimental World-Circling Spaceship. In 1948, Project RAND was separated from Douglas and became an independent non-profit organization, sponsored initially by the Ford Foundation, to 'further promote scientific, educational, and charitable purposes, all for the public welfare and security of the United States of America'. The ranged of topics has since expanded greatly. The acronym RAND actually stands for 'Research and Development'.
30. In the Lindahl problem, named after the Swedish economist Erik Robert Lindahl (1891–1960), it is asked how parties can contribute to the cost of a public good in proportion to the incremental benefit they derive from it.
31. In 1941, Paul Samuelson and Wolfgang Stolper postulated the Stolper–Samuelson theorem according to which under some assumptions such as constant returns and perfect competition, a rise in the relative price of a good will lead to a rise in the return to that factor which is used most intensively in the production of the good, and conversely, to a fall in the return to the other factor. Wolfgang F. Stolper and Paul A. Samuelson (1941).
32. Paul A. Samuelson (2004).
33. This is an allusion to Friedrich August von Hayek (1944). Hayek was awarded the Nobel Prize in 1974, together with Gunnar Myrdal – both received it 'for their pioneering work in the theory of money and economic fluctuations and for their penetrating analysis of the interdependence of economic, social and institutional phenomena'. With regard to Hayek, this is somewhat ironical, given that his major contributions are much rather to be found in his works in the field of social philosophy.
34. After the events of 17 June 1953, the suppressed widespread uprising against the East German government, Bertolt Brecht wrote in the famous poem 'Die Lösung' (the solution), one of his 'Buckower Elegien': 'Wäre es da nicht doch einfacher, die Regierung löste das Volk auf und wählte ein anderes?' – wouldn't it be simpler if government dissolved the people and elected a different one?
35. A liquidity trap is when people prefer to hold all their assets in cash, given that the nominal interest rate is too low, that is close or equal to zero. The classical tools of monetary policy, especially a further lowering of the interest rate, then don't work – but rather make things worse.
36. According to the Taylor rule, named after the American economist John B. Taylor, the central bank should change the nominal interest rate in response to divergences of actual GDP from potential GDP and divergences of actual rates of inflation from a target rate of inflation (John B. Taylor, 1993).

37. Pareto optimality, named after the Italian economist and sociologist Vilfredo Pareto (1848–1923), is a concept that refers to a situation in which none of the concerned parties can improve his or her welfare any further without impairing the other one's. In exchange relations, this demonstrates the optimal scope of mutually beneficial interaction.
38. William 'Willie' Sutton (1901–1980) was a prolific US bank robber. For his talent at executing robberies in disguises, he gained two nicknames, 'Willie the Actor' and 'Slick Willie'. He actually denied having uttered the famous quote and attributed it to the reporter.

Kenneth J. Arrow

Stanford University, Stanford, CA, USA

The Sveriges Riksbank Prize in Economic Sciences in Memory of Alfred Nobel 1972, shared with John R. Hicks, both 'for their pioneering contributions to general economic equilibrium theory and welfare theory'.

INTRODUCTION

It is not easy to see him. Not because he's short. Rather because the piles of books and papers scattered around his admittedly relatively narrow office in the Landau Building are so high. 'They've moved us here and now I'm trying to look through all my stuff and see what I can possibly throw out', says Kenneth J. Arrow, rising swiftly from behind one of the book piles, with an apologetic gesture. In spite of his 86 years, he seems physically quite fit and, no wonder, he prides himself in cycling to the office every day. The room is nice, bright, modern and new, but there is no way Arrow could possibly fit everything into the book shelves along the walls. 'Never mind', he says, laughing. He has a great warm open smile, and is eager to talk – which he then does at an amazing speed. Politely, he liberates a chair for me, opens a drawer next to himself for me to place the microphone in since there is no more space on the desk, of course – and off we go.[1]

In spite of his intellectual brilliance, his outstanding academic career, and even his 'Nobelity', Kenneth Joseph Arrow is self conscious in a rather unexpected way. Maybe this character trait, navigating between polite humility and self-asserting pride, has to do with the modest background that he comes from. Born in 1921 in New York City, he always had to assert himself. This case differs dramatically from that of Paul A. Samuelson, who is six years older, whose family was rather well-off until the Great Depression came along, who was able to go to the best universities right away and who, at Chicago, was pretty protected from anti-Semitism. Kenneth J. Arrow's path, in his younger years, was greatly overshadowed by the uncertainty and difficulties of this era. Interestingly, uncertainty would later on become a major topic of research for him. Due to the Great Depression, Arrow's father Harry had lost his position in a bank, the family survived on some odd jobs, and so, in preparing for a career, young Kenneth J. Arrow mostly looked out for something that would provide him with some financial stability. He went to a well-renowned, tuition-free college, City College of New York, which has forever made him a grateful friend of public education. Arrow seriously considered becoming a teacher, or an actuary, as the following interview reveals. It was more or less a coincidence and also the pressure of his teachers that drew him, via mathematics, to statistics, and from then on, under the influence of the great Harold Hotelling and Abraham Wald, toward economics as an academic science, even though the prevalent anti-Semitism at New York Universities didn't make the start easy for him.

After studying undergraduate mathematics at the City College of New York, Arrow thus enrolled at Columbia where he received his MA in mathematics in 1941, at age 20, and a Ph.D. in economics in 1951 – after four years in the US Army Air Corps, some courses at the New School, three years under Jacob Marschak at the Cowles Commission at the University of Chicago and at the RAND Corporation, until he moved on to Stanford in 1949. As he remembers in the following interview, it took him disparagingly long to come up with his own breakthrough idea for a dissertation – but this idea, triggered by a classroom discussion with John R. Hicks, then turned out to be a major breakthrough in social choice theory, precisely the one that brought him the Nobel Prize in 1972. In Stanford, finally, Arrow was tenured in 1953 as a Professor of Economics, Statistics and Operations Research. In 1962, he joined the Council of Economic Advisers. In 1968, he went to Harvard, but ultimately he returned to Stanford in 1979. Kenneth J. Arrow was awarded the John Bates Clark medal in 1957 and the von Neumann Prize by the Institute for Management Sciences and Operations Research in 1986.

Without being what may properly be called a generalist, Arrow has been active in a large variety of fields, ranging from social choice theory to production theory and health economics. Especially in the later years, most of his work has been involved with the production and use of information in some way or another. In all the fields that Arrow has been active in, his contributions are highly technical. He is famous for at least four major contributions: his dissertation, as already mentioned, *Social Choice and Individual Values*;[2] the path-breaking Arrow–Debreu theorem developed together with Gérard Debreu in the *Econometrica* paper named 'Existence of equilibrium for a competitive economy';[3] his monograph with Frank Hahn, *General Competitive Analysis*,[4] where the authors demonstrate the mathematical robustness of general equilibrium theory; and his work on risk and uncertainty, which can essentially be found in his book *Essays in the Theory of Optimal Risk Bearing*.[5]

All of these papers have triggered long debates and further work by others. This is especially true for his social choice paper which reformulated Condorcet's paradox on voting from 1785, which, however, Arrow wasn't aware of at the time of publication.[6] His logical treatment of the issue has puzzled the profession ever since it came out in print. In this monograph, Arrow demonstrated, using logical tools such as binary relations theory, that under a number of minimal, generally accepted requirements, the classical democratic procedure, that is majority voting, was incapable of aggregating non-identical individual preferences in a coherent way. Instead, it results in a never-ending cycle. This problem can only be solved through the violation of one of those requirements. In a way he showed that there is no such thing as a social indifference curve, as it has been used in welfare theory. The minimum requirements that he posited are transitivity (preferences must be consistent), Pareto efficiency (if everybody prefers one option individually, then the group as a whole does, too), independence of irrelevant alternatives, and non-dictatorship (nobody has a right to impose their particular choice on others). The resulting voting paradox comes as an attack on the majority voting rule. None of the work in the entire research industry in social welfare theory that followed up on Arrow ever proved him wrong. Rather, most of the subsequent work has focused on the question concerning just how relevant these findings are. For example, preference intensities are not taken into account – a point that Amartya Sen, Nobel Laureate in 1998, took up later on. Also, James M. Buchanan, Nobel Laureate in 1986, placed the theory into a dynamic context and pointed out that the democratic voting procedure is valuable precisely because cycling can prevent a 'consistent' exploitation of minorities and allows for social learning.[7] Thus it doesn't really matter whether static aggregation is coherent or not. As the reader will find in the interviews both with Kenneth J. Arrow and with James M. Buchanan, this issue is still not settled. Arrow, after his dissertation, sporadically returned to the subject, but his curiosity was quickly drawn to the next, different topic as usual.

This sheds an interesting light on the question of how and where Arrow got his inspiration. As the topical question of the present book is how the economic challenges of changing times, the evolution of economics as a field of science, and personal biographies all act together in the progress of economic theory as exemplified in the work of individual Nobel Laureates, this teaches us that there are very different approaches – and characters. In Arrow's case, these three lines didn't interact so much. In essence, it is probably fair to say that Kenneth J. Arrow is not really an economic policy person – but rather an extremely gifted mathematical logician with a good sense for the use of these technical tools in economic theory. Arrow views himself as someone who just looked out regularly for some logical puzzle to solve. As he recalls, those puzzles were usually brought to him by someone else who saw it but couldn't solve it. Neither the general economic picture of his country or the world ever really left a mark on his research agenda, nor his personal biography in a narrow sense. Arrow let himself be guided by whatever unsolved question theoretical progress left open for him to tackle. As he says, he has always been 'open to requests' – and this clearly explains why he has worked in so many different fields. And, as he confirms, he has also 'done things that were sort of implied in the literature'.

In the famous article producing the Arrow–Debreu theorem, Arrow managed to shake up the profession once again. The question was simply whether there can possibly be a unique mathematical solution to the hugely complex system of equations that describes the competitive economy as a whole, that is the Walrasian model. If there isn't such a unique solution, or root, then the whole logical system becomes empty, or meaningless. Arrow and Debreu had both worked on the question independently and ultimately teamed up to show mathematically that such a unique solution can indeed be guaranteed if there are forward markets in all goods and services. However, this was quite a restrictive requirement – but it is one that Arrow was able to relax later, in the treatise and reference textbook *General Competitive Analysis*, co-authored by Frank Hahn.

In his work on uncertainty and risk, Arrow has marked the profession by coming up with the twin concepts of adverse selection and moral hazard in insurance markets. Adverse selection means basically that if an insurer cannot distinguish between different risks, then bad risks tend to cluster (because they get coverage cheaper) and to drive out good risks (because coverage gets too expensive given the underlying risk). The result is a financial problem for the insurance company which may go as far as making some risks uninsurable. Moral hazard means that people behave exactly in the way they shouldn't: due to being covered, they engage in higher risks than they otherwise would. In both cases, with adverse selection and moral hazard, insurance produces socially costly disincentive effects and an unwarranted redistribution of income. Arrow also developed measures of risk aversion and modeled optimal insurance.

Besides that, Arrow has worked on inventory and production theory, as in *Studies in the Mathematical Theory of Inventory and Production*,[8] and he also was one of the four authors who effectively replaced the traditional Cobb–Douglas production function by introducing a CES function, that is a production function with the mathematically nice feature of having constant elasticities of substitution.[9] This was as important for growth theory as his work on 'learning by doing',[10] which ultimately led the profession into endogenous growth models.

INTERVIEW

What attracted you to economics originally, Professor Arrow? Was economics – or rather the economic situation, and the economic policies of the time – a topic at home?

Oh yes. The stock market crashed when I was eight years old. It didn't affect us immediately, but of course it did within a couple of years. So I was a teenager in the Great Depression. And my father's economic successes went down with it. So it was very much a topic of conversation.

What was your father's occupation?

He was working for a bank. The bank was having financial difficulties. It was taken over by another group, and they dismissed him. It took him five years before he found another good job. In the meantime, he did various odd things. He had a law degree, so he did some work for legal firms. We also had some things left over that we kept on selling. So I know exactly what poverty was. But even if you were well off, you couldn't help thinking about the economy. The Great Depression was all around us. You saw all that unemployment in the streets; the papers and newsreels were full of it. And the elections in 1932 entirely revolved around that. I even remember Roosevelt's inaugural address.[11]

In which way were those things discussed? Were those conversations more about the question how to make ends meet or rather about adequate government action?
We did talk about policy, but nobody knew what to do. So everything turned around the question what was wrong with the system and what needed to be done. Things like that.

Later, at university, you didn't tackle economics right away. You studied math. When, why and how did you switch? Was it more push or pull?
Well, that's hard to say. It was a long process. I had a general interest in all sorts of things, including history. I was a mathematics major, but I also took courses in economics. They weren't very good. They were more or less historical. We were required to take one, but I took a couple more. But also – and I don't know what the relative importance was – I was concerned about getting a job. I didn't look beyond college very much at that point. All I wanted was security. I wanted some kind of job that wasn't too dependent on business. Therefore, the idea of going into some kind of business was not very appealing to me. I was not the personality for it anyway. But there was one kind of exciting and secure position that I could think of, and that was being a high school teacher of mathematics.

Right. That should have been secure enough.
Well, not quite, as you will see. In order to be a teacher in New York City, you had to have taken education courses. So I took education courses. There I was what they called a practice teacher, meaning that I attended a class together with a teacher, and I'd take over now and then. It was one of the greatest education experiences of my life. New York State has – and I think it's still unique – state-wide examinations which you have to pass in order to obtain an academic high school diploma. It's called the Regents examinations. That's a very old institution in New York.[12] For some reason, no other state has ever adopted it. Nowadays, these exams are substitutes because of the federal legislation. In those days, many students would take plane geometry. There were two terms. At the end of that, you had to take the Regents examinations. The school didn't like to have many failures on its records. So if you failed, you could take the course over again. If you failed really badly, you were allowed to take plane geometry too, but only on the condition that you didn't take the Regents examinations. There is some genius in the American system. They created a situation in which a student recommended by a teacher could take a voluntary course after-hours, and if the teacher permitted, the student could eventually also take the Regents examination. It was a three hours course. In the end, I was assigned to teach this group on my own – the best of the worst.

So you were the second chance giver.

Yes. There I had people who wanted that course badly. Most of the time, motivating the students is a problem. Here, motivationally, there was no problem at all. They were eager; they had a craving. I was able to authorize two thirds of them to the exam, and they all passed. It was the biggest teaching success I've ever had in my entire life. The problem was something else, and I already knew during my college years that there was a chance of this. It all had to do with the Great Depression.

What was that?

The problem that made the high school teacher career not all that secure was that in 1932, they had given an examination for math teachers. So there was a list from which people were drawn as vacancies occurred. Those who remained on the list eventually got other jobs, but they weren't terribly good ones, given the Great Depression. So all of them wanted to be high school teachers, and nobody dropped off the list. The result was that they didn't give another examination. At college, I thought that by the time I would graduate, this situation would have changed. But in 1940, they were still working off the 1932 list. So during my second or third year at college, I realized that I had to think of something else. I continued my little work in education, but I started to look out for something else.

So what did you pick?

I thought, maybe statistics. I just didn't quite know what that was. The mathematics department gave a course in probability and statistics. I took it, simply to enhance my job chances with big companies or government. Those institutions had statisticians. Becoming a professor was a little outside what I was thinking. So I took this course. The teacher frankly didn't know too much, that was pretty obvious. Most of the teachers in the math department were good teachers, but this fellow wasn't. He had references, however. So I started reading on my own. Mathematical statistics was fairly new then. The basic papers started maybe around 1908/1910. Some of the great creators were still very active at that time. I got really fascinated with the logic. By the time I graduated, in 1940, the job situation was still not very good. So when I asked myself in my senior year, what do I do next, I thought – well, why not go to graduate school? I wasn't going to be drawn as a high school teacher anyway. My father, by that time, had a steady job. We weren't well off, but the situation was a little better than before.

How did you get through school financially?

I lived at home, and college was for free. I went to City College, created in 1847, and that was completely free then (it isn't any more nowadays). City

College had originally been created by the initiative of some merchants who thought it was important to supply free education for those who couldn't afford it. Admission was by grades, mechanically, because they couldn't afford to have their staff look at each application. At that time, of course, many people wanted to get in. Many couldn't afford tuition elsewhere. And it was also a question of anti-Semitism in colleges and universities.

Even in New York?
Oh, there is no question about it now. Especially at Columbia University, definitely. New York University didn't have the same prestige, and so they were probably a little more liberal. At Columbia, they were quite open about it. It was kind of a quota. The proportion of Jews at Columbia was higher than the number of Jews compared to the rest of the population, but still it was a lot less than the number of Jewish people who were qualified. That quota was ultimately revised – but only much later. By the way, anti-Semitism also blocked the road to faculty appointments, not just student applications, as I realized later. Well, when I came out of high school, I applied at Columbia. I was below what they required as a minimum age. And yet, I was called for an interview. I really had a very good high school record. I prepared for the interview carefully, and passed. But I did need a scholarship; we couldn't afford tuition. So I asked the interviewer, who was the assistant dean, some informational question about the deadline. 'Oh, I wouldn't bother', he said. 'You're not going to be admitted.' I didn't know it then, but some years later, somebody wrote a book on anti-Semitism at American universities, and this fellow was named. He was notorious for trying to keep the numbers of Jews down. In the end, I was admitted. But then it was too late to apply for a scholarship.

Oh no! Hadn't the guy said what he did, you would have applied for a stipend in time.
Probably. He just didn't tell me the truth. Had I been bolder, I would have complained, arguing that now that they had admitted me, they should also give me a scholarship. But you know, you take these things as given.

So instead, you went to City College.
Yes. There were a lot of students at City College who were very bright. It really was an exciting group to be with. The faculty, however, was mixed. The teaching load was heavy. It was 15 hours a week of teaching – which, even then, was pretty high. At any rate, City College wasn't a high prestige kind of place. But the students would meet after class and discuss the books and work through the hard parts. We were quite productive. And we were

all very violent arguers. I was not particularly political. I was leftist, but I wasn't affected by this adulation as much as others. My time was not spent at that, my time was spent studying. Also, I regarded myself as a socialist, not a communist. And from very early on, I took the anti-Stalinist side.

Those were the times. . .
There was a series of trials of the old Bolsheviks in the Soviet Union. Some people from the old Revolution days were brought before the courts. Nikolay Bukharin was the most famous, Grigori Sinoviev, Karl Radek, Mikhail Tomski, etc. It was pretty obvious that those were no real trials. Stalin had simply decided. He just sacrificed his old comrades.

You sensed the unlawfulness and illegitimacy of the whole enterprise.
Yes. It was really bad. Later, it turned out that it was even worse than I had thought. But from the beginning, I had a bad impression. After the war, there were a lot of ex-Soviets who somehow managed to get to the west. Listening to them, I realized that some of the worst charges against the Soviet Union were still understatements.

And now you went on to graduate school.
Yes. I wanted to study mathematical statistics. But that subject couldn't be studied. There was no department of statistics. It was not a recognized subject. Even today, it's not taught very widely. There are only two or three places in the US that have such a department. But I knew enough of the literature to be aware that Harold Hotelling[13] at Columbia was one of the great people. So I rather naively applied for a Ph.D. in mathematics, figuring it was the closest thing, and I'd study with Hotelling. When I got there, I found that Hotelling gave a course in mathematical economics in addition to courses in statistics. I was enrolled in mathematics and in mathematical statistics courses given by Hotelling and his assistant, a very great statistician, Abraham Wald. Hotelling had a personal grant from the Carnegie Corporation to hire a research assistant. And this was Wald.[14] In 1940, he was Hotelling's research assistant. He had been in the US for a year or two years. All the students knew that Wald was a great figure. Anyway, Hotelling gave this course in economics. I was fascinated by the subject. Otherwise I might have settled for becoming a statistician.

Again, how did you manage financially?
My father had borrowed money for me to go to graduate school. He knew somebody who knew somebody who was rather well off. It cost 400 dollars per year. Tuition has gone up much more rapidly than core inflation. Tuition is 30 000 dollars nowadays. Per year.

What did Hotelling teach in that economics class?
Actually, as I realized later, it was the least interesting part of what he had himself done. What he taught was essentially the theory of the firm and the theory of the consumer. Those were models in complete generality, with any number of goods. The problems were how to calculate the first order conditions, and the big thing that Hotelling was especially concerned with were the second order conditions, that is, in how you calculate a maximum. And I was a complete master in bordered Hessians.[15] However, as I began to know a little more economics, I was hit by the number of extremely original papers that Hotelling had written.

How was your interaction with Hotelling? Was he helpful?
Well, I impressed him as a good student. One day, Hotelling had some example he was very proud of, but he couldn't do it with linear functions. And so I proved that you could do it with linear functions. I walked up to him and showed him what I had worked out. It was quite easy as a matter of fact. He questioned me whether I was going to continue my graduate studies. So I asked him: 'Would you write a letter of recommendation for me?' He then told me that it would be useless. The department of mathematics had not the least interest in statistics, and they would probably not pay attention to his recommendation. Hotelling was a professor of economics. He had a Ph.D. in mathematics, though, quite pure mathematics by the way. He had been coming out of Stanford. He had written some papers which really were economics, but he also wrote some papers on statistics. He wrote a lot of important papers and had a reputation for his interest in economics. Columbia actually already had somebody who applied statistics to economics. But the fellow went crazy and had to be institutionalized. So they had a vacancy. And somehow, in 1931 or so, they had the idea of appointing Hotelling, which must have been a very daring move. He took the opportunity to try and create a statistics program. He was convinced that statistics should not be subordinate. He told us that over and over again. Anyway, upon my request, he said to me: 'If you should want to switch your enrolment to economics, usually I get a fellowship for a student of mine.' Well, I was obviously fascinated by his course – and so I was bought. This is what literally happened.

Weren't you afraid that this would pull you too far away from pure math?
Well, I was in statistics, so I had already made that step. And I knew I could do a Ph.D. in economics and still concentrate on statistics. But of course I had to take classes and qualify.

Did the probability of finding a job enter into your strategy again? Did you perhaps think that economics would open up more doors?

I didn't think too much about that question. What exactly the job opportunities were, I didn't know. I wasn't really calculating. In fact, I was still playing it safe. The new 'safe' idea was that I was going to be an actuary, and that was something I thought statistics would be useful for. To be an actuary, the Society of Actuaries gave examinations, and essentially all the insurance companies recognized them. There were nine examinations. The first four or five of them were essentially mathematics. I took a couple, to be on the safe side. They were very hard examinations. They were not so much deep, but tricky. So as I said, I was playing it safe. But of course I thought that with a Ph.D., I should also be able to have some academic job or to go and join some government institutions. I didn't know quite what, but I was aiming at something along these lines.

When you pick one career path rather than another, you always drop one. You sort of close a door that perhaps won't reopen. Were you afraid of closing doors?

I'm not a nightmarish type. I just take every day as it comes. There was a little idea of keeping doors open, but meanwhile, my next thing was that I had to write a term paper for my master's thesis. I was wrapped up in the immediate thing. I should mention something else. After I graduated from College, and before I started graduate school, in the summer, I was looking for a job. I thought that maybe I could work as a clerk at a department store. In 1940, there was still a lot of unemployment. Anyway, I went to a department store but they weren't hiring. So I walked out, and across the street I saw a sign of some insurance company. I walked in and asked whether they were looking for anybody. They said yes. They hired me as an actuarial clerk. That meant doing some elementary computations, calculating premiums. They specialized in disability policies. They had some methods of computing them. I was very fast, I picked it up immediately. I got paid 20 dollars a week. It taught me how those premiums are actually calculated. I realized something there that was very useful later. There are a lot of expenses. The idea that insurance represented an actuarially fair premium was wrong. There were two loadings, as they said. One was called safety loading, calculated according to what the tables say. This was life insurance premiums. Then they had another premium, just for the cost of running the business, which was non-trivial. It was not 1 percent, it was 15 percent. So I learnt that there was a gap there. But I didn't pay attention until 20 years later, when I realized the importance.

How did college continue?

I was now in my second year, in 1941/42, and I was in the economics department, taking all those economics classes. The place was a little bit weird, even by the standards of the time, in the sense that it was very anti-neoclassical. One of the results of this mood was that there was not a course in price theory, at any level, believe it or not. It was not that everybody was in the same mould, but the dominant figure there was Wesley Clair Mitchell.[16] In his course, he said that it was our duty to collect a lot of data. When you have collected enough data, then things will be clean. Mitchell was head of the NBER.[17]

What else did you discover?

There was a course in the history of economics. It was taught by a man who was very famous at the time, John Maurice Clark. He was the son of John Bates Clark.[18] This fellow was always apologetic, nervous, exactly what you'd expect from a person with an extremely strong father. I took his course in the history of economics. It was funny because every couple of lectures, he would say something very witty. But I couldn't even concentrate, I was so bored. He wrote beautifully, he had some very good ideas, but face to face, he was the dullest lecturer I have ever heard in my life. Then there was a course with Mitchell on business cycles. I realized that his ideas on statistics and what I was learning from Hotelling were very different, but I thought it would be interesting anyway. It turned out that Mitchell was on sabbatical leave, and a – to me then unknown – visiting professor named Arthur F. Burns[19] ran the course. Burns was one of the most brilliant people I've ever met. We had almost nothing in common in terms of our approach. But he respected me and I respected him.

Well, his political persuasions obviously were somewhat conservative, even though he proved to be almost a liberal Keynesian in practice. Talking of which, I imagine that business cycles must have been a very interesting field then. Those were already the days of the Keynesian revolution.

We spent a whole year, and finally, at the end of the year, I asked Burns: 'What about this fellow Keynes that I keep hearing of?' He just didn't mention Keynes. Later he wrote a piece criticizing Keynes.[20] He would take up these various theories, mainly to show that none of them worked, and then to explain the statistical methodology that he and Mitchell were developing. They published that later in the book *Measuring Business Cycles*[21] which I felt was just nonsense. It didn't seem to me that it was going to answer the questions they wanted to answer. But individual points were just very, very bright. Tjalling Koopmans[22] wrote a famous review of that, by the way. Burns had me report on sunspot theory. That is the part of business cycle theory that, by comparison, uses the most formal, sophisticated statistical methods. These people were talking about real sunspots. There were some quite distinguished people involved in this. Stanley Jevons started this back in 1882. And it is not nonsense. There is a sunspot cycle, and it does have some effect, at least on weather, and therefore on agricultural crops, which was not a minor matter at the time. Mind you, this is not what is called sunspots today, just as a figure of speech, such as in Shell/Cass.[23] They take it for granted that real sunspots don't matter, and therefore they use the term as an example of something that didn't matter or rather of something that is only believed to matter. Well, that was December 1941. And then, we were at war. I enlisted in the weather program, hoping to make use of my mathematical training. And then I had to wait until I was called up. Given this, I wanted to get through as fast as possible. I took my examinations in March and April. I didn't waste much time.

Did you have to go through the whole economics program?
Oh yes. Although they didn't have a course in price theory, you had to take an examination in price theory. The idea was that you go to a professor and agree on a topic, and then you get a reading list. And so I went to Clark. There was a big hot topic at the time, and that was imperfect competition. This was Chamberlin and Robinson and all that. It really was an early version of game theory. Then, Hotelling would examine me in statistics, and Burns in business cycle theory. I had to have two applied fields, one of which was business cycles and the other public finance, which I took with Robert Murray Haig. I also had to discharge an obligation in economic history. Ordinarily, this was met by taking the course. But I had no more room to take this course, because I was taking all these other things. So the professor of American economic history just gave me his reading list and gave me an examination later on. It was one of the most interesting exams I have ever had. He called me in, and gave me three questions. Then I would sit outside his office and think for 40 minutes or so. Then you were called back in and gave the answers. One of the questions was terrific. It was: What would be the imports and exports of what is now the US in 1725 and 1925? Using this information only, say what you can about the internal economic structure of the country. That was terrific. Another question was: If the South had been allowed to secede in 1861, what would be the effect on the trade patterns today? Obviously, who knows? Those were only questions to see how you defend yourself. I passed all my exams. The department thought very well of me. I had an especially good scholarship for the next years. Then I was called up to military service. But I got the fellowship when I returned from service.

How did you avoid being sent to combat?
I just didn't wait until I was drafted; I enlisted in the weather program right away. The Army used the civilian programs, and I was sent to the meteorology department at New York University. The department gave what would be an equivalent of a master's degree in weather forecasting. We were also drilled, which of course was not particularly helpful to our studies.

Was that part a good or a bad experience?
A good one. You see, drill was not exactly a major part of our life. We were basically academic. We had drill maybe two or three times a week, for a couple of hours. It was not a very serious matter. They just tried to put some kind of military gloss on this, and so we had dormitory inspection. They would come in and check whether your bed was made properly. One day, we had made great efforts to have everything orderly and clean. And somebody looks up at the chandelier and says, oh, oh, we forgot this, it may be dusty. And sure enough, the officer comes in, puts on a white glove, and reaches up. . .

But didn't you fall asleep intellectually?
Well, they assigned me to research. Some people say that's because I wasn't any good in the field. Anyway, it was not very productive; I didn't use much of my intellectual devices. I spent most of the war fitting regressions. The problem was predicting weather for the next 15 days, or even for the next month. The big thing was of course forecasting day by day. The fact is that you can't forecast for two weeks. But we tried. And I was using these statistical methods. They weren't very good, but I spent a lot of time at that. We were using big desk calculators. They cost about 600 dollars then, the equivalent to 8000 or 9000 dollars today. But everything they could do is what the cheapest calculator can do today. To fit one eight-variable regression took eight hours. Not because I was incompetent; on the contrary, I was very good at it. Still, I can't say I contributed much to the war. That bothers me.

But you didn't do much economics, either.
I did one really solid thing. Some people came with a question: When you navigate a plane, how do you use the winds to get from one place to another as fast as possible? The main point was not speed, but to save fuel. We were flying bombers from Newfoundland to Scotland. It was a 12-hour flight. This was the pre-jet era. I saw an interesting mathematical problem here. It was a branch of mathematics that I didn't know much about, but I read on it and solved it. That brought me my first published paper in a

journal in the US.[24] It was a calculus of variations problem. I developed on that and found how we could save an hour on the average, which is a lot compared with 12 hours. They never took it up. As far as I know, it is the basis of airline route setting today. It's all about catching the winds. But Air Force didn't pick it up then. I feel that my work experience wasn't terribly helpful.

At any rate, this wasn't pure mathematics, but another step in applied mathematics.
That's a typical characteristic of my work. I usually start with some definite problem and try to formalize it in a way where you use math. I've done that over and over again.

What happened after the war?
I was on leave in January 1946 and got discharged in April. The war had been over in August 1945, but we had to wait until we got our papers. I went back to graduate school. I had passed all the oral exams and was now in the dissertation phase. The chairman was Haig, the same professor of public finance as before. He told me: 'A dissertation is meant to be your master piece. Do you know what master piece means? The term originates in the medieval guilds. It means that you do a competent piece of work to show that you're qualified to be a master.' They urged me to finish my dissertation between April and October. Everybody thought I was very good. I thought I was very good as a student, too, but I wasn't at all sure I was capable of original work. A good deal of my education had been the fact that I had a desk in the library, in the stacks. It was near the economics, so I'd just pick up those books and read. So one day, I ran across John Hicks's *Value and Capital*.[25] In terms of visions, Hotelling was a little narrow. But Hicks gave a vision of the whole economy that excited me. On the other hand, I was a very critical person. I would say 'this is not very well done', 'this is an open question', 'he just sort of glossed over this point', etc. I was not a hero-worshipper.

You weren't shy, then.
I was a very polite person, though. Paul Samuelson tells these stories how he used to correct his professors. I assume that's true. But I wasn't that type.

How did you get started on logics?
This was when I was still at City College. I was in my last year there when the war broke out in September 1939. It so happened that there was a conference on logic, and people came. A man named Alfred Tarski, a

Polish logician, was caught here by the outbreak of the war. I had an interest in logic. There was no course in it, but I liked to read about it by myself. Now the philosophy department had a vacancy, but Tarski knew no English. He couldn't teach. He spent the fall term learning English and started teaching in February. He gave two courses. One was essentially a basic course. The other course was called 'the calculus of relations': X bears the relation r to Y or X is the father of Y or any of these things. He had developed a formalization of this whole process, and he introduced things like transitivity. I was a student in that class. The first lecture or two, we couldn't understand a word he was saying. A few of us would sit together afterwards and analyze what it was that made him so difficult to understand. We realized that the stresses in the sentences were wrong. But he had a very good sense of language. We also learnt a little bit how to listen to him, and he learnt to improve his English. I did very well in the course, and in the final exams, after 40 minutes, I had the exam. He was a little surprised, but I thought it was very easy. When you got on to the right wavelength, it wasn't hard at all. Anyway, Tarski gave me this whole idea about symbolic logic and the calculus of relations. He wanted to have a translation of an elementary textbook he had written. It was originally in Polish, but there was a German version, too. That version was being translated by a young German immigrant, Olaf Helmer. Tarski felt that his English was not quite up to proof-reading it, so he asked me. That summer, I was working at the insurance company, but I spared some time for proof-reading.

When were you able to make use of what you learnt about symbolic logic?
When I started studying economics, everybody was talking about preferences. That's orderings! That's what I had learned from Tarski. He had educated me to think about these kinds of logical things. The first instance came during my first year at graduate school. When I was back at Columbia, trying to work on a dissertation and trying to correct Hicks, Hicks himself came and gave a lecture. And he had some new idea. He wanted to maintain ordinalism, but he also wanted to have interpersonal comparisons. Suppose you have A and B. A has some goods, and B has some goods. Supposing that A prefers his goods to what B has, and B prefers A's goods to what he has, wouldn't you say that A is better off than B? That was a definition of being better off that only involved ordinal comparison. But then I had a question: 'Professor Hicks, if you say that A is better off than B, you'd like to be able to say that if A is better off than B and B is better off than C, then A is better off than C. But that doesn't follow from what you said. It is perfectly possible that A is better off than B and B is better off than C and C is better

off than A.' That's what later became my social choice paper.[26] It just came like that. At that point, however, it just struck me as a clever thing, but nothing serious, I didn't pay any attention. One of the aspects that bothered me with Hicks and with economic theory in general was firms maximizing profits. Now firms have many owners. It's true that they all want to maximize profits, so that shouldn't be a problem. But Hicks was emphasizing that expectations of the future really matter. So maximizing means maximizing the sum of discounted profits. Now suppose you and I or three of us own a firm, and we all want to maximize profits, but each of us have different ideas about what profits consist of, because we have different expectations. So how does a firm make a decision? Majority voting, obviously.

So that's the link between the theory of the firm and social choice! I see. You introduced one into the other.
That's not quite the end of the story. I remembered that we wanted this to be an ordering. If the firm is better off, you want to be able to say that there is a maximum. Majority voting has to lead to an ordering. It took about 15 minutes of doodling to realize that this isn't true. Of course I didn't realize then that Condorcet[27] had done the same thing in 1785. But I didn't discover that until about 1952.

That was after your dissertation was out.
Yes. I published it without knowing about Condorcet. But by that time, a professor at a conference had given me a reference to somebody named E.J. Nansen. Nansen had done it, too, and published a paper in Australia.[28] But in fact, the paradox was much older than that. Anyway, I was quite annoyed. Because I wanted a theory of the firm. I wasn't looking for a paradox. So I put this aside and still tried to build up my rewriting of Hicks. I was very unsatisfied with that. As a consequence, I still thought I was going to become an actuary. In fact, I even went for an interview and got an offer from an insurance company. Again, I had asked Hotelling for a letter of recommendation, which he gave me, but he also said he was very upset by this. He didn't want me to leave academia. The insurance company wanted me to join their staff right away, but I told them I needed to get this dissertation done before I'd do anything like this. Then, in 1946, there was a meeting of the American Statistical Societies at Cornell, and the Cowles Commission[29] had organized a few sessions. They invited me to participate with them. Wald was a close friend of Jacob Marschak, then the director of the Cowles Commission. They had been looking for people they could recommend who had the right statistical–economic mix. They were mainly interested in the econometric

simultaneous equations method. I went to this meeting, and there I got to know Koopmans. He then was very thin, a tall person, a very ascetic looking man. He had been in Geneva and had managed to get out before France fell. I knew that he had published a paper on a very interesting statistical point, and it was signed Pen Mutual Life Insurance Company. So I asked him how he had found working for an insurance company. And he just said, with his strong accent: 'Oh no, there is no music in it.' And the minute he said that, there was no further question in my mind of my joining an insurance company.

So that was a crucial moment.
Well, I'm sure I wouldn't have done it anyway. I would have come to the same conclusion without this. Koopmans just put it so well. Hotelling couldn't put things this way. I couldn't either. Anyway, a year later, I was still working on my dissertation, the Cowles Commission invited me again to work with them, and I went. But I felt very unhappy about my lack of progress. I was wondering whether I was really capable of having an original thought. I could critique, I was very smart, I could take the best economists and find what was wrong with what they were doing. But all this is part of being a bright student. That's not the same thing. At any rate, I now got into that Cowles atmosphere. They had a big emphasis on econometrics, but of course you needed a theory to fit the econometrics. It was a terrifically exciting group, with Leonid Hurwicz,[30] Lawrence Klein,[31] Koopmans, Marschak, and some others. I also met another graduate student there, and we were married within a few months.[32] We still are married. Her family was poor, too, and she had been a clerk in the agriculture department. There was a statistician there, Meyer Abraham Girshik, who had been trained by Hotelling. He didn't need a secretary, but a research assistant. So he got her to do the calculating, and he always said that she was much better at calculations than she was as a secretary. She finally got back to college, got a degree in statistics from George Washington University, and eventually became a graduate student. Through her, I got to know Girshik. He was Russian. He was totally anti-communist. Air Force created this project RAND.[33] It started as a project within one of the aircraft companies, and then it spun off as a separate corporation. Girshik was doing statistical work which was closely connected with what the Cowles Commission was drawing on. So he visited there and almost immediately asked me whether I wanted to spend some summers at RAND, getting paid pretty well. So I got there in the summer of 1948. I had already spent a year at the Cowles Commission. I was still this brilliant person, very active in the seminars, but I didn't really get anything done. Another year passed.

Everybody expected me to amount to something. I was the only one who was doubtful about this.

Did RAND give you fresh inspirations?
Well, at RAND, I went to the math division. Game theory was brand new then, and I learnt a lot about convex sets, supporting hyperplanes and all that. It was all very useful, but not immediately. My friend Helmer, the philosopher, was now hired. At RAND, they were aware that we didn't know what new wars are going to be like, with the atomic bomb, and so they wanted some free thinking and hired a philosopher. And one day, we had coffee together and he said to me: 'You know, I'm puzzled by one thing. We're trying to construct game theoretic models with the players being the Soviet Union and the US. But the Soviet Union is not a reality, it's only a construct. They are people, individuals with different interests.' I told him that Abram Bergson had written a paper explaining all this, coming up with the 'Social Welfare Function'.[34] He suggested that I write an exposition of this. I started writing. The theory of the firm came back to my mind, and I asked myself how we practically realize those social welfare functions. All you have is preferences. It must be a sophisticated kind of voting. It didn't look like majority voting would do it. Nothing looked good. Either you got intransitivity, or you got a situation where preferences were for things that were not feasible, that is, that didn't matter. About three or four days later, I saw that the voting paradox would be replicated, no matter what you did.

In fact, Helmer just pushed you to formulate something you already knew.
I had asked this question to Hicks, but I myself felt this was unimportant stuff. But now I had been forced to give an explanation.

That was a real breakthrough for you, I suppose, also psychologically speaking.
Oh yes. This was the first time I thought that I had done something.

You later published this as your dissertation using the term the 'possibility theorem'. In the literature, it is also known as the 'impossibility theorem', referring to the impossibility to aggregate preferences in a non-contradictory way.[35] Now what?
Oh, that was because Koopmans found the name 'impossibility theorem' too gloomy. But I think 'impossibility theorem' is more appropriate.

What did you do upon leaving RAND?
I went back to Chicago, now being an assistant professor half-time. Columbia helped the Cowles Commission out by appointing one of

their people half-time. I somehow had the feeling it was not a serious appointment, although technically, it was a regular one indeed. It was really tenure-track. The Cowles Commission was pretty broke, they needed help. It gave me some teaching experience. I taught statistics in the economics department in 1948/49. I already had one invitation from Stanford, but I wanted to get something done. Now things changed a little bit. A fellow named Al Bowker was brought to Stanford to organize statistics. He had been a fellow student at Columbia, and he had stayed on. Columbia had created a statistics department eventually. By the way, that's another complicated story. Originally, Hotelling had demanded it, but they would never do it. Then he got an offer from North Carolina (Chapel Hill) and left – and then Columbia built it, on Wald. Nobody ever understood why it happened this way. Anyway, Bowker came to the math department in Stanford in 1948 to organize a statistics program, and it was clear that it would be supported by the federal government. He induced Girshik to come here. Girshik was a star. He was interested and asked me whether I could come too. So he approached the economics department. There were opportunities because some people hadn't come back from the war. The people who organized everything wanted to change the department from a low-graded one to a classy one. When I was interviewed, I presented my brand new stuff. As a person, Albert Gailord Hart was the person with whom I was in contact. I don't think he understood what it was all about. He just seemed to think that if I said so it must be good. He was very nice to me, although I was told he was pretty arrogant with other people. And then I spent the next six months writing down all these ideas, giving a little historical background, reviewing the philosophy, connecting up with things in the literature, pointing out that people had come up with versions of this paradox or with extensions without seeing it in its totality, for example Scitovsky and Kaldor. I was really dying to get a dissertation of less than a hundred pages.[36] The typical size then was 300 pages. Mine turned out to be 105 pages in the end, and I was a little disappointed.

But you didn't go to Stanford at that point.
No, but I now felt I already had something, and then I was back in Chicago teaching statistics. In the post-war group, there were a lot of good students. The editor of the *Journal of Political Economy* asked me to write an article for the journal.[37] That was something I hadn't thought about. From that point on, I became much more productive. In other fields, that is. I didn't go back to social choice. I didn't continue that line. I became much more creative.

I guess you just sort of finally jumped off that starting block. But let me ask – why is it that you came back to social choice theory only sporadically? A lot has been written on that, following your path-breaking paper. You've triggered a huge debate. James Buchanan's reply,[38] for example, pointing to the good effects of cyclicality, deserves special attention, I think. Why didn't you follow up much?

On its own terms, my theory has never been subverted. And the result is a negative thing, it is not very encouraging. Political choice is raising a somewhat different set of issues. The idea of political choice is economically motivated. It is not a new idea. Hotelling, in his paper on spatial competition,[39] has it explicitly. Even von Neumann and Morgenstern discussed politics. In a sense, everybody is maximizing utility. I think Jim tried to argue that if you take account of politics, then the social choice theory just goes away. And that's just wrong. I can buy votes, but that doesn't change the problem. The problem is that in a multi-dimensional world, a voting equilibrium doesn't even exist. I had already been thinking of the one-dimensional case before writing my dissertation. I was idly talking to some friends and I drew it up on a napkin and showed that if people are just left to right,[40] then majority voting is going to be transitive. Before I got around to writing it up, I found that it had already been published by Duncan Black.[41] Obviously, he had found it years before I did. The one-dimensional case is just very different from the multi-dimensional case, and that's true as much in social choice theory as in political choice theory. Don't misunderstand me. Jim has started a terrific set of research on the question of motivations. The whole idea of explaining bureaucratic and legislative behaviour by maximization is just very well done. What they are maximizing is not always so clear. I have a theory that does actually accrue to one paper he wrote with Geoffrey Brennan. It circulated as 'the logic of the letters', but it was published under a different title.[42] The idea is that when you're voting, you're not really maximizing, you just express your feelings. Your vote doesn't really matter, and therefore it isn't rational to vote. And you know that. So if you do vote, you just express yourself.

Isn't there quite a difference between your approach and Buchanan's? It seems to me that Jim is more on a Hayekian track, talking about the prevention of minority exploitation[43] and at the same time referring to the creation of knowledge[44] in the political realm. He argues that in the political realm, knowledge comes into being through individual action that gets aggregated through political voting and then needs to undergo the reality test without being suppressed by persistent majorities. You seem to ask how you put the individual preferences together, while he asks on the basis of what the individual members of society can form, revise and express their preferences about collective action.

That may be. I guess what you're saying is that new knowledge comes out of social interaction. I haven't thought about it that way. Is that in Jim's work?

Well, I think so. And he also does say that there is no such thing as a social utility function that can be defined independently – not much more than an individual utility function by the way – because that is something that doesn't exist in any predetermined fashion 'out there'. On the contrary, you only find out about it as you act, that is, essentially as you trade.[45]

I'm sure that's true. People sometimes say that they don't know what they think until they've said it, you know. But mind you, even as a graduate student, I've never thought that utility theory implies consciousness. Of course you discover things and learn about your own preferences. This is a point that I haven't explored and that I probably should study more. It seems especially important from the point of view of innovation. By the way, what has always bothered me about Hayek is that all this local knowledge has to be transmitted before the process of social interaction can generate any new knowledge, but he doesn't show us how that is going to happen.

What would you consider to be your most important contribution?

In terms of originality, it was the social choice paper that we just talked about. In terms of contributions to economics, there were a couple of them. There is the 1963 paper on uncertainty and the welfare economics of medical care which is a favorite of mine.[46] A lot of what I have done has been the result of requests, like when Helmer asked me that important question. In the case of the 1963 paper, the context was the following. The Ford Foundation, which was then very generously supporting research, had a program officer named Victor R. Fuchs. He had the idea of taking applied subjects and getting a theorist who hadn't really worked on the area to write one paper, and a practical person to write another. They did it for health, for education and for welfare. He approached me, asking whether I would consider writing about the question of healthcare. That topic was very much on the agenda in those days. President Harry Truman had raised already the question about insurance. I didn't have any immediate reaction, but I was reading up on the question, since because of my statistical background, I was interested in uncertainty. A lot of my work has been dealing with uncertainty in one way or another. Also, if something is new, it gets me really excited. If it's something I have already been doing anyway, I lose interest. Quite frequently, even in recent years, I've been responding to challenges.

What do you mean by challenges?

Questions that give me tasks. The more outlandish they are, the more I'm likely to say yes. There is no doubt that I get a lot of my inspiration from other people's questions – questions that I never thought of before. That was true also for inventory theory, to take a different example. That was a very influential paper,[47] and it came to me as a request, too. Other things did not; some rather came from general literature. In the healthcare case, I diligently read a lot on the subject and saw that it was a theoretical question. The insurance market is a little imperfect because you insure against medical costs, but medical costs are not independent of the insured. Of course this is a common observation. Also, there was the question why physicians spent a lot of time on charity, giving free care. There was no law, but it was done. Hospitals were typically non-profit. There were many funny things around. Somehow it hit me that there was a common trait to all this. The two parties of the transaction don't have the same information. Other people were coming to this from different angles. Some people were studying the Soviet Union, analyzing how the managers at the factory level respond to the orders given by the central administration, and how can the latter know what goes on in the factories. And then it was realized that capitalist systems have those principal–agent problems as well. The big thing was asymmetric information. The reason I was prime to it was that I had written a purely theoretical paper a couple of years earlier, one of which I'm also very proud, on the optimal allocation of risk-bearing. Theoretically, it was about how to incorporate uncertainty into general equilibrium. Hicks had originally raised the question, but in effect, he closed it down by saying that people act as if prices are certain. But I had learned one thing from statistics, and that is that when you're uncertain, you may do things which you wouldn't do otherwise. People hedge in some ways. There is behaviour that is qualitatively different with uncertainty. The question is just how you incorporate this into modeling.

And how did you manage to find a way?

I can't say how exactly it hit me. I just happened to be accustomed to the idea that uncertainty means that there are states of the world which you don't know. So for each state, you have a bet. The perfect security then is a complicated combination of bets. The elementary idea is contingent securities. The ideal insurance therefore is a function of state. The problem is if I know the state and you don't, how can I guarantee that the payment will be right. It's as simple as that. Having this highly theoretical education, as soon as I saw a practical problem, I could see what was wrong with my theory. I didn't invent the theory to explain the practical problem, I had the theory first, and then I applied it and checked whether it worked. In this case, my theory didn't work, because it didn't allow for asymmetric information. And that's how I got the idea that asymmetric information was important. Anyway, I got invited to a conference in France on risk-bearing in 1952 and presented this stuff. The organizers wanted to publish my paper, and so I rushed through it and had it translated into French. It was extremely short.[48] Nine years later, some editor asked me for an English version.[49] That was easy, since I had originally written it in English. I shouldn't have published it in French right away. Anyway, after publication in English, it became quite influential.

Summing this up, the theoretical debate – with Hicks – gave a first impulse, then you saw a practical problem that theory couldn't answer, and then that triggered a new theory.
That's right. And then I realized that this problem didn't only matter for insurance, but between physician and patient, there was again the same kind of thing: how do I know the physician is doing the best thing for me? Given this fact, all the peculiar features of the health market could be understood. The pure theory assumptions just weren't satisfying.

One thing leads to another, as new theories are confronted with other theories and also with reality. I guess that's the course of intellectual progress.
Yes. My reaction to the development in connection with insurance and medical care was the importance of social institutions. Others went on in the direction of rational expectations, stressing the importance of prices as a signal.

You also worked on growth theory. You worked with Robert Solow on this idea of constant elasticities of substitution.[50]
We were four of us. Hollis Chenery and his student, now a well-known professor, Tsunahiko Watanabe, were looking at the share of labor in the same industry in different countries. With a Cobb–Douglas function, you'd expect the share of labor to be constant. Worker per unit of output should be inversely proportional to the wage rate, or put in logarithmic terms, the slope of the curve should be –1. Well, they found that the slope was not –1, but –¾. So they came to me and asked whether there was some theoretical explanation for this. I'm very open to requests. And so I started playing around with it, and for two weeks I couldn't solve it. Then I saw a most elementary method that I had just overlooked. Hendrik Houthakker mentioned that Bob Solow had developed a function that could be used. Solow had been tired with using the Cobb–Douglas function, but he didn't see the implications. So his part was probably the smallest.

Your openness to requests explains why you've worked in so many different fields.
Yes, but I also have done things that were sort of implied in the literature. I do have an ability to take things from different directions and see whether there is a connection. I can see things having parallels. What I've done tends to be small-scale. I don't go into big things such as laissez-faire.

What is progress in economic theory, in your view?
We're in a state of flux right now. Some of the many new ideas haven't been pushed enough yet, for example the social nature of economics. That really is an unexplored – or rather insufficiently explored – part of economics. People do influence each other not only through the market. But that's not part of most of our theories. Economics has a bias in that it is too individualistic. Behavioral economics is even more individualistic, with all its emphasis on cognitive failures. The same is true for experimental economics. Experiments are very good at suggesting new theories, but they have to be tested in the field. The experimental situation is always too far removed from the field. Anyway, we tend to neglect the fact that information is transferred between people not only through prices, but also in much more elementary ways, such as for example one person saying to another that today is the time to sell a specific share. This information is not spreading through the market, it's not shown in a price, but it's spreading verbally, through the social context. That's social behaviour. There are also certain norms which people follow even if it's not rational in the market. We need to concern ourselves more with this.

OK. Thank you, Professor.

NOTES

1. The interview was held on 27 June 2007.
2. Kenneth J. Arrow (1951a).
3. Kenneth J. Arrow and Gérard Debreu (1954).
4. Kenneth J. Arrow and Frank Hahn (1971).
5. Kenneth J. Arrow (1971).
6. See the interview with Kenneth J. Arrow in this book.
7. James M. Buchanan describes this as follows: 'It serves to insure that competing alternatives may be experimentally and provisionally adopted, and replaced by new compromise alternatives approved by a majority group of ever changing composition. This is the democratic choice process, whatever may be the consequence, for welfare economics and social welfare functions.' (James M. Buchanan, 1954, p. 119).
8. Kenneth J. Arrow et al. (1958).
9. Kenneth J. Arrow et al. (1961).
10. See, in particular, Kenneth J. Arrow (1962).

11. Franklin Delano Roosevelt, the 32nd President of the United States, announced his plans on a New Deal in his inaugural address on 4 March 1933. The New Deal was a program of government interventions aiming at a relaunch of the economy, relief for the poor and unemployed, and regulation of the banking system.

12. The Regents, designed and administered under the authority of the Board of Regents of the University of the State of New York. These exams were first administered in 1865. The original purpose of these tests was to distribute funds to encourage academic education.

13. Harold Hotelling (1895–1973) was a famous American statistician, who laid the groundwork for the modern neoclassical school, for general equilibrium theory, and for game theory.

14. Abraham Wald (1902–1950), of Romanian Jewish origin, had studied in Vienna with Carl Menger. In Vienna Wald worked on pure mathematics, mostly geometry, and on econometrics. Upon invitation by the Cowles Commission, he left Austria after the Nazi invasion in 1938 and came to the US.

15. A Hessian is the second derivative of a matrix. 'They now no longer teach this', says Arrow.

16. Wesley Clair Mitchell (1874–1948) was an economist especially known for his empirical work on business cycles and for directing research at the National Bureau of Economic Research (NBER) from 1920 until 1945.

17. The NBER is a private, non-profit research organization dedicated to the empirical study of economics. It is 'committed to undertaking and disseminating unbiased economic research among public policymakers, business professionals, and the academic community'. It publishes working papers and books. The NBER is located in Cambridge, Massachusetts, with branch offices in Palo Alto, California, and New York City.

18. John Bates Clark (1847–1938) taught economics at Columbia University. He is considered a pioneer of the marginalist revolution and an opponent of the Institutionalist school of economics. In honor of his work, the biennial John Bates Clark Medal which is awarded by the American Economic Association to 'that American economist under the age of forty who is adjudged to have made a significant contribution to economic thought and knowledge' is named after him. The medal is considered one of the most prestigious awards in economics.

19. Arthur F. Burns (1904–87) taught at Columbia and presided over the NBER. He also was the chairman of the US Council of Economic Advisers (1953–56) under President Dwight D. Eisenhower and Chairman of the Federal Reserve (1970–78). President Ronald Reagan sent him as ambassador to West Germany (1981–85).

20. 'The great and obvious virtue of the remedies proposed by the Keynesians is that they seek to relieve mass unemployment; their weakness is that they lean heavily on a speculative analysis of uncertain value.' Arthur F. Burns (1946, p. 12).

21. Arthur F. Burns and Wesley C. Mitchell (1946).

22. Tjalling C. Koopmans and Leonid Kantorovich were awarded the Nobel Prize in 1975 'for their contributions to the theory of optimum allocation of resources'.

23. Karl Shell and David Cass (1983).

24. Kenneth J. Arrow (1949).

25. John R. Hicks (1939). John R. Hicks and Kenneth J. Arrow shared a Nobel Prize in 1972, 'for their pioneering contributions to general economic equilibrium theory and welfare theory'.

26. This was his dissertation (Kenneth J. Arrow, 1951a).

27. The Marquis de Condorcet (1743–94) was a French philosopher, mathematician and political scientist, in line with the ideals of the Age of Enlightenment and rationalism. His paradox shows that majority preferences become intransitive with three or more options: it is possible for a majority to prefer A over B, another majority to prefer B over C, and another majority to prefer C over A (Condorcet, 1785).

28. E.J. Nansen (1883).

29. The Cowles Commission for Research in Economics was founded in Colorado Springs in 1932 by the businessman Alfred Cowles. It moved to the University of Chicago in 1939 (the directors being Theodore Yntema until 1943, Jacob Marschak until 1948, and then Tjalling Koopmans) and later on to Yale University in 1955, where it was renamed the 'Cowles Foundation'.
30. Leonid Hurwicz was awarded the Nobel Prize in 2007, together with Eric S. Maskin and Roger B. Myerson, 'for having laid the foundations of mechanism design theory'.
31. Lawrence Klein was awarded the Nobel Prize in 1980 'for the creation of economic models and their application to the analysis of economic fluctuations and economic policies'.
32. Arrow's wife is Selma Schweitzer.
33. The RAND Corporation is a research institution created originally in 1946 by the United States Army Air Forces as Project RAND, under contract to the Douglas Aircraft Company. In 1948, Project RAND was separated from Douglas and became an independent non-profit organization, sponsored initially by the Ford Foundation, to 'further promote scientific, educational, and charitable purposes, all for the public welfare and security of the United States of America'. The range of topics has since expanded greatly.
34. Abram Bergson (1938).
35. Those preferences which it is impossible to aggregate are also called 'cyclical'.
36. Kenneth J. Arrow (1951a).
37. Kenneth J. Arrow (1950).
38. James Buchanan explains that the majority principle can only be a workable instrument of political control and knowledge creation if cycling does in fact occur: 'It serves to insure that competing alternatives may be experimentally and provisionally adopted, and replaced by new compromise alternatives approved by a majority group of ever changing composition.' James M. Buchanan (1954, p. 119). James M. Buchanan was awarded the Nobel Prize in 1986 'for his development of the contractual and constitutional bases for the theory of economic and political decision-making'. See also Michael Wohlgemuth (2002, p. 232).
39. Harold Hotelling (1929).
40. He refers to what has become known as 'single-peakedness': If A, B and C are firmly ordered on the line, then the only votes possible are A>B>C, C>B>A, B>A>C, B>C>A (and not A>C>B and C>A>B). This generates transitivity.
41. Duncan Black (1948).
42. This theory is known as the 'expressive voting theory'. See Geoffrey Brennan and James M. Buchanan (1984).
43. See James M. Buchanan (1954), and Friedrich August von Hayek (1960, p. 109).
44. This refers to two papers by Friedrich August von Hayek, namely Friedrich August von Hayek (1937) and (1945).
45. Geoffrey Brennan and James M. Buchanan (1985/2000, pp. 23–37).
46. Kenneth J. Arrow (1963).
47. Kenneth J. Arrow et al. (1951).
48. Kenneth J. Arrow (1953).
49. Kenneth J. Arrow (1964).
50. Kenneth J. Arrow et al. (1961).

James M. Buchanan

*George Mason University,
Fairfax, VA, USA*

The Sveriges Riksbank Prize in Economic Sciences in Memory of Alfred Nobel 1986 'for his development of the contractual and constitutional bases for the theory of economic and political decision-making'.

INTRODUCTION

Sister knows how to behave herself. Bustling around, barking nervously, begging playfully for a little bit of tenderness, she instinctively senses what it means when the microphone is turned on. She settles on the sofa, her nose comfortably between her paws, and waits silently. Sister is the amber-haired dog that James M. Buchanan is now looking after faithfully, a couple of years after his wife Anne, to whom the dog belonged, passed away. The two have taken a liking to each other, comforting each other in their loneliness at the modest farmhouse on the vast piece of land near Blacksburg, Virginia, that the couple once bought and then expanded with the Nobel Prize money. 'When Sister was a puppy, before Anne got her, she was badly treated, they beat her up – so she is a poor, traumatized dog, and it took quite a while to give her some confidence back', explains Buchanan. He is fond of dogs generally, as the huge collection of little porcelain, wood and plastic dogs on and around his chimney piece shows.

Anyway, it turns out to be a long wait for Sister, as our conversations stretch out over two full days. It is not the first time that we meet, and the Nobel Laureate again seems to enjoy sharing his thoughts as he looks back and also ahead. For all his academic excellence, his intellectual rigor, his logical intransigence, and his strong convictions, Buchanan has remained a down-to-earth, open-minded, humane and moving personality. He also is a wonderful, generous story-teller, with his lovely Southern drawl, his naturally beautiful prose, a dry sense of humor and an excellent feeling for building up suspense. Nothing of what he says will need any editing later on, just a lot of shortening. Buchanan's elegant use of the language comes as no surprise to anybody who knows the writings of this prolific author, or at least the titles of some of his books: *The Calculus of Consent, The Limits of Liberty, Democracy in Deficit, The Reason of Rules* – this author truly is a master in the art of finding grasping titles in the form of alliteration. And, as he admits, he is sensitive to the joys of construction and composition, beyond the necessities of sheer analytical coherence. He feels himself to be a mixture of scientist and artist.[1] At lunchtime, Buchanan gets up and busies himself in the kitchen, where he prepares a simple sandwich and some Nescafé for us. After lunch, he retires for his usual nap, while I take seat in the classical rocking-chair out on the porch, enjoying the view and watching freshly washed and trimmed Sister disappear in the grass and the mud. She's having a great time, not anticipating the frown that she will earn later on.[2]

A lot has already been written about James McGill Buchanan's identity as an American Southerner – and that's not just for the anecdote. Being a Southerner means inheriting the trauma of being dominated, as the Southerners were by the Yankees up north, after the lost war of secession. This heritage, passed on to him mainly by his intellectually curious and ambitious, much admired mother, has endowed James M. Buchanan with a set of values that have directed all his thinking and his research. Buchanan was born in 1919, in the little rural town of Murfreesboro in the state of Tennessee. Coming from a very modest background, raised on a farm which he qualifies as being 'just a run-down operation', his childhood was dominated by poverty and his schooling was simple. Nevertheless, Buchanan engaged in higher studies at Middle Tennessee State Teacher's College and then, thanks to a fellowship, went on to the University of Tennessee. During the war, he joined the Navy. He experienced discrimination there for being a poor Southerner instead of being part of the East Coast establishment, which of course reinforced his innate deep aversion to any sort of arbitrary domination. Nevertheless, he liked life in the Navy a lot: 'the military life, the social life, the order'. After the war, a fellowship took him to the famous University of Chicago – a place which he picked mainly because he couldn't stand New York. At Chicago, the famous Frank Knight exerted great influence on him. He also discovered the writings of the Swedish economist Knut Wicksell, especially Wicksell's 'Finanztheoretische Untersuchungen', a 1896 dissertation providing 'a new principle of just taxation'.[3] This text, which Buchanan translated into English, was to become the basis of much of his own thinking. After receiving his Ph.D. from the University of Chicago in 1948, he took up teaching at the University of Tennessee (1948–51) and subsequently at Florida State University (1951–55), before spending a research year in Italy as a Fulbright scholar. Upon returning to the United States, he accepted a position as a Professor of Economics and director of the Center of Political Economy and Social Philosophy at the University of Virginia in Charlottesville. During this period, he co-founded the Public Choice school of thought, together with Gordon Tullock. Those were also the years when the Public Choice Society and the academic journal *Public Choice*[4] saw the light. After a stint at the University of California at Los Angeles in 1968, Buchanan returned to Virginia in 1969, as a Professor of Economics and general director of the Center for Study of Public Choice at Virginia Polytechnic Institute in Blacksburg. Interestingly, but in accordance with his experiences of discrimination in the Navy, Buchanan has never taken root at any great, Ivy-League University on the East Coast, but has preferred small places instead where he was granted the necessary leeway for his unorthodox approach. In 1983, he moved the Center from Blacksburg to George Mason University in Fairfax, on the doorsteps of the national capital. When he received the Nobel Prize in 1986, he was also serving as a President of the Mont Pèlerin Society, a rather loose international group of classical liberal scholars and intellectuals founded by Friedrich August von Hayek in 1947. These days, Buchanan spends almost all his time in Blacksburg on his property, taking advantage of his office at Virginia Tech only now and then.

As already mentioned, James M. Buchanan deserves notoriety for having been one of the founders of Public Choice theory and Constitutional Economics. Public Choice applies the tools of economic analysis to political, or 'non-market decision making'. This means that state, or government behavior is no longer artificially seen as being exogenous to economics, but is realistically made endogenous instead and raised to a topic of its own. The first path-breaking contribution to this field came in 1962 in the form of a joint monograph that Buchanan co-authored with Gordon Tullock, published under the title *The Calculus of Consent*.[5] In this treatise, the authors take up Knut Wicksell's basic underlying concepts such as methodological individualism, the image of man as a *homo oeconomicus*, and politics as exchange. They apply the usual neoclassical hypothesis of individual rational utility maximization to the whole area of collective choice. One of the novel, in those days still truly revolutionary, assumptions here is the idea that politicians and bureaucrats do not necessarily behave as 'benevolent dictators', but rather display the usual kind of purposive behavior, that is they pursue their own self-interest, and they react to incentives just like anybody else. In this book, Buchanan and Tullock also draw a crucial distinction between two different levels of collective decision making, namely the constitutional level and the level of ordinary, day-to-day politics.

Constitutional choice is the level where all the fundamental rules of the game are being laid down; this level is therefore of the utmost importance. The exchange process that takes place between citizens and the state is analogous to the one described theoretically by Thomas Hobbes in his famous *Leviathan*;[6] individuals confer a monopoly of coercion to the state in exchange for protective and productive services. While Hobbes still views this social contract as implying a complete and absolute transfer of all power, without recourse, Buchanan and Tullock take the opposite direction and view this process as one in which the rules of the game, including particularly the limits to state action, are being set. Consequently, all the rules determined at this level require unanimous consent. Instead of having everybody gather at the ballot box in person, however, Buchanan conjures up some fictitious social contract at this point, where all participants can be imagined behind a 'veil of ignorance'. John Rawls later proceeded along similar lines in his *Theory of Justice*.[7] Behind such a 'veil of ignorance', individual decisions are ideally not influenced by extrapolations on one's own position at some future point in time. Along the lines of the famous Kantian imperative, the decisive conjectural question now is whether the rules in question are of such a nature that they 'could have emerged from agreement by participants in an authentic constitutional convention', as Buchanan puts it in his Nobel Prize Lecture.[8] This holds true for the initial agreement on a constitution as much as for later constitutional reform. What may seem a serious practical limitation of Buchanan's approach here is due mainly to the purely normative, justificatory interest that is being pursued. As such, there are some clear prescriptions, though, for example that these rules must be designed to be general, that is fully non-discriminatory.

At the post-constitutional, or sub-constitutional, ordinary level of politics, variants of majority voting still turn out to be the usual procedure for collective decision making. Majority voting, however, has a major shortcoming that is often overlooked – an omission that unfortunately often leads to an uncritical sanctification of democracy in public discourse: minorities can systematically be dominated. In Buchanan's view, majority voting at the post-constitutional level is legitimate, only as long the rights of those minorities are guaranteed at the constitutional level and as long as there is at least a fictitious consensus about this constitution. To use Buchanan's metaphor again, this is the political game being played within the rules. At both levels, the political process is all about social cooperation aimed at achieving mutual advantage.

The fact that politicians and bureaucrats are just as much guided by self-interest as anybody else makes Buchanan pessimistic about the possibility of restraining government. As an outcome of ordinary politics, that is of the game within the rules, he sees a built-in bias towards large government, inevitably entailing large deficits and public debt. The only way to limit this is through adequate constitutional rules. In his *The Power to Tax*,[9] written jointly with Geoffrey Brennan, he suggests a series of constitutional rules and contrivances that avoid this. This book is particularly fun to read because it turns all the principles of optimal taxation theory upside down. And yet, it remains an open question as to why constitutional rules should not be biased in the same way as ordinary politics is. If the consensus requirement is only a fictitious one, one that only serves the purpose of normative justification, where then is the practical guarantee? Well, argues Buchanan in *The Reason of Rules*,[10] we should devote more effort to deriving those procedures. Even if the consensus requirement is a fictitious one, constitutional rules are usually abstract and universal enough to mimic the 'veil of ignorance' at least to some degree and to avoid discrimination. To bring this about in real life, however, probably requires somebody who behaves in an axiomatic, enlightened way, beyond his immediate self-interest. In his 'Notes on Nobelity', he talks of 'some ethic of constitutional responsibility' that is required here, 'some interest that extends beyond that which is of measured direct utility value to me'.[11] Even if, in Buchanan's contractual approach, there cannot logically be any real absolutes, those are the 'relatively absolute absolutes', according to a formula invented by Frank Knight, that is those elementary preferences and values that society cannot possibly do without.[12]

Coming back to the topical question of this book, exploring the sources of academic progress along the lines of the economic challenges of changing times, the evolution of economics as a field of science, and personal biographies, the case of James M. Buchanan is particularly intriguing. Clearly, unlike Kenneth J. Arrow or Robert M. Solow, he is not a puzzle solver but rather a system builder, someone who has come up with a whole new paradigm, an innovative way of looking at the world in general and at politics or collective choice in particular. As the following interview reveals in impressive clarity, the roots for this are to be found to a very large, dominating degree in his personal background, his personal experience and cultural inheritance as a Southerner. What interested Buchanan more than anything else, from the very outset, was how people can live in society without infringing on each other's rights. Others before him or alongside him have thought along similar lines, especially Friedrich August von Hayek. I cannot think of any other scholar endowed with such a deep longing for justice, with such a visceral, subjective disgust for domination and discrimination – and this is true as much for his own sake as for the sake of others. Buchanan's approach is strongly individualistic and decidedly subjectivist. All this makes him a pure classical liberal, and it comes as no surprise that he is thoroughly familiar with the works of classics such as Adam Smith, Knut Wicksell and the Austrian school of economics. Buchanan's heritage and disposition made his mind receptive to the work of those classics which he integrated, carrying their ideas further and developing an approach that was the logical next step in theory on the one hand, but also the necessary answer to the concrete political questions of the current times on the other hand. In this way, in this absolute landmark case, the three lines of inspiration all interacted, but there has been a strong predominance in the decisive influence of what I've called personal biography.

INTERVIEW

Professor Buchanan, I would like to start with the most obvious question: how did you get to be interested in economics in the first place? It's not such a straightforward choice, after all. One isn't usually confronted with economics at school, for example, so one does need some other kind of external instigation, be it from parents, or others.
There was no instigation at all. The Great Depression was on, and I could not afford to go to Vanderbilt College, which I was supposed to go to, and ultimately go to law school. So I had to stay home. The only place where I could go was to teacher's college which was in town. This was a small operation. You had to take all those education courses and so on. But I was a good student, and by the end of the second year, I was leading the pack in terms of grade records. I took three majors, part of it for convenience, part of it for interest. I had mathematics major, a literature major, and a social science major which included economics. At the end of my four years there, job openings being very scarce, I had only three options: I could have taught high school – and indeed I did some substitute teaching – or I could have worked in a bank, having an offer from a bank, or else my political science professor got me a fellowship at the University of Tennessee in economics. The fellowship could have been in anything, I

would have taken it because it dominated the other options. So that was my introduction to economics. It was pure luck.

Were you somehow prepared for that step, though? Was there some predis-position or other intellectual readiness for economics on your part? What was it like at home, for example? Did you talk about economic topics at all, in the sense of talking about scarcity or budget constraints as they were experienced in everyday life, especially in those tough times of the Great Depression?

I don't think so. My home environment wasn't like that, even though my mother was a brilliant woman, a just absolutely voracious reader, reading everything. She consumed everything from pulp fiction all the way to lit-erature. She was very disappointed that my high school didn't have Latin. She wanted me to take Latin, and she made me take French, which I didn't want to. She was interested in everything, literally everything. She came from a family of deputy sheriffs and preachers for the most part. They were what you would call upper middle class. My mother was really the dominant influence on me. My Dad read the newspaper, but he was not a leader in intellectual conversation at all. And yet, his family had more academic connections than my mother's family. His uncle was a historian at the University of Oklahoma. There is actually a street named after him. My Dad went two years to the University of Oklahoma and played football.

You lived on a farm.

Yes, we ran this farm. My grandfather on my father's side had been Governor of the state of Tennessee. That ruined him forever for farming, but we lived there. We had several tenants on the place, mostly black families. They were gradually moving out over the whole period. When his father died, my Dad was left with managing and running the farm, despite the fact that he didn't own it. It was owned by the whole family. As a result, he had no incentive to fix it up much, so it was just a run-down operation. We sold milk; that was our main cash crop. Then we had a little bit of cotton, and we had corn, all that standard stuff. My Dad was no natural farmer. He did a lot of odd jobs, carpenter or insulator work for example. His real love was to doctor animals, and he used to go around and help people with their animals.

Was that a poor life?

It was a very poor life, although I didn't realize that at the time. My mother had this very strong work ethic. She worked all the time. I got that from her, definitely. But my Dad really enjoyed loafing. I've never enjoyed loafing. My mother didn't enjoy loafing. But he would go down to the store and sit around with his buddies for hours and leave me do the work. He really was happy idle, not doing anything. That didn't transmit to me.

Your parents were an interesting match then!
They were an interesting match indeed. She taught school for nine years before she got married. She was the dominant intellectual force. He was a lot better looking man than she was a woman. He was a handsome man, and she was ordinary – but that was fine. He always deferred to her. He was in charge of the money, but he fully understood that she was brighter than he was. So she was ultimately the arbiter. He didn't suffer from that, he had no complex, he was very self-confident.

Was making ends meet difficult in those times? Was that a topic?
Well, my mother always complained that he didn't give her enough money to buy what she wanted to buy. But that was a perennial sort of a thing. We never went hungry, not even close to that. The only real impact that the whole of the Great Depression period had on our family in a narrow sense was that right in the middle of it, my mother's sister and her two boys moved in with us. This woman's husband had worked for a railroad and got laid off. His mother would let him come back, but not his family. So they were destitute. Obviously subsistent, we had to keep them. They lived there for about a year, until her husband got a job in Memphis. He came and packed them up and they left.

The goal for you was to get just some kind of good education and then move on?
It was not only a goal. It was kind of understood.

You were not supposed to become a farmer?
Oh no, never, never, never. My mother would have turned over in her grave forty times if I did. The idea was that I would just keep on going, doing the best I could. She had great ambitions for me. For example, every other boy in the whole school would have to take off and help pick the cotton or the corn or whatever. My mother wouldn't let me miss a day in school for work, oh no. So I went every day. I didn't mind, I enjoyed going to school. At all levels. I never found that to be a chore.

Did you have teachers that left a mark?
I had a good teacher for the 5th and 6th grade. She was a great fat woman. But she was a great teacher in the sense that she had a good relationship with all her students. During the course of the year, she would take them

home with her. It was always a big event. Three or four boys for example would get to go home with Miss Meyer and spend the night at her house. Her father ran a store down the road. They were a little bit more affluent than we were. She had things, and she was a good cook. I probably went to her house twice. One of those times, I remember distinctly, after supper, we were sitting around and she showed us one of those stereopticon things. You would look through them and you could see scenes from the holy land in three dimensions. That was something strange.

Then, later, at college, you took those three majors that you mentioned, mathematics, literature, and social science (economics). What exactly did they teach you in economics?
Nothing. Absolutely nothing. Our lecturer was a retired preacher or something like that, and he had not the foggiest notion what all this was about. And then I went to the University of Tennessee for a year, on that economics fellowship, and didn't learn economics either. Well, at that time economics was all institutional. We had one course on Roosevelt's New Deal. There were all these abbreviated agencies, the NRA, the FDS, etc. There was a good course on central banking, but no economic theory as such. We had a pretty good statistics course, but I didn't learn economics before I went to Chicago.

But that year must have triggered your interest, otherwise you wouldn't have gone on to Chicago.
No. Not really. As I said, the idea was to keep on going to school. I had a fellowship in statistics. That was, again, the one field where a fellowship was available, for the second year at Columbia. They had a good program there at that time.[13] But then, in March or April, my number came up to the top in the draft. I had to go and take Army physical exams. I had no problems there. Practically, I would have had to join the Army, but I started scratching around, trying to get in to officer's training for the Navy. However, my blood pressure was too high for that. I asked the doctors to let me come back for a test the next day. They agreed, and I went down to Nashville, back home. My Dad's cousin was one of the local doctors. We called him up on the golf course and told him the story. He said, well, you go back tomorrow. You estimate the best you can, and half an hour before the test, you take this pill. So I went. At some point, I figured it would be about half an hour, and I took the pill. But they immediately called me, and my blood pressure was still beyond the limit. And so I said, I'm just nervous, let me sit over there just a few minutes. Within less than half an hour, I got my blood pressure down, the doctor was amazed, and I got in to Navy officer's training.

Were they worried about high blood pressure in case you were in a submarine or something?
No, that was just arbitrary. It's just like everything else. They didn't care.

So the Navy saved you from becoming a statistician.
Oh yes. Had I been 4F,[14] I would have gone to Columbia, in order to work on a Ph.D. in statistics, I suppose. I am sure I would have enjoyed it. I have always thought that you can find any of these intellectual experiences rewarding. Going back to my time at teacher's college, I had to ride in and out ten miles every day, in order to milk those cows. Due to this farm work, I couldn't take courses that had labs late in the evening. So I couldn't take physics, and I had to take biology, where the labs were earlier in the day. But during the last year, I was able at last to take a sequence in physics. Had I been able to take that in my second year, I am sure I would have become a physicist. I was fascinated, absolutely fascinated. But it came too late in my studies. It also has a lot of parallels to economics.

Didn't you have a dream about what you wanted to become?
Not really. In those days, if you could survive and get a job, then you were content. I very vaguely remember that I used to think that by going to teacher's college, if I could be a professor at a college like that, this would be the ideal life. My political science professor, the one who got me the economics fellowship for the University of Tennessee – a worthless teacher, I didn't learn anything from him, but a nice fellow – had this nice little house on this nice little street in Murfreesboro, and he made 3600 dollars a year. At that time, that was a fabulous sum. And I thought, God, it would be wonderful to have someday a position like that. That's the only kind of ideal I remotely remember.

What did the Navy teach you?
Those were formative years, from the middle of 1941 to the end of 1945, and they were very, very good for me. Luck played a tremendous role here again. First of all, I went off to that officers' training school in New York. You had to be a college graduate for that. They trained us for three months. We went through the regular training in an accelerated way. At first, there was a boot camp, drills with rifles and marching and ropes and boats and things like that. Then we had courses in navigation, gunnery, seamanship, etc. We were about 600 boys. The locale was an old battleship from the Spanish-American war in the mud of the Hudson River, the 'SS Illinois'. We lived on board that ship. We'd have classes there or in a warehouse building on the dock. James Tobin was in the class directly after me. Anyway, during the first month, I experienced discrimination, and it just got me all upset. If there

is one thing I can't stand – and that's central – it's when somebody is treated unfairly, whether it's somebody else or whether it's me. A disproportionate number of us were from the South and the West, as opposed to the upper East. I experienced overt discrimination for being a non-Easterner, a non-establishmentarian. In the whole group of 600 boys, there were only about twenty who were graduates of Yale, Harvard, Princeton – all Ivy League. By the end of this first boot camp period, they had to select midshipman officers. Out of the 20 boys from the establishment universities, 12 or 13 were picked, against a background of a total of 600. It was overtly discriminatory towards those of us who were not members of the establishment. That made me into a flaming communist. I would have signed up immediately to the Communist Party had a recruiter come along. I had already had strong left-wing socialist leanings, but now it was stronger than ever. I think I felt this stronger than anybody else. Even today, there is a residue still there. I don't ever get rid of that. . . Anyway, no recruiter came along, and I didn't sign my name on any communist manifest. But I would have!

Where did those left-wing convictions come from? Was it just the usual incli-nation that we all share, at least while we're young, towards everything that sounds like justice and doing good?
No, it was more than that in my case. It was fundamentally due to a popu-list background. I grew up with all those pamphlets from the time in the 1890s when several American states went Populist[15] – pamphlets about the Wall Street Barons and the Rubber Barons and all this stuff. And of course, the Democrats ran the South at that time; it was a one-party system. Then I got interested in economics, and everybody in my peer group was a socialist. We didn't get the right picture about what was going on. Russia was an ideal for us all. I even started learning Russian.

Wow! But did you trust the government generally?
At that time I still implicitly held to this image that somehow the state was benevolent. I didn't start raising those kinds of questions until much later.

Well, let's get back to your Navy experience. How did that continue?
I was very, very lucky again. We had orders already as to where we were going to report next. I had orders to report to the Naval Communications School in Connecticut, to become a communication expert. But after Pearl Harbor, four of us had our orders changed. We were now supposed to go to Naval War College in Newport, Rhode Island. We were the only junior officers ever to go to War College. There, we would have a fascinating five weeks' course in operations plot, and then we would go and report to the staff of Chester W. Nimitz in Pearl Harbor. In Pearl Harbor, our job

was to keep the maps going, and to keep track where all the ships were. I was senior among the group in the sense that my grades were better than the others, and so I moved up to be assistant operations officer by the time the war was over. I actually had a part in writing up the official report on the Battle of Midway, our crucial battle in the Pacific. It had of course been just chaos and confusion. So we did empirical research, sorting out what plane sank what ship etc., night and day, and we wrote this report.

How much fighting did you experience? This sounds like you were somewhat remote.

Oh yes, we were several stories underground, actually. We had one operations officer, a captain, who felt that we shouldn't be ordered out to sea unless we had sea duty ourselves. But he did order us to spend at least a little time at sea. So I went out with the 5th fleet on the 'Indianapolis' for the invasion of the Marshall Islands. We bombarded the shore, and they brought the Japanese back on board. All in all, it took not quite six weeks. That was my total exposure to actual fighting. Then in December 1944, we moved our headquarters to Guam, and sat there for the last eight months of the war.

When the war ended, did you consider staying in the Navy?

Oh yes, very strongly. The most difficult decision that I've ever made was whether to get out of the Navy or stay in it. They tried to get me to stay; they thought I could do well in the Navy. I was very tempted, because I liked the military life very much, the social life, the order. In academia, I didn't know how good I would be, so I took a big chance when I decided to go back to academia.

But what exactly convinced you to leave then?

I think it was fundamentally this idea that a reserve officer who has gone through these short three months of training and then got promoted to be an officer would still be always be secondary to those that had gone through the regular program. Another factor that wouldn't help was the absence of sea duty – I had only those six weeks.

So you left the Navy and went on to Chicago to take up your academic life again. Why Chicago?

I had this fellowship to Columbia, but I didn't like New York. New York without any money is not a very good place now and never was, even in those days. My undergraduate professor that I mentioned before had taken his Ph.D. in political science at Chicago, around 1938. He had conveyed to me the intellectual excitement of the place. I agree with this to this day. It is the most exciting atmosphere in the world, there is no question about that. I had no idea about the department of economics, no idea whether it was good or bad or indifferent. Had I known that it was a market-oriented department, I would probably have gone somewhere else.

Who was there, at the department, and left a mark on you?
Frank Knight[16] was there, and he was certainly a dominant influence in my career. He became a role model. He was teaching the price theory course and the history of thought course. Jacob Viner had already decided to leave Chicago and did so in 1946, but I still took his course in international trade. He drove everybody insane, he was so tough. Viner felt it was his obligatory duty to make every student feel worthless and small. Just the opposite of Theodore W. Shultz[17] whose teaching habits I picked up. His idea was never to put down students, he rather said, well, Mr. So-and-so, there might be something in what you're saying. . . Viner would just crush you. Then, the year that I finished my course, in 1947, Milton Friedman came and joined the faculty. The graduate adviser recommended that even though I had taken the price theory course already with Knight, I should take it again with Friedman, because it was quite different and better. That was very good, he was very thorough.

And that was the end of your socialist inclinations, I guess. They must have turned you around?
And in a hurry. We were about 30 people in Knight's course in price theory. Fifteen switched over completely within six to eight weeks, and 15 stayed exactly the way they were. They were socialist to start with and they were socialist when they came out. There was no distinction in the grades, it was no question of who was intelligent and who wasn't, it was rather that, somehow or another, you were preconditioned. And for some reason, I was preconditioned to buy into the workings of the market – which was something I had not really understood at all until I took Knight's course.

Is being a Southerner, and therefore loving independence, part of that precondition?
Oh yes, no doubt about that.

Could you explain this a little, please? The American Civil war lay way behind; you didn't experience those times yourself. You didn't suffer from any kind of repression, did you? After all, you have been living in a free country. So why that 'Southern' urge towards independence?
It all goes back to my mother. She was an intellectual force. She had grown up in this Southern culture. She hated Abraham Lincoln with a passion. That was three generations before her, but it still was very strong in her

way of thinking. The slavery part didn't enter the picture. But Lincoln, as the personification of the Yankees, had imposed the war on the South. That feeling was very strong in my background. This was coupled with the populist influence, which went against the moneyed interest of Wall Street and the Eastern establishment. I really had to rethink my views on all that. This change has been hard for me to undergo, but I have come to admire Lincoln more and more and more.

Back to Chicago. What did you learn in the economic thought course? Was it there that you got in touch with the Scottish Enlightenment, with Adam Smith?
Yes. Frank Knight's course was really a course on Adam Smith. He, however, concentrated on how relative prices get formed. What was neglected altogether was the second principle by Smith in his *Wealth of Nations*,[18] namely the idea that the way an economy grows is by extending the market. I rediscovered that part of Smith only in the eighties, and I have been working on that for 20 years now. That's something very few people have picked up. My question is why, if you extend the market, you get a disproportionate increase in the value of the total product, even if there are no economies of scale, no externalities etc. The neoclassical paradigm will tell you, erroneously, that you won't. But I think we got the answer to that now. The economy will still grow disproportionately as you extend the market because you have stochastic demand. In that case, it becomes worthwhile to produce something only if the market reaches some critical size, so that there is enough demand to cater to.[19]

Then you're reintroducing economies of scale through the back door, from the consumption side rather than from the production side.
Yes, you can't get away from that.

Did the Theory of Moral Sentiments[20] *have any effect on you?*
No, and not even to this day.

Let's come back to your time as a Ph.D. student at Chicago. Did you have much interaction with your teachers?
With Frank Knight, I did. Not with others. Again, I was very lucky. I am not sure that Knight was very accessible to many people, but he sure was to me. It was partly because he liked me, and partly because we shared a comparable background. Once a rapport was established between Knight and me in this personal way, I spent hours in his office, talking to him, just chatting away. What I got from Knight was not so much specifics, but the idea that everything is up for grabs, that is, you challenge everything, you don't accept any authority. There is nothing sacrosanct.

And how did you pick your themes for study and research? What drove you toward public finance in the first place?

The public finance part was due to the fact that I became the graduate assistant of our public finance professor. And so I wrote a master's thesis on how the state of Tennessee allocated its tax money amongst the counties. So I already had one leg up, and then it was a natural for me to write my dissertation on fiscal federalism, that is, about how states with independent taxing power and federal government interact. So I was in public finance and just stayed. By the way, there was a course taught at Chicago on public debt. When we were handed out this very thick bibliography on public debt, I thought we were supposed to read the stuff, and so I started to read. I read, and I read, and I read. When I found out that nobody else was reading these materials, I felt really foolish. And yet, foolish but lucky – because when, nine years later, I all of a sudden realized that everything I had learnt about public debt was wrong and set out to write my book,[21] at least I was sure I had read everything.

What was the political climate at University? How did Keynesianism affect Chicago?

There was not much of that, really. Keynesian teachings had not fully arrived there. We did have a course in macroeconomics that Jacob Marschak taught, and I guess you could say it was Keynesian-oriented, but that tendency was sublimated. And my colleague Don Patinkin started to work on the Pigouvian effect.[22] But basically, Chicago was not dominated by Keynesian models at all.

Are you saying that Chicago was trying to resist Keynesianism and did it so well that there wasn't even much of a debate going on?

Yes. They thought it wasn't even worth bothering. Just as an illustration of how much a world apart Chicago was, let me tell you this. I remember very distinctly that in the summer of 1948 – I was about ready to leave Chicago – they put Lloyd Metzler on faculty. And so with a friend, we went in to audit the course, just to see what he was saying. Metzler started the course out by saying: 'There are two types of economics being taught in the world today. There is Chicago, and there is the rest of the world. I'm going to teach you what the rest of the world is teaching, not Chicago.' And then he started all this Keynesian stuff.

How did you escape the mathematization fad?

I had an undergraduate major in mathematics, and therefore my graduate adviser at Chicago told me I didn't need any further class. So I skipped that, which is a little unfortunate for me. Had I had a little less background, I might have been more receptive. I have never been negative on mathematics, as a matter of fact, but I never felt like I needed to use it much.

Where did you get the idea to endogenize and analyze state action? I know that stumbling over Wicksell's Finanztheoretische Untersuchungen[23] *in the old Harper Library at Chicago in 1948 was crucial, almost an epiphany, because he formulated many ideas that you had, too. When did you learn German in the first place?*
We had to know German and French in order to get a Ph.D. at the time. You had to have a reading knowledge in both, and you had to pass a test. I had French at high school, and I learnt German on my own. I just got myself some grammars and books. I learnt enough to read economics. But that wasn't really enough to translate Wicksell, which I absolutely wanted to do. I did start, but Elizabeth Henderson helped me a lot in it.

But why did you flash so immediately upon reading Wicksell? Where did the idea to apply the choice paradigm to politics come from? What made you a contractarian? Was it the result of discussions with other people or did it just develop in your own head?
It certainly wasn't from talking with anybody. I don't know how these things come about. I guess underneath it all – and this goes back to my being a Southerner – I was searching for an explanatory logic that would make it legitimate for somebody to coerce somebody else. Philosophically, I am an anarchist in a way, and very much an individualist. You need to have a justification for being able to coerce other people if you take this view that I start with. Then, with my approach, you can conceptualize a collective order to which people agree, and it's not coercion but some kind of contract if people agree to it.

Hypothetically.
Hypothetical consent gives you one criterion that is better than saying 'I want it' or 'Gods want it' or a thing like that. It gives you at least a means to lay out where we should stand normatively. This is Adam Smith's impartial spectator, or John Rawls's position behind the 'veil of ignorance'. It's a better starting point for normative questions than any other alternative, but of course it does subject itself to corruption. Real agreement is the only test, but it's very costly. Anyway, looking back, it just seems so obvious that there was this huge gap – you could drive a truck through it – in the way people felt about the state and politics. Somehow we needed to explain activities on the part of the collective. Nobody paid attention to that. If you look at public finance in the 1940s, it's amazing

that nobody was worrying about this. Economics was dominated by this Keynesian digression, and macroeconomics came in, and government was supposedly benevolent. So this was a natural gap that needed to be filled. I guess I was also influenced, more than I realized, by Antonio de Viti de Marco's one book that had been translated into English,[24] in which he talked about the model of the state. Several of us who came in to Public Choice had come from Public Finance and had been influenced by the Italians. Following up on that reading, at any rate, my first article in 1949[25] was nothing more than a plea for public finance economists to at least pay attention and model the state in one way or another – either as an organic, benevolent being, or as a set of individuals. Everything would depend on that.

What happened once your Ph.D. thesis was written?
The terms of the extra fellowship I had at Chicago were such that I was supposed to return to the South for at least the length of the fellowship or else pay the money back. So I went to Tennessee first, from 1948 to 1951, on faculty. In 1951, I got an offer from Florida State University. Earl J. Hamilton, then at Chicago, was responsible for that. Florida State was just moving from an all-girls university to co-education, building up its faculty real fast. I chose to go there, I don't know why. But it was the critically best decision that I ever made. There were two fellows on the faculty there, Clark Allen and Marshall Colberg, both of whom had an idea of what modern academia was all about, which was something nobody at Tennessee had. They understood that you need to publish. We all three wrote a textbook together.[26] So I all of a sudden metamorphosed into somebody who was interested in writing pieces. It just happened while I was at Florida State. And then, Duncan Black and Kenneth Arrow came along with their ideas. I was never interested in the exact workings of majority rule, nor was I ever interested in the social welfare function. But Arrow in particular, in 1951, generated a huge amount of discussion.[27] I was dissatisfied with the whole tone of that discourse. It really got me upset, it didn't seem appropriate at all. Underneath it all, both Black and Arrow had this notion that if we could generate a social ordering or welfare function, that would be good. To me, it was just the other way around. Their ideal was a structure of preferences we wouldn't want to have. We need to avoid dominance, and so we actually want to have a cycle. The two best pieces I've ever written were published in those years, in 1954, while I was at Florida State. Earl Hamilton, then the editor, published that in the *Journal of Political Economy*.[28] They were critiques of the whole Arrow discourse, attacking the notion of the social welfare function. It made no sense to me, and still makes no sense for me. I could

never understand what Paul Samuelson and Abram Bergson were driving at.[29] I just couldn't understand this underlying desire to have a social ordering somehow. So I wrote these pieces that nobody really understood and nobody but Amartya Sen[30] has ever understood. Anyway, that was a critical turn in my career.

How receptive was academia?
Nobody paid any attention to it at the time. But when I go back over my stuff myself, I really think it was the best I've ever done.

What was the driving force behind these two pieces that you wrote?
I didn't like the implications of some of the discourse here. I saw it as an attempt to justify or legitimate the majority imposing its will on the minority. That's what goes all the way back to the 'Southerner' thing. I really thought in terms of wanting to protect the minority against the tyranny of the majority. I wanted to minimize coercion of man by man. If you take the implications of the Black and Arrow stuff, and if you find a dominant majority, then you just keep on imposing on the minority. That was what I was reacting against. That's a strong underneath value for me. I've always been very sensitive to minorities being oppressed. That plus the Wicksell idea gave me some outlook for a way of legitimizing collective action, instead of becoming a pure anarchist. Then I shifted again during my Italian year (1955),[31] which reinforced a lot of these notions. The Italians paid a lot of attention to how you modeled the state. That put me in a framework of thinking in terms of the collective, that is, in terms of that sector of the economy as opposed to the market. That year was also important in a value sense. It made me willing emotionally to challenge some of the sacrosanct precepts of American democracy. It is deeply embedded in a lot of people, and certainly was in me, that you don't look at the state and collective action in a critical way. Quite to the contrary, there is this awe, the state just has got to be benevolent. The Italians just stripped all that away. They had no respect for the state, no respect for politicians, no respect for politics. That was useful for me, because it allowed me to pull that part of my thinking up. Otherwise it might have remained buried.

But what made you more or less abandon the standard allocational aspects and turn to the analysis of the rule level instead?
Before I went to Italy, in 1954, I spent the summer at the RAND Corporation. I was very much imbued with the standard neoclassical approach. Beginning about that time, for example, there was the discussion in the US about President Dwight D. Eisenhower's plan to build interstate highways. I had already published a little piece in the *National*

Tax Journal[32] about highway pricing, and I decided to write a book on highway economics. I got half of that book done. Then my stay in Italy came through, and I lost interest in the highway topic. I abandoned it completely. I was much more motivated to write my book on public debt, by clarifying this terrible confusion about opportunity cost, and bringing everything back to individual choice. I was determined to do that. The allocational type standard economic stuff didn't seem to appeal to me at all any more when I came back from Italy, and so I shifted away. The debt book was a precursor to my *Cost and Choice*[33] book later, and it also ties in with the collective action idea. After Italy, I went to the University of Virginia at Charlottesville. And there, a strong reinforcer of that Italian emphasis was Rutledge Vining. He had a big influence on me. He had also been a student of Frank Knight. Knight had insisted on rules, and Vining had picked that up. You don't choose anything but rules – that was Vining's emphasis, and of course I picked that up. This way, I started thinking about alternative rules and constitutions and so forth and so on. That turn came in the mid-fifties.

So it was crucial to have intellectual exchanges.
Oh yes, it was. And then in 1958, Gordon Tullock came on board on a post-doctoral fellowship. This is another side-influence. Tullock had personally been influenced by Joseph Schumpeter's book *Capitalism, Socialism, and Democracy*.[34] I had not been at all, even though you can see in Schumpeter a lot of precursory ideas to what Public Choice later developed. Gordon was also friendly with Anthony Downs, who had written his thesis under Arrow.[35] So Gordon wrote this thing on majority rule, published in 1959.[36] That year, Tullock and I gave little pieces at the Mont Pèlerin meeting at Oxford. We were both talking about rules and constitutions. Those were some seeds for the *Calculus of Consent*.[37] We went back to the States after that meeting. Tullock went off on the faculty of foreign relations at South Carolina University, and I got a Ford Foundation fellowship to spend a year off and got away from teaching and administrative duties. It was during that academic year 1959/1960 that we wrote that book, sending chapters back and forth between Charlottesville and South Carolina.

What was the reaction to that path-breaking work of yours when it came out?
It got surprisingly good reviews. The political scientists seemed to be a little bit scared of it. I didn't think we were doing anything revolutionary. We were just taking James Madison's notions, putting them into modern terminology, and that was all. It was implicitly a defense of the American structure of political decision making, as opposed to parliamentary

majoritarian structure that all political scientists idealized, and so it was an attack on the majority rule.

When did you discover Friedrich August von Hayek? Was his approach to the knowledge problem decisive in forming your approach?
He had no influence on me at all at that stage. This only started much later. We knew that Hayek had written *The Road to Serfdom*,[38] but we didn't pay any attention to it. Ludwig von Mises and his *Human Action*[39] however had an influence on Tullock. Not on me. All the radical subjectivism bits that I have came more closely from the London group, from Jack Wiseman and George Shackle. Mises turned it all into tautology in a way.

The individualism bits are absolutely crucial to your work as a starting point. But in what is this rooted? Not in any kind of natural rights, I suppose.
Well, I guess this is what philosophers nowadays call 'ontological individualism'.[40] It seems to me that you have to be an ontological individualist. I don't see how you could be anything else. It is not a question of norms; it is also not just a logical starting point. It's a fact. An individual, that's what you are. That's how I look at it. In welfare economic terms, even if all the elements in your utility function are derived from the benefit of the tribe, they are still yours.

So when did Hayek show up as an influence on you?
That didn't come in until the sixties. I did fully learn from Hayek the distinction between what I later called moral community and moral order and moral anarchy – this is about the sense that our genetic predisposition is all for the insider tribe.[41] That was his main influence on me. He thought a lot about that jump from the tribe to the extended society, where we treat strangers just like we treat members of our own tribe. How we learn to do that – that remained a mystery to him. To everybody. And it is a mystery. That's where he theoretically lapsed back into some process of cultural evolution.

What about the idea of universalizable rules and generality?
That came from him, too, but later. Also, Hayek's 'catallactic'[42] idea of a spontaneous order in the market place reinforced the notion I had picked up on my own and also from some of the writers of the nineteenth century. Michael Polanyi's *Logic of Liberty*[43] was also an important influence. My theme was that we should concentrate on exchange, not choice. Of course you choose when you exchange, but what is central is the institution of exchange.[44]

Let's turn to The Power to Tax,[45] *another important, well-known and also fun-to-read book of yours. What was the genesis of that?*
Well, Geoffrey Brennan had just arrived, and we had found some common ground. At the same time, somebody was organizing a Festschrift in honor of Joe Peckman, who had been the tax man for the Brookings Institution for many years.[46] Peckman had been one of the main advocates for broadening the tax base. For that Festschrift, Brennan and I wrote a piece together in praise of loopholes,[47] arguing that if you really had a completely broad base, there was, by definition, no way to escape it. The existence of a loophole, however, would limit by how much you could raise the tax rate if you want to maximize revenue, because otherwise, people would go through the loophole. We thought it was kind of a neat idea. It was just a logical solution to a little logical puzzle. We then expanded that idea into a book. *The Power to Tax* was a book strictly developing one single idea.

Many people must have been stirred up by that book, with you turning everything upside down.
Yes. Richard Musgrave,[48] for example, was very upset about that book.

You co-authored a lot, compared to other people. Is that an indication that the driving force in your creativity was cooperation?
Yes, but it wasn't uniform, my co-authors served different functions. There were several co-authors who were there because they had technical competences that I didn't have, Roger Faith, for example, and Dwight Lee, to some extent. Geoffrey Brennan is different in the sense that he and I can sit together for half an hour and come up with lots of ideas. When I see him for half a day I get more stimulation than from most people in a lifetime. With Gordon Tullock, he was brilliant but I had to bring the discipline to bear. Other co-authors were people who had inchoate ideas but I had to kind of pull them out. Other ideas would just come out of ordinary discussion, sometimes even in class.

How would you describe the process by which you come from one topic to the next? Has that been linear?
I would say that it's logical gaps in the theory that need to be filled. You proceed as you tend to clarify what seems to be a biding confusion.

How come you were optimistic about the possibility to influence, or rather to improve the way people live together in society, by means of adequate rules and constitutions? I know that you don't pick outcomes, but rules. At the same time, rules are also outcomes, and insofar. . .
. . . it is an infinite regress. Yes.

How do you get out of that?
You can't get out of it at all. You can talk about policies within a set of existing rules or institutions. You can posit that those rules or institutions are 'relatively absolute absolutes',[49] which is an evasion in a way, and then you compare policy options and you can say this one is better than that one, given some efficiency norms or value norms. When you move on to the level of the rules, you can analyze different sets, and you try to judge comparative sets of outcomes generated by different sets of rules. And finally, you can also move up to the John Rawls level in order to normatively decide on the principles for deriving the rules. For my part, I'm willing – and that distinguishes me from Rawls[50] – to stop with procedures, whereas he even wants to define specifically what would emerge from them.

Coming back to your sources of inspiration, was there ever any public policy problem out there that you were called to solve?
I've never been much of a public policy wonk nor engaged myself in advocating one policy rather than another. With one exception, and that was a failure. I did get involved in the balanced budget amendment proposals. I testified a few times in different state legislatures. Otherwise, I have done no consulting, except one time, when William Baumol thought I might be interested to testify before the state commerce commission, on the pricing of barge traffic and real traffic. They were regulating all these prices. The argument was pure marginal cost pricing. So I wrote a 24-page brief, and it paid a huge amount of money. But it was never used and never amounted to anything. I think the barge people finally gained the case. That taught me a lesson. If you get tempted, you can cram a lot of money, but it's not worth it. Money doesn't mean that much to me, you know.

I rather meant that sometimes topics for research may come up in connection with policy debates in the public.
Oh yes, and I was involved in some of that. For example, I did want to see Europe go into a federal structure, so that the states would maintain their existence and their powers, while ensuring free trade and full mobility of capital and labor across borders. I wrote that paper for a conference in Paris in 1990, called 'Europe's constitutional opportunity'.[51] Then I spun off from that the whole idea of European federalism, and produced many different papers on that. However, I was too optimistic. I made two mistakes in that paper. I thought that due to the demise of communism, the old-fashioned socialist position and central planning had much less power than it did. On the other side I assumed that the federalism idea was so obvious that it wouldn't generate much opposition, especially from the

British. The federalism thing just seemed so natural. Well, some of my stuff has always been triggered by these ongoing issues. And still is. I really ought to get involved and say something about free trade, insisting on the strength of the Smithian logic as opposed to the Ricardian one[52] – in order to get this huge protectionist sentiment down in this country.

Summing up, I guess we can say that you had all these different sources of inspiration – personal background, logical gaps in theory, policy challenges, challenges from papers by other researchers that you reacted to, and, finally, discussions with peers. So it's been kind of a mixture, and none of them was dominant.

That's correct. In my case, there was more drift than dominance. Looking back, much of it looks more coherent than I ever dreamed it would be, writing what I did for different purposes, in different times and contexts. As you drift along, you just get interested in more things. I enjoy working out an idea and writing it out. The joy of construction and composition is important for me, in addition to the logical coherence. Many of my colleagues don't know how to write. It is no longer fun to read economics at all.

Is there still something out there that cries for explanation? You've created a paradigm shift. Other people did it in other fields. Is there still something that needs to be done? Or has progress come to a point where there is nothing more to be asked and answered?

Well, we haven't learnt yet to live together peacefully... But I don't know what progress really means. Anyway, I think we need to have faith in the fact that there is more out there to be explained. Even the paradigms that we now have, including subjective value theory, for example, are only provisional. Some physicist might believe that ultimately, we will be able to explain everything. To me, that is utterly stupid, just like saying that an atheist is equally dogmatic as a Texas Baptist. It seems to me that, if you accept evolution, you can still not expect your dog to get up and start talking German. And that's because your dog is not genetically programmed to do that. We are human animals, and we are equally bound. There are whole realms of discourse out there that we cannot reach, by definition. There are always going to be limits beyond which we cannot go. Knowing that they are there, you can always hope to move a little closer – but that's all.

Thank you, Professor.

NOTES

1. James M. Buchanan (1992b, p. 99).
2. The interview was held on 23–24 June, 2007.
3. Knut Wicksell (1896).
4. The journal was at first published under the somewhat clumsy name 'Papers on Non-Market Decision Making'.
5. James M. Buchanan and Gordon Tullock (1962).
6. Thomas Hobbes (1651).
7. John Rawls (1971).
8. James M. Buchanan (1986/92).
9. Geoffrey Brennan and James M. Buchanan (1980).
10. James M. Buchanan/Geoffrey Brennan (1985).
11. James M. Buchanan (2001).
12. 'Existing preference functions and the institutions generated by past choices are "relatively absolute absolutes", subject to change, but only through time – change that might be influenced only marginally by choices made now.' (Geoffrey Brennan and James M. Buchanan, 1985, p. 85).
13. Harold Hotelling had created this program in the 1930s. See the interview with Kenneth J. Arrow in this book.
14. Permanently referred from the Army.
15. The Populist Party was a political party in the US in the late nineteenth century. It flourished particularly among western farmers, based on its opposition to the gold standard.
16. The economist Frank Knight (1885–1972) presided over the Department of Economics at the University of Chicago jointly with Jacob Viner from the 1920s to the late 1940s. He is well known still today for his famous distinction between 'risk' (randomness with knowable probabilities) and 'uncertainty' (randomness with unknowable probabilities). He argued in favor of laissez-faire not for utilitarian reasons, but rather because it holds individual freedom as an absolute good.
17. Theodore W. Shultz (1902–98) was awarded the Nobel Memorial Prize in Economic Sciences in 1979, together with W. Arthur Lewis, for 'their pioneering research into economic development research with particular consideration of the problems of developing countries'.
18. Adam Smith (1776).
19. James M. Buchanan (2008).
20. Adam Smith (1759).
21. James M. Buchanan (1958).
22. The Pigou effect is the wealth effect on consumption that takes place as prices fall. A lower price level leads to a greater existing private wealth of nominal value, leading to a rise in consumption. See Alvin H. Hansen (1951) and Don Patinkin (1948).
23. Knut Wicksell (1896). A major portion of the book has been translated by James M. Buchanan and Elizabeth Henderson as 'A new principle of just taxation' (Wicksell, 1958).
24. Antonio de Viti de Marco (1936).
25. James M. Buchanan (1949).
26. Clark L. Allen et al. (1954).
27. Kenneth J. Arrow (1951). See the interview with Kenneth J. Arrow in this book.
28. James M. Buchanan (1954a and 1954b). Both of these essays are reprinted in James M. Buchanan (1960, pp. 75–104).
29. Paul A. Samuelson (1956). For a later reiteration, see Paul A. Samuelson (1977).
30. Amartya Sen was awarded the Nobel Prize in 1998 'for his contributions to welfare economics'.
31. During the academic year 1955–1956, James M. Buchanan had a Fulbright Research Scholarship for Italy.

32. James M. Buchanan (1952).
33. James M. Buchanan (1969b).
34. Joseph A. Schumpeter (1942).
35. Anthony Downs (1957).
36. Gordon Tullock (1959).
37. James M. Buchanan and Gordon Tullock (1962).
38. Friedrich August von Hayek (1944). Friedrich August von Hayek was awarded the Nobel Prize in 1974, together with Gunnar Myrdal – both received it 'for their pioneering work in the theory of money and economic fluctuations and for their penetrating analysis of the interdependence of economic, social and institutional phenomena'.
39. Ludwig von Mises (1949).
40. The philosophical view sometimes called ontological individualism is the thesis that social or historical groups, processes, and events are but complexes of individuals and individual actions.
41. See Friedrich August von Hayek (1952), especially chapters 8–10. Later on, Hayek states this again explicitly in his epilogue to Friedrich August von Hayek (1979, pp. 153–76).
42. Catallaxy is exchange, that is friendly interaction between people. Hayek explains his liking of that term especially well in a chapter named 'The market order or catallaxy' in Friedrich August von Hayek (1976, pp. 107–32). He uses the term to describe 'the order brought about by the mutual adjustment of many individual economies in a market' (pp. 108–9). He derived the word from the Greek verb katallasso (καταλλάσσω) which means not only 'to exchange' but also 'to admit in the community' and 'to change from enemy into friend'. It seems, however, that it was the English logician, theological writer and Anglican Archbishop of Dublin, Richard Whately (1787–1863), who had originally coined the term 'catallactics', in Richard Whately (1831).
43. Michael Polanyi (1951).
44. See James M. Buchanan (1969a).
45. Geoffrey Brennan and James M. Buchanan (1980).
46. Henry J. Aaron and Michael J. Boskin (1980).
47. James M. Buchanan and Geoffrey Brennan (1980).
48. Richard A. Musgrave (1910–2007) was an eminent scholar in public finance. He systematized his field by dividing it into the three classical subdivisions of allocation, distribution and stabilization policy. He also invented the idea of 'merit wants' that should be provided for by the state.
49. This term, which has been used a lot by Frank Knight, Henry Simons, George Stigler and others at Chicago, is a pragmatic tool used by James M. Buchanan in order to clearly separate the stage of constitutional choice from the later stage of political choice within the constitutional framework. 'Faced with a set of collective alternatives or options at t_0, the individual recognizes that both preferences and constraints embodied in the historical record are fixed. These are not within the set of choice variables under the control of the decision makers acting within the decision rules. Existing preference functions and the institutions generated by past choices are "relatively absolute absolutes", subject to change, but only through time – change that might be influenced only marginally by choices made now.' In Geoffrey Brennan and James M. Buchanan (1985, p. 85).
50. John Rawls (1971). James M. Buchanan wrote a review of that book (James M. Buchanan, 1972). He later dealt with the issue again in James M. Buchanan (1976).
51. James M. Buchanan (1990).
52. Along the lines of James M. Buchanan and Yong Yoon (2002).

Robert M. Solow

*Massachusetts Institute
of Technology (MIT),
Cambridge, MA, USA*

The Sveriges Riksbank Prize in Economic Sciences in Memory of Alfred Nobel 1987 'for his contributions to the theory of economic growth'.

INTRODUCTION

It is raining cats and dogs. It's June, but nevertheless, the raindrops fall out of the dark clouds above Boston in this particularly distasteful horizontal manner. In spite of my umbrella, I'm soaking wet as soon as I get off the subway at Kendall. As I jog towards the corner of Wadsworth Street and Memorial Drive and head on to the grey building which hosts the Sloan School of Business, Robert M. Solow, who has already arrived, kindly holds the door open for me so as to avoid any further soaking. He's slim and trim as ever, very busy in spite of his 83 years, and looking forward to his three month long summer vacation which he is going to spend with his numerous family at Martha's Vineyard, as every year, in the house that he has bought with the money from the Nobel Prize. He lets me dry off a little and then invites me into his small cubicle right next door to Paul A. Samuelson's office. It was a 'geographical coincidence', as he likes to say, that originally placed him in this office that was once designed for an assistant professor, and he has never wanted to change that fate. It is hard to imagine, however, that there has been enough space in this tiny room for all the innovative ideas he has poured out ever since 1949, which was the year when he left Harvard and joined Paul A. Samuelson in the endeavor to create a new and successful department right next door. They have been office neighbors, sparring partners and pals for almost sixty years. It's an interesting, uneven pair – the quirky, dominant and self-confident Paul A. Samuelson on the one hand, and the sweet, patient and humble Robert M. Solow on the other hand. What unites them, of course, is their mathematical and rather eclectic Keynesian/neo-Keynesian approach. Solow first inquires for some news about Germany – he speaks the language and has always been interested in the economic policy there, worried especially by the ECB's relatively tight monetary policy which he considers as counterproductive. He then makes a quick phone call to his pharmacist, where he will pick some medication up later on. And now we're all set.[1]

Robert Merton Solow is a perfect example of how teaching and research are not contradicting each other but can go hand in hand in an ideal way. George Akerlof, Nobel Laureate of the year 2002, is not alone when he says 'He is a wonderful person, and a fantastic teacher (who gave really superb classes). I owe a great deal to him.'[2] Solow is naturally drawn towards young people, and he likes to explain things. There is something paternal about him, a well-tempered sense of humor and a humane kindness that allows for no arrogance whatsoever on his side. This may have to do with the fact that Solow seems to have found happiness early in life, both in his personal life and in his career – and that he knows how to enjoy life in all its facets and aspects. The only thing that can make him lose his temper is foolish economic policy. And foolish economic policy, to Solow, the liberal, egalitarian, interventionist Keynesian, most of the time means dogmatic monetarism and/or free-market economics. Just like Samuelson and most mainstream economists nowadays, Solow prefers to picture himself simply as a pragmatic economist, beyond all 'ideologies', choosing a Keynesian, that is demand-side oriented approach when adequate, and also a supply-side oriented approach when adequate. His firm belief is that no economic system is as efficient as capitalism, but since markets happen to malfunction, government has a role to play there. Without having illusions about the perfectibility of government, he still claims active control:

> There are times when there will be inflation and governments ought to try to control it. There are times when there will be prolonged unemployment and governments ought to try to fix that. I also think that there's every reason to

believe that, in order to fix problems like that, fiscal policy, as well as monetary policy, is both necessary and effective.[3]

Robert M. Solow was born in 1924 in Brooklyn, New York, as the son of a Jewish fur trader. His family originated in Russia. After high school, he was admitted to Harvard, where he started out studying sociology and anthropology. During the war, he served in the Army. Unlike most of his colleagues, he didn't spend his time doing research in some government or military institution, but was sent mainly to Sicily, North Africa and Italy for combat. When he was released, he continued his studies at Harvard, focusing now on economics, following the advice of his then newly wedded wife. At Harvard, he was strongly influenced by Wassily Leontief, whose research assistant he became, Leontief eventually becoming a Nobel laureate himself, in 1973. Solow graduated in 1947, became an assistant professor at MIT in 1949, spent a year at Columbia, and finally received his Ph.D. from Harvard in 1951, with a dissertation about the dynamics of the income distribution among families. This thesis brought him the David A. Wells Prize.[4] By then, however, he had moved away from Leontief's field of research, being attracted more by questions of development and growth. As he explains, there were two questions that truly intrigued him: how the Great Depression had come about and whether another depression was going to follow after the war.

Ever since the 1950s, Solow has remained faithful to MIT. For more than twenty years, he served as the department head. Even though he joined and supported Samuelson in the promotion of the formal approach to economics, he claims never having pursued the mathematics for the mathematics. 'I knew I wanted to do economics mathematically, and economic theory in particular, but not with enormous mathematical artillery. I pursued the study of mathematics itself only until I figured it was so that I wouldn't struggle with the economics', he says. Also, in spite of the technicality of his field, his prose has always remained highly readable. From 1961 to 1962, Solow served as a senior economist at the Council of Economic Advisers to President John F. Kennedy, a man whom he greatly admired, as the interview documents. From 1968 to 1970, he was a member of the President's Commission on Income Maintenance. From 1975 to 1981, Solow served as a member of the Board of the Federal Reserve Bank of Boston. He was awarded the John Bates Clark Medal in 1961 and the Seidman Award in Political Economy in 1983, and he has become a member of the Ordre pour le mérite in 1995.

Three of Solow's relatively early contributions have made a lasting impact on growth theory, triggering a host of subsequent research endeavors. The first important contribution was his 1956 paper named 'A contribution to the theory of economic growth',[5] in which he presents a neoclassical mathematical model that later on became a classic: the Solow growth model. In the meantime, it has been extended by the introduction of other production factors and even by the inclusion of stochastic features. The Solow growth model is an extension of the Harrod–Domar model, adding labor as a production factor. Its essential features are diminishing returns for capital and labor individually, constant returns for both – substitutable – production factors combined, and a time-varying technology variable. This model predicts that an increase in the savings rate does not affect steady-state growth rate, that countries with higher rates of labor force growth have lower steady-state levels of capital input per worker and output per worker, and, most importantly, in the steady state, both capital input per worker and output per worker grow at the rate of technological progress. At this point, he didn't yet try to explain what this technology variable really meant, what the nature of technology was or where its continued change came from. This was just the first door that Solow opened for the analysis of technological change as a motor for economic growth, something that somewhat later became famous as the 'Solow residual', as it was dubbed. Solow concentrated more squarely on technological change in his 1957 paper, 'Technical change and the aggregate production function',[6] where he found a way to decompose the sources of economic growth into technological change and the increase of physical inputs. In his 1960 paper, 'Investment and technological progress',[7] he also introduces a method which allows us to view technological progress as incorporated into subsequent generations of capital: the famous 'vintage capital' approach. Both these papers laid the groundwork for 'growth accounting'. With the 1962 paper on 'Substitution and fixed proportions in the theory of capital',[8] a further refinement followed: the famous type of growth model named 'putty clay'.[9]

Together with Paul A. Samuelson, in a 1960 paper,[10] Solow was also responsible for popularizing the idea of the Phillips curve in the United States, according to which there is a trade-off between unemployment and inflation – an idea that came under attack later on, mainly by Milton Friedman and Edmund Phelps.[11] Also, he was engaged in the 'Cambridge Controversy' in capital theory between Joan Robinson, Piero Sraffa and Nicholas Kaldor in Cambridge, England, on the one hand and Paul A. Samuelson and himself in Cambridge, Massachusetts, on the other hand. In his 1963 book *Capital Theory and the Rate of Return*,[12] Solow insists that the important thing for capital theory is the determination of the rate of return on capital, not the – extremely difficult – measurement of capital itself, which however had been the bone of contention. Solow also provided a new approach to the Keynesian idea of wage stickiness by explaining that cutting wages might not be in the employer's interest as productivity might shrink as a consequence and costs might rise.[13] This was an important contribution to the neo-Keynesian efficiency wage theory.

Among all the Nobel Laureates interviewed for this book, Robert M. Solow was the fastest to fully understand what it was that I was trying to get at. Having reflected a lot on himself and the main sources of his own inspiration before, he was able to give very clear answers right away. As it turned out, the Great Depression was crucial once again, both as a puzzling economic situation, an unsuccessfully answered policy challenge, a situation that economic theory didn't have a satisfying explanation for, and an unfortunate personal experience. This background first and fundamentally drew Solow's attention to economics as a social science. As he says in the following interview, there

> was the widespread fear that the end of the war would be followed by another Depression. . . I certainly was interested in that and wanted to understand it. That led me into Keynesian economics. The other question that was in the air was economic development, given that the British Empire was dissolved. I got interested in the theory of economic growth in that way.

This is, so to speak, the explanation for the long run. From then on, however, once he was on that track, in the short run, Solow went ahead in a way that was in some sense inherent in theory itself, almost dictated by it. He filled up one gap after the other. Borrowing Thomas S. Kuhn's famous term, Robert M. Solow calls himself a 'puzzle solver'.[14] For him, progress simply means: 'you solve more puzzles'. Of course, those puzzles change as time goes by. What is puzzling is something that remains unexplained either because the theoretical framework isn't encompassing enough for the given situation or because the situation has changed in an important way. In the course of Solow's long and fascinating academic career, he has experienced both. Thus it is probably fair to say that even beyond the initial moment when he discovered his interest in economics, he was propelled forward by forces along all the three major interacting lines of inspiration: the real economic challenges as they occurred, personal experience, and the evolution of economics as an academic field. While the latter may indeed have developed a strong dynamic of its own, as Solow indicates, it can by no means have been unrelated to the other sources of inspiration. Motivation and inspiration are usually fed from various different sources.

INTERVIEW

What drew you into economics in the first place, Professor Solow?
I arrived at Harvard College in September 1940. I had no idea what I was going to study. I was 16 years old and vaguely thought I might be interested in biology. I had grown up during the Great Depression, and I had heard that there were jobs available for biologists in the US forest service. I thought I might as well do something where there would be employment.

So it wasn't the beauty of biology as a science that attracted you?
No, not at all. I was never fascinated by biology. I took a lecture course in my freshman year and I was not terribly good. I had trouble in the laboratories. I'm terrible at drawing, and when we were instructed to draw what we saw under the microscope, I did very badly.

Well, and so biology had to turn out a dead end, I can see that. But why economics instead? Was your family affected by the Great Depression? Had that experience already set you on the economics track, in some way?
Yes, I think so. The Depression had made a deep impression on me, and that did have some importance for my interest in the business cycle and unemployment. My father was a furrier. We were never impoverished during the Depression, but as a boy, in the 1930s, I was totally conscious of the fact that all my mother and father talked about together was where the next dollar would come from. The Depression affected my family in a very drastic way in the sense that the only job that my father could find at one point in the fur trade involved his going to the Soviet Union, buying furs. They held major auctions of furs in Leningrad and elsewhere. So my father was absent for long periods, and once even for years at a time, because he got trapped in Russia. He was able to send letters through the diplomatic channel, so we heard from him all the time – but still, he was away two or three years.

What happened next? How did you make up your mind?
I drifted – and that's the right word – into a field that was then called at Harvard the 'area of the social sciences', which was meant to be interdisciplinary. Why did I do that? Because, having grown up during the Depression, and the war having started in 1939, it was pretty clear to me that society wasn't functioning very well. And that, I was really motivated to go into. I took courses in sociology, anthropology and economics. I found that moderately interesting, economics not more than the others. Then, two years later, when I was 18 years old, I left Harvard and volunteered for the Army. Whether it was because I thought it was so important

to defeat Hitler or because I was bored, I don't know. Both motives were there. By this time, of course, in 1942, the US was involved in the war, and Pearl Harbor had happened. So I was in the war for three years.[15] In July 1945 I came back, and got married one week after I arrived – to the original girl[16] – and then, in August, the Military publicized a system of points for who would get discharged from the Army in what order. We were married two days earlier and were planning to go to Cape Cod for a week of honeymoon. We had the radio on in our hotel room, and I sat listening to the point system and adding up the point value of my months of service, of combat, and my one decoration. Then I turned to my wife and said: 'I'm out! I've got enough points, I'm going to be discharged!' Since we were in Boston on our way to the Cape, I thought that while we were here, I'd better let the Harvard people know immediately that I was going to go back to school in September. But what was I going to tell them I was going to study? And so I asked my wife of two days: 'You studied economics. Was it interesting?' And she said: 'Yes, it was'. And so I said: 'Okay, we'll try that'. I marched over to the economics department and told them that one month later, I would be back as a student.

You make it sound as if the decision for economics came totally out of the blue. Was that really so?
Well, I certainly was not going to study physics, and I knew I was not going to study biology, but I could have become a sociologist or an anthropologist. However, I found sociology a little soft. I think that somewhere in my mind, I probably already had the notion – which turned out to be right – that if I was going to be a social scientist of some kind, I would like a rigorous social science. The analytical aspect of economics already appealed to me. That must have been so. It was not really a matter of chance. But if my wife had said 'oh, no, economics was terribly boring', I would probably have found something else to do.

Did you still think about job opportunities?
No, I was no longer thinking about that at all. I was just thinking that I had another year and a half to go at college, and I needed to find a focus. I had to choose, and I had to choose then. And so I chose economics.

How was it then, when you started? Were you happy with your chosen field?
At Harvard College in those days, every student had a tutor, whom you met once a week. He would suggest something to read, and you read it, and the next week he came back, and you discussed it with him for 30 minutes. My tutor was Wassily Leontief.[17] That was not my choice, he was allocated to me. I had actually had one lecture course from Leontief

before I joined the Army, which was called 'Structure of the American economy'.[18] Leontief gave me things to read, and he knew exactly what he was doing, I imagine. One of the things I read was Johann von Thünens's *Isolirter Staat*.[19] I found that was very interesting. I could read it in German, and so I did. Wassily would say to me: 'Why don't you read such-and-such. Oh, no, no, you can't read that, because you don't know any calculus', and sold me something else. And the second time, he would say something similar.

Incentives through frustration, was that his strategy?
Well, yes, I figured that if there was good stuff and weak stuff, I wanted to read the good stuff. So I started studying mathematics. I had been excellent in math in high school, maybe my best subject, but I had no particular interest in studying mathematics. I never had any interest in being a mathematician. It's too abstract for me – although I could conceivably have made a life as an applied mathematician. Anyway, when I was up to it, I started reading the good stuff, and I liked it a lot.

What was the good stuff?
John Hicks, for example, and his *Value and Capital*.[20] And then I read papers on the business cycle, by people like Jan Tinbergen.[21] And of course, I also read some of Leontief's work on input output analysis. I took to this, and liked it. I ended up wanting to do economics mathematically, although it is certainly not true of me as a kid or as a young person that I was fascinated by the math and simply wanted to find an application for it. There is a saying according to which, to a child with a hammer, the whole world looks like a nail. I think some people are like that, but that was not the case with me. I was doing economics before I took a year or two of mathematics to pick enough to do more than just read. I knew I wanted to do economics mathematically, and economic theory in particular, but not with enormous mathematical artillery. I pursued the study of mathematics itself only until I figured it was so that I wouldn't struggle with the economics. I just wanted one thing more than what I needed. And that was where I stopped.

Can you remember some guiding questions that were in the air and that attracted you?
Oh yes, I can. There were two of them. The first was – and that moved me away from Leontief, who would have liked me to do extensions of his own work – the widespread fear that the end of the war would be followed by another Depression. That fear was natural, because after all, the war had been preceded by one. In 1940, the unemployment rate in the US was 14

percent. I certainly was interested in that and wanted to understand it. That led me into Keynesian economics. The other question that was in the air was economic development, given that the British Empire was dissolved. I had never been interested in the study of developing economies, but I got interested in the theory of economic growth in that way. It was an extension in this worldwide interest in the question how economies grow in the long run. So that was my story.

When did it occur to you that you might actually have an academic career?
Fairly early on. In fact, I can advertise myself as an early feminist in this respect. Two years after the war, I finished my undergraduate degree at Harvard, and I had to decide what to do next. I wasn't yet settled on becoming an academic. I talked about this with my wife, and she said: 'I think you want to stay on at graduate school and do a Ph.D.'. And I agreed: 'I will if you will'. So we both enrolled as Ph.D. students. Shortly after, when I realized that I was good at this, that I got excellent grades, that I understood things quickly, and that I had thoughts about things that I might work out myself – by then, I had probably essentially decided that I would do an academic career. And then, at the end of that Ph.D. era, I had two job offers and didn't look for anything else. One was an assistant professorship at MIT, and one was that I could be a teaching assistant at Harvard – which was almost insulting. By then, I had certainly settled implicitly on being an academic.

Did you ever ask yourself where you wanted to be in 10 years' time?
Oh no. I am not a planner. My wife is. Most people are systematic planners, few are like me. I never ask myself that question. Not even then. And even when asked to plan, I resist it. I always focus on the things that I have to do now.

Coming back to your Ph.D. thesis, how did you choose your topic?
When I came to write my thesis in 1948, I chose a topic which, in a way, was methodologically determined. In the course of learning economics and doing a graduate degree in economics, I had got interested in probability and statistics – mostly because I have never been very much interested in pure theory. I always wanted to do theoretical work with an application clearly in mind. So I needed to know statistics. However, the teaching of statistics at the Harvard economics department in the late 1940s was a joke. It was awful. Little as I knew, I knew garbage when I saw it. And I saw it there. Fortunately for me, the statistician Charles Frederick ('Fred') Mosteller had been appointed in the sociology department. He taught a one semester mathematical statistics course that I took, and I liked it. So I

asked him if he would arrange a reading course with me. Fred did that. So I really got interested in probability and statistics, even for its own sake. It's fascinating. In a way, probability is maybe the single most successful mathematical model of anything that human beings have discovered. I thought that I could write a Ph.D. thesis producing a model of the size distribution of income. This enabled me to make use of probabilistic and statistical methods. In order to do that, actually, I spent a year with a fellowship in New York at Columbia, where there was an excellent statistics department, with Abraham Wald,[22] and Jack Wolfowitz, the father of Paul Wolfowitz. And even before I finished my Ph.D. thesis, I was offered this job at MIT. And of course, I took it, and I began teaching when I came back from Columbia.

How was that new life at MIT? What kind of new impulses did you get there?
I began teaching in 1950, and most of my teaching was in statistics. I was an assistant professor in statistics. But I also taught a share of the macroeconomics course – and I taught that for the next 49 years. I quickly became acquainted with Evsey Domar's 1946 paper,[23] and I looked at Roy Harrod's earlier paper[24] and his book,[25] and I started thinking about questions of economic growth. A little later, Paul Samuelson and Robert Dorfman and I agreed with the RAND Corporation to write a book on linear programming in economics. We did that, and it was published in 1958,[26] even though all the work had been done by 1956. It just took a long time to write up. In connection with that, I got some more different angles on growth. You could do a dynamic Leontief kind of thing, and that's what I did. So this is the way I got interested in thinking about long-term growth.

I would like to understand what exactly drove you towards that level of mathematization, apart from your very obvious talent. Why not a more verbal field, a philosophical approach?
I like precision. I like to know exactly what is. When I think I have demonstrated something, or when I have come to a conclusion, I like to know exactly what conclusion I have come to and why I should believe this, if it is something about the real world. I think I was attracted into economics in part exactly because of the possibility of being a social scientist, but having some precision, some rigor, some exactness. And also, as Paul Samuelson likes to say, 50 years ago, there were still a lot of fairly easy things that nobody had thought of before. The use of economics was not yet as wholly converted to mathematical modeling. In fact, not at all. I remember getting involved in a controversy in the *Review of Economics and Statistics*, rather early. This person wrote a methodological, anti-mathematical

piece, and a number of people and I wrote replies.[27] I was already arguing that the right way to do economics was model-building, and that meant mathematically – not for the sake of the math, but because that's the way you can pose a precise question and try to find a precise answer. I never had any doubts about that, from those early days. The other thing was, as Paul Samuelson likes to say, that there were a lot of low-hanging fruit to be picked, and that is true. There were a lot of things that were not well understood. And so you could make an economic model of this, so that all would become clear. Sometimes it turned out to be nonsense. So there were intellectual victories to be had. Now, of course, it's much harder because we have had 50 years of bright young people doing economics in the meantime. Probably anything that is fairly easy and straightforward has already been done. So I was luckier than somebody who is getting a Ph.D. in economics today.

Has there really been so much progress that there are really fewer questions out there now?
It's not that there are fewer questions, but there are now more difficult, more refined questions. Those are questions that turn on little things rather than big things. Let me give you an example that in a way defined my own career as an economist. The question was what would become of the Harrod–Domar growth model if you allow explicitly for the substitution between capital and labor. That's not a little teeny-tiny question, that's a big question. In 1955, or whenever I was working on that, no one had thought to ask it, and no one had thought to answer it.

Those shortcomings in the model that struck you, did they occur to you alone, or was it broadly being discussed in academia?
It was certainly not being discussed. There may have been other people who were thinking about it, but it had not been written about. Trevor Swan, for example, an Australian, also published a paper on roughly the same subject.[28] He was a superb economist. A brilliant guy. Terrific. His paper contains the germs of the same model. But Trevor was not asking the same question I was asking. He thought he was writing a paper whose audience was Joan Robinson, and people in Cambridge, England. I was writing a paper whose audience were readers of Harrod and Domar. Immediately after those papers appeared, there was a burst of literature. There were hundreds of papers written. I once looked up how many articles on growth theory appeared in the years 1958/59/60. There were hundreds. It clearly struck a topic that was of a lot of interest in the economics profession. But you know, if I hadn't done that, somebody else would have done it. It's not so difficult, you just needed to ask yourself the right question.

Sometimes, time is just ripe for some specific new idea, and so it springs up from various sides, with different people tackling it, sometimes even without any interaction.
Absolutely. If you look at academic economists – but it is true of other fields as well – mostly what stimulates the writing of a paper is some other paper. In fact, I think that's what I didn't like ever about mathematics for its own sake. Pure mathematicians are never thinking about anything else than what somebody else has written. The great triumph in mathematics is a way of taking two papers that exist in the literature that seem unrelated, and showing that they are in fact related. That's a nice intellectual game, but it never struck me.

But how would you define progress in economic theory, really?
Amongst economists, there are two ideal types. One kind you could call system-builders, such as Gérard Debreu,[29] and then there are puzzle solvers.[30] I am a puzzle solver. I don't know how system builders define progress, but for me, it is simple: you solve more puzzles. You find something strange and not quite easy to understand, and then you try to get closer to understanding it. The accumulation of the solutions that you find is progress. Sometimes the right answer to a puzzle changes, because circumstances change, or institutions change, or attitudes change. Very likely, we will never run out of puzzles to solve. As you can see, I have a very non-grandiose picture of progress in economics. It means more and more little things that you are able to understand. And understand doesn't necessarily mean predict. Understanding is just kind of a confident belief that you could give a correct answer to the question what would happen if you changed some variable or other. What your understanding may lead to may be this unpredictability. Some economists perceive their profession as pursuing a theory of everything. I am not.

Is progress in economic theory a random walk?
Yes, I think there is an element of that. But it's not a pure random walk, there tends to be a direction. The direction comes both internally and externally. It comes, thank God, partly from problems in the real world: here is a puzzle, here is something in the actual economy that nobody seems to understand. But there is also the fact that someone writes a really interesting paper and has an interesting idea, and then people are attracted to extend that. So it goes both ways. A bright idea can occur to almost anyone anywhere on almost any subject, and that will have an effect on the literature. At the same time, the literature is also responding to what it sees out there as a real problem. It is clear, for example, that the coming of the computer age and the shift of economic activity from goods to services

(except in Germany which continues to want to manufacture wherever it can) has set off a whole bunch of questions that it is very hard to get a grip on, and when someone writes an interesting paper in that context, other people will refine it. But it's all moving in a direction that is determined by something out there. The Great Depression was a prime example of this. It gave rise to Keynesian economics, and that of course then gave rise to non-Keynesian economics. It's not an accident that there was an enormous burst of interest in the business cycle during the Great Depression. How could you not? The discovery of the Third World after the Second World War, the break-up of the British Empire and the French colonies in Africa were also events that got the whole economic development literature going and affected the growth literature. It goes both ways, and has to. I don't think there is any alternative. None of the two is dominant. They are both essential. From time to time, there will be situations in which it is clear that the external impulse is the dominant one, and sometimes, it will be clear that it is the internal one. That's just the way the world works.

As you were always interested in real world problems, you obviously tended more to that side of the causality, I guess.
A little more. And again, the experience of the Great Depression had a role in that. It really was a major event for my generation. Considering Germany, you could argue that, had it not been for the Great Depression, Hitler would never have risen to power. Events like that clearly shape the direction in which economics moves. If you look at successive quarterly issues of a learned journal, most papers are inspired by other papers. Although some of it is methodological in a rather good sense. A lot of what appears in American journals now comes from the fact that economists now have access to very large datasets and they have the computational power to deal with them. That opens up lots of questions, but they are real questions, questions about life that you couldn't ask before because you didn't have the data – or if you had the data, you couldn't do the calculations.

Let's go back to past, that is, to the Harrod–Domar model and to your extensions. What was the next question that came up and why?
The thing about the Harrod–Domar model that made me want to think further about it was that the typical conclusion from that version of growth theory was that growth in a capitalist economy is very unstable. And certainly, anyone whose beliefs about growth in the industrial capitalist economy were formed by reading Harrod and Domar would expect history to consist of a series of catastrophes, periods in which there was hopeless excess demand and inflation, followed by periods in which there was hopeless deficient demand and depression. But in spite of the 1930s,

that was not the true history of capitalism. And by the 1950s, we had already had a decade with minor business cycles, but that was all, and the trend was upward. And so, I definitely was saying to myself that there has to be something wrong with these theories. They don't correspond to what you see. My mental process was not to say 'these models do not allow for input substitution, but we know that input substitution is possible, so we should improve them'. My train of thought was rather that these models say that a capitalist economy is inherently unstable, but it is not. So there has to be something either in these models that shouldn't be there or not in there that should be there, and what would that be? And I thought a bit. If you ask yourself that question and your mind is full of Harrod–Domar, pretty soon you observe that one thing that is lacking here is the fact that, both on the production and the consumption side, the economy can adapt to changes in savings rates. In the Domar sense, it can't. That should not be a difficult conclusion to come to. The question was just how to work this out, how to produce the logic of this to make it transparent, so that you could actually see what was going on. That gave me the first paper.[31] Then, the natural question for me was how this stacks up to the history of the American economy. I began looking at long runs of data. It looked a little bit peculiar, and so I developed further a way of separating out the sources of growth, that is, growth of labor, accumulation of capital, and the rest, the 'residual'. That led me, one year later, to that 1957 paper.[32] It was a semi-failure, even though it ran along the same lines. The conclusion of two papers I had written was that the long-run growth of the economy is determined entirely by the residual. That was a disappointment. What I would have liked to have found was an easy way of making the economy grow faster, something that policy could do something about. Technological progress, however, is kind of mechanical, and what do you do? It doesn't lead anywhere. Of course, you can finance research and development – but that's all very indirect and uncertain. So I was looking for something that was left out, something that would provide that kind of lever that could influence the growth rate more directly. It occurred to me that something had indeed been left out, and that was the fact that most technical progress needs investment to become real. Certainly, Harrod and Domar had gone under the obvious presumption that if you could invest more, you would grow faster. The startling thing that came out of the model, however, was that if you invested more, the economy would grow faster for a while, but then the growth rate would revert back to what was determined by technological progress. But given that technological progress, in order to have any effect on the economy at all, almost always needs capital investment, maybe that link, made explicit, would lead to a result that you could tell Congress. And so I tried to model that. I called it 'embodiment', by a very bad word, which has stuck, for better or worse. I worked out a model like that and found that I could find a way, requiring some assumptions that I didn't like a lot. It was a model that one could actually make work and apply.[33] But it didn't have the result I was looking for. It was still true that this embodiment affected the short-run consequences of having more or less investment, but it did not affect long-run consequences. On playing around, I ended up understanding why that was so. But the model didn't do what I wanted it to do, and the idea fell flat. Nobody followed it up. It seemed to be very hard to find an empirical counterpart of that phenomenon. It went away, until some eight years ago, some other people revived the idea and did begin to find some empirical counterparts. But it's a good example of a piece of theory aiming at producing an insight into the world. Anyway, I continued to work on growth.

Your liking for real-world problems ultimately drew you to Washington, right? What was your motivation for going out to work for the Council of Economic Advisers during a year?

It's quite amusing how that came about. In 1960, after John F. Kennedy had been elected President, but in the interval before the administration changed, the phone rang in our house in Concord, Massachusetts, fairly late at night, close to midnight. I was already asleep and had to get up to answer the phone. On the other end were Walter Heller,[34] Kermit Gordon[35] and James Tobin.[36] My first words to them were: 'What are you doing up at this hour?' They wanted me to come and join the staff of the Council. And I said 'I'll think about it'. But I really had no interest in doing it. It was too remote from my teaching. They emphasized, actually, that I could be the ivory tower economist in the Council, so that I could work on theory, and that they would do the everyday work. But I was not interested in doing that. So I went back to bed and told my wife what the call was about, and I told her that I didn't want to do it. But she said: 'You know, during the whole of the Eisenhower administration, I have heard you complain about how lousy the economic policy is. Why don't you put your money where your mouth is?' I had no answer. So I checked with my department chairman and I asked for a leave of absence. I was there for about two days, and I discovered that this ivory tower economist idea was for the birds. Nevertheless, I had a wonderful year. I never worked harder in my life. It was painful in some ways because Walter Heller, the chairman, was a night-owl. He would hang around the White House all day, and whenever an economic question came up he'd ask Kennedy whether he'd like a memorandum on that. And then he'd come back at 5p.m. and we'd have a night's work to do, and I'd call home and tell them. I remember one day I called home and my six-year-old son picked the phone up. I could hear him saying 'Mom, it's Dad, he's going to tell you that he's not coming home again'. And that was what I was calling to tell them. But I enjoyed my work a lot.

Were there new ideas for your own research springing up from that?
Yes. This work got me interested in short-run economics, particularly in unemployment. It was a matter of chance, in a way. When we arrived there in January 1961, we had to produce some sort of miniature economic report. We needed to have this document testified before Congress in five weeks' time. Within our internal division of labor, I was told to do the piece on unemployment. The unemployment in early 1961 was around 6 percent. I had never done any labor economics. There was also circulating at the time, very much like today, the idea that a rise in unemployment was inevitable, and that it was the consequence of automation. We didn't think that was true, but I had to dig into the question anyway. I spent those weeks working like a dog to produce a serious position on the rise in unemployment and what might be done about it. That gave me another interest that I have had ever since – that is, the macroeconomic side of the labor market, of employment and unemployment. I was at the Council only for one year, but the next year, I was commuting to Washington to help out. I then went on working on both sides of that street, the short-run and the long-run side of macroeconomics.

How was the interaction with Kennedy?
Kennedy was a dream president for economists, because he cared. Walter Heller, because he was a good soul, made it a practice to put a little note on every memo he sent to the President saying that the underlying work had been done by Arthur Okun or Bob Solow or someone else. Usually, it was one of us two. And Kennedy would call you up! He would say 'I'm reading this memo that I understand you have something to do with, and I've got to the middle of page 2, and it says this. I don't understand why this should be, so could you please explain it to me?' Oh my God, you die for a president who would do that! And I met him a couple of times, even though I was not a member of the Council; I was just a staff person. Later, I could have been a member or even chairman of the Council, but I never wanted that. Anyway, when there were meetings at the White House about economics, and if I was the guy who had done the work, then I would be invited along. I also met Kennedy on other occasions. I never was a strong Kennedy supporter when he was running, by the way. I had voted for him, yes, because I certainly wasn't going to vote for Nixon! I liked him. He had a good sense of humor about himself, which is always important. And he wanted to understand things. That was very gratifying. After Kennedy

was shot and Lyndon Johnson became president, the word came to the Council that he never read more than half a page, so you better kept your memos short. Johnson wasn't interested. He wanted to act. But he had a reasonably good mind, not a reflective mind, but also not like the ignoramus George Bush. Johnson was a real tragedy, a genuine Greek tragedy. I think he would have been a great president had it not been for the Vietnam War. He was effective, his heart was in the right place, and he would have done the right things, but he was destroyed by not being willing or able to extricate himself from the Vietnam War. It was a tragedy for the world.

What happened after your Washington episode?
In 1963, I don't know how that happened, but I was allowed to take a sabbatical leave. I spent that year in Cambridge, England, fighting with Joan Robinson.

Was that the time of that famous Cambridge controversy?[37]
Yes, exactly. I had already been involved in that controversy earlier. I had written a learned journal paper responding to something that Joan had written.[38] For me, it was a natural to get involved in, because my contribution to growth theory involved the substitution of labor and capital in the production function, and Joan had attacked that very idea. So I felt obliged to respond. I wrote this paper, and there had been some backing and forthing.[39] Then, in 1963, I planned to spend my sabbatical year in Oxford. Why Oxford, I can't remember, but probably because I had read novels about what a dream of a beautiful place it is. And so I thought, why don't we move the family to Oxford? The annual convention of the American Economic Association was held in Washington that year. On that occasion, I had a cup of coffee with Nicholas Kaldor, whom I had never met before. But we knew each other's name from all that squabble with Joan. In the course of the conversation, I mentioned to Nickie that I was going to spend the following year in Oxford. And he inferred that I was afraid to come to Cambridge. And so I said 'I'll come to Cambridge'. Obviously, males don't react well to that kind of thing. So I spent the year in Cambridge, much of it engaged in that fruitless squabble with Joan. It occupied a lot of my time. I did a certain amount of work that I would not have done was it not for Joan Robinson. But I came to the conclusion that the whole controversy was mostly smoke. It was more about ideology than about technical economics, and so I tried to disengage myself from that as much as I could. I think there wasn't anything very useful in it. The one intellectual problem that was unsolved – and still is unsolved because it is just too hard – I knew I wasn't able to do much with. So I just came back here to MIT and did my normal work.

What was that one question?

If you think of growth as an uninterrupted, smooth process, and if the economy is in some kind of a natural equilibrium all the time, then you can give a fairly complete analysis of that. But when a surprise happens, a shock of some kind, a war, maybe a big invention, any kind of a disturbance, then the existing real capital – machinery, and buildings, computers, telephones, and all that – has to be revalued in smooth equilibrium conditions. This is what capital theory is about. You can talk in pretty precise terms about what the value of a capital good is. The reason why, when a disturbance occurs, you cannot do that any more, is because the value of the capital good depends on the present discounted value of its future earnings. The essence of the surprise is that you thought you knew what your earnings would be but it turns out that you don't. And then the question is to understand in exact detail what happens then and how the economy does or does not get back to a different equilibrium state. You have to be able to get a grip on how capital goods are valued under such circumstances of real uncertainty, that is, uncertainty that cannot be described by probabilities. That's very difficult. I have never had a very good idea. Nobody else has ever had one either. That's a very important question, it's not esoteric. Maybe a dozen times in what I've written I have commented, just to keep people's minds on it, that we have a theory of growth, and we have several short-run macro theories, but for any one of them, the problem is how you connect the two. That's unsolved. The deep reason why it is unsolved is that you don't know how to treat investment in those circumstances. It's not that there is some piece of mathematics that I don't know, or that other people don't know, or that we don't know where to look for it. The problem is conceptual. It's a problem about economic life that doesn't have any obvious answer. If God were thinking about this question, he might perhaps say that there isn't any answer to that: 'There is confusion, and everybody is confused in their own way. Why would you expect there to be an evaluation of capital that you could use in a model, poor human fool?' That may indeed be the right answer.

What did experience teach you in that respect?

Experiences differ. There is no uniform pattern. We do know that unless there are political disturbances and unless society collapses in some way, capitalist economies do eventually get back to the kind of equilibrium that it is fair to describe by a growth model. But the exact way of doing that. . . well, it's a real problem. It's like the medical profession facing a disease it just doesn't understand.

Would you agree that you can only push dynamics so far? The real upheavals are hard to explain.

Yes. And it may also be that one upheaval is different from another. It matters what the source of the disturbance is, it matters what the exact circumstances are in which it happens, etc. But I think that for macroeconomics, the key problem now is what I call the macroeconomics of the middle run. James Tobin described himself as a Keynesian in the short run and a neoclassical economist in the long run. I would describe me exactly the same. Jim and I tended to think alike. Robert Lucas once said that this was a logical impossibility, for the short run is always now and the long run is always now, too, and so there is no time in the middle run. Well, I have what I thought was a very good analogy answer to that, apart from saying that this is how I feel and that's the way I think I think. Here comes the analogy. When I was younger, I was a small boat sailor. I know perfectly well that the world is a sphere. If I were sailing for days on end, I should think of myself as sailing on a sphere. On the other hand, when I go out on Martha's Vineyard Sound, I navigate my boat as if the water is as flat as is this desk. Somehow you have to connect these two things and you do. You sail as if you're on flat water, and then, every once in a while, you make a little correction. I think we have to do the same in economics. That is a problem that macro people still can't tackle. We don't have a good way of dealing with this.

And yet, let me ask – are you happy with the way growth theory is being done nowadays?

I think there is a line of progress. What matters is whether errors get corrected. This is a big question in all sciences. The big change in my field was this so-called endogenous growth theory. It was an attempt to include technological change, as an extension to human capital as distinct of physical capital. I think that's an absolutely right thing to do, but it doesn't offer any real intellectual problem. There is nothing really problematic about that. But understanding technological progress is a very difficult thing. When that movement first got started with the two papers of Paul Romer[40] and Robert Lucas,[41] the first thing the economics profession did was to run with the ball in the wrong direction. These were the days of the so-called AK growth models.[42] In those models, you have to suppose that there are exactly constant returns to capital. It attracted a lot of attention, and many people followed suit, because it gave you very powerful results very quickly. It was a terrific temptation. Some people who were using these types of models would make the claim that if you reduce the tax on capital, you can increase the steady state growth rate of the economy. That's a pretty powerful thing to say. If you told me that by paying some cost, I could increase the steady state growth rate of the American economy by 0.2 percent per year, I would be willing to pay an enormous cost to do that, because over a long period of time, that's gigantic! Those results, however, depended on the absence of diminishing or increasing returns. From the very beginning, I thought that was very foolish, and I said so. Eventually, after a few years, it disappeared, and hardly anybody does that any more. Then what really interested Paul Romer was trying to understand the evolution of technology.[43] Again, I think the literature on that was over-simplistic. It made very powerful assumptions in order to get where it wanted to go, and provided no justifications for those assumptions at all. It seems to me that if you make a very powerful assumption, you at least owe the community a discussion why it is not a foolish assumption to make. But there was none of that. Eventually, the economists who were working in this area, including Romer, got around to say – to themselves – that the model of technological change that they were using wouldn't quite do, and that they had to think more carefully about the direction and the rate of technological change. There is a lot more work going on along those lines nowadays. My MIT colleague Daron Acemoglu and other people are working on this, and they are making slow progress. It's got to be slow, because it's a harder problem than the others. We don't have an understanding of science as a production process, and we don't have data.

Last question: what do you think about other new economic approaches such as experimental and behavioral economics, for example?
I like experimental and behavioral economics. I think it is a wonderful corrective to the easy belief that greed, rationality and equilibrium explain everything. But what it lacks is any kind of theory. It has reduced the puzzle-solving aspect, and so it is going a little too far. What it now needs is a little more generality. It is not enough to observe that people do certain things in economic decision-making that clearly violate the assumptions of greed and rationality. What we need now is something relating these observations.

Thank you, Professor.

NOTES

1. The interview was held on 4 June, 2007.
2. See the interview with George A. Akerlof in this volume.
3. This quote is taken from an interview with *The Region*, recorded in September 2002, currently available at http://minneapolisfed.org/pubs/region/02-09/solow.cfm.
4. In a funny anecdote, Solow admits in his Nobel autobiography that he actually never

benefited from the Wells Prize: '(it) offered publication in book form and $500 (in 1951 prices!) upon completion. When I reread the thesis, however, I thought that I could do it better. But I never returned to that work and the thesis remains unpublished (and the check uncashed).' (See www.nobel.se.)

5. Robert M. Solow (1956).
6. Robert M. Solow (1957).
7. Robert M. Solow (1960).
8. Robert M. Solow (1962).
9. The term 'putty clay technology' refers to the rates of substitution, implying meta-phorically that putty can be moulded at will before baking, but once baked, it becomes hardened clay and it is impossible to further influence its shape.
10. Paul A. Samuelson and Robert M. Solow (1960).
11. See the interview with Edmund S. Phelps in this book.
12. Robert M. Solow (1963).
13. Robert M. Solow (1979).
14. See Thomas S. Kuhn (1962/1970 pp. 35–42).
15. Robert M. Solow joined the Army Signal Corps and served in Africa, Sicily and Italy.
16. Barbara Lewis.
17. Wassily Leontief was awarded the Nobel Prize in 1973 'for the development of the input–output method and for its application to important economic problems'.
18. Wassily Leontief (1941).
19. In this book, Thünen (1783–1850) develops a pattern of land use, combining spatial economics and the theory of rent (Johann Heinrich von Thünen, 1826).
20. John R. Hicks (1939). John Hicks was awarded the Nobel Prize in 1972, together with Kenneth Arrow, 'for their pioneering contributions to general economic equilibrium theory and welfare theory'.
21. Jan Tinbergen was awarded the Nobel Prize in 1969, together with Ragnar Frisch, the two of them 'for having developed and applied dynamic models for the analysis of eco-nomic processes'.
22. See the interview with Kenneth J. Arrow in this book.
23. Evsey Domar (1946).
24. Roy Harrod (1939).
25. Roy Harrod (1948).
26. Robert Dorfman et al. (1958).
27. This was a debate launched by RAND Corporation economist David Novick, com-plaining that 'the present trend to mathematics as a language had cut off a large part of the fraternity from an ability either to read or understand much of the new thinking' (David Novick, (1954). A number of prominent mathematical economists stood up to rebut the criticism in the same journal: Laurence Klein, James Duesenberry, John Chipman, Jan Tinbergen, Robert M. Solow, Robert Dorfman, Tjalling Koopmans and Paul A. Samuelson. Solow just states that mathematics 'is simply an immensely pow-erful and efficient device or vocabulary for thinking about certain kinds of problems' (Robert M. Solow, (1954, p. 373).
28. Trevor Swan (1956).
29. Gérard Debreu was awarded the Nobel Prize in 1983, 'for having incorporated new analytical methods into economic theory and for his rigorous reformulation of the theory of general equilibrium'.
30. This differentiation is apparently analogous, but fundamentally different, from Friedrich August von Hayek's distinction between the 'master of his subject', that is, someone who has excellent memory and therefore all-encompassing knowledge of a field, and the 'puzzler', that is, someone who, lacking this type of perfect memory, has to think through everything on his own – which however may make him more creative, allowing him to discover unconventional avenues that others may not see. See Friedrich August von Hayek (1978).
31. Robert M. Solow (1956).

32. Robert M. Solow (1957).
33. See Robert M. Solow (1960).
34. Walter Heller (1915–87) was the chairman of the Council of Economic Advisers (1961–64).
35. Kermit Gordon (1916–76) was Director of the United States Bureau of the Budget (1962–65) and President of the Brookings Institution.
36. James Tobin (1918–2002) was awarded the Nobel Prize in 1981 'for his analysis of financial markets and their relations to expenditure decisions, employment, production and prices'.
37. The Cambridge controversy took place mainly between economists Joan Robinson, Nicholas Kaldor and Piero Sraffa at the University of Cambridge in the UK and Paul A. Samuelson and Robert M. Solow at MIT in Cambridge, Massachusetts, in the US. It was all about the measurement or evaluation of capital.
38. Robert M. Solow (1958).
39. Eventually, Robert M. Solow came up with his definite argument, according to which it is more important to understand how the rate of return on capital is determined than to measure capital itself. See Robert M. Solow (1963).
40. Paul M. Romer (1986).
41. Robert Lucas Jr. (1988).
42. Those so-called 'AK models' assume that output is the product of capital, K, and a constant positive level of technology, A.
43. Paul M. Romer (1990).

Gary S. Becker

University of Chicago, IL, USA

The Sveriges Riksbank Prize in Economic Sciences in Memory of Alfred Nobel 1992 'for having extended the domain of microeconomic analysis to a wide range of human behavior and interaction, including nonmarket behavior'.

INTRODUCTION

Finally, Gary S. Becker turns around the corner, walking leisurely, hands in his pockets. He sits down with me in the lobby of the New Otani Hotel in Tokyo, Japan, where we both attend the 60th Anniversary General Meeting of the Mont Pèlerin Society – the famous platform for debate between classical liberal thinkers from diverse backgrounds and fields of research that Friedrich August von Hayek initiated in 1947. Becker, who had served as president of the Mont Pèlerin Society 1990–92, was the head of the program committee this time, much to the benefit of the meeting. The conference program shows that he has brought many of his friends and co-authors – amongst them Edward Lazear, now head of the Council of Economic Advisers to the American President. Gary Becker tries out the sofa first and then switches over to the not so soft chair where he finds a more comfortable position. His back aches a bit; he blames it on an overdose of exercise in the hotel gym. Sports are still very high on his priority list, just like in his younger years. However, and as usual, Becker looks a bit frail with his extremely slender body, his almost translucent skin and his crown of white hair – but his energy is impressive, just as much as his efficiency.[1]

Gary Becker likes quick, precise questions, and he gives quick, precise answers in a very polite way, without however giving away too much. Becker doesn't waste his time. He doesn't over-invest – obviously, he is too much aware of the opportunity costs. And thus he is not the type of person for a long warm-up. Anyway, we don't really need one, since we have met before, repeatedly. We met for the first time in 2000, at a meeting of the Mont Pèlerin Society in Santiago, Chile; I interviewed him a couple of times for my former newspaper, *Frankfurter Allgemeine Zeitung*, once in 2002 and once in 2003; there was some email backing and forthing to commemorate Milton Friedman who passed away in 2006; and Becker also was one of the first Nobel Laureates who agreed to participate in my book. However, even though his overall readiness was clearly there and very generous from the very beginning, time was not. Gary Becker turned out to be extremely difficult to get hold of. His agenda is full, he still travels a lot, and he doesn't always check his email, and so one trip to Chicago to meet him there turned out fruitless. We thus performed a true, albeit exquisitely friendly fox and hare run for almost two years until we now finally managed to get together. By the sound of light piano music in the background, we set out to conjure up the past as well as we can.

Although he was born in Pottsville, Pennsylvania in 1930, Gary Stanley Becker can be described as a quintessential Brooklynite – a Jewish intellectual, very cultivated, witty, rather European in style. His family moved to Brooklyn when he was four years old. His father was a pretty successful businessman who had come from Canada when he was only 16 years old; his mother had come from an Eastern European family. Neither had much schooling. They were parents to two daughters and two sons. After completing high school, Gary Becker undertook undergraduate studies at Princeton University. His intellectual appetite not being satisfied with the usual undergraduate courses, he took a number of graduate courses as well, and ran across Jacob Viner, who had been at Chicago before coming to Princeton. Jointly with Frank Knight, Viner had presided over the Department of Economics at Chicago from the 1920s to the late 1940s. Viner was a controversial figure – a very knowledgeable and widely read economist, but not extremely original, if we are to trust Friedrich August von Hayek[2] – and he was a very tough, demanding teacher. As James Buchanan remembers, Viner tended to 'crush' his students. Becker, whom Viner complimented as having been his best student ever, didn't mind – just like Evsey Domar, who says 'Viner was superb because he was extremely nasty. He would write a statement on the board, challenge us to comment on it, and then make fools of those who tried.'[3] In an interesting parallel, Becker became a tough academic teacher himself. Terry Anderson from PERC,[4] for example, still glows with admiration when remembering his visit to the University of Chicago many years later, when Becker was already rather famous and he himself a well-respected economist. He had an initial conversation with Becker – who 'just minced' him with his sharp remarks.

Gary Becker earned his BA at Princeton with the grade 'summa cum laude'. He then decided to move on to Chicago, where he got under the influence of Milton Friedman, the short but nonetheless towering figure of the Chicago School of Economics who was to have a great impact on Becker's thinking ever since. 'In everything he did, he was just magnificent', remembers Becker. While his first two papers dealt with more conventional topics of trade and monetary theory,[5] Becker now began to pursue his own idiosyncratic and immensely creative path, fearlessly applying the economic approach to broader social questions. This is the 'vintage Becker: controversial, important, unpopular, and almost certainly correct', as Steven Levitt describes him.[6] This new approach opened up a whole new horizon for economic theory; it was a major revolution. The basis of all this is rational choice theory, by which purposive behaviour is assumed, implying that people aim to maximize utility as they conceive it and therefore tend to weigh the prospective cost and benefits in their decisions as well as they can, whatever field these decisions may concern. Here, Becker of course also had Milton Friedman's explicit support.[7] Nonetheless, this extension of the economic approach to non-monetary issues has been highly controversial and 'hence, at the outset, (it) met with scepticism and even distrust', as Assar Lindbeck mentioned in his Nobel presentation speech in 1992.[8] It was decried as 'economic imperialism' – a term which was meant nastily in those days, but which American economists nowadays have grown to use with almost complete self-confidence.[9] A more subtle criticism might object to the method of adding diverse non-monetary elements into people's modeled utility functions, for this might ultimately result in a logical circle, allowing to explain almost anything if only the relevant underlying assumption has been made.

Under Milton Friedman's supervision, Gary Becker wrote his doctoral thesis on discrimination[10] – a topic that was at the center of lively public debate in those days even before the heyday of affirmative action.[11] Becker sought to explain the persisting wage differentials between Blacks and

Whites, and solved the theoretical puzzle by introducing a parameter describing a 'taste' for racial segregation into the utility functions of both employers and employees. Discrimination is costly and harms both sides, but it can be maintained in a cartel situation. Globalization, however, by breaking up national monopolies or cartels, makes this increasingly difficult, as Becker pointed out at the Mont Pèlerin Society meeting in Tokyo.

After obtaining his Ph.D., Becker first remained at Chicago, teaching there for three more years, but then accepted an offer by Columbia University in New York City and by the National Bureau for Economic Research (NBER). In Manhattan, Gary Becker thus initiated his work on human capital; the path-breaking book that he published on this topic was actually an outgrowth of his research project for the NBER.[12] Becker broke away from the often unquestioned assumption that labor was all homogeneous. The idea was basically that human capital can be accumulated through schooling and labor training, and that the underlying choice is just another investment decision.

While these were fruitful years, Becker ventured back out to Chicago in 1969 as a guest professor with a grant from the Ford Foundation and finally decided to go back entirely in 1970. As he says in his Nobel Autobiography, he was beginning to feel intellectually stale at Columbia. He was also worn out by the student revolts of 1968, affected by his loss of his first wife in 1970, and tired of commuting in and out of the New York suburbs. At Chicago, he joined the faculty in a department that had in the meantime added George Stigler, who was to become a close friend,[13] and Harry G. Johnson. Here, he took up his work on crime, culminating in his well-known paper 'Crime and punishment', another revolution in the field.[14] He then started his work on the allocation of time, exploring the division of labor within a family. This burgeoned out into various different aspects concerning the family, going beyond the questions of birth rates and family size that he had been working on earlier, now touching also upon issues such as marriage, divorce, investments in child education, women's labor participation, the valuation of household work and so on. Instead of simply considering the family as a black box household, as was done in conventional theory, Becker decided to look at the inner workings of that unit, applying the usual tools of production theory. The two major works on this vast topic were his *Economic Approach to Family Behaviour*[15] and the later, complementary and also more comprehensive *Treatise on the Family*.[16]

In 1983, the Sociology Department at Chicago offered Becker a joint appointment, which was something he likes to interpret as a signal to the sociology profession that his rational choice approach was an acceptable theoretical paradigm. Ever since 1985, Gary Becker has expanded his domain beyond the scope of theoretical papers and textbooks, to include a monthly column for *Business Week* (discontinued in 2004) and a regular appearance on a common blog with Judge Richard Posner,[17] who is his sparring partner and in some ways his counterpart.

It is much easier to analyze the impact that Gary Becker's work has had than to get a feeling for the influences that generated his ideas. His impact cannot be overrated. Meant in a non-pejorative way, economic imperialism is now an undeniable fact: Becker has successfully extended the economic approach to all aspects of human life by focusing it on its very core, namely on individual choices and how they play themselves out in social interaction. This has refreshed almost all existing fields of research and sparked numerous new fields, including new interdisciplinary approaches together with sociology, anthropology and psychology. Much of labor economics, institutional economics and even behavioral economics wouldn't have developed without Becker having widened the horizon and scope of the discipline. Becker has continued the tradition of the Chicago School of Economics, and he has greatly influenced his own group of students and co-authors, ranging from Steven Levitt to Edward Lazear, and from Kevin Murphy to Edward Glaeser.

As for his own inspiration, Gary Becker has been the most reluctant one of the interviewees in this book to engage in an after-the-fact analysis and story-telling. In our conversation, he didn't reveal much about his private life other than childhood, and so no direct inferences can be made. But there certainly are some connections, given the daily-life character of many questions that he has addressed in his work. Some of his topics may have come to him from his own private life. But then, these intellectual ways to rationalize some personal puzzles or decision problems do only become relevant for the larger public insofar as they describe universalizable theories. Otherwise, much in his itinerary seems indeed to have been due to pure accident (he first took an economics course simply because he had to) and luck (without Viner's advice, he might not have gone to Chicago). Becker's taste for social questions seems to have originated in family discussions when he was growing up, without any dramatic background triggering this concern directly. Intelligence and excellence then propelled him further ahead, combined with the guts to do things that might be controversial, to end up at the University of Chicago. At Chicago, his destiny awaited him: Milton Friedman. It is no exaggeration to say that Friedman's influence on Becker was all-encompassing and decisive. Friedman showed him how economics can be done, he taught him to see how vastly the logical approach could be extended, and he supported him as Becker went ahead. It was only Becker's pronounced taste for independence that urged him to move away from Chicago for a period of 12 years. This may also be an important factor directing his path: his happiness with puzzling away on his own, his unwillingness to join the crowd. There is wisdom beyond the crowd.

INTERVIEW

Professor Becker, have you benefited from any kind of predisposition for economics, perhaps from your family background and upbringing?
That's hard to tell. My father was a businessman. He was pretty well-to-do. We also had a lot of discussions in the household, some of them with my father, but especially between my sisters, my brother, and myself. I also read the stock papers to my father when I was 13 or 14, because his eyes were failing and he couldn't read them any more. Maybe that's how I got an appreciation for business at that time.

Didn't you find those stock papers rather boring?
Very boring. That's true. I felt this obligation to help my father out, but I had no interest in this myself, absolutely no interest.

Then this obligation should logically have distanced you from economics, rather than drawing you any closer.
I also took a high-school course in economics. That was a very bad course. I had to take some course, I took this one purely by accident, and it certainly didn't generate any interest. But at some point I did begin to develop – and I can't really explain how, maybe through my elder sister and the discussions we had in the household – a desire to do something for society. This desire to make a contribution in some way did begin to emerge, even though I then still had no way to know how to do it. It certainly came around age 16 or 17, and it continued to grow stronger as I became more serious about learning more subjects at school, including philosophy and mathematics. I have always been interested in mathematics. It's hard to know what exactly the causal mechanisms were that made me end up in economics. What the elements were that put you on some track rather than another, that's a hard thing to know in general. I can't see any other influence than the discussions we had at home. My friends just played sports. All they were mainly interested in was sports.

You were 15 years old when the war ended. Did that period affect you in any way – the American war effort, perhaps, the concerns about post-war reconstruction in Europe, or the more general economic repercussions?
Not very much, not more than any other typical American had been affected, of course. I remember how I heard about Pearl Harbor.[18] I was

11 years old at that time. I remember this because we were listening to a big football game on the radio with my father, and I found it really annoying when there was this announcement about the attack on Pearl Harbor. Later, we heard about some people from the neighborhood who had been killed in the war. Daily life wasn't so much affected otherwise; there was some rationing, we had to cut down on some expenses, but that was pretty much it. This was nothing compared to people in Europe or in Japan. My brother was drafted towards the end of the war. He was engaged in the occupying forces in Japan. All in all, I can't remember the war as having had any major impact on my interest. But then, at high school, I became more serious in school, and teachers began to stress subjects of social science, and they were discussing this with us. I had this sort of awakening when I was 16 years old, and I began to develop a keen interest in these types of social questions. So I started reducing my athletic activities, whatever they amounted to,[19] to the benefit of math and other intellectual activities.

Mathematics and philosophy are not exactly the same things, however. And liking calculus is not necessarily the same thing as being interested in social issues. How did you bridge that gap?
In the beginning, these had been separate interests. But then, in the first course I took in economics as a freshman at Princeton, we had a textbook – and that was Paul Samuelson's.[20] It was fascinating. What impressed me about that famous textbook was that in the last quarter of that book, in those days (and it is probably much more now), he had a mathematical formulation of economics. That was the part of the whole course that really attracted me the most. To me the question was how I could use mathematics – which I liked and was pretty good at – to discuss social questions. So Samuelson's book actually built the bridge.

Essentially, you happened to have a talent in math and an interest in social issues. And the insight that you could combine both was what made you pick economics at university.
Right. I majored in math and economics for my BA at Princeton. I graduated in three years. I had accelerated my undergraduate curriculum. . .

Why did you do that?
I wanted to be financially independent early. You know, I can't say I came from a poor family, and I can't say I came from a very wealthy family either. The truth is that we were a pretty well-to-do family. But I didn't like the idea that I was dependent. I wanted to be independent and actually

help my father out that way. So I decided to accelerate my undergraduate studies to three years, which meant that whatever I was going to do, I'd do it quicker. I don't know whether it was a wise decision in that respect, but that's what I did. And then, during the last year in economics, my third year, I began to lose interest in economics.

How come?
Well, it wasn't dealing with the social questions that I was interested in.

What was it dealing with, the way it was being taught?
It was taught very formally, without applications.

Was it more macroeconomics than microeconomics?
No, it had a lot of microeconomics, but it wasn't taught in a way that showed the current theory was useful for understanding the world in those days. I was just plain dissatisfied with that. So I looked at sociology. I never took a sociology course but I spoke to some sociologists and read some books on sociology, especially by Talcott Parsons,[21] who was really a great figure in those days. However, I decided it was too difficult. I found I had great difficulty comprehending what people like Talcott Parsons were saying and what it all amounted to. And so I reverted back and started graduate school in economics, again in Princeton.

What did you find so difficult about sociology?
I couldn't see the logical structure so clearly. That was my problem.

That certainly was due to sociology, not you.
Maybe. Anyway, that was my feeling. I decided sociology was too difficult for me and so I went back to economics. I wasn't 100 percent happy about that, but I thought this was a better field for me.

Did you have teachers at this point who helped you make a decision or who even perhaps tried to lure you into economics?
Princeton had some pretty good teachers. But the person who influenced me the most was a professor who had been at Chicago before, Jacob Viner,[22] who was a very famous economist at the time. He had moved from Chicago to Princeton and now taught graduate courses at Princeton. I took a lot of graduate courses there, even though I was still doing undergraduate studies. So I took two graduate courses taught by Viner and liked them a lot.[23] Most courses were a waste of time in retrospect, but these were quite good.

Did he also influence you later on? Did he recommend that you go on doing post-graduate studies?
He didn't recommend anything directly. But at the end of my undergraduate studies at Princeton, I asked him for advice where to go on studying. I had a Fulbright fellowship for Cambridge University in the UK, something like that also for the London School of Economics, and also very good fellowships for Harvard and Chicago. And I remember asking him, 'Professor Viner, what do you think I should do?' He didn't recommend Cambridge. He just said: 'Cambridge makes witty people wittier.' That was his expression, I still remember it to this day. That's what he said. And so I acknowledged, 'Well, I'm not that witty.' I think he gave me a good advice this way. Cambridge wasn't a place for me at that time. My choice then rather quickly came down to Chicago or Harvard. It was really difficult to decide where to go. Milton Friedman[24] from Chicago had come to speak at Princeton once, but I wasn't that impressed by his talk. Everything just seemed too simple. The paper he was presenting was actually a very profound one on flexible exchange rates which is still very famous in the field.[25] But it seemed too simple to me. So I went up to visit Harvard. But I didn't like the attitude of people at the department there. They thought they obviously had the best department. It wasn't that great a department; people were rather conventional in terms of their work. Apart from that, Chicago also just happened to be a newer place for me in the Mid-West. I had been living on the East coast my whole life, and Chicago seemed to me more experimental. The Cowles Commission[26] was there, too, with an interesting mathematical group. So that's why I went to Chicago, and they gave me a very good fellowship. To be fair, I must say that Harvard would have given me a very good fellowship, too. I would like to be able to say that I went to Chicago expressly in order to join Milton Friedman or some of the other great figures, but that simply wouldn't be true.

When did it occur to you that you might become a professional economist, doing research full time and for a living?
Well, once I was at graduate school in Chicago, I felt I would become a professor. I still remember the time when I told my mother: 'I want to become a professor'. I was maybe 20 or 21 years old. And she said: 'But you will only make 10,000 dollars a year!' And I answered, 'well, that's enough, that will be enough for me'. My father was more encouraging. Actually, my mother wasn't really discouraging either. So at that time, I already was thinking of becoming a professor. You see, I had had a very good record at Princeton, and at Chicago, I had already published a couple of articles.[27] That's when I made the decision to stay in economics and go on in academia.

Let's turn to your topics and approaches more specifically. The rational choice approach[28] is the basis of what you are doing. When did that come to you, when did you settle on this fundamental paradigm as the core around which everything else should be built?
It was actually a gradual process. Certainly Milton Friedman had a great influence on me here. He was by far the greatest living teacher I have ever had. He really opened my eyes to economics as a powerful engine of analysis. Milton Friedman was just number one. He was a great man. He used rational choice himself, but he didn't use it to discuss such a broad range of problems. Anyway, I got on that when I did my work on racial discrimination.[29] But I didn't at that time fully see the progress that could be arrived at. As I said, it came gradually. As I worked on types of problems such as racial discrimination and fertility, and finally human capital, I began to get a feel that this could be a pretty powerful tool for a wide range of problems. It was a gradual process.

How did the topic of discrimination arise? Did anybody suggest that to you?
I can't even remember. But no, nobody suggested it to me. In fact, most of my teachers weren't happy I was working on that. I somehow got the topic, and when I gave my teachers an outline of my thesis at its very early stages, Milton Friedman thought it was promising; another Mont Pèlerin Society member and a very fine labor economist, H. Gregg Lewis,[30] thought it was promising; and Theodore W. Shultz,[31] another Nobel Prize winner, also thought it was promising. But that was it. Most of the faculty of the economics department at Chicago didn't like it. In order for me to go ahead, they insisted that somebody from the sociology department should be put on my committee. Which was what we did. I really can't say the topic was suggested to me by anyone on the economics faculty by any means, but I had some strong support from a minority of the members of the department. These were the members I respected the most.

Who did you interact most with at that stage?
Milton Friedman and H. Gregg Lewis were the people I interacted the most with. They were both on my committee. Milton Friedman – you know, in everything he did, he was just magnificent. He gave great lectures. He was the dominant catalyst in the group. And H. Gregg Lewis really was an unsung outstanding economist, although he never published a lot.

Did Frank Knight[32] play a role?
We didn't have much personal interaction. He was pretty old at that time. I took three of his courses, which we used to call Knight I, II and III,

whatever the exact title was. We students also liked to say, which was true, that whatever topic Knight started, he would come around to religion. Why religion? Well, while he was explicitly very hostile to religion, Knight saw that it had a lot of relevance for economic problems.[33] Knight had a lot of important ideas, and I certainly appreciated those. He was a great economist.

You once tried out some ideas which were actually precursors of Public Choice theory,[34] but Knight dissuaded the Journal of Political Economy *from publishing it. That wasn't very helpful – and it must have been pretty frustrating.*

That's true. It was an early Public Choice paper called 'Competition in democracy'. I had sent it to the *JPE* and they were inclined to take it, and the reviewing process was under way. I still have a copy of Knight's review. He opposed it. And so, since they had a policy of not publishing anything unless it was exceptional, they decided not to publish my paper. I think Knight didn't really understand what I was doing in that paper. I'll give you another story as well, which you might not know. I took a handwritten version of that same paper and showed it to Friedrich August von Hayek,[35] who was at Chicago at that moment. He just gave it back to me, saying that he didn't read handwritten essays. The problem was that I wasn't typing in those days. So I never had an opportunity to get his comments.

Not very encouraging either. Did you drop it then?

Well, partly. I then revised the paper a little bit, and it eventually got published in the first issue of the *Journal of Law and Economics*.[36] Aaron Director[37] liked it. He wanted me to publish it, and that's what we did.

But you didn't follow up much on this topic.

No, not until much later, in the eighties, when I turned to special interest groups and their role in the political process.[38]

Even small decisions by other people have great influences, apparently. Who knows in which direction you would have gone otherwise. . . had Knight and Hayek not been so discouraging, maybe you would have become a Public Choice theorist and would never have come around to dealing with discrimination, human capital and the family.

Well, I dropped it partly because I was discouraged, but partly also because my interests moved elsewhere. Of course it was a shame that *JPE* didn't publish that very early paper at that time. They really should have. It was a mistake on their part. But I can't complain, I did OK nevertheless.

The topic of discrimination came to me instead, on which I wrote my thesis,[30] and growing out of my interaction with Milton Friedman, I even published a little paper together with him in the *JPE*.[40] I stayed at Chicago for six years, teaching as an assistant professor for the last three years. In the end, I decided that it would be better for me to become more independent. Milton Friedman was great, but he was just such a dominant intellectual influence. I wanted to be on my own. So I decided to move east and to commute from the suburbs of New York City to the University of Columbia. I was also going to do some work for the National Bureau of Economic Research (NBER), which was based right in New York City. They needed a topic, and so I said that I would like to work on the economics of education. They accepted it. They had a small grant for me to do research on it, and that's how I started working explicitly on human capital.[41]

Did the notion 'human capital' already exist in those days?
Oh yes. Theodore W. Shultz had been working on human capital and had used the term. In Chicago, there was some excitement about it. Not much anywhere else to speak of.

The next big block of topics was the family. How did that come about?
I had taken on to the economics of fertility quite early on, in 1960.[42] Then I dropped that topic. However, when I was working on a paper about the allocation of time later on,[43] that brought me back to the questions about fertility, women's labor force, and those type of questions. I didn't do much more with that before the early seventies, but then I started to work out the theory of marriage and decided to devote myself to the economics of the family.

Why did you pick exactly that topic?
(*Laughter*). Again, that is a difficult question that is hard for me to answer. I remember sitting in a hotel room one morning, starting to think about this question who marries whom. Why do more educated people tend to marry more educated people? Why do high IQ people marry high IQ people? Why is that? Why do you see that kind of thing? I started to work out a theory of marriage, and I got one insight as to why that pattern operates. And then I started to look at other aspects of marriage.[44] When you talk about marriage, you must also talk about divorce, that's a natural corollary. I looked into different types of marriage; I worked on fertility and looked at the choice of having children;[45] I worked on human capital. So all these things just grew together, and then I wrote my book on the family.[46]

Did some of these correlated issues spring up from conversations at university?

At that time I was at Columbia. Some of my work I discussed with some of my colleagues at Columbia. Especially with Jacob Mincer.[47] I had helped to persuade him to come to Columbia. He was an outstanding economist. He also did work on human capital and other related areas. He and I had a workshop together where we had a lot of discussions. Mincer wasn't interested in marriage and so on, but he was interested in labor participation and fertility, for example.

And that workshop, did that provide fresh ideas? Were there any students who put you on new tracks and gave you unexpected impulses?

We had very good students indeed. And therefore, in my paper on the allocation of time,[48] I mention in the very beginning that this was the result of much of a cooperative effort. As I said, at Columbia, we had some great students, and there was Mincer, of course, who also worked on the questions I was interested in. We certainly had an influence on what they were doing, I think that is true. One of the greatest articles on the economics of health care was written by one of my students, Michael Grossman.[49] His thesis at our department was basically an application of human capital analysis to the health area. It was very influential in health economics. I really had some outstanding students, some of them working in law and economics. The interaction with students, a couple of faculty and the NBER was very important, both ways.

Why is it that you were not attracted by other fields within economics that might have satisfied your mathematical appetite as well, such as growth theory which was booming in those days, or social choice theory, for example?

You just cannot do too many different things. I was working on problems that had been neglected a lot in economics, and which I found important, given my general interest in society. I was working on marriage, education and crime. Those were important social questions about which I thought I had something to say. Had I had more time, I would certainly have liked to follow up on more things, but time is scarce. That's of course the foundation of the theory of the allocation of time: you cannot do everything.

Was it not also the fact that you preferred to be a big fish in a small pond rather than being one more fish in a big pond?

Right, I preferred to be on my own here. I'm not someone who likes working in a crowded area. That certainly is relevant, I agree.

But swimming more or less alone, you did encounter a lot of resistance.
A lot of resistance. Enormous resistance

How did that affect you? Did that stimulate you or did you suffer?
Nobody liked what I did. But I had a few things that saved me. One was
that people whom I respected enormously, such as Milton Friedman,
Theodore W. Shultz and George Stigler,[50] whom I got to know very well
when I was back at Chicago, liked what I was doing and thought it was
interesting. They didn't like everything I was doing, but they liked my
approach generally. The other thing was that I also had a lot of confidence
that what I was doing was important. Until this day, I can't understand
the criticisms that I received from some very eminent economist for my
work on marriage. George Stigler had sent my paper out to him as a
referee. And I don't want to give the name, but that Nobel Laureate who
was asked to read my work was very negative, and he said: 'don't publish
this'. I couldn't understand this and still cannot. It was such an important
topic which we shouldn't leave to the sociologists; they aren't going far
with these problems. And I had something to say on it. That confidence
in myself, combined with a very important wave of support from people I
respected, enabled me to take the criticism and to deal with the feeling that
I wasn't recognized maybe enough at first. Of course I was hoping that in
the long run, I would be recognized.

Well, you have been. . . .
(*Laughter*). Yes, I was. More than I deserve.

*You encountered violent criticism mainly for two reasons: for your exten-
sion of the economic approach to non-monetary issues, which got decried as
'economic imperialism', and for the rational choice approach itself. Much of
that criticism came and still comes from non-economists, but some also came
from within the discipline in those days. What do you say to people who criticize you on these grounds? Is the rationality assumption merely a heuristic
tool that serves to find out what the mechanisms are and how incentives work
– or do you actually believe that people are purely rational and calculating,
beyond viewing them as simply purposive agents?*
The rationality assumption is indeed basically a tool. The goal in some of
my work has been to expand the concept of what is rational to include a
lot of other behavior that is excluded otherwise. If you think that being
rational means selfish individuals, coldly calculating, only worrying about
themselves and about their monetary benefits, then that's obviously a caricature. It is a caricature that maybe sometimes some economists use, but
it is a caricature. What I wanted to do was to expand the notion so that

we can consider people with other feelings such as love, altruism toward other people, hatred, and all these things. People worry about other things than money. People worry about family. People do harm, people commit crimes. I wanted to expand the concept of rationality so that more ordinary aspects of life could be mirrored, aspects that you see as you look around. That was my approach. There are miscalculations and people make mistakes in their lives, alright, but in spite of that, the rational choice approach is still a very powerful engine of analysis that helps us understand a lot of the problems of the world.

What do you think about behavioral economics? Do you think it is useful even though it questions the rationality assumption? Can it teach us anything at all?
There are three different aspects about behavioral economics. One is that in this approach, you can extend the concept of people's preferences, so that their utility includes equity and so on. I certainly accept that. I have done some of that myself, and some people have been doing this for a long time. Doing this is useful in some instances, although maybe not in others. Another aspect is about all those psychological quirks and deviations. I think that has taught us something. On the other hand, third, I think there is sometimes confusion in this kind of literature between what is important at the individual level and what is important at the group level, which is the way economists look at these things – the market level, so to speak. There are all those quirks that are unimportant at the group level because they cancel out. They don't survive, just like discrimination. A lot of discrimination doesn't survive due to market forces. In many cases, there is done too little of that sort of market analysis. But on the whole, I think behavioral economics has added some insights, and it is a useful contribution to economics in general – if its limits are accepted, and if the role of market forces is not overlooked. I just have these two provisos.

How did your political persuasions develop? Have you always sided with the market – or did you start out as a socialist like almost every young person?
I was a socialist, that's true. Even my father, although he was a pretty successful businessman, strongly supported interventionist-type candidates. We had some arguments about that. But what really influenced me and pulled me away from socialism were essentially two things: Milton Friedman and economics. Studying economics, at the end of my sophomore year at Princeton, I remember I debated somebody about markets versus socialism. And I was on the market side. I had already shifted away from socialism. Entering Princeton, I was a socialist. Two years or so later,

I was no longer a socialist. Three years later, I decided to go to Chicago. I still had an uneasy feeling. Even though I had the basic principles why I should lean in that direction, I still was missing the theory. I then got that at Chicago.

Did you ever have time then to look at purely philosophical issues more closely?
Well, studying at Chicago, at least in those days, we got in touch with a lot of philosophy within economics, regarding for example the foundations of liberty. My professors were big on that. I read a number of the philosophers, and I certainly did get involved with philosophical thinking, absolutely. I attended Hayek's seminars.

What was he like as a teacher?
I didn't get to know him well. He wasn't really in the economics department, he was at the Committee on Social Thought.[51] His seminars were very light-touch, he didn't try to dominate them. In his seminars, there were interesting, some great speakers. Hayek was very gentlemanly. I began to read some of his work, the *Road to Serfdom*,[52] of course, and the *Constitution of Liberty*[53] somewhat later. I wish I had had more contact with him. I really didn't have enough contact with him. I tried, I gave him a paper to have a look at, but he didn't want to read it, and that sort of put me off a little bit. He wasn't very influential in the economics department simply because he wasn't in the economics department, and so graduate students didn't get to see and listen to him. In that sense he didn't have much of an influence on the students at Chicago. I was fortunate, I had heard of him, and I went to his seminars. So at least I had some more intellectual contact.

If you had to designate the one person that clearly had the greatest influence on you, the one person who gave you the most insights and impulses, who would that be? Not Hayek, obviously. Must have been Friedman.
Of course. No question.

Would you describe yourself as a person who would get most of his ideas in front of a sheet of paper, or while reading, or in conversation?
That's hard to tell. Remember, sometimes, it's just sitting in a hotel room.

Were you with someone?
Oh no, I was alone. I was traveling to something, can't remember where and to what. What triggered the theory of crime was that I had to go to an

examination at the University of Chicago, I was running late, and I had to decide whether to park my car legally or illegally. That got me started on thinking about rational crime.[54] And so I started to think through the question considering the probability of getting caught, doing all kinds of calculations, taking into account the interaction between the police, society and the criminal etc. I hadn't thought about this at all before that. You might say that was a chance event, but somehow my mind was prepared for it, who knows why. I don't believe I got too many of my ideas explicitly from reading. Certainly, I got my approach to economics from lectures and from reading. That background influence was of course enormous. As for real-world experiences – well, as far as current events are concerned, I can't believe they did have any significant influence, other than perhaps concerning the topics of crime and so on. But it's really hard to know.

What about the political debate? Was that ever a source of inspiration?
In anything that I consider my more important work. . . well, racial discrimination was a big issue, definitely. I wouldn't have gotten involved in that if I hadn't been aware that there was a big problem out there, in the US. That certainly was a factor. The same is true for the question of addiction, on which I did some later work.[55] I was aware of the problem, and so I went into that issue. Thus there was an influence. But generally, my work never came from being involved in the public debate and then using that to work out some theory. That never was a major factor.

It was rather just 'in the air'.
Yes.

Are the private and the professional Gary Becker the same? Are they exactly identical or is there a clear-cut dividing line between the two?
Oh sure, they're different. Which is true for most people – it is one thing how you are in your private life and it is another thing how you are in your professional life, even though I live a rational private life, too. I like to think about what I'm doing. That's true both for the private and the professional Gary Becker. You see, I met my wife and I really felt attracted to her, like everybody else would. I didn't sit down to write down an equation and decide whether I wanted to get married. That doesn't mean it wasn't a rational decision nevertheless, and it has been a good marriage. I just happen to be a person who likes to think through decisions. I have always been pretty organized myself. That's the rational Gary Becker. I like to approach problems that way. But we make a lot of our major decisions under much uncertainty, and I'm aware of that. You cannot plan it

all through. For example, I went to Princeton – but I could have gone to MIT. I then went to Chicago – but I could have gone to Harvard. All those were lucky decisions, you know. And then, when I went to Columbia, which was a good decision, too. I could have gone to a couple of other places. I met my wife completely by accident. There is a lot of uncertainty in the world. The question is how you respond to this uncertainty and whether you are able to take advantage of the opportunities that come up. Life is a lot about lucky decisions.

Last question about progress in economic theory. What does progress consist of and where should we go in the future?
I'm always reluctant to say where we should go. If I did, this would be as if an elder statesman was telling everybody else what they should be doing. I don't want to do that. I have no agenda for where we should go and what areas should be the most important ones. As for the past, I think there has been a lot of progress in economic theory since I was a graduate student. Just think of a lot of areas that have developed in the meantime, and all the new techniques that have been worked out – for example human capital theory, family economics, Public Choice theory, and informational economics. I could go on quoting things that have constituted progress in economic theory. And I think that will continue. A lot of my students say that all the important things have been worked out already. But that's nonsense. Anybody in research can find new questions. There are still a lot of things we don't understand about the world. Right now, I'm working a lot on higher education, trying to figure out why women are advancing so much in higher education. There are also a few other topics, such as population growth etc. But I can't say where exactly the next series of breakthroughs is going to appear. When people say something like that I'm usually very skeptical. This is very hard to predict. Somebody will come up with some good ideas, and then that will influence other people. But I do know there still is a lot we don't understand about the real world, and so therefore there will inevitably be progress in the next 10 or 20 years. Inevitably, we will get better insights into human behavior. We will build on the theories we have, and so they will obviously change over time. Theory is an evolving structure, and it will continue to evolve. In that process, we won't eliminate everything we have, by no means. There will always be the fundamental elements, that is, rational choice and markets. They will always be around to guide us. But theory will be modified in various ways. That's how I look at the future.

Thank you, Professor.

NOTES

1. The interview was held on 12 September 2008.
2. See Friedrich August von Hayek (1978).
3. Evsey Domar (1992, p. 121).
4. Property and Environment Research Center, based in Bozeman, Montana.
5. Gary S. Becker (1952) and Gary S. Becker and William Baumol (1952).
6. Steven D. Levitt (2006).
7. Milton Friedman himself has a very famous paper defending rational choice theory, arguing that people and firms make decisions 'as if' they apply subjective expected utility maximization under perfect information (Milton Friedman, 1953b).
8. Nobel Foundation (1992).
9. Edward P. Lazear (1999/2000).
10. Gary S. Becker (1957).
11. 'Affirmative action' means measures to increase the representation of minorities in areas of employment, education and business from which they have been historically excluded. Some of those steps involve controversial preferential selection in order to correct for past discrimination. Affirmative action is an idea that originated in the Civil Rights Act in 1964 and became an inflammatory public issue in the 1970s.
12. Gary S. Becker (1964).
13. They co-authored two articles (Gary S. Becker and George Stigler, 1974 and George Stigler and Gary S. Becker, 1977).
14. Gary S. Becker (1968).
15. Gary S. Becker (1976).
16. Gary S. Becker (1981).
17. Richard Allen Posner is currently a judge on the United States Court of Appeals for the Seventh Circuit in Chicago. He helped start the law and economics movement while teaching at the University of Chicago Law School (1969–81); he currently still serves as a lecturer at the Law School. He founded the *Journal of Legal Studies*. The website, created in 2004, is at www.becker-posner-blog.com.
18. The attack on Pearl Harbor was a surprise attack of the Japanese navy against the US naval base in Hawaii, on 7 December 1941. It turned around public opinion to favor US participation in World War II.
19. It was mainly handball.
20. Paul A. Samuelson (1948).
21. Talcott Parsons (1902–79), an influential American sociologist on the faculty of Harvard University, was well-known for his theoretical approach called structural functionalism, trying to integrate all the social sciences into one overarching framework.
22. Jacob Viner (1892–1970) taught economics at the University of Chicago until 1946 and at Princeton until 1960. One of the leading lights of the early Chicago School and a staunch opponent to John Maynard Keynes, Viner was well-known himself mainly for his theory of the firm, his theory of trade and some contributions to the history of economic thought.
23. Viner had a reputation for his notoriously rough and tough teaching habits. See the interview with James M. Buchanan in this volume: 'Viner would just crush you.'
24. Milton Friedman (1912–2006) was awarded the Nobel Prize in 1976 'for his achievements in the fields of consumption analysis, monetary history and theory and for his demonstration of the complexity of stabilization policy'.
25. Milton Friedman (1953a).
26. The Cowles Commission for Research in Economics was founded in Colorado Springs in 1932 by the businessman Alfred Cowles. It moved to the University of Chicago in 1939 and later on to Yale University in 1955, where it was renamed the 'Cowles Foundation'.
27. Gary Becker had received his BA at Princeton in 1951 and his MA at Chicago in 1952.

The papers he is referring to are Gary S. Becker (1952) and Gary S. Becker and William Baumol (1952).

28. Rational choice theory can be described as an approach to economic and other social behavior that starts from the idea that individuals tend to optimize their actions according to their preferences and constraints – they act in a purposive way, balancing good and bad effects as well as they can. Rational choice theory is decision theory, focusing on notions such as incentives and opportunity cost. Rational choice theory is thus a facet of the more general approach of methodological individualism.

29. Gary S. Becker (1957).

30. H. Gregg Lewis (1914–92) was one of the earliest Chicago 'economic imperialists', teaching there from 1939 to 1975, and subsequently at Duke University in Durham, North Carolina.

31. Theodore W. Shultz (1902–98) was awarded the Nobel Memorial Prize in Economic Sciences in 1979, together with W. Arthur Lewis, for 'their pioneering research into economic development research with particular consideration of the problems of developing countries'.

32. Frank Knight (1885–1972) was a greatly influential American economist. One of his more famous students is James M. Buchanan. Jointly with Jacob Viner, Knight presided over the Department of Economics at the University of Chicago from the 1920s to the late 1940s. Friedrich August von Hayek famously described – and distinguished – the two, Knight and Viner, as 'two types of mind': Viner on the one hand, 'very much a "master of his subject"', he wrote, that is, someone who has excellent memory and therefore encompassing knowledge of a field, and Knight on the other hand, 'a puzzler if there ever was one', that is, someone who, lacking this type of all-absorbing memory, has to think through everything on his own – which however may make him more creative, allowing him to discover unconventional avenues that others may not see. See Friedrich August von Hayek (1978, pp. 50–56).

33. See Frank H. Knight and Thornton W. Merriam (1945).

34. Public Choice theory is an application of the tools of economic analysis to political, or 'non-market decision making'. This means that government behavior is no longer seen as being exogenous to economics, but is made endogenous instead and becomes a topic of its own. See the interview with James Buchanan, one of the founders of the Public Choice school, in this volume.

35. Friedrich August von Hayek was awarded the Nobel Prize in 1974, together with Gunnar Myrdal – both received it 'for their pioneering work in the theory of money and economic fluctuations and for their penetrating analysis of the interdependence of economic, social and institutional phenomena'.

36. Gary S. Becker (1958).

37. Aaron Director (1901–2004), Milton Friedman's brother-in-law, was a professor of economics at the University of Chicago Law School. He was a founder of the field of law and economics and also created the *Journal of Law and Economics*, which he co-edited with Ronald Coase.

38. See Gary S. Becker (1983 and 1985).

39. Gary S. Becker (1957).

40. Milton Friedman and Gary S. Becker (1957).

41. The result was Gary S. Becker (1964).

42. Gary S. Becker (1960b).

43. Gary S. Becker (1965).

44. Gary S. Becker (1973 and 1974).

45. See Gary S. Becker and H. Gregg Lewis (1973).

46. Gary S. Becker (1976 and 1981).

47. Jacob Mincer (1922–2006), a Polish emigrant to the US, was an early and famous leading figure of labor economics. He taught at Columbia from 1959.

48. Gary S. Becker (1965).

49. Michael Grossman, born 1942, teaches at the City University of New York and does research at the National Bureau of Economic Research (Michael Grossman, 1972).
50. George Stigler (1911–91) was another leading figure of the Chicago School of Economics. He received the Nobel Memorial Prize for Economics in 1982, for his 'seminal studies of industrial structures, functioning of markets and causes and effects of public regulation'.
51. The Committee on Social Thought was one of several interdisciplinary Ph.D.-granting committees at the University of Chicago, started in 1941 by the historian John Nef, the economist Frank Knight, the anthropologist Robert Redfield and University President Robert Maynard Hutchins.
52. Friedrich August von Hayek (1944).
53. Friedrich August von Hayek (1960).
54. Gary S. Becker (1968).
55. Gary S. Becker and Kevin M. Murphy (1986).

Douglass C. North

Washington University,
St Louis, MO, USA

The Sveriges Riksbank Prize in Economic Sciences in Memory of Alfred Nobel 1993 shared with Robert W. Fogel both 'for having renewed research in economic history by applying economic theory and quantitative methods in order to explain economic and institutional change'.

INTRODUCTION

The door to Douglass C. North's office at Eliot Hall, the Economics Building, is wide open. From his desk, behind piles of books, he waves at me as I peek in. I make an attempt at reminding him who I am, but he just barks at me: 'I know who you are, Karen, come on in'. North is his usual refreshingly unorthodox self, looking like the quintessential rough, weather-worn and robust sailor. Fittingly, he is dressed in a casual way, wearing jeans and a Norwegian sweater. As usual, too, he is talking fast, pouring out his most recent ideas and hunches, challenging and pushing his counterpart at any unexpected moment, and all that in an extremely witty style, sometimes so funny that he makes one bend over with laughter. 'You're lucky that I'm here,' he throws at me with a cheeky grin, 'I had of course forgotten, but Elisabeth reminded me this morning.' Elisabeth Willard Case, his 'wife, companion, critic and editor', as he likes to describe her,[1] carefully keeps track of her husband's multiple engagements. Which is not a trivial task. In spite of his 87 years, he is constantly over-booked. Slowing down just isn't fun, obviously. Right now, since he has just returned from a longer absence including a conference in Singapore, he wants to look through some of his mail before we start talking. As he digs through the piles of envelopes that Fannie Batt, the department sec-retary, has just brought upstairs, he finds a check worth $500 – a speaker's honorarium from some conference on the New Institutional Economics, the field of research that he once co-founded. 'Oh no', he says with a frown, 'they keep sending me these', tears it up and throws it in the bin. 'They need the money more than I do.' This isn't just a fluke. Indeed, Douglass C. North has a reputation for refusing what he considers undeserved or inap-propriate pay. Legend – which is probably true – has it that he even refused salary raises from his university for decades, feeling that he was earning enough. North is different.[2]

His non-conventional ways are mirrored in his biography. While not having an intellectual family background, Douglass Cecil North still grew up with a very wide, international horizon, and thus was able to pick up enriching influences from many different directions. His story is an amazing one for the era we're talking about; and it is absolutely enjoyable to read and discover it in the following interview. He was born in Cambridge, Massachusetts, in 1920. His father was a manager at the Metropolitan Life Insurance Company – a job that caused the family to move time and again as he climbed the career ladder. Thus, Douglass C. North went to elementary and secondary school in Ottawa, Canada; to private schools in Lausanne, Switzerland, in New York City and on Long Island; and finally to high school in Wallingford, Connecticut. He studied political science, philosophy and economics at the University of California at Berkeley, which laid the groundwork for the interdisciplinary approach that he was later to develop. At Berkeley, North formed strong Marxian beliefs and mil-itated for peace, as he recalls. Upon his graduation, he joined the Merchant Marine for what turned out to be quite a rough but rewarding adventure.

Coming back after the war, he decided to drop his much-cherished dream of becoming a photographer and to pursue further studies in eco-nomics instead, with nothing but the clear idea that he wanted to improve the world. Only in his postgraduate studies did he start to embrace the historical perspective. As he worked on his dissertation on the history of insurance companies in the United States, much to the concern of his father, he won a scholarship and spent a year doing research at Columbia University and Harvard. At Harvard, he came into contact with Joseph Schumpeter, who had a major influence on him. North obtained his Ph.D. from Berkeley in 1952 – six years after he had started teaching, and two years after he had obtained tenure as a professor of economics at the University of Washington in Seattle, In 1956/57, he spent a year at the National Bureau for Economic Research (NBER) as a research associate. On this occasion, he met the famous Simon Kuznets, who was to become a Nobel Laureate in 1971. Since 1961, North then also served as the Director of the Institute of Economic Research at the University of Washington. For 20 years, from 1967 to 1987, he was a member of the board of directors at the NBER. In 1966/67, he spent a year in Geneva as a Ford Faculty Fellow; that year was responsible for focusing him ever more on the analysis of institutions. In 1979 he spent a year at Rice University at Houston, Texas; and in 1981–82, two years in Cambridge, England. Finally, after retiring from his post in Seattle in 1983, he accepted a chair at Washington University at St Louis (WUStL), where there was an attractive group of young political scientists and economists who were attempting to develop new models of political economy. Here, North created the Center in Political Economy. This is where he still is these days – except for the summers, which he usually spends at his summer home in Michigan.

The unorthodoxy started with Douglass C. North not being drawn into the Keynesian revolution as such, but getting interested in the historical perspective instead, which he then tried to get hold of with mathematical, statistical and other quantitative means. While being a severe critic of what he views as over-mathematization and over-formalization of economics as it is today, quantitative methods did play an important role in his own career. He is famous for thus having launched a new field of economics, namely 'new economic history' or 'cliometrics', together with Robert W. Fogel, his co-laureate. The whole cliometric adventure really began at a joint conference of the NBER and the Economic History Association in 1957. Cliometrics – named after Clio, the Greek muse of history – is the discipline that endeavors to measure history. It implies, in a broader sense, 'the use of quantitative techniques, hypothesis testing, economic theory and counterfactual analysis to explain economic growth and decline', as the Nobel Committee puts it.[3] While the underlying economic theory was still neoclassic, the major innovation here was the incorporation of large volumes of quantitative data into the analysis of historical economic performance. The first path-breaking piece that North wrote in this field was his quantitative study of the US growth performance 1790–1860, published in 1961.[4] This study had its roots in an export base model that North had formulated earlier in the context of a project concerning the US balance of payments – a project that he had worked on with Simon Kuznets at the NBER.[5] Another piece that North wrote some years later about the sources of productivity change in ocean shipping 1600–1850[6] gave him an excellent reputation as a quantitative historian. At the same time, this paper already incorporates and anticipates North's later focus on institutions: one of the major findings – and one with more general validity – is that organizational changes had played a greater role than pure technical change. Until this day, this is one of the most quoted studies in economic history.

During his year at Geneva in the late 1960s, North grew more and more interested in European history. This, however, proved to be more complicated than he had thought. The difference was, as he says, that 'the US has always been a market economy to some extent', and so the traditional, static neoclassical approach, with its accent on price theory, abstracting from any kinds of disruptions or frictions, worked fine to explain what had happened throughout its history. 'But Europe? How could you talk about feudalism and the manorial system with neoclassical theory? This is where I realized that we need to develop a better body of theory to confront the crucial issues. That's what got me into trying to figure out and understand institutions.' Only institutions – rule of law, property rights, competition, political institutions and government – can explain why some countries had been successful and others lagged behind economically. In some cases, institutions have evolved that minimize transaction costs, that is the direct and indirect cost of entering into mutually beneficial exchange, and these countries flourish economically. Others don't. So what are these necessary institutions? Arriving at this puzzle, Douglass C. North embarked on the second major part of his innovative career, ultimately launching the new (or revived) field of institutional economics. This field builds on neoclassical economics but fills its empty gaps, dealing explicitly with phenomena such as transactions costs, bounded rationality, and so on. As North says, he had 'become convinced that you need a new theory that would concern itself with how economies evolve through time. And that didn't exist.' Ultimately, this brought him also back to the United States, with two books: *Institutional Change and American Economic Growth*,[7] co-authored by Lance Davis, in 1971, and *The Rise of the Western World*, co-authored by Robert Thomas.[8] North and Thomas, for example, find precisely that England's advance over countries like Spain had been propelled by the institutions that had developed, with property rights in the first and foremost role. It is in this book that North talks explicitly about incentives for the first time.

But if there are good and bad sets of institutions, why is that so? How come? This question links the New Institutional Economics to adjacent fields already familiar to North, such as sociology, social philosophy, psychology, political theory and especially Public Choice. This merger of disciplines into one interdisciplinary approach focusing on social interaction and evolution in all its various aspects over time is emblematic of both the unorthodoxy and the specific richness of North's research. It is as vast, fascinating and demanding as it is relevant or rather: essential. It is social science at its all-encompassing best. A major work is North's 1981 book *Structure and Change in Economic History*,[9] which he himself considers to be the best book he's ever written. It provides what may be called a unified Public Choice theory based on property rights and transaction costs that accounts, for example, for the transition from the hunter-gatherer economy to agriculture. North describes how inefficient institutions can in fact emerge and persist. Then, in his great 1990 book on *Institutions, Institutional Change, and Economic Performance*,[10] North asks why some countries are rich while others remain poor. Searching for answers, he looks especially at the relationship between politics, institutions and economic performance. Given that voters are 'rationally ignorant', they don't monitor politics perfectly, with the result that bad institutions can persist. To make everything more difficult, North also hints at a phenomenon called 'path dependence':[11] once a country is on a given track, it is not easy to get away from it. Cultural heritage isn't easy to change or transplant. Also, overall economic performance doesn't just depend on formal institutions alone. Still more important are informal institutions, that is customs, conventions, beliefs, norms, common prejudices and so on. So we have still not reached the end of the story: 'I realized that institutions come out of beliefs, and so I had to try and understand how beliefs are formed, and that takes you to how minds and brains work', says North. In order then to find out how the mind and brain work, how beliefs are formed and why they shape the way in which institutions are created, some insights from cognitive science seem needed. Consequently, North has helped create a program at WUStL that focuses on philosophy, the neurosciences and psychology (PNP). In the meantime, many researchers have taken up his ideas; a whole movement has come into being. In 1997, ISNIE has been created, the International Society for the New Institutional Economics. Douglass C. North served as ISNIE's second president, after Ronald Coase, Nobel Laureate of the year 1991.

When it comes to pinpointing the sources of his inspiration, Douglass C. North is hard to categorize – which doesn't come as a surprise with an unorthodox person like him. His family background wasn't intellectual at all, and so his interest in the issues that later became his areas of research can't seem to have been promoted much at home. However, he mentions how the Great Depression triggered his interest in economics, even though his family wasn't too dramatically affected by the crisis. The only instance where his personal biography seems to have played some prominent role was in the choice of his dissertation topic (the history of insurance in the United States) – although, as he recalls, this was rather to his father's dismay. His choice of topics also wasn't helped by current events, given that he decided to look far back. And it's also not as if his area of study was an already established, booming, fashionable one, where everybody was engaged in discussions through which new fruitful avenues sprang up regularly – and this is true for both aspects of economic history, that is for cliometrics as much as institutional economics. On the contrary, North started both avenues mostly from scratch, coming from nowhere. 'In terms of where my ideas come from, I have been very much a loner', he says. 'My driving force all my life has been that I was dissatisfied with the theory that we have to explain economic history and economic development. And I still am. I'm never satisfied with what I know.' The problem is that the more one knows, the harder this groping for more inevitably becomes. The air gets thinner and thinner up there.

INTERVIEW

I would like to know what it was that got you hooked on economics. Was economics a topic at home with your family, when you grew up?
No. My father never even graduated from high school, nor did my mother. He was the classic self-made man who started out as an office boy at the Metropolitan Life Insurance Company and ended up as Vice-President. My mother came out of a very rich Italian family, but they didn't believe in having their daughters educated, and so she didn't get much education at all. I never talked economics to them, and we never even thought about economics as a matter of fact.

Not at all? Not even remotely, when, for example, there was a sudden price hike for some good? Didn't you then discuss possible reasons?
No.

Nothing?
Well, we must have. I mean in family discussions, but certainly nothing that I can remember. It had nothing to do with how I evolved to become an economist.

What were topics at home then? Politics?
Well, yes, I guess, standard family kind of things, I don't remember much, but politics quite a bit.

What was the influence that your family had, then?
My mother was a fascinating woman, and I am enormously in her debt. She didn't like the educational system in the United States. By the time I was getting older, my father made lots of money, and so she took me to Europe to live. We lived in London, Paris and Lausanne. I went to school

in Lausanne for a year, to the Lycée Jacquard. All those things had a big influence on me. Then when we came back, we lived in Ottawa, Canada. My father then was head of the Metropolitan Life Insurance Company in Canada. When we came back, I went to lots of schools. I was in six different schools in seven years or something like that. We moved all over the place. Finally, when I got ready to go to high school, I got a very good education at a church school in Connecticut. It was so good that during my first years at college, I didn't have to do any work.

How did you pick the college to go to?
Well, I was accepted for Harvard, but then my father was made head of the West coast office of his company. In those days – it was the 1930s – 3000 miles from everybody wasn't good. And so I went to the University of California at Berkeley instead. I didn't go to Stanford because my brother was at Stanford and I didn't want to go to the same place he did. So you see all those rational ways by which I got started.

What did you major in?
I had a triple major, political science, economics and philosophy. I got a C average in all of them.

Oh my goodness.
Well, that was because in my sophomore and junior year, I became a radical. I headed the Labor board and welfare council; I led peace marches and things like that.

How did that happen?
I don't really know how that happened. Somehow or other I got involved. I guess the big reason is that the Great Depression was on, and I began to be interested in what was going on. There were no good answers in standard economics in those days; it was just boring and stupid. Then I discovered Karl Marx, and he had answers to everything. In fact, he had all the right questions but not very good answers. But it took me long years to find that out.

How did you discover Marx? Where you surrounded by left-wingers?
No. In fact, in college, I had joined a fraternity, and they almost threw me out when I became a left-winger. I was an outcast.

But how else did you pick up the idea that the solutions might be found on the left-hand side of the political spectrum?
Well, it was the Great Depression, and we had 25 percent of the American labor force unemployed. You were surrounded by problems related to

that every day, even though personally, I was living a life of comfort. Actually, even my father went broke three times during the Depression, but I never knew it. He cornered the Cuban sugar market just in 1929, which was a bad time to corner the Cuban sugar market.[12] He did things like that, he was crazy. But he kept his job with the Metropolitan Life Insurance Company. I don't know how anyone could avoid being a radical in those days, as surrounded by problems as we were. And so I drifted into being a Marxist. Not a Communist, a Marxist. That's a big difference.

Did you really understand Marx's labor theory of value?
Oh yes. I was a serious student of Marx. I read his *Capital*. Not many people have read that book, but I did. I read lots of Marx. That was a big influence on my life, and it still is. I'm not a Marxist any more, but still, he had an enormous impact. Anyway, I went through school and thus became a leader in left-wing activities. Then, World War II came along.

Did you fight?
By that time, I was a pacifist; I didn't want to kill anybody. So I went to sea. I joined the Merchant Marine. People could shoot at me but I wouldn't shoot back. I signed up as a cadet and was given two months of basic training doing nothing that I can remember. Then I was assigned to a ship, and the captain told me: 'I don't believe in cadets, so you'll just be a deck-hand'. I hadn't ever done any work in my life before that, so that was quite an experience. We had been to sea two days when the captain called me up on the bridge and said: 'North, you went to college. Well, we're lost. I'll give you 24 hours to learn to navigate.' What had happened was that they were turning out one ship a day at the shipyards, and they had to staff them. They took seamen, mostly Scandinavians who were on ships, and they had to promote them to captains and mates. Our captain had had a couple of years of school, but the first mate had never been to school. And he was supposed to be the navigator. Nobody knew how to navigate. So I stayed up all night and read an 1810 book on navigation. That book, by the way, is still in print. I got up the next day and was ready to navigate. I got the ship from San Francisco, California, to Melbourne, Australia. In 38 days.

Incredible. What kind of practical and analytical skills were needed for navigation?
Well, you had to learn how to use the sextant, you had to learn enough spherical trigonometry in order to be able to take sights and do the

calculations. I loved it. It was a natural for me. I had a wonderful time. Of course I also moved out of being a deck-hand which I didn't like being. I got a cabin in the officers' quarters and had a much easier time. All I had to do was navigate. When I came back from my second voyage, I had enough time to sit for my third mate license, and then I went back to sea as a third mate. So that's what I did the next 3.5 years. That took me through to 1944.

Did you ever get into dangerous situations?
Oh sure. I was very lucky that I was in the Pacific, not the Atlantic. The Atlantic had an enormous percentage of casualties. In fact, we loaded to go to Murmansk around Christmas time 1942.[13] At the last minute, the US invaded the Solomon Islands. So they unloaded us to load us up again to Solomon. Out of that convoy to Murmansk of 91 ships, 30 made it. I wouldn't be here if the invasion of the Solomon Islands hadn't come along.

Lucky indeed.
Also in another respect. In the Merchant Marine, when we got to a port, like Port Moresby in New Guinea for example, we didn't have anything to do. We couldn't go ashore during the night. So we played poker all night. The only rule was that when air raid attacks came, you withdrew what was in the pot. You couldn't run, though, because there was no place to go. If they hit us, we would be blown to pieces anyway, because we carried high-octane gas, kind of a thousand pound bomb. I won a lot of money playing poker. I won 2500 dollars, which in 1942/43 was an enormous amount of money. I think the highest I ever got in terms of salary was 90 dollars a month. I sent the money home to my mother, and she wondered how I could possibly have become such a good poker player. I wasn't a good poker player, though. I just followed a very simple rule: I stayed sober all night. I'd drink one beer, but the rest of us would all drink four or five bottles of Australian ale, which was 12 percent alcohol. By midnight, I was winning hands down. I kept telling them they were crazy. It didn't bother them a bit.

Then after the war, what happened?
I went back and debated whether to become a photographer or an economist. Oh, actually, I left out that very important part of my life. When I was 14, my father gave me a camera, and I became a very serious photographer. In the summer of 1941, between my junior and senior years at college, I had lived with migrants in the Central Valley. I moved with them. I stayed with them Monday through Friday, and on Friday

night, I would go home and work in the dark room. I was working for Dorothea Lange from the Farm Security Administration. Photography really became a very serious part of my life. After the war, I figured that the best way to save the world – and I still wanted to save the world – was probably as an economist, however. Dorothea's husband, Paul Taylor, was an economist at the University of California at Berkeley. They used to argue with each other in front of me as to whether I was to become a photographer or an economist. Paul won. When he did win, he said: 'Doug, you must promise that you won't take another photograph until you've made it as an economist.' And I did. For 25 years, I didn't take another photograph.

What did your parents think?
My father always wanted me to go into the Metropolitan Life Insurance Company and get rich and do all those things I had no interest in doing. Indeed, my Ph.D. dissertation was a muckraking attack on life insurance companies, something that my father wasn't enthusiastic about, to put it mildly. Actually, it wasn't a bad dissertation.

But your parents probably liked your becoming an economist better than the idea of a career as a photographer.
Oh yes. It seemed more respectable for a living. Being a photographer was not something my parents found very respectable.

So where did you go, once you had set your mind on becoming an economist?
I came back from the Merchant Marine in January 1946. When I applied to graduate school in economics, nobody would take me, given my C averages as an undergraduate. Everybody thought I would never be any good. But at Berkeley, where I had been as an undergraduate, they at least agreed to give me one semester, and if I became any good, I could stay on. So that's what I did. I enrolled in February 1946. At Berkeley, I got straight As and ended up with a Ph.D. And with the money I had won at poker in the Merchant Marine, I bought a ranch in Northern California.

What a luxury.
I bought it for 1600 dollars, and I lived there in the summers. It had 160 acres, a five-room log cabin, a blacksmith's shop, 180 walnut trees, and a vineyard. Taking care of that was actually a big job. To get to the ranch, you had to drive up on the highway 101 to Garberville, go over the top of the mountain and down on the other side, then you had to leave your car

at some village store, walk down to the river, canoe three miles upstream, hike up to the top of the mountain, and that's where my ranch was. It was a wonderful place. Of course, you had to be young for that. The ranch just had one small failure which I didn't know about at the time: It had a rattlesnake right under the house. I found that out the hard way. Anyway, I worked my butt off during all fall, winter and spring down at Berkeley doing my graduate work and then went up there during the summers, taking care of the ranch and reading the rest of the day. It was a great place. Eventually, all my fellow graduate students and teachers came up and visited me there. They were all jealous.

Who were your teachers?
I had three professors who influenced me at the time: Robert Brady, who was a cantankerous left-winger, but not a Marxist; Leo Rogin, who was really the intellectual, a very brilliant guy, all of us graduate students thought he was terrific; and Melvin M. ('M.M.') Knight, who was Frank Knight's[14] brother. M.M. Knight became my thesis adviser by a fluke. When I decided to write my thesis on life insurance, I went to the American economic historian Sanford Mosk, but he rejected me: 'North, you're never going to be any good'. I was still a radical, and I guess he didn't like that. And so I did my dissertation under M.M. Knight, and when I got elected the president of the Economic History Association a few years later, I sent Sanford Mosk an invitation to come.

What did you learn with M.M. Knight?
His brother, Frank Knight, was a very famous economist. He did have a big influence later in my life. M.M. Knight didn't believe in economic theory, but he knew an enormous amount. He was a very exciting person, but he didn't like theory. His economic history was story-telling through time. It was very good, endless story-telling. M.M. Knight told damn good stories. I'm still impressed. I learnt a lot from him – but not much theory. Obviously, there was a lot of implicit theory in it, even though he didn't think so. But there was.

He just didn't make it explicit.
Right. I finished my graduate work in the fall of 1950 and started to write my thesis. I went back to live in New York for this. That's where all the life insurance companies are, and so that's where I had to do my research, including at Metro Life – to which my father had strong objections, of course. That year was very useful and important because I got to know a lot of people who influenced me, such as the sociologist Robert Merton

from Columbia University, and Talcott Parsons, another sociologist at Harvard.

I guess that's when Joseph Schumpeter also left a decisive mark on you?
Yes. It happened because from New York, I went up there to Harvard and got very friendly with the whole entrepreneurial school of Arthur Cole at Harvard. All this was important. When I finally got my first job at the University of Washington in Seattle in the fall of 1950, I hadn't yet finished my dissertation. Then there was a guy who had arrived the same year, Don Gordon. He was a good economist, and we played chess every day from 12 to 2 p.m. I beat him at chess all the time, and he taught me economics. I knew so little economics that, when I graduated, I had just memorized all the right answers for the exams and reproduced them. I didn't know any economics, not even simple price theory.

So Don Gordon was a major influence in your intellectual development.
Yes. He had a very powerful influence on my life, because he really taught me economics. And that also was the last step in my getting rid of Marxism. As I re-learned theory, I became a very rigid neoclassical, Chicago type economist. Typically, there is nothing worse than when you have lost your way and you pick up the next thing. In my case, this made me a right-wing reactionary.

Oh, did it? And price theory was enough to turn you away from Marxism and into a right-wing reactionary? That's amazing.
I'm not sure I have a good answer to that. On the one hand, I found that Marxism was insufficient to answer a lot of mundane questions of economics, such as prices. On the other hand, the pressing issues that Marxism raises were still out there and couldn't be answered by standard economic theory.

What about the calculation debate? Friedrich August von Hayek's 'division of knowledge'?[15] The evolution of institutions?
You're ahead of me. That came later in my life. The reason is that in the meantime, this contradiction directed my research interests, and we launched the so-called cliometric revolution. Having become a confirmed, very rigorous neoclassical economist, I thought we should apply economic theory and quantitative methods to history. And so I did. Two of my students, Lance Davis and Jon Hughes, had gone to Purdue and created an annual meeting on cliometrics,[16] although this wasn't what we called it in those days. This revolutionized economic history. It took a while, of course, but I became a big cliometrician.

Your first book, The Economic Growth of the United States 1790 to 1860,[17] *is very much of a classic nowadays*
Yes. I also studied the sources of productivity change in ocean shipping 1600–1850.[18] All that gave me a reputation as a serious quantitative economic historian. But let's jump to where you want to sneak me up anyway. . .[19] In 1966, I had gone to Geneva, Switzerland, for a year as a Ford Faculty Fellow. And there, I decided to switch from American economic history, on which I had written several works, to European economic history. But that confronted me with a puzzle. You can write all American economic history using simple price theory. The US has always been a market economy to some extent, one which became more and more a market economy. So just using a simple theory of markets could tell the story of a lot of what had happened in the US alright. But Europe? How could you talk about feudalism and the manorial system with neoclassical theory? This is where I realized that we need to develop a better body of theory to confront the crucial issues. That's what got me into trying to figure out and understand institutions and all that jazz that I've been doing ever since.

Who did you interact with in Geneva? Where there any important influences?
No. I had a good time, but the Swiss were so cold. In fact, I never got invited even to the home of any Swiss fellow professor at the University of Geneva.

So if it wasn't conversations with fellow researchers, what else was it that brought about your shift in interest?
I just couldn't make sense out of history. The problem is that economic theory is static. It is not concerned with change over time. I've become convinced by this that you need a new theory that would concern itself with how economies evolve through time. And that didn't exist. So I began to bumble and bumble around. I'm a good bumbler. And I bumbled through quite a long time.

How did you manage to persuade people that this was a good avenue?
Oh, when I started, I was all alone. Nobody had an interest in this. They all thought it was crazy enough. I had a good reputation as a cliometrician. I had done good quantitative stuff. And so they said: 'North, you're crazy, you're throwing away a reputation to pursue this will-o'-the-wisp, you don't even know where you're going!' And that was true, I didn't know where I was going. I started out, I knew I had to concern myself with change through time. I had to concern myself with the vehicle for change,

that is, with institutions and the way they evolve. Then, later, I realized that institutions come out of beliefs, and so I had to try and understand how beliefs are formed, and that takes you to how minds and brains work. And that's been going on ever since.

That's the toughest question of all. But let's turn back to the question about your sources of inspiration. In Geneva, where your paradigm shift took place, if I may say so, you were pretty much alone. But you've also published a lot with co-authors. May I infer from this that you didn't produce all your ideas exclusively as a loner, from within, but some of them also through intellectual exchange? Did interaction matter?
Well, I guess. I'm sure I have learnt a lot from other people, but those influences are hard to specify. It is true that I have had co-authors, and I enjoy working with them. But in terms of where my ideas come from, I have been very much a loner. My driving force all my life has been that I was dissatisfied with the theory that we have to explain economic history and economic development. And I still am. I'm never satisfied with what I know.

So where did that take you in those days?
There were two different kinds of developments in my thinking. One was continuing on this path. The first book that I wrote that applied the idea was with Lance Davis, called *Institutional Change and American Economic Growth*.[20] Lance was a terrible person to work with. He was impossible, obstreperous, ornery and difficult. Anyway, the book caused a stir. That was part of what I was doing.

And what was the other part?
When I returned from Europe in 1961, I became chairman of the economics department at the University of Washington in Seattle. I decided that we should go back and see how we teach freshman economics. That freshman year had 800 students, it was a giant class. And I was doing standard economic theory, you know: neoclassical graphs, supply curves, demand elasticities and all this stuff. In about the sixth lecture I was giving, I was talking about agriculture and perfect competition. A black kid got up in the back of the room and yelled: 'That's a lot of bullshit'. So I said: 'Alright, come on up here and tell everybody why it's a lot of bullshit.' He did. He was very articulate. He became a good friend years later, but boy, at that moment, I wanted to slink off with my tail between my legs. . . He got up and pointed out that agriculture was not at all perfectly competitive because prices were programmed and all. I went home that night realizing that I had to think about how to deal with economics in a way so as to confront these issues. I was up all night drinking brandy, mostly.

I'm sure that was fruitful.

Oh yes! The next day, I got up before the class and said: 'I've just been an advisor of the Seattle City Council', which was true, 'on how much they should spend on preventing violence. What they said was they should spent 20 million dollars a year. What that means is that you're going to allow 28 murders. That's the same thing.' Well, that got me the class's attention. And that started me on something that is still in print today: *The Economics of Public Issues*.[21] It's now in the fifteenth edition, and it's produced 1.7 million copies. I wrote it together with a guy named Roger Miller, who was at the University of Washington at that time. The deal we had was that I would write all the articles in rough draft and he would polish them. I did a new one every day, for class. By the end of the semester, Roger took the manuscript to a publisher, but everybody said: 'This is not the way how you teach economics. You teach economics with supply curves and demand curves and all that stuff.' So nobody was interested. Finally, we did find a publisher, and with our book, he ran out of print within the first six weeks. And it's been growing ever since. This was a way to teach economics that was so much better than training people to learn a lot of abstract concepts. You just take a basic issue, you run with it and show how you can make sense out of some economic theory.

Don't you need both, abstract theory and practical applications?

Yes, but this is the way you should start teaching economics. You should try to get people interested, by showing that it has relevance and that the logic behind it makes sense to understand things that are really important. I stumbled on it by accident, the accident being that black kid making a fool out of me. It worked very well. And it changed my life. What I wanted then was an economics department that really was concerned with how you get people to understand things rather than just formal theory.

Why was that important to you?

I guess that's a hangover from my Marxist days. I wanted to save the world. I'm still trying to save the world. Not very successfully, you understand, but I'm still trying to save it.

Some people are more interested in the intellectual beauty of some exercise, rather than the practical relevance.

Not me. And indeed, I object violently to the way economics is still practiced today, including here in this department.[22] It is abstract high-level theory with formal mathematics. It's elegant, you can formalize it, and you can write mathematical equations. But it doesn't do anything. It doesn't solve problems. It's so far removed from the issues you're concerned with. Realizing this has started me on a track that I'm still on.

How did you react to the Keynesian revolution? Did it hit you at all?
The Keynesian revolution came on when I was a graduate student. After the war, Keynes was the big thing. I went through all that, I learnt Keynes. That was useful. Remember, I was a semi-Marxist. So I sort of liked Keynes, because that was at least a step in the right direction. He was concerned with unemployment and other real real-life problems rather than the kind of crap that I got and still get from some of my colleagues in economics all over the place.

But you didn't get caught up in the struggle between Chicago and the Keynesians?
Oh yes. After I became chairman of the economics department at the University of Washington in Seattle, the department was split right down in the middle between Chicagoans and non-Chicagoans. Since I was looked down on as being both a Chicagoan and anti-Chicago – both at the same time, which is a neat trick – I could talk to both sides. I never had a department meeting, because they would have killed each other. It was really violent. I can't believe how strongly people felt about theory. I was chairman for 12 years, and I turned us into one of the top 20 departments of economics in the United States. I did it by never ever having a department meeting. I made decisions myself, after consulting with both sides separately, trying to reconcile what we did. I did reasonably well. Of course, when I left in 1983 and they had another chairman, the department fell apart. But that's another matter.

I mentioned Friedrich August von Hayek earlier. Did he leave a mark on you?
Oh yes. While I was at University of Washington in Seattle, I was very flattered when I once got a note from Hayek saying that he would like to come and talk with me. He had read *The Rise of the Western World*,[23] and he thought it was a very interesting book. He came to Seattle and spent two days with me. We had a good time and I really enjoyed him. But I wish I had known then what I have learned since, so that I could have appreciated his visit more appropriately. I had never read his stuff on cognitive science in those days. He still seems to me the greatest economist of the twentieth century, and by a long way. If you look for people who really want to try and understand the world, Hayek came closer to that ideal than anybody who has ever lived.

Let's turn back to theory. What were your next steps?
My book *Structure and Change in Economic History*[24] is the best book I ever wrote. I wrote that in 1980. I'm very fond of it. I was starting to think out exactly what it was all about. I still hadn't gotten around much of the cognitive science stuff; that came much later. But I had realized that you had to learn political theory in order to see how institutions work. So I was moving away from economics and kind of spanned economics and politics and sociology, since you had to learn about norms. Writing this book forced me to think carefully and thoroughly about institutional change. I suspect this is why I got the Nobel Prize in 1993. By then, institutional economics was becoming a hot subject.

It was very timely, too, given the rise of the iron curtain which came about.
That's right. Anyway, in 1983, I left Seattle and came to St Louis. By that time, I was very interested in politics, in political theory and political economy. There was a very bright group of young professors here at the Washington University at St Louis. So I came here with the idea of creating a Center of Political Economy. Which I did.[25] That was a good move. I was forced again to think along new lines. Once you begin to ask yourself how you can mesh politics and economics, you have to start thinking all over again. The Center was a good way to embark on all that. Barry Weingast was here at the time, before he moved to the Business School and eventually went to Stanford. We have written the most cited article in political science together.[26] At any rate, after having moved here, I really got serious about cognitive science. With cognitive science, once again, I had to think anew about the things I already had. I helped create a PNP Program here: Philosophy, Neurosciences and Psychology. It still exists on this campus. I co-taught courses in cognitive science and economics. This moved me along the path which I have been on ever since, trying to find out how the mind and brain work, how beliefs are formed and why they shape the way in which institutions are created. In that context, I also worked a lot with Vernon Smith, by the way, who was in Arizona then, before he went to George Mason University. We were very close for quite a long time. Usually, I would bring problems, and then we would do experiments together. I learned a lot from him and his group. I nominated him for the Nobel Prize. Which he did get.[27]

What about the group of researchers within ISNIE, the International Society for the New Institutional Economics, which you helped to create as well, in 1997?
Oh yes. At that moment, Ronald Coase[28] had a big influence on me. He and I both got honorary degrees at the University of Cologne, Germany, in 1988. It was the first honorary degree I ever got. At the end of the ceremony,

each of us had to give a talk about what we were doing. And he gave a Coase theorem kind of talk. I gave a talk on how you could take Coasean theory and with transaction cost, you could revolutionize the way in which societies evolve through time by reducing transaction costs. Ronald came over and said: 'You know, I never thought about that'. He hadn't really taken his own ideas anywhere beyond their original scope. I had always thought that the Coase theorem was interesting – because it was wrong. The Coase theorem should have told you that human beings always attempt to solve interaction problems by maximizing the returns of the players. Of course, that's not the way economics works at all. But it should. If economic theory was about rational and calculating behavior, then it should. This is precisely what has always been the focus of my attention, that is, the question why it doesn't. This gets you into belief systems and how they are incompatible with each other. Anyway, in 1997, Lee Benham, my colleague here at the Washington University at St Louis, said: 'We should create a new organization'. So he called the first meeting, and Ronald and I joined forces. He was the first president of ISNIE, I was second. Ever since, ISNIE has gone great guns. That was a big success. I'm not sure everything they do is very interesting. But that's because all organizations, when you form them, start out being revolutionary, but end up being very conservative. I'm still a revolutionary. I'm still trying to figure out how to make sense of the world. I'm not going to get much further in my life, but I've got fun trying to get there.

And now? What are you up to?
Today, I'm still going. I got an offer from George Mason University last year. Vernon Smith had just left. All the rest of his group were still there. I was very much tempted to go. But they wanted me to completely restructure and reorganize the whole affair. But then I thought, at 87, I shouldn't do that any more. So I eventually turned down the offer. Now, I have a new book coming out with Barry Weingast from Stanford and John Wallis, a former student of mine, now teaching at the University of Maryland: *A Conceptual Framework for Interpreting Recorded Human History.*[29] How do you like that for a modest title? That's a really revolutionary book, carrying all those different elements forward, trying to integrate everything into a whole new framework for thinking about how economies and societies work. It is not just economics. It is political theory, social theory, economic theory and cognitive science. We've just finished writing it.

One final statement, perhaps, summing up: what is economics, Professor North?
Economics is a very narrow field that, by itself, I don't think is very interesting. It asks how people, given some utility function, can always improve

their lot. That's not very interesting. It's only a little tiny piece of the action. The real action gets you to worry about social norms, how belief systems work etc. It gets you into a complex world.

We might call it social interaction theory, perhaps. Thank you, Professor.

NOTES

1. See the Autobiography by Douglass C. North at the Nobel website, www.nobel.se.
2. This interview was held on 25 March, 2008.
3. See www.nobel.se.
4. Douglass C. North (1961).
5. This work had already led to another, preliminary paper, namely Douglass C. North (1960).
6. Douglass C. North (1968).
7. Lance E. Davis and Douglass C. North (1971).
8. Douglass C. North and Robert P. Thomas (1973).
9. Douglass C. North (1981).
10. Douglass C. North (1990).
11. The phenomenon of path dependence was first described by Paul A. David (1985).
12. In 1929, the Great Depression broke out, and the Cuban economy, concentrated on sugar production, suffered the immediate consequences of the worldwide breakdown of demand. Buying in those days meant not being able to resell afterwards.
13. From 1941 to 1945, forty convoys, with a total of more than 800 ships, including 350 under the US flag, started on the Murmansk run. Ninety-seven of those ships were sunk by bombs, torpedoes, mines and the elements. They carried more than 22 000 aircraft, 375 000 trucks, 8700 tractors, 51 500 jeeps, 1900 locomotives, 343 700 tons of explosives and other equipment.
14. Frank Knight (1885–1972) was an influential American economist. Jointly with Jacob Viner, he presided over the Department of Economics at the University of Chicago from the 1920s to the late 1940s.
15. See, in particular, Friedrich August von Hayek (1945). Hayek was awarded the Nobel Prize in 1974, together with Gunnar Myrdal – both received it 'for their pioneering work in the theory of money and economic fluctuations and for their penetrating analysis of the interdependence of economic, social and institutional phenomena'.
16. 'Cliometrics' is a term created after Clio, the Greek muse of history.
17. Douglass C. North (1961).
18. Douglass C. North (1968).
19. Douglass C. North refers to the interviewer's intention to find out how his interest in institutions came about.
20. Lance E. Davis and Douglass C. North (1971).
21. Roger LeRoy Miller and Douglass C. North (1971). There is also a more recent new edition, co-authored now by Daniel K. Benjamin (Roger LeRoy Miller et al. 2007).
22. Douglass C. North is referring to the economics department at the Washington University of St Louis.
23. Douglass C. North and Robert P. Thomas (1973).
24. Douglass C. North (1981).
25. The Center is still operating. Douglass C. North served as director from 1984 to 1990.
26. Douglass C. North and Barry R. Weingast (1989).

27. Vernon Smith was awarded the Nobel Prize in 2002, together with Daniel Kahnemann, 'for having established laboratory experiments as a tool in empirical economic analysis, especially in the study of alternative market mechanisms'.
28. Ronald Coase was awarded the Nobel Prize in 1991 'for his discovery and clarification of the significance of transaction costs and property rights for the institutional structure and functioning of the economy'. He is famous, among other things, for what George Stigler has labeled the 'Coase theorem'. This theorem, the name of which has stuck, states that when trade in an externality (such as water pollution) is possible and there are no transaction costs, negotiations will lead to an efficient outcome, regardless of the initial allocation of property rights: if the upstream farmer is initially endowed with the right to pollute, then the downstream farmer can pay him to stop polluting, or if the downstream farmer owns a right to clear water, then the upstream farmer can compensate him and thereby buy off his right. In his academic papers, Coase often proceeds in counterintuitive ways – and in this case, the reverse side of the coin is of course that since negotiations are never free of friction and effort, that is since transaction costs are not zero, the initial allocation of property rights does matter (Ronald H. Coase, 1960).
29. There already exists a NBER working paper on that topic by the three authors: Douglass C. North et al. (2006).

Reinhard Selten

Universität Bonn, Germany

The Sveriges Riksbank Prize in Economic Sciences in Memory of Alfred Nobel 1994 shared with John Harsanyi and John Nash, all three 'for their pioneering analysis of equilibria in the theory of non-cooperative games'.

INTRODUCTION

It's not trivial to find Reinhard Selten's office at the University of Bonn – but at least it's easier than finding one's way to his laboratory in experimental economics, hidden somewhere deep down in the basement. The 'Juridicum' – the law and economics building – is not only run-down and chaotic, notwithstanding its square shape, it also has a pretty complicated layout. Selten's office itself is simple and functional, free of any traces of modernity. All the heavy computer equipment is downstairs in the lab, not here. Selten speaks with a soft, almost feeble voice, as if he doubts that anybody could truly be interested in his personal story. Most of the time, his sentences end with the formula 'isn't it', asking for confirmation. While fully aware of the value of his own contributions, the first and only German Nobel Laureate in economics remains an extremely humble, polite and gentle character. He is more at ease talking about theory than about himself, but as time goes by and as the conversation moves forward, he opens up a little. But research is his addiction.[1] And so his talk easily veers toward the abstract and then gets carried away – and that's true also for his lectures. As generations of students have witnessed, his demanding lectures prove his genius as much as his unorthodox, complicated ways. In the classroom, he is famous for his highly complex transparencies, for example: they are usually handwritten, Selten's uneven letters densely covering all available space, using up to four different colors indicating four different levels of meaning. Selten is truly the quintessential professor, outwardly a little bit disorganized, but inwardly extremely rigorous in his thinking. Vernon Smith, Nobel Laureate of 2002, another pioneer in experimental economics, characterizes him as 'a wonderful man with an intense curiosity'.[2]

Reinhard Selten's biography is an extremely moving one, as the following conversation will show. Given the circumstances, Selten's career has been a most unlikely one. Born in 1930 in Breslau, a then German city that is now part of Poland, Reinhard Selten suffered the consequences of his half-Jewish origins. His Jewish father, who had run reading circles as a very successful business, had to sell his operations under Nazi law, and passed away in 1942. The children were forced out of school as early as at age 14 – so that their education was far from what it could, and should, have been. Very quickly, however, Reinhard Selten developed a keen interest in mathematics. Everything the gifted child learnt at that age, however, was necessarily self-taught. When he was 15, the war came to an end, and together with his mother and siblings, he fled the approaching Soviet army. The family sought refuge first in Saxony, then in Austria and finally in West Germany, in Hessia. Life continued to be difficult even then, being characterized mainly by bitter poverty, hard physical work on a farm, and other odd jobs – but ultimately, after two years out of school, Reinhard Selten was able to continue with his education. As he likes to point out, he had to walk to and from school more than three hours every day, which gave him not only enough time to solve plenty of mathematical puzzles in his mind, but which also taught him to enjoy nature. After graduating from high school in 1951, however, Selten moved on to the city of Frankfurt where he studied mathematics and also explored other disciplines such as economics and psychology. He was the first student who was allowed to take his mathematics diploma with a minor not from the natural sciences: he chose mathematical economics. He specialized in experimental economics, exploring the limits of rationality, and in game theory. After his master's degree in 1957, Selten got a job as a research assistant, doing essentially experimental research on behalf of the German Science Foundation (Deutsche Forschungsgemeinschaft, DFG).[3] Selten received his Ph.D., still in mathematics, in 1961.[4] Coincidentally, he was introduced to Oskar Morgenstern in Frankfurt, whose major work he had already studied on his own. Morgenstern arranged for him to come to Princeton, USA, for a conference. This is where he met John Harsanyi, who would be his partner in research on bargaining under incomplete information, his co-author and his Nobel co-laureate later on. In 1965, he took part in a legendary three-week-long international workshop on game theory in Jerusalem, reuniting all the emerging first-class researchers in game theory. From 1967 to 1968, Selten then was a visiting researcher at the University of California at Berkeley, California. Clearly preferring Germany for living, he came back from overseas, completed his 'habilitation' dissertation required for obtaining tenure, in Germany in 1968,[5] and accepted a professorship at the Freie Universität Berlin in 1969. Selten stayed there throughout the really 'hot years' of student revolts, until the year 1972, when he moved on to the more peaceful, provincial Universität Bielefeld. In 1984, he left for the Universität Bonn where he found better conditions for creating the – now rather famous – laboratory: the Laboratorium für experimentelle Wirtschaftsforschung. Since his retirement in 1997, he has remained the academic coordinator of this laboratory. Reinhard Selten is a member of the Ordre pour le mérite. He has a pronounced passion for hiking, for plants, for cats, and for the artificial language Esperanto.

Reinhard Selten is a pioneer both in game theory and in experimental economics. Game theory is a mathematical field dedicated to the analysis of interactions between individuals, taking into account that individual decisions are interdependent. Unfortunately, the name 'game theory' gives a somewhat non-serious flavor to this field, which essentially deals with strategic interaction – which makes it relevant for highly serious and relevant questions ranging as widely as from military conflict,[6] including nuclear deterrence, to price-setting behavior in oligopolistic markets, which is one of the areas that initially attracted Selten. The earliest work in this context was done by Auguste Cournot in 1838.[7] The first major work in modern game theory, however, applied to economics, was John von Neumann and Oskar Morgenstern's 1944 book *Theory of Games and Economic Behaviour*,[8] distinguishing between coalitional games between three or more agents and zero-sum two-person games. Selten had read this book during his first years at Frankfurt University. Given that cooperative games crucially rely on agreements that must be enforced some way, the next step in the development of this field then logically had to be the analysis of the more general class of non-cooperative games, combining both possibilities of cooperation and competition. In a seemingly paradoxical sense, cooperative games now came to be viewed as a sub-class of non-cooperative games. The next concept that came up was the idea of a non-cooperative finite game without any communication between the players, introduced by John Nash, Selten's highly controversial co-laureate.[9] Nash identified and formalized the set of optimal strategies for all parties as an equilibrium situation. In his honor, this set of strategies that nobody has an interest to move away from unilaterally, is named 'Nash equilibrium'. Subsequently, Reinhard Selten entered the scene to refine the Nash equilibrium concept for analyzing dynamic strategic interaction, focusing on the stability and robustness of the equilibrium. This greatly increased the relevance of the concept for economic policy, thereby opening up also a whole new branch of worthwhile academic research. Selten distinguished between games in 'extensive' or 'normal' form. In the normal form, players choose their strategies simultaneously, knowing about the strategies of others. In the extensive form, however, that is in a succession of moves, the situation is quite different. Here, one must distinguish between different stages of a game and pay attention to the timing of individual moves as much as to the information that is available at each stage. The question about the stability of such equilibrium is then multiplied and logically becomes a question about the stability of the strategic equilibria at each individual stage – that is the subgames – of the game. This procedure allows ruling out 'irrelevant' equilibria, that is equilibria based on empty threats. This is crucial if a general rationality assumption is made. The Nash equilibrium at each stage then is the 'subgame perfect equilibrium' – and this is precisely the concept and term that Reinhard Selten has coined in his two 1965 papers on an oligopoly model with demand inertia,[10] both of which are in German. Selten produced another paper in 1975, this time in English, further refining the criteria for a stable Nash equilibrium. Here, he introduced the concept of 'trembling-hand' perfectness – a concept which allows for small strategical mistakes (a 'trembling hand') without causing the equilibrium to break down.[11]

In later years, Reinhard Selten has concentrated more and more on experimental economics, thereby picking up a center of interest that he had since his beginnings and tackling the rationality premise that he himself had been using in his own subgame perfect equilibrium concept. Accordingly, Selten calls himself a 'methodological dualist'. The field of experimental economics aims at finding out how people behave, going beyond the traditional neoclassical model that uses perfect rationality as a heuristic device. In the Bonn laboratory, Selten tries to develop a host of descriptive theories showing how – boundedly rational – people behave and decide in oligopoly markets, auctions or bargaining situations. As he says in his Nobel Autobiography, it is his 'goal to help to build up a descriptive branch of decision and game theory which takes the limited rationality of human behavior seriously'.[12]

When it comes to the fundamental question directing this book, namely through which interacting channels it is that outstanding scholars receive their inspiration, Reinhard Selten is another case of his own. His personal background is one that made an intellectual career exceedingly difficult and quite implausible – but fortunately, that could not deter him. And in that sense, his personal background may, in a negative sense, have been absolutely crucial. Not only has Selten inherited from his father the stubbornness to go ahead in what he deems a good avenue, against all odds. As he himself points out in the interview, his difficult background may have shaped his character, teaching him to be rebellious.

> More than anything else, the effect was that I have always mistrusted majority opinion. I have always had to think independently. That was true for politics in those days, and I also applied that insight to my research later on. Actually, I've never been swimming with the crowd. Game theory has become the mainstream later on, but when I started out with it, it was but a tiny streamlet.

Once he was set on his off-mainstream track, Selten's further research agenda then seems to have evolved according to the advances made in his field generally. A self-propelling process was then set in motion, as closer logical scrutiny showed that new concepts needed more and more refinement. As a rule, it is probably fair to say that those challenges endogenous to theory tend to become more and more detailed over time – or else, quite to the contrary, there is a flip-back to much more fundamental, overarching challenges, for example drawing the entire approach into question. Selten experienced and worked his way through both, coming up with more and more refinements of the Nash equilibrium on the one hand and turning to the new field of experimental economics on the other hand in order to overthrow and supplant the traditional rationality hypothesis. Both these lines are theory-endogenous, however. None of them is triggered directly by any confrontation with current economic policy or the economic situation in general. Reinhard Selten is the quintessential scientist. Research can be not only a vocation, but an addiction, too – and at any rate the only thinkable way to spend one's life.

INTERVIEW

Professor Selten, I would like to find out what it was that originally raised your interest in the questions which later became your field of research. So please let me ask – what was it that led you first towards mathematics and then later on to game theory and experimental economics? To what extent has your childhood and upbringing left a mark here? How has your way of thinking evolved? I suppose my intellectual evolution began at high school. As soon as mathematics was taught at school, I noticed that I seemed to have a talent for it. From age 15 onward, I self-taught myself mathematics.[13] I always had my nose in some kinds of calculations. And later, of course, I studied mathematics. But the math that was taught at university was completely different from the one I knew from school. At any rate, I was well aware from the beginning that I wasn't going to stick with mathematics. However, the fact that I'm today doing what I'm doing has been brought about to some extent by the outer circumstances and coincidences of life. My interests have always been pretty wide, and so it would have been just as natural for me to get hooked by something else than economics.

Was mathematical talent a widespread feature in the Selten family?
No.

So you were different, so to speak
I don't know. You see, there are people who do actually have a talent, but they never grow aware of it because they don't even get in touch with the things that they have a talent for. And apart from that, talent is something that can be passed on from one generation to the next only to a very limited degree, even though some genetic core can probably not be denied.

And what about academic antecedents in your family? George Akerlof, for example, told me that he just couldn't imagine anything but an academic career, given that he didn't simply know anything else from home.
That's not my case. Not at all. My mother had only been to a commercial high school, and the emphasis there was on commerce. My father only had three years of schooling anyway. He was blind, and so he had to go to a school for the blind for three years. All blind people had to learn the trade either of a basket maker or of a broom maker. And that was all the education he got. My grandparents had not received any academic training either. My father's father was in the realty business. My mother's father was a grade school teacher. In those days, you didn't have to go to university in order to become a grade school instructor. In those days, elementary school teachers were educated in a 'teachers' education institute' which offered a specialized high school and college curriculum. Anyway, only a tiny percentage of the German population – less than 1 percent – received a high school education before World War II, and out of that 1 percent, only very few went on to university. Life was very different in those days. It was pure luck that my life finally took an academic turn. I would perhaps have dreamed of something like that, but it was utterly impossible to pursue it actively.

Your father wasn't an academic, alright, but he was brilliant in other ways: he started a very successful business. He had an ingenious idea: the reading circle.
In those days, the reading circle was totally different from what we know today. Today, we're of course still familiar with the reading circle – think of the magazines that you find in the doctor's waiting room or at the hairdresser's. But in those days, many private households had subscribed to a reading circle. An assortment of magazines was lent for one week, recollected and lent out again. My father, by the way, wasn't the first to come up with that idea. There already existed a reading circle in Berlin when he started his business in Breslau and other medium sized cities in Silesia. There were subsidiaries in Gleiwitz and Liegnitz.

He managed to do that in spite of his handicap?
Yes. His first wife had helped him create the business. At first, they did everything by themselves. Then the business grew, and my father hired employees. Many people were needed – in order to deliver the magazines, to acquire new clients, and to work at the office. Specifically, you always had to erase the crossword puzzle that people had filled in. Those magazines were used 10 to 20 times. The newer, the higher was the lending fee.

Did you ever have to help out in the business? Erasing the crosswords, perhaps?
No, I was still too little for that. My father had to give up his business in Breslau as early as 1934. We then moved to Gleiwitz, given that he could keep his subsidiary there for a while. Minorities were protected there, due to a contract with the League of Nations. Actually, that contract was meant to provide special protection for the German minority in Poland and the Polish minority in Germany, but the formulation of the text was such that Jews benefited as well. For this reason, they couldn't take away my father's business in Gleiwitz at first. Later, of course, he was forced to sell it too. After all, his business had to do with the German Reich press. And that was just inconceivable.

How did your family manage to subsist?
Well, since my father was forced to sell his business, he had some money. We just had to live off our bank accounts.

Those were left untouched? They didn't take your financial capital away?
No. My father still had sold his business in an absolutely regular way, and so he could keep the proceeds. Had we emigrated, however – and we did have such ideas indeed – he would have lost half his fortune due to the

'Reichsfluchtsteuer'.[14] Furthermore, if you went to Switzerland in those days, you weren't allowed to accept a job there. That means that if you really wanted to go away, you had better be very wealthy. In that respect, the choice was very difficult.

Was there an open debate about emigration in your family? How concrete was the idea?
Nobody discussed this with me, of course. I was too young. But my father and my mother obviously had spoken about this. My father had transferred his fortune to my mother, given that she wasn't Jewish. I even remember overhearing some exchanges about that. She didn't want this, but he explained that it was necessary, since otherwise, the money would be lost.

What bitter times.
It was relatively bearable, after all, given that my parents had what was called a 'privileged mixed marriage'. Which doesn't mean it was free of disadvantages, but it was bearable. The scary thing was just that everything went downhill. Politics always managed to come up with yet something else that would make the situation worse for us. After the war, the situation was bad, too, but at least, the tendency was upwards.

May I infer from this that your conversation with your parents and siblings at home turned more around politics than around economics?
Well, not much either, because politics was dangerous. Especially when talking with children, adults had to be careful and not say too much, so that the kids wouldn't repeat anything critical in public. I knew what the matter was with us, though. And the older I grew, the more I was made part of those conversations. But in the end, I was only a child.

How much did you have to suffer the disadvantages of your situation at school, or in public life?
The situation at school was critical. On one occasion, I was being threatened in a rather scary way, during a couple of days, because I was half Jewish and said so. That was really difficult. It cooled down, however. I went to a private high school. When I started there, they made me skip the first year right away. So I joined an already existing class, not a newly constituted class.

Also in terms of the subjects, that must have been quite a challenge.
Well, at home, I had been taken care of by a very good governess. She was Jewish and had no other professional opportunities. She lived in our house. She made sure that we did our homework rapidly. When she wasn't

there any more, I used to sit there all afternoon and doze. With her, everything was efficient. She also even taught us English long before I was admitted to high school.

How shall I picture the Selten household, from a material point of view? If you had a tutor living with the family, that seems rather well-to-do.
Yes, but it was not a bourgeois household. In those earlier days, most academics came from families with a very good financial background. But in our case, our wealth didn't go that far. Yes, we employed people in the household, but a proper governess would normally have been beyond our means. In the case of this lady, things were different; she had found refuge in our family. When asked about my father's profession, by the way, I always say that he was a bookseller. That was indeed his title officially. But he was a little more than that. He was a bookseller who had some 20 employees.

He was a true entrepreneur, and a successful one, it seems to me.
Yes. Once the war had broken out, however, everything became worse and worse. We had to move several times. Whenever somebody who was affiliated with the Party happened to like our apartment, we had to move out. Every time we had to move, the new apartment was worse than the old one. Our last apartment was in a street where they had concentrated Jewish families.

Did your father have to experience all that?
No, not up to the very end. He died in 1942, from a serious illness. Between my parents, there was an age difference of 22 years.

How did you continue with your education?
At age 14, mandatory schooling was over for half-Jewish children. Which means that as the summer holidays began, I had to leave school. At first, I just spent my days helping out at home. It was difficult to find anything. The only career open to me was that of an unskilled worker. I was denied the right to learn a real profession. Then we got in touch with this man who lived in our house and traded in petroleum. He wanted to have me join his business – not officially, of course, and not as a real apprentice, but he did want to teach me something. He wanted to help us. This was supposed to happen in February 1945. But at that time, we weren't there any more.

You escaped the Russians.
Originally, my mother wanted to stay. For us, after all, it was a good thing that Germany lost the war. It was like a ray of light. But then my mother

realized that more and more German soldiers came to Breslau, and the City was declared a fortress. She inferred that heavy and long fighting would take place there. That's in fact what eventually happened. And so we went away.

Were you officially 'allowed' to leave at that point?
When everybody started to escape, we could hide our 'special' status rather easily. Many people on the run had no papers at all, and nobody asked for any. Everything was dissolving. We managed to catch one of the last outgoing trains. That was not evident. People had been urged to leave the city on foot. But we somehow managed.

What was your destination?
Oh well, one didn't really have a destination. One traveled wherever the train would go. At first, we didn't even know where our train was heading. Then we heard it was going to Dresden. We had been on board this train for three days. My mother didn't like the idea of another big city, and so we got off at Bautzen. We found accommodation in a village nearby. We could see Dresden going up in flames. It had been a very wise decision to get off the train at Bautzen.

That was already the second wise decision that your mother made.
Yes, but we couldn't stay there, the front came closer and closer. So we climbed on yet another train and were on the rails again for three or four days. And finally, we were in Austria.

But you didn't want to stay there either. Or couldn't you?
The area was under Russian occupation. But more fundamentally, we really wanted to go to Germany. The people we were staying with in Austria helped us, and it's clear enough that they also wanted to get rid of us. At the border, some Austrians smuggled us back to Germany on illegal footpaths. At that time, the Americans didn't let anybody enter their occupation zone any more.

But you didn't have family in the West?
Yes we did. My father's sister, my aunt, lived in Frankfurt. She had always managed to successfully conceal her Jewish origins. With the help of the Catholic Church, she had been baptized. Beyond that, it was her tactics to always talk in a way that nobody would take her seriously. She behaved as if she wasn't fully in her mind. It was rather odd. But she was very clever, and she made it. However, we didn't manage to get to Frankfurt.

Why?

Because they lost me at the Wuerzburg train station. In those days, the stops would be really long. We still had a couple of food ration cards, and I wanted to use them and just briefly ventured out to buy some bread rolls. When I was back on the platform, the train was gone. So I continued on to Frankfurt on my own. The rest of the family had gotten off their train in Kassel. My brother then came looking for me, and he eventually found me in some waiting room.

Oh my goodness.

We then all traveled together to a Hessian village near Kassel, not far from Melsungen. It was always the same thing: the refugees would arrive, the mayor would allocate them to different homes, and the families were not really happy. It had been like that in Bautzen, too. Now we shared only one room. At some point, the mayor saw to it that we got a little more space and better accommodation.

When did you get back to school?

Not immediately. In Austria, I had already been working in agriculture, and here I had to do it again. School only began in the spring of 1946. At that point, I had been out of school for two years. For this reason, my mother decided to enroll me at a level at which I had already been before, and so I lost another year. But two years out of school – that means that you forget everything. I had lost all my Latin, for example. I was really frightened.

Didn't you feel that going back to school amounted to some kind of inner liberation nonetheless, because things took off again?

Of course. My activities as a farmer – or rather as a farmer's help – had been tough. I was a pure city child; I wasn't really suited to these kinds of things. Accordingly, I didn't have much prestige (*laughter*).

Were you able to make some valuable experiences nevertheless? Did that period teach you something you wouldn't want to miss now, looking back?

My period in agriculture did provide me with some insights and more understanding. In Austria, for example, those farm people lived under really primitive conditions. Everybody ate from the same bowl. The farmer himself actually wasn't really poor, he owned a lot of land, and the family had plenty of food. That was important in those days. I was paid in foodstuffs. In Germany, in our village, conditions were not as primitive. The farms were smaller, and the farmers lived better.

But let me ask again – did this period shape you in some way? Was there something about it that has proved useful in the meantime? Discipline, or getting up early, perhaps, I don't know?
No. The only thing that happened was that I lived the life of another era for a while, especially in Austria. It was as if you went back a century. It was visual instruction. Afterwards, I found it easier to imagine how people live in underdeveloped countries. I was able to better understand life and to be more aware of the advantages of civilization. The worst part was lice and fleas. You even get used to that. But I found the whole thing rather unpleasant.

At least, there was no threat to your life, right?
Well, I got sick, I suffered from scabies. But well. It sure was interesting. And over time, I almost had gotten used to my life as a farmer's help. But then, things didn't stay the way they were.

And school finally started. Did you run across teachers who recognized your talent and helped you develop it?
Not really. Of course, as soon as my mathematical talent began to show, I found some support. But I was always rebellious, always contradicting everybody. Especially in our German class.

Why? Can you explain?
Psychologically speaking, it seems that one's position it the sequence of siblings does account for something. My brother is three years older than I am, and he always told me how stupid I was. Of course I knew less than he did. By the way, psychological studies show that those academic researchers who are number two children or even farther down the line tend to be more rebellious than those who were a first-born or only child. These tend to be pretty conservative, not only in their political persuasions, but even in their academic orientation. Dissidents can be found more frequently in the group of number two children. Younger siblings just don't swallow so easily what the older ones tell them. So that's one element. The other element may have been our political outsider position.

Was there some kind of public discourse about the latter, once the war was over?
Little. Mind you, National Socialism and anti-Semitism weren't over once the war had come to an end. All these things still existed in the population, and be it only latently. And so, our 'special status' didn't vanish from one day to the other. Today, that's over, finally, but in those days, no.

How come the village knew these things about you?
I never remained silent on our origins.

The bitter experiences that you had to endure probably also account for your rebelliousness.
More than anything else, the effect was that I have always mistrusted majority opinion. I have always had to think independently. That was true for politics in those days, and I also applied that insight to my research later on. Actually, I've never been swimming with the crowd. Game theory has become the mainstream later on, but when I started out with it, it was but a tiny streamlet.

And how was life in your Hessian village?
Well, as refugees, we were of course in an uncomfortable position. My mother had to rely on welfare benefits for many years. As time went by, the situation did somewhat improve. I gave many private lessons in order to expand our budget a little. Then, one year before graduating from high school, I was hired at a subsidiary of the America House. It was sort of a book lending outlet, almost a library. While still going to school, I had a full-time job there, eight hours a day. I just did my homework there. The library was open even on Saturdays and Sundays. It brought me in contact with many interesting books, for example with a textbook on the history of ideas in economics. And there was the *Fortune* magazine. In one of the copies, I found an article that confronted me with game theory for the first time, in popular prose. That job was pure bliss for me, for in those days, it wasn't so easy to get hold of books and magazines. The learning conditions were not what they are today.

By then, it was clear to you that you'd finish high school, I suppose.
Yes.

And how about university? Didn't you face financial problems? Conceivably, it might have been more important to earn real money immediately, rather than investing more years in education.
Well, yes, there were financial problems. But the situation improved. My father had owned stocks before the war. After the war, there was no stock trading going on, there was no stock exchange. But all that came back after the currency reform in 1948. Monetary assets were devalued drastically, down to approximately 6.5 percent. But that wasn't the case with stocks. We had owned many shares that were now irretrievably lost, such as shares in the capital of some industrial plants in Silesia. But we also had some stocks from the West. And out of those, we got dividends.

It wasn't much, but the value of the shares also increased over time. And then, sometime in the fifties, my mother also received some transfers in the context of the official reparation schemes. And then, ultimately, we even got money out of the German burden equalization scheme.[15] So the situation was bearable, if not very good. As a student, I also had different jobs. I lived on 150 marks a month, rent and fare included. That wasn't much. Most students had a lot more. But I managed.

Were you a lodger?
Yes. For a long time, I shared a room with someone. He was a policeman. It was a rather small room, and cheap. It cost 15, 20 marks. When the landlady wanted to make me pay 25 marks, I moved out. I could get something better for 25 marks.

At the beginning, you studied mathematics.
Yes. If you were looking for an applied field, something where you could put mathematics to practical use, in those days you would usually think of physics. There was almost nothing else. But I always observed the announcements in economics, and went to some lectures. That's how I found my teacher, Ewald Burger. He also gave a course in mathematics for economists. Once he even came up with a seminar in game theory for economists. I knew what that was; I had read the fundamental work by von Neumann and Morgenstern.[16] So I participated, even if the seminar wasn't for mathematicians. Apparently, I impressed him, and so he suggested I write my master's thesis with him, in that field of game theory. I already had passed my 'Vordiplom', my intermediate exams. By the way, those Vordiplom exams in math were awfully difficult. I worked very hard, day and night, for three months. Never in my life have I had to pass any exam as difficult as this one. Only my driver's license test came second.

What was so difficult about it? Or did you simply put yourself under too much pressure?
Two fellow students, both very gifted and successful, had told me I was going to fail. And I took that very seriously. In those days, German university was organized in such a way that you just never knew precisely where you stood, whether you were good or bad. Today, the students have to take tests all the time – but not in those days. The only thing that was mandatory was the oral exams for the 'Vordiplom'. There was the possibility to take tests before that, but I never managed to do that.

And then you had to face the truth.
I passed my exams relatively well. I wasn't bad.

By then, did it occur to you that you should aim at an academic career?
Oh no, I couldn't expect to have an academic career. As a student you
cannot yet envisage such a thing. One idea that I had was that I might
become a science reporter. But I have no aptitude for journalism, as I
realized early enough, fortunately. Anyhow, during my studies and also at
school I delved into things that were none of my business, that is, not relevant for the exams. At university I took some courses in psychology, which
is something that had strictly nothing to do with my curriculum. I did all
kinds of things in which I didn't have to take exams. That's probably the
reason why it took me longer to graduate than the average student.

*Do you think you wouldn't have been satisfied with mathematics in the long
run?*
I wouldn't say that. Mathematics was the field in which I had been especially good at school. But that was the school level, of course. All those
who are outstanding at school then come together at university. And all of
a sudden, you are no longer all that good in comparison to the others. But
I did want to get through it.

*But what about the subject? After all mathematics is only a logical instru-
ment. Weren't you unhappy with this instrumentality?*
Yes, a little more connection with society, that's something I would have
liked. I read the newspapers assiduously and have always been interested
in politics. The natural sciences could also have tempted me, astronomy
for example. But in those days, there was practically only astrophysics.
And physics was something I had great difficulties with.

*Astrophysics is certainly an exciting field, but it doesn't have so much to do
with people.*
Yes, it doesn't have much to do with people. And I was more attracted by
social questions. Economics is good for that. Psychology would have been
good, too. There were other subjects as well. But I continued with mathematics, and even wrote my doctoral thesis in that field. But at that time I
was already enrolled in the economics department. When I was working
on my master's thesis, I had produced more than it could contain. And so
my teacher said: 'So much will go into the master's thesis; we will keep the
rest for the doctoral dissertation.' The dissertation then somehow went
much faster than the master's thesis.

How influential was Heinz Sauermann,[17] your doctoral adviser?
Sauermann was well-known in Germany, but not really internationally.
He did write some textbooks. And after the war he was one of those who

introduced Keynesianism in Germany and made it popular. His own contributions have remained relatively unknown. But there are some things that are known, for example two papers that we wrote together.[18] In some ways they are fundamental. His views on economic theory have influenced me, especially in macroeconomics, even though sometimes you don't realize you're taking something in that is going to guide you in a certain direction. Sauermann had a very good feeling for the future of economics. He always showed us the right way. He himself didn't have enough knowledge of mathematics to use all the new things in his own work. But he knew what was coming, and that he should set his people to work on that.

Those were the days when the Keynesian theory was being formalized, especially in the US. In that sense, with Sauermann, you were indeed in the front row of science.
Yes. Sauermann was committed to that. He promoted mathematization, while most economists in Germany watched this development with a great deal of skepticism. In those days, some economics professor told me: 'Mathematics brought into economics – that doesn't have a future at all' (*laughter*). Many German economics professors shared this opinion.

Time has proven them wrong. Today, the economic mainstream is extremely mathematical.
That's true, but we really had to fight tough battles for this mathematization. In those days, we were clearly in the role of the dissidents. It wasn't easy to get mathematical economics accepted.

Throughout your academic career, you've always placed yourself in such a dissident's position, falling out of the mainstream first with game theory and then also with experimental economics.
Yes. For a pretty long time, game theory wasn't especially salient even within mathematical economics. The common belief was that this field wasn't ever going to take off. With experiments, it was pretty much the same. I began working on it very early and became a pioneer. In this case even more than before, people laughed at me and didn't take me seriously. But I don't mind. Very early in my career, I had studied Herbert Simon's work on bounded rationality.[19] Sauermann and I then jointly wrote a paper on that.[20] We also touched upon that topic in our joint paper on experiments.[21] The idea of bounded rationality is something I never lost sight of. This is something I've worked on a lot – almost as much as on game theory, albeit with less success. It's just more difficult.

Apart from that, it's probably also not easy when you're more or less all alone in your field. It's of course extremely honourable to be a pioneer but hard. And lonely.

In this case, the point was not just the math, but rather that a new theoretical concept was needed. Incidentally, I was awarded the Nobel Prize for my work in game theory precisely for having developed something conceptual;[22] not for the mathematics underlying it. I wouldn't have expected to receive the Prize, by the way. Ken Binmore once said that in game theory, five people would qualify for the Nobel Prize, namely Robert Aumann,[23] Lloyd Shapley,[24] John Nash,[25] John Harsanyi,[26] and Reinhard Selten. Given this group, my personal forecast would have been Aumann and Shapley. Aumann has indeed been awarded the Nobel Prize in the meantime, but Shapley still hasn't. This is strange in a way, given that he really was the leading game theorist. It seems, however, that the members of the Nobel Committee looked out for the theoretical development that had the most repercussions in economic science. And those indeed were not the cooperative games, which were predominant in the sixties and seventies and for which Shapley is famous, but rather the non-cooperative games that we were promoting. The multi-stage games and incomplete information in particular have brought about the whole scientific revolution. And in doing that, of course, I found myself once more in the dissident's role.

What drew you to game theory in the first place? Was it its logical appeal or rather a view to practical applications?
Game theory is extraordinarily exciting because it pictures both cooperation and conflict. In a sense, game theory is dramatic. And that's fascinating.

That means it wasn't the appeal of formalization as such that attracted you, but instead it was the light that this approach is able to shed on human interaction.
Of course. This instrument of analysis is of particular importance for politics. Game theory really does provide you with an insight into human interaction. Today, however, I have to admit that the exclusively rationalistic approach is not really sustainable. At the time when I did my master's degree, I was at first a naive rationalist, too, even though I had taken some classes in psychology. Of course, nobody believed that the idea according to which people are fully rational should be taken literally. But we did think that this assumption brought us relatively close to how decisions are made, in the sense that it was at least a pretty good approximation of reality. That's something some people still insist on today, and in some

contexts, it is indeed sustainable. But in many other contexts it isn't. We must learn how to better understand in which cases the assumption of perfect rationality is sustainable and in which it isn't. As I went on with my work, I was more interested in bounded rationality and its implications. But at the same time, I also continued to work on the basis of the assumption of perfect rationality, and that's what I got the Nobel Prize for.

And why was it that you focused on non-cooperative games? Was there just more music in it than in cooperative games?
I had already dealt with cooperative theory in my master's thesis and in my doctoral dissertation.[27] In those days, however, I already used the extensive form. It made me recognize the difference it makes whether you use the normal or the extensive form.[28] And so I realized earlier than others that something could be done there – because of the perfectness problem.[29] When I then gained more ground with the perfectness problem, I also noticed that it could lead to further advances in economic theory. Mind you, my 1965 paper[30] was actually on the oligopoly problem. That was an application. My definition of the subgame perfect equilibrium didn't fill more than half a page in it. I had always been fascinated by the oligopoly problem and just hoped to contribute something to oligopoly theory. In order to tackle this problem, I needed the instrument of the subgame perfect equilibrium.

Why was the oligopoly problem so fascinating for you? Was it because of its direct practical implications or mainly because there was still room to push the logic somewhat further?
The oligopoly problem is fascinating because it is directly connected with game theory. There are only a handful of players who interact. Another thing that attracted me was the fact that traditional oligopoly theory had produced tons of theories that all claimed to be based on the assumption of rational behavior. But they were all very different from one another, so the whole thing couldn't be quite true. That's what made me think that we should just do experiments and see how people behave in reality. I knew experimental techniques from psychology. In those experiments, you could see fairly rapidly that the results had nothing to do with the results that you would expect on the basis of rational theory. Notwithstanding this, you still always need an analytical solution for your problem, even when this must be based on false premises such as the assumption of full rationality. That's always been a concern of mine. You need a benchmark to confront the data that you gain from experiments. In the long run, however, this is not satisfactory. We have to get away from the rationality

assumption. The way it is set up right now, game theory is more adequate for biology.

Don't we need both, the heuristic instrument as much as the empirical observation of reality? I remember you once said of yourself that you are a dualist in this sense.

The traditional normative theory does in fact reflect something about human thinking. The underlying kind of rationality is one that people would like to attain if only they could. It is something that looks appealing and rewarding. However, it is a fact that such a kind of rationality is not practically possible. So we have to put up with less. Nature just doesn't cooperate. The human brain isn't made for this ideal kind of rationality. This is an insight that now finally begins to spread in academia. Of course, from a philosophical point of view, it is necessary to fully explore the idea of perfect rationality. It just turns out that this idea, as laid out in Bayesian theory, is not satisfactory even from a normative standpoint. There are severe shortcomings in this respect. This is well known in the literature, but nothing is done to overcome the problem. The academic business of today has sort of settled into working with a specific toolkit and then analyzing economic problems with it, for example with the utility concept by von Neumann and Morgenstern.[31] It is true that this concept has been very important for the development of game theory. But when you look at applications of game theory, you see that in most of these models, all that is being maximized is expected profits, under the assumption of risk neutrality. When you look closer, you see that this kind of utility theory is not at all satisfactory from a normative standpoint, that is philosophically. One example is how we deal with time in our models. It is not only important whether something is uncertain. My colleague Robin Pope[32] has made me aware of the fact that it also matters how long an uncertain event remains uncertain, and at what point the uncertainty will be over. Imagine somebody who takes a test whether he or she has cancer or not. It may matter greatly to that person at which point of time he or she will know the results. It may matter for some decisions that need to be made. Traditional theory abstracts from this. But this point is relevant – and be it only because somebody who doesn't have certainty usually just can't stop worrying. Of course nobody can really change a terrible fate, and usually you can't even prepare for it properly. But still, we want to know about it as early as possible. And so, the fact that there are different probabilities for different scenarios is not the only thing that matters. It is also relevant to know when it will be that uncertainty will turn into certainty. There is some literature on this, but it hasn't been acknowledged much in economics. Of course, this is not surprising, given that we hardly seem to pay much attention to the theory of expected utility and we just assume risk neutrality.

Economic theory is becoming more and more complex, isn't it?
Rationalistic economic theory as we know it currently only enables us to tackle problems when we are able to simplify them. More complex problems can't be solved this way. As a consequence, you have to radically simplify and then hope that more complex problems can be solved in a similar way as those toy problems of ours. Maybe you can construct some kind of analogy. From a rationalistic point of view, of course, there is no justification for basing anything on analogies. It doesn't happen frequently that you can solve concrete, real problems thanks to this kind of a toolkit.

But isn't complexity reduction crucial if you want to be able to say at least something?
That's correct. But there is no justification for assuming that an entrepreneur makes his decisions in a fully rational way if his problem is one you can't possibly solve with rational means. And just think of the theory of rational expectations in its original variant. You had to suppose that everybody actually knows the model of our economy and optimizes within this framework, fully expecting everybody else to do so as well. The funny thing is that all economic agents are assumed to know the model, but economists disagree what this model really consists of. According to their own assumptions, they just have to go down to the street and ask someone at random, given that people supposedly know it all. How should such an approach be able to deal with real-life problems? If such a simplistic approach survives and even grows dominant, then that's a problem, not a solution. What's more, if it happens to solve real-life problems, then we seriously have to ask how this can possibly be.

How receptive were your peers to your pioneer work? I guess your own attention was very much directed towards the US in those days.
Fifteen years after the von Neumann/Morgenstern book[33] was published, most people felt that nothing would come of this new line of research that had originally looked so promising. I then usually explained that you only had to look at the economic journals to realize that you'd always find at least one paper using game theory. They hadn't even noticed. This probably simply has to do with the fact that you have to specialize, and then you follow only remotely what goes on in other fields. It just took time. And the younger people were needed. It was only in the eighties that game theory really made its way. And ever since, the mainstream of economics has been on my heels again.

You always tried to escape the mainstream, but by doing so, you eventually ended up creating a new one. That's funny. Actually, how did your speciali-zation beyond the mainstream pay off in the academic labor market? Has it made things easier – or rather more difficult?

The whole recruitment procedure was different in those days. In Germany, there was no such thing as an application. The recruitment commission of some university would gather and review who was available in the desired field. The market was smaller than nowadays. We were much fewer people. Among the young scholars, I had the reputation of being one of the best. I was known for being a mathematical oligopoly theorist and a game theorist. Game theory wasn't very advanced yet, but people were well aware that it was a difficult and interesting thing. It did have a certain standing. Three universities were interested in having me. I then decided to go to Berlin, in 1969.

In 1969 – oh, politically speaking, those were hot years, especially in Berlin.

Yes. I can say that I participated in the heroic days there. It had already been wild in Frankfurt, by the way. I could never deliver my 'Habilitationsvortrag'.[34] It had been publicly announced several times but they always had to cancel it due to some student boycotts. In the end, the university administration just sent me the document without me giving the lecture. It just wasn't feasible.

In the meantime, things have calmed down significantly on this front. Given that you stayed in Germany, then, how did you create your international network?

In 1961, I was invited to a conference on game theory at Princeton University. That was thanks to Oskar Morgenstern. From very early on, he had shown some interest in me. He had once been to Frankfurt University, to some seminar, and I intervened a lot during the discussion. He liked it. He came to Frankfurt regularly and always tried to meet up with me. He even organized a flight ticket for me, via the MATS.[35] Those were the times of the propeller engines. The flight to the US took 19 hours, with two stops for refueling. At that conference, I met John Harsanyi. We had been working on similar things, starting from differ-ent angles. We became friends. He even wanted me to come to the US, to Detroit. But then he himself left and went to the University of California at Berkeley. Another event that was really good was the game theoretic workshop in Jerusalem, in 1965. It lasted three weeks, with 17 people. We didn't have a predefined program. You just went, and if somebody wanted to present a paper, then we would spontaneously agree to gather again at a given time and listen. We had huge discussions, especially about

Harsanyi's concept of incomplete information. I supported him a lot. We worked jointly later, too. In 1967/68 I also went to Berkeley, as a Visiting Professor. I didn't even have my *habilitation* yet. At Berkeley, I worked not only with Harsanyi, but also with Tom Marschak, on the price setting behavior of firms in the general equilibrium model. I also worked experimentally, among others with Austin Hoggatt. I got many useful contacts in the US.

Did it never occur to you that you might move there permanently? Maybe you would have found even more sources of inspiration over there?
I have never been so much interested in sources of inspiration. I'm not so dependent on external inspiration. And besides, I tend to find contacts and stimulation wherever I am. It's true, I could have gone to the US. I got several offers, in 1961 for Detroit and later for Stanford, for example. But I didn't really want to go. I wanted to have a career in Germany first. And I didn't like the American way of life. For example, one thing was that I didn't drive a car until very late. I was 41 years old when I finally got my driver's license.

So it actually was a cultural decision.
Yes. It also had to do with the German language. That has always been important to me. And I would also have missed the German highlands, with well-signaled hiking trails, inns and cafés.

That's true, the infrastructure is different here and there.
Germany has just been more in line with my personal preferences. Especially in those days. Today, things have changed somewhat. Some kind of Europeanization of the US has taken place in the meantime – not just an Americanization of Europe. Some differences still persist, but they are less drastic. Anyway, I had my job in Germany, and it was a good one.

I guess much depends on how exactly you generate new ideas. If you depend a lot on discussions with other scholars, then it may be helpful to be more or less in the same place.
Of course you need discussions. I do too. That is important. But it's something you also get at conferences, when you present your stuff. By the way, those scholars with whom you interact most are typically never in the same location. You meet on purpose and talk in a focused way. It's not so easy to discuss things in detail with people at the same university. With your immediate colleagues, topics such as the department, administration and new appointments always block the agenda. You don't talk

much about your science; you rather talk about the internal politics of the university. That's why the closest collaboration is always between people from different places. That's no coincidence.

Would you characterize yourself as a lone tinkerer or as a team person?
I do like to work with others. I often take co-authors, even when I could very well do it on my own. In the case of experimental studies, somebody has to program the procedures. That's something I have never learned. Of course I could still set myself to work and learn it. But I don't need to. By the way, I still write mostly on paper, with a simple pencil. I prefer not to use a computer.

That's interesting, given that our thinking processes are very much connected with how we write. And how do the concrete topics spring up that you choose to work on?
Nowadays, much is a result of strategic planning. Often times, the question is for which kind of project there will be funds available. That kind of consideration does give the whole enterprise a concrete direction. But more fundamentally, one's research topics do have something to do with the long-run interests that one pursues.

Are you a quick and efficient worker?
No. Everything takes forever with me. The book that I've written jointly with John Harsanyi has taken us 18 years. And now I'm writing another book, and the 18 years are already over. We've gotten quite far, but it will take some more time, perhaps another two years. I'm very slow. That's another reason why it's good for me to be at the margin. When you swim in the mainstream, you've got to be fast. But I need to take my time. Everything I do is very long-run.

In what kind of topics do you feel an urge to make progress in the years to come?
I absolutely want to arrive at some breakthroughs in the field of bounded rationality. I do have a ten-year research project running, started in May 2006. We just completed a first study. That's very important. We're concentrating on the issues of formation of goals and aspiration adaptation. Sauermann and I wrote a paper on aspiration adaptation within the firm as early as in 1962.[36] That paper did receive some attention, even in business administration. It was often cited for a while, but then almost fell into oblivion. Then, in 1998, I came back to that subject in the *Journal of Mathematical Psychology*.[37] Psychologists usually like our way of modeling bounded rationality. But for many years, I thought it to be a major

shortcoming that we haven't checked things experimentally. So that's what we're catching up with right now. We have one experiment that depicts a complex dynamic monopoly problem. It confirms the aspiration adaptation theory. But sure enough, a theory like that can never encompass everything. It can only describe the typical behavior of a successful person. But that's already very nice.

Those results provide new impulses as well, right?
Sure. The researcher in game theory or in experimental economics always meets with one kind of resistance, and that is empirical testing. But he or she also has to be sensitive to the other kind of resistance that you meet with: and that's mathematical logic. Our creativity always has to find its way within the framework of that which is mathematically correct.

Thank you, Professor.

NOTES

1. The interview with Reinhard Selten was held on 10 September, 2007.
2. See the Vernon L. Smith questionnaire in this volume.
3. This gave rise, among others works, to a paper published jointly with his dissertation adviser, Heinz Sauermann (Heinz Sauermann and Reinhard Selten, 1959).
4. Reinhard Selten (1961).
5. Reinhard Selten (1970).
6. This topic was the particular area of contributions by Thomas Schelling, Nobel Laureate of 2005.
7. Auguste Cournot, or rather, more precisely, Antoine Augustin Cournot (1801–77), was a French economist, philosopher and mathematician. His major work was Auguste Cournot, *Recherches sur les Principes Mathématiques de la Théorie des Richesses* (1838).
8. John von Neumann and Oskar Morgenstern (1944).
9. John Nash was highly controversial not within the field of economics, where his outstanding contributions are being recognized beyond any question, but rather within the Royal Swedish Academy. As Mark Perlman and Morgan Marietta write, the problem with Nash was that his relevant contributions were more than 40 years past; that he was a mathematician seeing his major contributions himself as not being in the field of economics, but in mathematics; the fact that his career had been overshadowed and interrupted by schizophrenia; and that it was not clear whether he would be able to participate in the traditional Nobel Award Ceremony. The vote was tight – and the ultimate, tragic consequence was that Assar Lindbeck, the last member of the original Nobel Committee from 1969, when the Swedish Riksbank first instituted the award, and in 'many respects one of the fathers of the Prize', was sacked in a rather disreputable way. See Mark Perlman/Morgan Marietta (1994).
10. Reinhard Selten (1965).
11. Reinhard Selten (1975).
12. Available at www.nobel.se.
13. At age 14, as a half-Jewish boy in Breslau, then part of Nazi Germany, Reinhard Selten was forced to leave school.

14. This was the 'escape tax' by which the Nazis enriched themselves to the detriment of the Jews who left Germany,
15. This 'Lastenausgleich' was agreed upon in 1952.
16. John von Neumann and Oskar Morgenstern (1944).
17. Heinz Sauermann (1905–81) was a rather influential German economist, based in Frankfurt, who greatly promoted mathematization in the post-war years. He was the first president of the Economic Council to the German Ministry for Economic Affairs.
18. See below.
19. Herbert Simon was awarded the Nobel Prize in 1978 'for his pioneering research into the decision-making process within economic organizations'. See in particular Herbert Simon (1947 and 1957).
20. Reinhard Selten and Heinz Sauermann (1962).
21. Heinz Sauermann and Reinhard Selten (1959).
22. The Nobel Committee pointed out that Selten 'was the first to refine the Nash equilibrium concept for analyzing dynamic strategic interaction. He has also applied these refined concepts to analyses of competition with only a few sellers.' See www.nobel.se.
23. Robert Aumann was awarded the Nobel Prize jointly with Thomas Schelling in 2005 'for having enhanced our understanding of conflict and cooperation through game-theory analysis'.
24. Lloyd Shapley is an American mathematician and economist, Professor Emeritus at University of California, Los Angeles, affiliated with departments of Mathematics and Economics. He has contributed to the fields of mathematical economics and especially game theory.
25. John Nash was awarded the Nobel Prize jointly with Reinhard Selten and John Harsanyi in 1994 'for their pioneering analysis of equilibria in the theory of non-cooperative games'.
26. See note 25.
27. Reinhard Selten (1961).
28. In its extensive form, a game is modeled as a sequence of separate individual moves – while in the normal form, all decisions are viewed as taking place simultaneously, that is within the framework of a one-shot game.
29. What is meant here is the possibility to reach a Nash equilibrium, that is a strategic equilibrium, in which no player can gain any further advantage by modifying his strategy unilaterally. In the extensive form, that is in a succession of moves, the question about the stability of such equilibrium is multiplied and logically becomes a question about the stability of the strategic equilibria at each individual stage – that is, the sub-games – of the game. The Nash equilibrium at each stage then is the 'subgame perfect equilibrium'.
30. Reinhard Selten (1965).
31. The concept of expected utility or 'von Neumann/Morgenstern utility' transfers the traditional concept of utility into a world with uncertainty. Basically, it is a cardinal utility concept based on preferences concerning lotteries. See in this context Reinhard Selten (2001).
32. Currently at Bonn University under a German National Science Foundation award.
33. John von Neumann and Oskar Morgenstern (1944).
34. The *'Habilitationsvortrag'* is the public lecture one traditionally has to give in Germany upon one's earning the right to teach at university (*habilitation*).
35. The Military Air Transport System was a command of the US Air Force from 1948 to 1965.
36. Reinhard Selten and Heinz Sauermann (1962).
37. Reinhard Selten (1998).

George A. Akerlof

University of California at Berkeley, CA, USA

The Sveriges Riksbank Prize in Economic Sciences in Memory of Alfred Nobel 2001 shared with A. Michael Spence and Joseph E. Stiglitz, all three 'for their analysis of markets with asymmetric information'.

INTRODUCTION

'Let's not stay here in the office. Everything is grey here. They even painted the walls grey, did you see? I hate grey. I just hate it. Let's go outside and get some light and air'. It's true, it's a warm sunny day, so why stay indoors for our interview? George A. Akerlof seems to have itchy feet anyway. He's visibly uneasy at first. Constantly in motion. Almost a little shy, tense. And also, whether it's about those freshly painted grey walls in the hallway at Berkeley's Evans Hall that truly disturb his aesthetic sense, or about some possible nuisances that others might suffer – George Akerlof is permanently tuned to the world around him. He's always trying to be helpful, and his very receptive radar system never gives him a break. He's gentle, sensitive and considerate to a point to make you feel guilty. When we sit down at the Caffe Strada on Bancroft Way, nice steaming café lattes in front, it's not for long. After only a couple of minutes, he interrupts himself: 'Are you sure your microphone is strong enough? It's pretty noisy here.' He's right, the tape will be awful. We move. We find a somewhat better spot, but there is a group of students working whom we might disturb. We look for yet another spot; eventually we find one, sit down and take up talking again. Until, twenty minutes later, a group of colleagues sit down at the table next to us. Akerlof jumps up in boyish excitement, greets them warmly, shakes hands, chats a while – and then makes us move again. This time, we settle in the most remote corner of the café. We continue our conversation, but when he suddenly realizes that a student girl next to us is doing some homework, the friendly Nobel Laureate of the year 2001 jumps up again and asks her whether we're making too much noise. 'Oh no, don't worry', she puts his mind at rest. Akerlof's narrative is humble, funny, with a strong undercurrent of self-irony. He makes absolutely no fuss about himself – he just happens to have this passion for economics.[1]

If the academic career path was not at all a straightforward option for some, given the unfavorable circumstances – in George Arthur Akerlof's case, on the contrary, it was difficult to avoid. His family background is heavily academic, albeit in the natural sciences. Born in 1940 in New Haven, Connecticut, his Swedish-born father was an associate professor of chemistry on the Yale faculty. His parents had met at a department picnic, his mother being herself a graduate student of chemistry. She came from an academic family of German Jewish descent; her father had established the first clinic in cardiology in the United States at Johns Hopkins and later became chairman of the department of pharmacology at the University of Minnesota medical school. Her brother was a chemist at the University of Wisconsin. And George Akerlof's own brother, Carl, became a physicist. Unlike the rest of the family, however, George Akerlof was more interested in 'social things' early on, as he says, and when he was at high school, he already had decided that he wanted to be a professor of economics one day. If he aimed that high, it was, as he admits with a smile, because he simply 'didn't know that there were all kinds of other things you could do as an economist. It seemed to me that most economists were professors. Being an economist was being a professor. It was automatic.' Following his father's professional moves, George Akerlof went to school first in Pittsburgh, then in Washington, DC, and finally Princeton. He went to college at Yale, like his brother, but majoring in mathematics and economics. In Akerlof's view, getting more mathematics at that stage than the usual economist has proven extremely useful. As he says, this advance over others just gave him more freedom in developing his own ideas and models. While not being interested in the mathematics for the mathematics, he maintains that 'the use of mathematics has advanced economics to a state where we have a mutual language'. At Yale,

Akerlof thus received what he calls 'a very good standard economics education' that prepared him well to go on to MIT where he finally received his economics Ph.D. in 1966. In his thesis papers, he attempted to provide sound micro-foundations for Keynesian economics.[2] His doctoral adviser was Robert M. Solow. Subsequently, Akerlof was hired as an assistant professor at the University of California at Berkeley. He spent one year in India and a couple of months at Harvard, only to come back to Berkeley in 1970 first as an associate professor and finally, ever since 1977, as a tenured full professor. In 1973–74, he served as a senior staff economist for the Council of Economic Advisers. In 1977–78, he spent a year as a visiting research economist on the board of governors of the Federal Reserve System. Frustrated with not being promoted, he left Berkeley in 1978 together with his newly-wedded second wife and future co-author Janet L. Yellen.[3] Until 1980, Akerlof taught Money and Banking at the London School of Economics, but then the couple returned to Berkeley. When Janet Yellen became a member of the Board of Governors of the Federal Reserve System in 1994, the family moved to Washington. Akerlof became a Senior Fellow of the Brookings Institution and at first continued to teach part-time at Berkeley, finally taking up more and more household and childcare duties. In 1999, the family moved back to Berkeley.

George Akerlof's approach to economics has three characteristic features. One is his acute interest in social, sociological and socio-anthropological questions. This may explain his pronounced liberal world view – which, however, he dresses up as 'libertarianism' in a way that philosophers may find puzzling: 'If people have more income, on the average they are freer to do what they want, and that does make them happier. . . the libertarian aspect [is] that you aim at getting people freedoms. The maximum freedom that you can have, which includes freedom from want, increases their welfare.'[4] At any rate, Akerlof admits that Keynesian macroeconomics had intuitive appeal to him. As a child, he almost anticipated the purchasing power argument: 'My thought was that, if [my father] didn't get another job and we stopped spending our money, then other families would also stop spending their money, etc.' A second decisive feature, intertwined with the first, is the point that Akerlof starts his analyses from, namely the suspicion that markets may fail or at least not fully clear. Throughout his career, Akerlof has remained a steadfast neo-Keynesian, that is someone who stays within the Keynesian school of thought insofar as he is predominantly concerned with unemployment and highly skeptical about the market's tendency towards equilibrium, while using a neoclassical model toolkit. The third characteristic feature is his method of situational analysis.[5] This method characterizes most of the theoretical approaches to economics nowadays. George Akerlof has a pretty garden metaphor when he explains why he prefers this situational approach:

> You can have a French garden, where there is some grand order to everything. [People assume some axioms, and then they derive principles.] And then there is an English garden, where there is seemingly no order. The English garden approach is how to make order out of something that seems pretty chaotic. . . [you] look at the world out there, and from those detailed stories, you can then construct a more general theory.

Akerlof's first major contribution came after his Ph.D. thesis. It was the first article that he wrote at Berkeley, it was only 13 pages long, and it ultimately brought him Nobel fame. It was the 1970 'Lemons' paper[6] – a piece that has given a huge boost to one area of research ever since: the economics of information. As such, economics of information had been around before,[7] of course, but Akerlof now drew the attention particularly to the problem of asymmetry. It started out with a theoretical concern that bothered the engineers of growth models, namely that there was no way as yet to take the quality of capital into account. Quality was the issue. Taking the example of used cars, Akerlof showed that, *ceteris paribus*, asymmetric information between sellers and buyers can prevent the market from clearing; in other words, there will simply be no transaction. Given that they cannot distinguish between a high-quality and a low-quality car, buyers are only ready to pay an average price. The average price, however, is not enough to cover the cost for high-quality cars. The result is that a seller will not even try to sell high-quality cars any more. Instead, he will concentrate on 'lemons' right away. The bad cars thus drive out the good ones, similar to Gresham's law on currencies.[8] This is a prime example of 'adverse selection',[9] which can of course also arise in other markets – and this problem is the reason why market institutions such as professional dealers (who have a reputation to lose), franchising systems, chain stores, brands, certificates, product guarantees, and publicity have emerged.[10] All of these institutions are crucial in generating and communicating information. As Akerlof recalls elsewhere, the paper was ready for publication in 1967, but it was rejected first by the *American Economic Review*, then by the *Review of Economic Studies*, for its 'triviality', and finally also by the *Journal of Political Economy*. Finally, it was accepted by the *Quarterly Journal of Economics*.[11] Once the importance of such information asymmetries was stated and acknowledged in the profession, more new approaches – especially by Akerlof's co-laureates Joseph E. Stiglitz and Michael Spence – came up showing how the market eventually deals with the problem, that is how information that is 'local' still ends up being transmitted through prices. Stiglitz is famous for his work on 'screening', Spence for his 'signaling' devices.

Another important contribution has been in the field of efficiency wage theory. It was Akerlof who came up with the idea that firms may pay wage rates that exceed the market-clearing level in order to promote their employees' effort, productivity and loyalty – thereby, however, creating unemployment in the overall economy. If productivity thus hinges on the real wage, the usual neoclassical response to unemployment – lower real wages – turns out ineffective or, worse, even counterproductive. Akerlof's first paper in this context was 'A theory of social customs of which unemployment may be one consequence',[12] in 1980, and a second important one was 'Labour contracts as partial gift exchange',[13] in 1982. The theory was summed up in a joint monograph with Janet Yellen, 'Efficiency wage models of the labor market'.[14] In 1991, together with Janet Yellen and a couple of co-authors, Akerlof then analyzed the East German case, imagining – and anticipating correctly – that upon reunification, the exchange rate might be wrong, causing severe disruptions in the labor market. He therefore advocated self-effacing wage subsidies in 'East Germany in from the cold'.[15] The wage subsidies were supposed to phase out as wages rose, vanishing completely once West German wage levels were reached in the East as well. The paper caused quite a stir, but the idea wasn't really put into practice.

Akerlof has also been dealing with monetary issues. For example, he has attempted to provide a micro-foundation for the connection between money supply and output.[16] He has tried to give a new interpretation for the long-run Phillips curve as well, claiming that there may be a permanent trade-off between inflation and unemployment in the presence of low inflation.[17] In recent years, he has also concentrated on sociological phenomena, analyzing, for example, why it is that, with similar resources but different backgrounds concerning ethnic or racial identity, some schools perform better than others,[18] or what kind of difference identity then makes in the labor market, in terms of providing an important supplement to monetary compensation.[19]

The insights from the interview with George A. Akerlof are again remarkable. In his case, the intellectual personal (family) background played a pivotal role in making him an academic. His choice of economics, however, was an act of dissidence. He chose economics because he was interested in 'social things', as he puts it – which he mainly just claims to be his 'personal thing', a character trait of his own, triggered by nothing in particular except, perhaps, worries about his father losing his job, and a general liberal world view. His research agenda later on was indeed a reflection of both the advances made in economic theory, especially in macroeconomics, and the issues that came up in current politics, for example rising unemployment. As he says, he usually learns a lot through academic interaction and discussion; he is not a loner in the ivory tower. As a person, Akerlof is driven by an intense curiosity. He has an extraordinarily acute innate radar and therefore notices everything around him – and he feels the urge to try to understand and explain what he sees, following his 'English garden' approach. All of that takes place within the general motivation that he has for all his endeavors, namely to try to 'contribute to making people's lives better, and to get it right'. That's what he claims for the entire profession. 'We actually have a duty to get it right.' Making the world a little better requires serious qualified research.

INTERVIEW

What I would like to find out is what guided you where you went. So let me ask, Professor Akerlof: what triggered your interest in economics? Was it a topic at home, for example? I am aware that as a young person, you wanted to do something that not everybody else in your family was doing. That ruled out chemistry. That's fair enough, but even given this, economics is not a self-evident choice.
I have always been interested in economics, at least as long as I can remember. I think I started out with economics in a very libertarian view which I still sort of have, even though, as I have grown older, I have begun to qualify this view more. The libertarian view means that the one thing one can do to make people happier is to free them from constraints, to get them more choices, so that they can improve their lot. There is a lot of literature saying that happiness doesn't solely depend on income, but yet, I think one has got to believe that if people have more income, on the average they are freer to do what they want, and that does make them happier. I have thought that for a very long time.

It's interesting that you should call this 'libertarian'. I thought that libertarians were not so much focused on incomes, but rather on rights.
Well, it's libertarianism in a rather loose sense.

To me, what you describe sounds more like liberalism than libertarianism.
Yes, it may be more liberal than libertarian. But I do feel that it has this libertarian aspect, that is, that you aim at getting people freedoms. The maximum freedom that you can have, which includes freedom from want, increases their welfare. This recognition has the spirit of economics, that is, it acknowledges that people are better off when they have more freedoms.

I don't want to say that I agree with every libertarian on every issue. But I think that this is one of the fundamental aims of economists: you want to get people more choice. So I thought that getting people the income they need to live is a major goal. The one problem that attracted my interest early on was unemployment.

Is that really a topic for children? Usually, kids are interested in animals, cars, etc. At some point, something special must have aroused your economic awareness in an acute way.
I'm not sure that children don't think about things like unemployment.

Well, maybe if their father is unemployed. But otherwise?
I always thought that there was a chance that my father could be unemployed. And in 1951, he did lose his job, and I was wondering not just about whether he would get another job, but also what would happen to the rest of the economy if he didn't get another job. My thought was that, if he didn't get another job and we stopped spending our money, then other families would also stop spending their money, etc.

Wow! That's Keynesianism in a nutshell. Where did you get that?
I've always found it straightforward, and I still do. It just seems utterly natural. However, at the time, I was only eleven years old, and I forgot to note that my family would continue to spend three-quarters or one half of what they were currently spending, so I forgot about the multiplier. Or rather, I made it a little bit too large.

Amazing. Were these things topics at home or with friends?
Friends, no, and I don't remember that my family was particularly interested. We did talk about politics at home, but I don't think either one of my parents or my brother actually knew what economists really did.

So you had a very strong interest in economics from very early on. Did that interest get reinforced at school?
Yes, I continued to be interested. When I was in high school, for example, I wrote my senior history thesis on an economic subject. And the first real book in economics that I read was John Kenneth Galbraith's *Great Crash.*[20] I remember reading that in high school. But economics as such wasn't taught in high school. At that time, I was quite interested in history. I was potentially interested in being a historian, aiming at an economic interpretation of history. So in high school, I already had a strong interest in economics, even though I didn't know what it was before I finally took my first course. When I went to college and was asked what I

wanted to be one day, I remember saying that I wanted to be a professor of economics.

Oh come on. I was going to ask you that later: most people study economics because they are interested in the topic, in the theory, because they are curious and looking for explanations of real world problems. But they don't necessarily have the goal of pursuing an academic career to start with.
I didn't know that there were all kinds of other things you could do as an economist. It seemed to me that most economists were professors. Being an economist was being a professor. Remember, I grew up in Princeton, New Jersey. My best friend's mother worked in the economics department. She had a Master's degree in economics, and she turned out the papers on international trade. From that extent, I knew that there were economists, and they did such things as did professors. It was automatic.

And what about your interest in history?
There are economists of different stripes. I have always been interested in economics as reflected in history. So I combined both, economics and history. Here is an observation that can serve as an example: when I graduated from middle school, when I was 14 years old, I got to write an editorial for the school newspaper, and I wrote about how terrible it was that people had worked on the pyramids etc. The whole thing was about economics, the use of power, and economic justice. From that early age, that's probably the only relic that I have left. When I went to university, it was just natural; I was very pleased to take a course in economics.

Did your teachers at high school or college recognize your interest and foster it?
No. They taught their courses straight. I don't think that anybody ever noticed that I had any particular interest. Still, I had very good teaching in high school, at Lawrenceville, where I went as a day boy. But none of the lessons, even in history, were very much focused on economics. There just wasn't much about economics. The economic interpretation of history was rather my personal thing, my own point of view.

What about people around you, especially at college? Weren't you evolving in some small group of friends that would debate issues of economic policy, in a highly politicized way, like many people at that age?
No. In college, I spent a great deal of time on the *Yale Daily News*. My rationalization of this was that if you were going to work on history, you should know how the news is actually created.

Didn't you also think you would enjoy it?
Yes, of course.

But you dropped the news business, ultimately. Did you ever seriously consider that avenue as a profession?
It did look like a possibility. But I realized that my comparative advantage was rather in being an economic theorist, rather than in working as a reporter.

And then, the next step was university. Why did you pick Yale?
I went to Yale because my brother had gone to Yale, so that was where I was supposed to go. It just wasn't a choice. I did consider Harvard briefly, that's true, but I was warned by the assistant principal in Lawrenceville. The school didn't want people to apply to more than one place. Given that he knew I was probably going to end up at Yale, he tried to divert me from applying to a second place. I also think that Harvard had some kind of quota at that time, and therefore the school wanted only those kids to apply for Harvard who were really determined to go there. Also, my teacher he had worked in the commissions at Yale, he very much liked Yale, and he identified with Yale. Also, he thought Harvard was more conservative than Yale. In the late fifties, Harvard was still very much identified with Roosevelt.[21] And he didn't identify with Roosevelt. That's my theory.

What kind of atmosphere did you experience at Yale?
That's hard for me to answer. Yale had a very mixed culture. The people that I associated most with were the group of people of the *News*. They were wonderful. They were very much interested in politics and everything that was going on in the world. At that time, I had the same kind of criticism of the news as I do now have of the economics profession. I felt that our newspaper was much too much an official paper. It didn't get at the underlying issues. And that was my complaint about economic history, too: somehow history was written too much from the point of view of an official tale. There was too much stuff like presidential biography, and too little emphasis on the social and economic aspects. My interest in the news was the same thing. You wanted to get at the underlying social causes of everything. So I didn't write official stories, and instead I tended to write non-official stories that I had brought up. I wanted to do human interest stories, on the one hand. Also, on the more serious side of social issues, at this time, a friend of mine and I went south, and we covered the activity during one of those very first sit-ins. It certainly reflects an interest in social causes, and in the inequality between blacks and whites – which was then even worse than it is now. This was very early, in the spring of 1959. What

attracted our attention in this case was that some students had been fire-
hosed in one of the Carolinas, and that had been written about in the news.
So a friend of mine and I decided to go down south, talk to people, and
write it up for the *Yale Daily News*. We did a lot of fascinating things.

*It is very true that history tends to deliver official stories only, without
digging deeper, without much consideration for individuals. It is interesting
that this bothered you, in both approaches, in history but also in economics
– and in the news!*
Every economist probably thinks history should be told from below. At
any rate, I was combining economics and history. There are a lot of economists who do have a very historical view. But not all.

Why is that?
I guess a lot of economists have a view according to which what they do
is theory, and most of them are now attracted by mathematical problems.
And therefore, much of economics is now written in a very a-historic
way, which I think is a mistake. One of the guiding principles of what I've
written is that I just try to generalize from some small historical observation. It's like history in a microcosm. I try to argue from those examples. I
feel that most economists approach things from the opposite end. They try
to establish principles, and then they argue from those principles, whereas
I try to look at the world and then to establish a pattern.

*But how far can such a generalization go? Would you establish laws or just
conjectures?*
There are two types of gardens you can cultivate. You can have a French
garden, where there is some grand order to everything. And then there is
an English garden, where there is seemingly no order. The English garden
approach is how to make order out of something that seems pretty chaotic.
There is a big difference between the two. The usual, standard economic
model, the French garden model, comes from physics. People assume
some axioms, and then they derive principles. But I want to do something
different. I want to take and observe the world, and then I draw conclusions of general interest from those observations which are just examples.
It's a very different methodology.

*I understand that. But how encompassing are those conclusions? Are you
aiming at an all-encompassing 'theory of everything', applicable to past and
future events, or just at explanatory elements that allow you to understand
specific observable phenomena?*
I'm not sure I'm taking an aim. I try to describe the world, and when
I get a good description, then that's useful. I don't want to claim that

it should be all-encompassing. I'm perfectly happy if it explains classes of phenomena that you can then also use to explain other phenomena. What I want to do is take examples that help us understand other markets as well, as I did in 'the market for lemons'.[22] The example that I used in the 'market for lemons' was what was happening in the automobile market. What happened there was asymmetric information. For that reason, used cars tended not to trade. You can use that principle, derived from an observation in the automobile market, to understand many other markets as well. That is actually how I do think. It seems to me that it makes life very much easier if you think about examples that you are familiar with. There, you can dissect exactly what is happening. When you take very simple stories and examples, you know that you've gotten right the correspondence between the mathematics and the example. What I do in seminars is, rather than to listen to endless mathematical derivations which I can only do my best to understand, I give myself an example of what some person or paper is trying to explain, and then I ask myself whether or not that example fits the mathematics. It's surprising how often one can find that the mathematics actually does not fit what people are trying to explain. This is the major way in which I generate ideas. I take some phenomenon, and I try to give the most specific possible example of it that I can. Then I look at it, viewing it as an English garden, and I try to find out which order to put on that. To a surprising extent, standard economics, which is top down, has not put the right order on it. It has been too restrictive. It restricts our notions of what we see. So even now, there is a surprising degree of economics that is wrong.

Tell me more about classes at Yale, please.
Classes at Yale were quite good. They taught what, for the time, was probably as good a course in economics as one could get. I can remember an essay that I wrote when I went to MIT later. It was the type of essay that too many students write. It was. . . well, I had now had courses in mathematics and as a consequence, I thought that economics needed to me more precise. When I later discovered – not exactly by myself – what actually economics was, I realized however that lack of precision was not the major problem with economics. People do start off with general principles that look nice when they are written down on a page, but then they neglect things that become very important when you look at markets in detail. Life is more complicated than in the standard neoclassical approach. Anyway, at Yale, what we got was, I think, a very good standard economics education, and so I was well prepared when I went on to MIT in 1962. At the time, most graduate students majored in economics and some

other social science fields. I had majored jointly in math and in economics, however, and the math really made a difference. It was good if you had a background in mathematics.

In what sense?
In a way, that freed me from having to accept the standard mathematical formulations in the economics textbooks. When I had an idea, I didn't have to go back to the standard mathematics. Basically, I could do my own mathematics. I had more freedom than other people to create my own approach. Actually, I think there is a duality between the mathematics and the economics. Having this good mathematical background made me free to choose. Then, during my first year at graduate school, I took a course at Harvard from a truly great mathematician, Raoul Bott. He taught a course in algebraic topology. He didn't just teach mathematics as formulas. He sort of taught you how to see where the heart of a problem was. He taught you how to differentiate between the core of a proof and all the window-dressing. I learnt something very valuable from him. And then, at MIT, there was one person who gave really superb classes, and that was Robert Solow.[23] He is a wonderful person, and a fantastic teacher. I owe a great deal to him.

And he became your doctoral supervisor. What did you learn from him?
At the time, he pioneered growth theory. He didn't just accept the simple model of growth. He developed new models that were very close to this English garden style that I mentioned. They are rather hard to do. One of them was the vintage capital model.[24] The idea is that capital isn't all the same; in some cases, you don't get increases in productivity unless you have capital of a certain 'vintage', embodying some specific level of technology. This is the type of thing I've always wanted to do with the English garden approach: to look at the world out there, and from those detailed stories, you can then construct a more general theory. And then, Solow did another type of model, which was even more influential on me: putty clay.[25] Before you build the capital, you can choose any capital–labor ratio. But once you build the capital, you have sort of fixed the capital–labor ratio, and you cannot modify it any more. He taught us how to analyze such models. That was a new algebra. Solow freed us to use new algebras to look at problems. The correspondence between all this and the algebra that you need to analyze the economics of information is really very close. Actually, I combined what I had learnt from Bott with what I had learnt from Solow. MIT was extremely good at teaching people about models and how to build them.

But how did you get from 'putty clay' to 'lemons'?
Initially, when I worked on the 'market for lemons', my question was really about variations in the business cycle. In the US, 1959 was a very big year for cars. The car companies had price wars trying to sell as many cars as possible, but at some point, people had just already bought their cars. The real question for me was: why in fact did the volatility in the demand for cars cause so much volatility in the economy in general? If you produce a car and can't sell it, why would that create so much trouble for the economy? So I tried to write that. I was not successful in writing that paper, but then I discovered that my observation was interesting on its own, due to the information aspect. By the way, at MIT, Solow had already given us a primer on the economics of information.

Asymmetric information is a strikingly simple idea. It's amazing that nobody should have thought about that before. . . What encouraged you to write that paper?
I don't think I've ever been encouraged to do it. I didn't tell any faculty members at MIT that I was going to write this. I only mentioned it to my friend Joe Stiglitz[26] and to John Neuhaus. I never wrote that paper before my first year at Berkeley.

What were the reactions then? Was everybody stunned – or did people find the idea too simple? Or maybe did they say that you stopped your analysis a little too early, before the really interesting market adaptation actually takes place?
There are two reasons why people had not thought of this before. One reason is that they had not seen the importance of the asymmetry of information, and they thought that, insofar as people do have asymmetric information, that just adds variants. The second thing was that this asymmetry of information refers to quality. Almost all economics then, however, was written not about quality, but about price. The reason why everybody thought that you could just write about price was that you could talk about price for a unit of quality, and so there was a simple way to translate problems of information and problems of quality back into the old economics. With uncertainty, for the most part, the old economics looks like the new. With quality, the old economics looks pretty much like the new, too. Given that there was an easy way to switch the model, given that you could in fact deal with quality without changing the model, you really had to come from the other end. You had to say that you didn't like the old model and you didn't like the results – and you had to go about it from backwards and ask what you needed to say in order to not get

those results. Relatively few people are willing to do that. In this case, I started out with the result that I wanted, which was 'the market doesn't work'. That was perfectly appropriate, because the market does indeed not always work. Then I could take an example, analyze it, and say why it is that the market doesn't work.

Critics would say that you are describing only subsets of human interaction or rather that you're too much focusing on individual markets where markets are substitutes between themselves. If one market doesn't function, this very fact incorporates a new element of knowledge which will spread, and new markets will spring up elsewhere. People will just find different channels to sell their cars.

That may be so, but then that's part of the economics that explains the market structure. I'm perfectly happy that people will find ways to make an end-run around these problems. But in order to understand what exactly the market structure is going to be, you have to understand what the central problem is that you start with. And that may be very difficult. There may be situations in which things are fungible and people can make an end-run around problems, but there are others where it's extremely difficult. We have that problem with health insurance. There are many areas, too, where we have these problems. It is an important area in economics.

You said you never discussed this idea much with anybody at MIT. But how did you work it out? How do you work generally – in a more or less lonely, inward-looking, isolated way, or with a lot of interaction and discussion?

I always have a list of projects. I start out with the best ones, and then, out of ten projects, numbers 7 to 10 usually drop off. In developing my ideas, then, yes, I tend to be somewhat interactive. When I arrived here at Berkeley, I did discuss the 'lemons' idea with my colleague Tom Rothenberg. I'm not 100 percent sure that I would have made this my first project, but he really liked it, and so it did become number one on my list. So this was the first paper I wrote when I came here. I think I always do interact with somebody. I do talk a lot with people. For example, I have written a lot of papers with Janet Yellen.[27] However, some of my topics have been long-standing ideas. In the case of 'market for lemons', the long-standing part of it was that I was dissatisfied with the way economics was dealing with issues of quality. This was exactly what Solow was doing in his papers, too. He was talking about quality of capital and showing how that made the difference. He applied it to growth theory, and I wanted to go a little bit further and apply it to much more everyday supply-and-demand economics. Quality matters.

You seem to be much more a micro person than Solow, however.
I have always been a macroeconomist.

But you micro-founded it.
Yes, that's it. I've always found that there should be micro-foundations to macroeconomics. And especially, I wanted a micro-foundation to unemployment. The 'market for lemons' started out from that program.

Is that the road how you got to 'efficiency wages' and all that?
Yes, what triggered that concept was my concern with the micro-foundations of unemployment. It took me a very long time to come to a conclusion there – and the one I came to is one that is very hard for an economist to draw. It is the following: if there is unemployment that is involuntary, then there can only be one reason. And that reason is that people are paying wages which are higher than the market-clearing level. It's odd that it took so long. But you simply had to draw that conclusion at some stage. Otherwise, the concept of unemployment didn't mean what we think it does mean. Once you arrive at that conclusion, though, then there are all kinds of stories as to why people would pay wages that are in excess of market clearing.

Well, that's very convincing. But what precisely was the origin of that idea?
When I was in graduate school, many of my friends were interested in economic development. In their opinion, development economics was not one of the strongest fields. But I thought that, as an economic theorist, I should have an interest in this subject. In 1967/68, I went to India for a year. There was a project by Steve Marglin to allocate the waters of the Bhakra-Nangal dam in northern Punjab. I worked on that project but I wasn't very successful. What I was supposed to do was to make a prediction of the rainwater in the dam. Yet I discovered that the water mainly didn't come from the previous monsoon but it depended on the winter melt, that is, it depended on whether it was a warm or a cold winter. And so, being consistent with my interest in history, I spent my year reading about and thinking about Indian history and society. The one thing that came up and that I have always wanted to find out about, now and then, was why markets sometimes didn't clear. In India, there was a pretty striking example of markets that didn't clear, and that was the caste system. So I wrote a paper about the caste system.[28] It may or may not be a good paper, but it gave an equilibrium in which markets don't clear. The reason why the labor market doesn't clear is some form of social custom. Then, later, I wrote other papers in which unemployment was a result of markets that don't clear because of the social system. And I think that this really

is the fundamental reason. The social system determines what people feel should be a fair wage, and this socially accepted 'fair' wage may be higher than the market clearing one. Here again you can see how I proceed analytically: the Indian caste system had a specific economic property that was mathematically interesting, and then I modeled that, and the resulting model could explain other things as well.

When you say 'mathematically interesting', you mean that it was separable?
What I mean is just that supply doesn't match demand.

You mentioned your wife Janet before. What is it like to have a partner who works in the same field? I guess it can be either wonderful or strenuous. . .
We got married in 1978, and then we went to the London School of Economics, where I got a professorship. I had tenure here at Berkeley, but I was not promoted, and so we went. Initially, Janet and I didn't work together. But we were both interested in macroeconomics, and at some point, we started working together. We almost always agree totally on almost everything in economics. By the way, she had written something very similar to the 'Market for lemons': her paper on bundling.[29] It's very much in the same genre. There is only one area in which we initially disagreed. We disagreed on the benefits of trade.

In which way?
Well, I think we're both converging towards the middle now, after thirty years. We both now see the benefits of trade but we also see that trade can affect the income distribution and be disruptive for poorer people. Janet and I – oh yes, it always was great fun to work together. We started to work together probably in something like 1982/83, and we continued to do so until she went to the Board of Governors of the Federal Reserve – at which point I was devastated to lose her as a co-author.

Was she your preferred co-author? Your cooperation must have been very intense, given that you could work together something like 24 hours a day, as a couple. . .
Yes. But I don't think we ever did that. All our papers were fun. But the paper that was most fun was probably the Germany paper.[30]

That is a very well known paper. But tell me, how did your work influence the way you'd interact? Would you wake up and sit at the breakfast table and debate papers?
I don't know. We talk about economics a lot. How much we talked about our papers as opposed to other economic issues, I don't know. At any

rate, you can't work on very formal, macroeconomic papers all around the clock. In the case of the Germany paper and the paper on abortion,[31] that was different, we talked a lot. Talking of which – the abortion paper is really interesting. The results may actually be correct. The question was why there are so many single-headed households. The answer is that, in the old days, if a woman got pregnant, the guy had to marry her. But then, once abortion became legal and the pill was invented, that custom broke down and women were in a much worse bargaining position when they got pregnant. It's actually a shame that this custom broke down. Families that are single-headed, and especially families that are planned to be single-headed, are a great source of poverty. It's much more difficult to raise children that way.

Right. But, returning to the German question, how did you get attracted to that at all?
It was for a wrong reason. East Germany was in the news a lot when we started writing that paper. That was when many people started leaving the country, to the Czech Republic. We looked at that migration and just thought that when East Germany would be united with West Germany, if there wasn't the right exchange rate, there would also be a lot of migration. So we did a model asking what would then happen if the exchange rate was wrong. Now this turned out to be exactly the case, but we had no reason to know that at the time. We were actually very lucky. And so, when Germany was reunified, the exchange rate turned out to be totally wrong, and we had a model for the questions that followed. That paper was really a great deal of fun. At first, it was more empirical. And we were able to make a good prediction as to what East German goods would be likely to sell and which wouldn't. We ran across the concept of 'Richtungskoeffizient',[32] and we said to ourselves that if there was such a thing at an aggregate, macroeconomic level, we could guess at one at the disaggregate level as well.

In that paper, you advocate wage subsidies. That recommendation was very controversial. It still hasn't yet been fully put into practice, but now, Germany is slowly moving in that direction.
The initial political attempt went very much in our direction. The 'Treuhandanstalt',[33] the German Trust Agency, would give companies subsidies if they employed a certain number of people. That was the equivalent to what we were recommending. What happened, though, was that big industries went in, and then, several years later, they wanted to get rid of some of their employees and cancelled their agreement. That's my interpretation.

In that specific case, but also generally, what is it that drives you? Is it the desire to understand? Or rather the drive to help change the world?
It is my view that if economists want to be taken seriously, they should contribute to making people's lives better, and to get it right. We actually have a duty to get it right. And intellectual beauty is only a corollary there. That's also the reason why I teach macroeconomics. The reason why I teach macroeconomics is that one thing the government can do and has responsibility for, is to create the background market conditions in which people can live healthy, comfortable lives. One thing that government can do is to see that unemployment is fairly low. That's just what every good Keynesian economist believes. As I've gotten older, I've realized that we need to analyze these questions in a more microeconomic way. It's microeconomic policies which make a difference.

I guess your definition of progress in economic theory also runs along these lines?
In the last century, we made one major bit of progress. We explained how, if you get into a depression, you get out of it. It is actually shocking if you go back to the 1930s, how poor an understanding people had of unemployment. If economics had been more advanced in the 1930s, we might never have had the Great Depression, and we might never have had World War II, too. We could have avoided a huge amount of suffering. We could easily have had deficit spending which would have taken us out of the depression. Now we understand that. So there is a great deal of macroeconomics now which minimizes the effects of demand fluctuations. But basically, macroeconomics does have the right structure. Today, we would know what to do. That is a major contribution. And that's due to Keynes, of course.

What are the major open questions then? What do we need to address urgently?
I think we must enlarge our horizon. The way economic theory is now structured is such that people's motivations are supposed to be fundamentally economic. Motivations may also include other things such as status, some non-economic goals. But for the most part, motivations are economic. And the way people deal with problems tends to be cognitive. Insofar as economists have dealt with psychology, it has therefore been cognitive psychology. But this misses the major theoretical structure in sociology. Sociologists do not deny that people have economic motivations. But they acknowledge that people also have motivations that economists usually do not take into account. People have ideas as to what they and others should do and shouldn't do: norms. Those are mostly left out in economics. Economists usually interpret norms as some sort

of equilibrium, or else the norms play a role in terms of information. But in fact norms are something that enters directly into the utility function. They are something people care about. These norms are really important. They affect how almost any economic institution or market works. There are relatively few areas in economics where they do not play a role. This is where economics still fails to answer major questions.

In your work, do you also deal with the question of where those norms come from? How they come into being?
A little bit. This is where the English garden style of economics comes back into play. People say that you have to talk about these norms, and they ask where they come from. Now my answer is that we should base our theory and our models on observations. I rather like to substitute for a theoretical answer where these norms come from by the observation that these norms do exist and that they are unlikely to change.

I guess you also have to distinguish between different mentalities. Norms are not the same in the US, in Germany, and in India.
If they are different, then that means that economists are making an error by not taking that into account. You have to be careful not to apply German norms to India. And we should not apply norms regarding democracy to the people in Iraq. If you do that, you are likely to make a mistake. And you can make really bad mistakes.

How can you build in norms into economic theory?
You can build in norms very practically in order to explain gender relations, relations at the workplace, or in the household. Other fields are economics of schooling, because education depends largely on what people think they ought to do, or the economics of institutions, or even macroeconomics. Economists usually look at causality in the sense of some kind of exogenous change. That's very different from causality as function. But what you really want to know is, when there is change, why there is change. That's a totally different notion of causality. We do that with a small example, such as schools, and then we expand that to a more universal level, such as institutions in general. Some institutions may not work just because they are not economically viable. Otherwise, good or bad norms can make all the difference.

Institutions and norms are very different, though, in that you can modify institutions relatively easily, but not norms. The practical consequence is that some institutions, as beautifully as they may be designed, will not work because the norms cannot follow suit.

Well, that's true. But you need to find out which of the two has to change in the first place. The current economic analysis tends to blind us to the fact that we need certain norms to get things to work.

Can we – and are we allowed to – change social norms?
Well, if you view the norms as a problem, then you probably have to. At any rate, it's difficult.

The peculiar thing about progress in many fields is that there seems to be a time for certain paradigm shifts. They seem to come about when the time is ripe. This leads to peculiarities such as the law of decreasing marginal utility having been found more or less at the same moment in four different countries.[34]
That may be true; I'll have to think about that. Well, some research agendas may indeed come up and generate paradigm shifts because with the traditional, top down French garden approach in economics, people don't get viable solutions. There is something about those solutions that makes them unsatisfactory. And then some people will spring loose from the cognitive tradition and will try something different, mathematical eco-nomics, for example. As a result of this pattern of progress, we can now consider phenomena in ways in which we couldn't consider them before. That's what I mean by freedom. In order to get new solutions, you have to free yourself from the older, from all previous non-mathematical tradi-tion, or otherwise you will end up basically with what everybody else had been doing before.

Doesn't economics run the risk of over-mathematization – nowadays? Can't we have economics without mathematics any more?
Probably not. And that's one of the successes of mathematical economics. Actually, we have only put simple mathematical structures on what other people would have thought of as rather complicated problems. That's very useful.

Sure, but math is only a tool. But can it give you inspiration about what goes on in social interaction?
Well, in many other social sciences, much of the debates turn a lot around meaning. They serve to clarify notions and definitions. Economists, however, tend not to argue about 'what do you mean?' The use of math-ematics has advanced economics to a state where we have a mutual language.

Thank you, Professor.

NOTES

1. The interview was held on 29 June 2007.
2. One of the papers that constitute his thesis was published as George A. Akerlof (1967).
3. Janet Louise Yellen, an economist with a Ph.D. from Yale, is currently president of the Federal Reserve Bank of San Francisco. She taught economics at the University of California at Berkeley, at Harvard and at the LSE. She served as chair of President Bill Clinton's Council of Economic Advisers from 1997 to 1999, and was a member of the Federal Reserve System's Board of Governors from 1994 to 1997.
4. Libertarianism typically concentrates on 'negative' individual freedom, that is on the absence of coercion exerted by others, but also and especially by the state. In essence, negative individual freedom means the protection of property rights, freedom of contract, and rule of law. What George A. Akerlof refers to here is the fundamentally different 'positive' freedom, that is the factual individual capability to achieve one's goals – and that has to do with money. See David Boaz (1998).
5. For a contextualization of this Popperian term, see Bruce Caldwell (2004, p. 388).
6. George A. Akerlof (1970).
7. George J. Stigler (1961).
8. Thomas Gresham (1519–79) was a financier and economic adviser to Queen Elizabeth I. His law is commonly stated as follows: 'Bad money drives out good'. Gresham made this observation with respect to the bad quality of the British coinage. The previous monarchs, Henry VIII and Edward VI, had forced the populace to accept debased coinage through their legal tender laws. The parallel is exact for the 'driving out' effect but incorrect insofar as market participants are able to distinguish good and bad money, but not good and bad cars.
9. See also Kenneth J. Arrow (1971).
10. Some classical liberals criticize the economics of information school on the grounds that instead of acknowledging that the market is a 'marvel' in assembling given local knowledge and in generating new knowledge from there, as Friedrich August von Hayek pointed out, they start from the idea that markets just don't manage to pass on the relevant information. This, however, is imprecise, and the criticism is unwarranted. The economics of information school can easily be subsumed to the Hayekian approach. Using Hayek's terminology, one may say that the proponents of this approach start from the idea that all knowledge is local and different, and then analyze in detail how exactly the process of 'division of knowledge' takes place, that is how it is that all these bits of information get assembled and dispersed in market transactions. While Hayek's is an n-stage dynamic model, Akerlof's model would be just a static picture of $t = 0$ in it – and that's probably what the 'triviality' criticism really meant. What is genuinely interesting is what follows in stages $t > 0$, and that is what the economics of information school really addresses. Given that this theoretical progress is framed as situational analysis, in Karl Popper's terminology, this enhanced explanatory power may however come at the price of less predictive power, as Bruce Caldwell points out. See Caldwell (2004, p. 393). There is of course undeniably a methodological difference in that the modern economics of information approach is couched in neoclassical equilibrium terms, while Hayek's approach transcends this. In a truly dynamic approach, the notion of equilibrium becomes meaningless. While one needs to be aware of this, I consider this however not to be terribly relevant if one looks at the compatibility of the two perspectives. Then there is also an ideological difference between those who talk about market failure and those who don't, preferring to look at the dynamics of markets as 'discovery procedures'. But this again isn't terribly relevant. It does not automatically imply a similar difference between those who do research in the economics of information and those who follow up on the division of knowledge idea. These two can be in harmony – even though, it is true, Akerlof and the other 2001 laureates clearly are market skeptics. Jörgen W. Weibull from the Nobel Committee also gives us an example to the contrary

in his presentation speech, concluding that 'Adam Smith's invisible hand does not always work as effectively as traditional economics had us believe' (available under www.nobel.se). For the 'division of knowledge', see Friedrich August von Hayek (1937, 1945, 1968/1978).

11. George A. Akerlof (2003).
12. George A. Akerlof (1980).
13. George A. Akerlof (1982).
14. George A. Akerlof and Janet L. Yellen (1986).
15. George A. Akerlof et al. (1991).
16. George A. Akerlof and Janet L. Yellen (1985) and George A. Akerlof (2001/2).
17. George A. Akerlof et al. (1996, 2000).
18. George A. Akerlof and Rachel E. Kranton (2002).
19. George A. Akerlof and Rachel E. Kranton (2005).
20. John Kenneth Galbraith (1954).
21. Franklin Delano Roosevelt (1882–1945) was the 32nd President of the United States. He was himself a Harvard alumnus. During the Great Depression of the 1930s, Roosevelt created the New Deal – a program of government interventions aiming at a relaunch of the economy, relief for the poor and unemployed, and regulation of the banking system. The New Deal is controversial until this day. See, for example, Amity Shlaes (2007).
22. This is probably Akerlof's most famous paper (George A. Akerlof, 1970).
23. Robert M. Solow was awarded the Nobel Prize in 1987 'for his contributions to the theory of growth'.
24. This idea was the result of a path-breaking paper by Robert M. Solow (1960).
25. The term 'putty clay technology' refers to the fact that putty can be moulded at will before baking, but once baked, it becomes hardened clay and it is impossible to further influence its shape (Robert M. Solow, 1962).
26. Joseph Stiglitz was awarded the Nobel Prize together with George Akerlof and Michael Spence in 2001, all of them 'for their analyses of markets with asymmetric information'.
27. Janet Louise Yellen, George Akerlof's wife since 1978, is also an economic scholar and currently president of the Federal Reserve Bank of San Francisco. Earlier, she taught economics at the University of California at Berkeley, at Harvard and at the London School of Economics. She holds a Ph.D. in economics from Yale University (1971). In addition, she served as chair of President Bill Clinton's Council of Economic Advisers from 1997 to 1999, and was a member of the Federal Reserve System's Board of Governors from 1994 to 1997.
28. George A. Akerlof (1976).
29. William Adams and Janet L. Yellen (1976).
30. That paper, in which the authors advocate wage subsidies, received a lot of attention internationally and started a still ongoing controversy in Germany (George A. Akerlof et al., 1991).
31. George A. Akerlof et al. (1996b).
32. 'Richtungskoeffizient', translatable as 'direction coefficient' or 'slope', is a notion related to trade with the GDR. It captures domestic resource costs. It was used to convert to GDR marks those profits or losses resulting from exchanges in convertible currency.
33. The 'Treuhandanstalt' was created by law in the summer of 1990, while the GDR was formally still in existence. Its main function was to sell or to transfer all publicly owned enterprises and assets of the East German economy into private hands. It was dissolved in 1994, with some spin-offs still existing today.
34. Hermann Heinrich Gossen, Stanley Jevons, Carl Menger and Léon Walras all came to that conclusion in the second half of the nineteenth century, in Germany, Britain, Austria and Switzerland. As Francis Edgeworth formulates, 'they have contemplated in different aspects the same fundamental conception: that value in exchange is neither

simply identical with, nor wholly different from, value in use, but corresponds to the utility of the last, the least useful, portion of the commodities exchanged. "Nützlichkeit des letzten Mengentheilchens", "Degree of Final Utility", "Grenznutzen", and "Rareté" – in different tongues and various terminology they proclaim the one essential truth which will for ever be associated with the names of Gossen, Jevons, Menger and Walras' (Francis Ysidro Edgeworth, 1889, p. 434). It is now widely agreed that Gossen was actually first (Hermann Heinrich Gossen, 1854).

Vernon L. Smith

*George Mason University,
Fairfax, VA, USA*

*Reprinted with kind permission of
Bernd Kramer.*

The Sveriges Riksbank Prize in Economic Sciences in Memory of Alfred
Nobel 2002 shared with Daniel Kahnemann 'for having established laboratory experiments as a tool in empirical economic analysis, especially in
the study of alternative market mechanisms'.

INTRODUCTION

We're supposed to meet in the lobby of the Westward Look Hotel in
Tucson, Arizona. It's the only hotel that I know here; I had once been there
for a seminar, and so I've taken residence there once again. 'The Westward
Look is my favorite spot in Tucson anyway', Vernon L. Smith had written
in an email, and so it was decided. A little before 10 a.m. on Saturday
morning, a hot, muggy day coming up, I'm downstairs, looking out for the
80-year-old with the legendary pony tail. But nobody's there who matches
this description. I wander around, venturing out in the driveway, coming
back in, out and around the pool. Half an hour goes by. Finally a man,
perhaps in his sixties, with short dark blonde hair, slim and trim, dressed
in tight jeans and a red Hawaiian shirt, rises from one of the couches and
comes over to me. 'Are you Karen?' Yes – and, unbelievable but true, he is
Vernon L. Smith. He had been there all the while. 'But where's your pony

tail?' I ask in a tone of reproach, apologizing immediately. He grins and says: 'Gone.' His characteristic numerous silver rings are still there, but I hadn't seen them from the distance. I feel terrible about having made him wait. But Vernon L. Smith doesn't mind, he is a patient person, and he's not in a hurry anyway: his third wife and soul mate, Candace Allen Smith, is away up in the North-East for a conference. We end up talking two full days. Which is surprising only to the extent that I naively thought I already knew everything about him, given that I had been allowed beforehand to read the 700-page draft of his breathtakingly moving, dramatic memoirs, *Discovery*.[1] But reading is passive, conversation is active – interactive even – and therefore much richer. We toss around a host of ideas and considerations together. It's a lot of fun. Vernon is kind, open-minded, deep and takes one seriously. And he enjoys one-to-one conversations.[2] After a long discussion on Saturday, Vernon is back at the hotel on Sunday morning, fresh and beaming, bringing hot coffee from Starbuck's and some fruit juice. I feel spoiled.[3]

Vernon Lomax Smith is another 'unlikely' case in the sense that neither his family background nor the economic circumstances of his youth seemed to allow for, let alone promote the kind of career that he has had. Vernon L. Smith was born in 1927, in the years leading to the Great Depression, in Wichita, Kansas, as the son of a machinist. Nobody in his family really was an academic. Vernon is the only child that his father, Vernon Chessman Smith, had with his mother, Lulu Belle Lomax, who had already had two daughters from an earlier marriage and had been widowed at age 22. Her first husband was a fireman on the Santa Fe railroad who was killed in an accident. The life insurance money provided to the family was invested in a farm near Milan, Kansas. In 1932, Vernon Chessman Smith lost his job, like many others during the Great Depression, and the family moved to the farm for survival. Vernon L. Smith has good memories from these times, as he makes clear in the interview. Farm life was poor and tedious, but fun for a child – and a good school for life. In 1934, the family lost the farm to the mortgage bank, and the family had to move back to Wichita. Fortunately, Vernon L. Smith's father had been hired again by then. Besides going to school, young Vernon started working in the ninth grade, first at a drug store, then at a restaurant and soda fountain, and finally, at age 16, while continuing his high school curriculum, at Boeing Aircraft. In 1944, Vernon started going to college – first to Friend's University, a Quaker college, studying physics, chemistry, calculus, astronomy and literature, and then to the renowned California Institute of Technology (Cal Tech), majoring first in physics but then switching to electrical engineering. At this time, however, he had already taken

a course in economics and had also stumbled over a very contradictory pair of books, namely Paul Samuelson's *Foundations*[4] and Ludwig
von Mises's *Human Action*.[5] Intrigued, he enrolled for graduate studies
of economics at the University of Kansas. He then was accepted at
Harvard for postgraduate studies, and received a scholarship free of
tuition. At Cambridge, he got in touch with foremost Keynesians such
as Alvin Hansen and Paul Samuelson, with Austrians such as Gottfried
Haberler and Fritz Machlup, but also with Edward Chamberlin – his
major source of inspiration. In 1955, Vernon L. Smith received his Ph.D.,
with a thesis on investment and production.[6] Subsequently, Smith joined
the economics research group at Purdue University in West Lafayette,
Indiana. In 1958, he was promoted to associate professor and received
tenure in 1961 while spending a year at Stanford at the same time. In
1967, he switched to Brown University in Providence, mainly in order to
enable his first wife, Joyce Harkleroad, to start her own career. In 1968,
he moved on to the University of Massachusetts in Boston. In 1972–73,
he spent a year at the Center for Advanced Study of the Behavioral
Sciences (CASBS) at Stanford as a visiting scholar, and the subsequent
two years at Cal Tech. In 1975, Smith joined the faculty at the University
of Arizona at Tucson and also married for a second time: his companion
Carol Breckner. He stayed in Tucson until 2001 when he was called to
join George Mason University in Fairfax, Virginia, where he created
the Interdisciplinary Center for Experimental Science. He also became a
research fellow at the Mercatus Center in Washington. Upon 'Nobelity',
he founded the International Foundation of Research in Experimental
Economics (IFREE).[7] In 2007, he left the Washington area and moved
to California together with his team: Chapman University at Orange
has committed to building a new Economic Science Institute, with a
brand-new purpose-built laboratory for experimental studies and an
annual budget of 4 million dollars. Beyond the Nobel Prize, Vernon
L. Smith has received numerous other awards throughout his distinguished career, the Adam Smith Award from the Association for Private
Enterprise Education (1995), the Distinguished Alumni Award from Cal
Tech, and the Hayek Medal from the German Friedrich August von
Hayek Gesellschaft (2008).

   Vernon Smith's mother had been a socialist, much embittered and
confirmed in her leftist leanings after the family lost the farm to the
mortgage bank in 1934. But this didn't prejudice her son forever. He
quickly realized that the economy isn't the same thing as engineering,
and that socialism, for lack of knowledge and inability to generate
relevant new knowledge, just cannot work. Today, Vernon L. Smith is
a deeply convinced free-market person, if not a libertarian[8] – not only

because he recognizes the efficiency of free markets that he has proved already in his first experiments, but also for a more philosophical reason. Friedrich August von Hayek's idea of the 'division of knowledge', building on Adam Smith's idea of a 'division of labor', has had found deep resonance in him. This is not to say that these two authors actually guided him throughout his career – on the contrary, it was only after 40 years of his own work that his own insights made him rediscover his namesake, the other Scottish Enlightenment philosophers, and Hayek. As Smith says,

> I first had to discover certain things for myself, and essentially it was the behavior I observed in human subjects in my laboratory study of markets that motivated me eventually to study Hayek seriously. Reading with the eyes of a new mind, I was able to appreciate an enormous depth of understanding in the work of Hayek that would have escaped me if I had not had this personal experience in the laboratory.[9]

This description is not without some reminder of Hayek's characterizations of the 'puzzler': a person who has perhaps not all the material of his field at hand, for lack of memory or reading, but precisely because he has to think things through on his own and on his own terms, he may discover unconventional new avenues.[10] Vernon L. Smith is such a puzzler – but he's not a loner.

How does this clear commitment to markets and the trust in the knowledge-assembling and knowledge-generating abilities of spontaneous, free interaction square with his experiments and with the market-design recommendations that he derives from them? Some libertarians mistrust Smith because his testing of market performance always implies some equilibrium benchmark, while in a Hayekian dynamic evolutionary setting, the very notion of equilibrium is meaningless – and because his endeavor to design specific markets, especially for public goods, may seem like a perfect example for the sin of constructivism. One answer is that in the short run (which, by the way, doesn't necessarily refer to time, but just to the unit of analysis), the equilibrium notion isn't meaningless. And the other answer is that trying to understand the workings of markets and other spontaneous orders, and seeing how exogenous rule changes affect them, doesn't mean that we may only sit still and observe. As Smith himself puts it in his Nobel Lecture, experimental economics is there to help people make rational choices in adequate settings, insofar as it necessarily is of course somewhat constructivist – like any set of rules that are collectively chosen. But that constructivism comes not only with the desire to do away with purely political distortions, but it comes also with a heavy dose of humility, because then of course, the implemented market design has to undergo the evolutionary market test. 'We understand little about how rule systems for social interaction and markets emerge, but it is possible in the laboratory to do variations on the rules, and thus to study that which is not.'[11]

The all-decisive impulse for Vernon L. Smith's career in launching experiments goes back to Edward Chamberlin.[12] In his introductory class at Harvard, in 1952, Chamberlin used a little experiment to show that with imperfect competition, markets don't clear. Although the students didn't take that little experiment very seriously, and even though Vernon L. Smith was to show the contrary later on, this experience 'really changed my life', as he says in the following interview. His own experiments, conducted at Purdue University, showed that markets do exactly what price theory predicts for them; there always was convergence to equilibrium. The profession however wasn't quite ready to take this new approach seriously. The resulting paper, 'An experimental study of competitive market behavior',[13] one of the two papers that were going to bring Vernon L. Smith the Nobel Prize in 2002, was rejected and needed two revisions before it could finally be published in the *Journal of Political Economy*, as he now recalls with a smile. Smith also found out that in order to make those experiments realistic, it is helpful to pay – and be they small – financial rewards.[14] His second major contribution then was the theory of induced valuation which he explained in a seminal paper named 'Experimental economics: Induced value theory'[15] which serves as a guiding handbook for experimental research still today.

Later on, he concentrated more on specific market design, relying on his insight that the institutional form of a market influences the way it functions. In that context, his laboratory became the 'wind tunnel' for testing proposed institutional mechanisms. One particular issue of this field is auctions. Different auction forms have different influences on outcomes, as Smith found out in some path-breaking pieces such as the 1976 paper on 'Bidding and auctioning institutions'[16] and the 1980 paper on 'Incentives and behaviour in English, Dutch, and sealed-bid auctions'.[17] For example, the average sale price tends to be higher in English and sealed-bid second-price auctions than in sealed-bid first-price auctions.[18] This work has been extremely influential. Dealing with market design also led his research group into consulting, especially for stock exchanges and for public utility companies. As Smith emphasizes in our interview, this wasn't just for the money, however, but 'it has really been important. It's been a critical part of what we do. That's where we find answers to the questions of how what we found in the laboratory works out in the field.' Beyond his paradigmatic field of experimental economics, Vernon L. Smith has worked in diverse areas, ranging from capital theory and finance to natural resource economics. On top of that, he has regularly come back to more philosophical areas such as social choice.[19]

As we have seen, Vernon L. Smith's ideas sprang from a range of different influences. People mattered greatly: family, teachers and collaborators. Although his family background was not an intellectual one, Smith claims that his father's work ethic and can-do knowledge as well as his mother's interest in political and social issues were instrumental. The Great Depression and the hardship it brought to the family also triggered his interest in these matters. His heritage and childhood have given him intellectual curiosity, the ability to work hard and to stand steadfast on firm ground even if surrounded by something new; and last, but not least, the guts to deviate from the mainstream. Then, good teachers and inspiring classes were essential, especially Richard Howey at Kansas and Edward Chamberlin at Harvard. Chamberlin's class was Smith's epiphany, even though in an indirect and not immediately effective way. Later on, much was due to Smith's innate – pathological or not – extraordinary capacity to concentrate, as he stresses, and of course to the fresh ideas generated by team work. While the economic situation as such didn't seem to play much of a role, economic policy did. It was actually the background against which all of Smith's research could take place: subsequent to the economic liberalization trend throughout the world, there was a growing interest in questions concerning how those liberalized markets, especially the utilities, should be regulated. Since the field was new, it also developed that dynamism of its own kind that invariably results as gaps in the theory show up. When theory doesn't withstand the confrontation with reality, these gaps need to be identified – and filled. It is through this continuous process of theory, theory rebuttal and theory refinement that progress takes place.

INTERVIEW

Is there any key to your academic interests that may already be found in your youth, Vernon?
I didn't know economics existed until I was an undergraduate at Cal Tech. Initially, I was interested in studying science and engineering. In that respect, my father's influence was pretty strong. Neither of my parents had an education beyond eighth grade. But he was a skilled machinist and had a lot of can-do knowledge; he could make anything of almost anything. It was that environment that took me to Cal Tech. My mother, on the other hand, was always very active in political and social affairs in the community. I think that ultimately developed my interest in economics.

Did you discuss economic topics at home at all, given the rising unemployment and poverty in the times of the Great Depression?
Within the family and with our friends, especially those connected with the socialist movement, it was clear that all the problems of the world were connected with the profit motive. This was the source of the country's problems and the world's difficulties. Essentially, this was why you had wars and why you had poverty. Later, in college, I was fascinated by the idea that you could actually study these things, that it needn't be only a matter of opinion. You could actually base your opinions on analysis, on investigation, on some kind of understanding about how society and how the economy works.

And not even high school helped you discover economics?
All through elementary school and high school, education was just concentrated on acquiring reading, writing and mathematical skills. And even that wasn't very strong. So, in order to get into Cal Tech, I had to go to Friend's University for a year, focusing entirely on mathematics, physics and chemistry. I also took a course in astronomy. My interest in experimental economics, I think, was in a way a return to my curiosity about how things actually work, in this case what the connection really is between theory of equilibrium economics and what actions people take in markets. It started as simply a curiosity about how to teach economics.

As a child, you spent two years on a farm, between age five and seven. Under the effects of the Great Depression, your family had to move out there, to a place in which your mother earlier had invested the life insurance of her late first husband, in order to assure your sheer subsistence. Did that situation make you ask more fundamental questions about the economy?
It was a great learning experience. Production was in the home. All this activity you were in direct contact with. Work was not something you went off for to somewhere else, and brought home income. We had moved to the farm because my father was laid off. On a farm, at least, you could raise food – which is what we did. It was a self-sufficient existence. The only cash crop was grain. Work was all about doing things, and so it was the opposite of a traditional academic stimulus. My only relative that had some education was my mother's uncle. He had a law degree from the University of Kansas. That was very early in the nineteenth century. He had a leg injury and wasn't useful on the farm, that's why he studied and practiced law. He was our only intellectual in the family. But still, my mother was interested in a lot of things, and she read. There were always books at home. Back in town, she was a member of a study club,

a group of women that would get together, read books and discuss them. Educational activities, either practical or intellectual, were going on all the time in my upbringing.

Your parents having little education, they seem to have been very much in favor of your pushing your studies a little further.
I don't know where that came from, but it was always taken for granted that I would go to college, even though my two sisters didn't. But in those days, girls didn't do that. When I was 16, however, I went out for some more working experience; I worked for Boeing for 15 months. I had already worked since I was twelve, for a local neighborhood drug-store at first, where I did deliveries on my bicycle and eventually learned how to operate the fountain. And then, after high school, I worked for a restaurant that had a fountain. When you start to work early, you have skills, and you find work more easily. They didn't pay very well; a dollar a day was common for that kind of work by the late 1930s and early 1940s. But this work experience helped me get the job at Boeing. The other thing that helped was the fact that at high school, I had studied electricity.

Why Boeing?
They had built a new plant to build the B-29. It was the first of a new generation of pressurized airplanes that would fly much higher than the old ones. It was still a propeller airplane, however, of course. I was in the functional Testing Department, earning 5.60 dollars per day. There were a lot of women working at Boeing, because the men were in the military. Also, there weren't any laws that prevented you from going to work at age 16. Nowadays, that would be considered child exploitation. But thanks goodness I was 'exploited'. I learnt to be responsible, to deliver as an employee, to be punctual and all these things. Actually, I had already learnt these things before I even went to Boeing. Still, that was a very good experience. It ended because I wanted to go to college [at Friend's University, Wichita, Kansas], study for a year, get prepared and then move on to Cal Tech. I had already decided that and then did exactly that. I was lucky enough to escape the military draft – mainly due to my young age (I only turned 18 in 1945) and my poor eyesight, which had also prevented me from joining the Merchant Marine.[20]

It is quite intriguing and somewhat surprising that you had an intellectual appetite at all, given that you were such a practical, hands-on person.
That's true. But I think that's also what drove me later to try and find out how this economic theory might actually work. That's an important

influence in my wanting to do this first experiment and then being sucked in to the vortex created by the results – results that didn't seem right according to the conventional wisdom of the time.

One thing at a time. . . We'll come to that in a moment. For now, back to Cal Tech. That must have been quite a challenge.
It was extremely hard work. The advantage for me of going there was that I learnt study skills and work skills in academic pursuits that were critical later on. I had been doing very well at Friend's, but at Cal Tech, everybody really was outstanding. There were a number of students that were better than I was, they were really brilliant. It was an inspiring place. I took chemistry classes with Linus Pauling[21] – he was a marvelous teacher, he had people spellbound in the big lecture hall. J. Robert Oppenheimer[22] taught physics, Fritz Zwicky[23] astronomy. My parents paid the tuition, and I also worked part-time.

You had been majoring in physics but switched to electrical engineering. Why was that?
Basically in order to avoid one specific, very hard class. I didn't want to take a run at that.

Understandable. But then you took an economics class, and that turned you around much more substantially. How did that come about?
Well, already by the time when I was a junior, and certainly as a sophomore, I wasn't so sure that I wanted to stay in physics. I didn't yet know what else to do, but as a senior, I started venturing a little into history and economics. The program at Cal Tech had a lot of social sciences – for example history, a little bit of economics, and philosophy. Economics was taught by an assistant professor, using some of those old, mainly institutional textbooks, but he supplemented the lectures with micro- and macroeconomics. So I was introduced to Keynesian economics, too. As a result of that course, I was getting really curious about economics, and I went to the library. There, I stumbled over Paul Samuelson's *Foundations*.[24] Also, I decided to subscribe to the *Quarterly Journal of Economics*. One of the first issues had a paper by Hollis B. Chenery[25] on Engineering Production Functions.

That was something for you!
Well, Samuelson's book indicated that economics was just physics, and Chenery showed that it was actually just engineering. Little did I know. . . . At any rate, all that got me intrigued, and I decided to go back to Kansas after my graduation and enroll for an MA in economics at the University

of Kansas. I figured that this additional step would enable me to make a decision whether I really wanted to go on with economics.

That move from the natural sciences to social sciences was a major switch.
That's right. The social sciences at Cal Tech had introduced me to a new world, completely different from the purely technical field. That just intrigued me.

Did you ever ask yourself to what kind of career that would be leading, whether you would be able to find a job with that kind of education?
I don't think I did. The science classes that I took did satisfy my immediate aspirations, but I didn't see it as a career. Economics was intriguing, and at very low cost, I could go back to the University of Kansas, supporting myself. I also had some scholarship support there. During the second year there, I started to teach as an assistant instructor. I taught economic history. That's a great way of learning things, by the way: by teaching them. You just need to stay ahead of the class. Generally, the economics program was very stimulating. From Richard Howey, I took price theory, mathematical economics, imperfect competition, and the development of economic thought.

Did math always come easy?
The Cal Tech experience really made that part of economics easy for me. Of course, you can have mathematical abilities, but the modeling skills don't necessarily transfer. But I found that I really enjoyed modeling in economics. Upon that experience at Kansas, I never looked back, and stayed in economics. Forever.

What was the next step after Kansas?
I had applied for graduate studies at Harvard, MIT, Stanford, Chicago and Carnegie Tech. I was accepted at all those universities. But in 1952, when I started, the scholarship at Harvard was the best, net of tuition. Also, you could take additional classes at MIT, and that of course was an advantage. So, during my second year, I took Paul Samuelson's micro course.

In terms of the development of economic theory, those were very interesting times.
Oh yes. I had Alvin Hansen[26] in macroeconomics. He actually was very optimistic that you could finance most of government from an expansion of money supply. The non-Keynesian contingent at Harvard were Wassily Leontief[27] and Gottfried Haberler.[28] Leontief had come from Russia,

and Haberler from Vienna, a young member of the Austrian school. Alexander Gerschenkron gave lectures in economic history which I liked Econometrics was taught by Guy Orcutt. However, Harvard wasn't very strong in mathematical economics. Mathematization was rather a new wave coming from MIT. Harvard was more traditional, with more emphasis on monetary theory. It was about right for me. I was there only for three years, because I had a family coming on. By the time I received my degree, I had three children, and therefore, I wasn't going to be a professional student.

Considering your own original thinking concerning market structure and market design, what did Harvard give you?
I had sat in on Edward Chamberlin's[29] introductory class at Harvard, in 1952. I didn't take it for credit because I had already had this very good imperfect competition class by Richard Howey back at Kansas. But Chamberlin gave me the decisive idea to use experiments. I didn't build on it before my time at Purdue University, but it really changed my life.

As a matter of fact, you received the Nobel Prize for 'having established laboratory experiments as a tool in empirical economic analysis, especially in the study of alternative market mechanisms'.[30] So what exactly did Chamberlin do in his class to the effect that the idea eventually occurred to you that one could study different market designs?
Chamberlin had done a little experiment in order to introduce us to monopolistic competition, intending to show us that markets couldn't always be trusted to be competitive. He might have gotten that from Eugen von Böhm-Bawerk,[31] by the way. There is a lot of good stuff in Austrian economics that hasn't been picked up for many decades. Anyway, and to be true, the reaction among students to Chamberlin's experiment actually was: 'What is this silly little demonstration?' Not that any of us doubted that he was right in saying that perfect competition was an unreal, impossible kind of ideal, abstract thing, but we thought that didn't really add anything. So, being peer-impressionable, I didn't question that at all. And then somehow, in the middle of the night, in 1956 at Purdue, I wake up and I have this idea.

In the middle of the night?
Oh yes. I was teaching 'Principles of economics' at that time, and I had a problem that attracted my curiosity: how do supply and demand actually connect to the actions that people take in markets? What's the relationship? If students had asked me, I wouldn't have been able to answer. Fortunately, students were usually reluctant to ask, and if they did ask, we

usually gave them answers such as 'this is a world without frictions' etc. – nothing to answer the question. We came up with those stories because we didn't know what the answer was. We just defined the problem away. That bothered me. I suddenly realized that Chamberlin, in his experiment, was trying to show a connection. Here was supply and demand, and he was having people do things. And that launched me. I thought – well, there is actually nothing wrong with an experiment, hey, that's fine! The problem was the way things were being done. If you want to show that perfect competition is unrealistic, you need to take an institution that might be more competitive. That would be a way to trade stocks and commodities, for example. Out of anywhere, the conventional wisdom was that those would be competitive markets – although I wouldn't claim that the economists knew why, although for one thing, there are large numbers and small traders. And so I wondered how they trade. That's not what you typically learn as an economist. And so I learnt about the structure of trading and the rules, and I then realized – I'll do experiments! The neat thing is that if you read the works of Friedrich August von Hayek[32] along with a program where students are engaged in those experiments, they really get it, they really see what he is talking about. For example, we often times do experiments with completely different kinds of markets that have never existed in history. But that they have never existed doesn't mean we can't do experiments about them. And Hayek has this wonderful quote in the *Law, Legislation, and Liberty* that runs more or less as follows: 'The proper study of social science is the study of what is not.'[33] This quote absolutely gives me chills. That's exactly what we do when we ask what would happen if we changed the rules that we have inherited. One thing this kind of analysis can always do is to tell you why the existing rules are the way they are.

How were the first experiments that you did received by the academic community? You were placing yourself way out of mainstream, after all.
I had support from my colleagues at Purdue University. It was a very nurturing, supportive community. Our recruiting strategy was basically to concentrate on economic historians instead of hiring people in various applied fields. A lot of new things came out of that strategy, in terms of quantitative methods, mathematical economics, econometrics, and cliometrics[34] in economic history – and experimental economics in my case. Nobody expected you to do anything that looked like traditional, old-style economics. We were all young, new Ph.D.s, assistant professors, some from Stanford, Chicago, Johns Hopkins, and Harvard. Economics was mainly a teaching service department on behalf of the large engineering and science program at Purdue. The reason why I had gone there was that

there was a real commitment to build a real economics department and, later, a business college in its own right.

And what about the reactions from the wider academic community?
They had no idea why anybody would be doing experimental economics. My first paper, 'An experimental study of competitive market behavior', was published in the *Journal of Political Economy* (*JPE*).[35] I had sent it out in 1960. By the time I got the paper back with two negative reviews and a rebuttal, a new editor had taken over. That was the Canadian economist Harry G. Johnson. He was the last editor of the *JPE* who read everything that came in. It wasn't a clear rejection; he left the door open for me. By that time I had done more work and wanted to revise the paper anyway, and he invited me to do that. So I ultimately resubmitted, and he sent the paper out to two referees, but the reports were negative again. Johnson wanted to know what my response would be, and so I wrote one. He admitted that before he became the new editor of *JPE*, he had been one of the two referees that had turned down the first version. But now I had convinced him. And so, in the end, he decided to publish it without further revisions.

What did they object to at first? Anything serious?
Oh, it was all off-the-wall stuff, such as the group for the experiment being too small, students in the group having systematic behavioral biases, etc. Nobody was thinking about these things the same way I was. To the average person the whole approach was new, it was strange, it wasn't economic, and somehow it couldn't be right. After that 1962 paper, however, it became easier. I had another paper in *Quarterly Journal of Economics* in 1964,[36] another one in *JPE* in 1965,[37] one in the *Journal of Business* in 1967.[38] At that time, it was as if my approach had a certain novelty. It was not as if journals were being inundated with manuscripts of that sort, and there was more tolerance. But still, it was only five papers in eight years. The field didn't start to really take off until the seventies, particularly after I went to the Center for Advanced Study of the Behavioral Sciences (CASBS) at Stanford as a visiting scholar in 1972–73, and during the following two years at Cal Tech. Those were important years.

In their official statement for the Nobel Prize, the Swedish Academy of Sciences expressly mentions your 1976 paper on 'induced valuation'.[39] What prompted you to come up with this paper which turned out to be a seminal contribution?
No one was doing experiments at that time, nobody saw a point in doing them – but I did. I found that there were things in it that I couldn't

learn otherwise. So I did more and more reading in the philosophy of science, and I thought about the methodology of the sort of thing we were doing. And that led me to realize that the thing that was driving the whole enterprise was what I came to call the 'theory of induced valuation'. If you take the standard revealed preference or utility function where people value two commodities x and y, and we have results that show that indifference curves are independent of a positive transformation of the utility function, then, as I realized, if you make the amount of payment a function of the amount of goods that someone ends a trading period with, then they only have to have a utility from money, and that means that utility is associated with x and y. This was a way of controlling the demand environment, so long as people weren't saturated with money. I taught that in 1963, 1964, 1965, when I was first teaching our graduate workshop. And also, which is perhaps more prosaic, Charles Plott[40] had come up to me and told me that, given that we had been using this approach for a long time, we needed something to cite, and so I should write something down. And so I did. Plott and I had a lot of interaction about our research, even on our fishing trips. He had come out of the Public Choice tradition in Virginia; Jim Buchanan[41] had been his dissertation adviser. He now had gotten interested in experimental economics and started to use the method of induced valuation in looking at voting systems. He really created the field of experimental political economy.

How did your ideas spring up – while working jointly with someone such as Charles Plott, or rather individually?
The interactions with Plott got me into joint research; that was really the beginning of it. He was a very important source of inspiration. He was also very good at placing papers. I often times gave up too early, but Charlie would always insist and be successful. For example, we worked together, and also with Ross Miller, on a market setting allowing for allocation over time, with cycling demand.[42] This was the first introduction of asset trading. That was necessary because you had to be able to hold an inventory of the flow commodity. Then, later, during the foundation building years in the late seventies and eighties at the University of Arizona, Arlington Williams and I did more experiments for which we had developed some computer software. In the experiments, people could now interact on the computer. We had used it for double auctions, but now we realized that this program could actually be easily modified and used for asset trading. By that time, our ideas came faster than we could implement them. The field now really took off. Charles Plott even got NASA money for some project.

In your approach, what is more important – to know how people actually behave (the behavioral aspects) or what the impact of specific market structures is as such?
I don't think you can rank them by order of importance. It's all about the interaction of both. In experiments, you create an environment, you bring in an institution, and then the open question is how people behave and how that behavior responds either to changes in the environment or to the institutional rules. These questions now become addressable. Behavior is important, but it's institutions, the rules that ultimately matter, because they in turn affect behavior.

Have you never been attracted by the kind of psychological approach that Daniel Kahnemann,[43] your co-laureate, stands for?
No. Kahnemann is interested in individual decision making where the circumstances are entirely defined. It's not about interaction – even though nobody is an isolated decision maker in this world! And yet, his field is only about choices between gambles, with fixed pay-offs and probabilities. It's concerned with how individual people think and decide in a context of uncertainty. The maintained hypothesis in psychology is that people aren't rational, and therefore the system can't be rational either – whereas we economists have learned that institutions matter. Well laid-out institutions can help people with rational decision-making. Therefore, I actually believe that a lot of the current work in cognitive psychology is likely to be affected by experiments with repeat interactive decision making experiences.

You have mentioned stock exchanges earlier. They also function under rule systems which may or may not undergo change. How easy has it been to change rules in the sense of introducing electronic trading, for example?
It took forever. I thought electronic trading was feasible in the early sixties, but that innovation got used in the market only 35 years later, due to the resistance coming from the owners. Actually, we were consulting with the Chicago Mercantile Exchange. Over the years, they have been more innovative than the Chicago Board of Trade. They've developed the first electronic trading system. But the problem was that the traders own the Exchange; they are the members. Introducing electronic trading necessarily put their trading activities out of business. So we needed a compromise, and in the end, they introduced electronic trading only off-hours, during the night, so that they could keep the old-fashioned way of trading during the day. But that couldn't work, and finally they got rid of that. I guess the reason for the breakthrough was competition from other exchanges. Of course, the exchange as a firm is more valuable with this innovation,

without the labor intensive kind of trading, and the members then earn their income through their ownership, not through trading. They finally realized it.

What about your work on airlines – pricing and slot allocation, for example?[44]
That's a case where you have indivisibilities. That creates some challenges. For example, double auctions may not work, and you have to find other institutions. Sometimes, these other institutions tend to be very hard on the firms, and competition becomes brutal, given the declining cost. That's exactly the case with airlines. Through experimentation, you can learn to find the price menus as a function of the characteristics of the flight pattern. For you really want to fill the airplane because the flight cost doesn't depend much on the number of people on the plane – fuel, crew, distance, they are all the same. In these markets, there is a terrible downward pressure on prices. That's also why you get those incredible price differences from one passenger to another. It turns out that prices are not set the usual way, simply at marginal cost, but planes are filled with low-cost passengers first, who have an incentive to buy early, so that the company can plan ahead, and then you hike up the price as much as you can for the other passengers. It doesn't look like a standard model of competition. The usual way of thinking about pricing just doesn't work here.

This sounds like a good topic to do consulting with.
Oh no. We have been pushing this since the early eighties. But airlines are not interested, and the Federal Aviation Agency (FAA) isn't either when it comes to slot allocation. The FAA's general attitude is 'use it or lose it'. The idea of turning slots into tradable rights just seems to run counter to some American tradition. The only time when starting and landing rights are really bought and sold is when a company goes bankrupt and the vultures come in. They are more interested in the remaining slots than in the airplanes as a valuable resource.

But you have done a lot of consulting. On whose initiative did that usually take place – or, put differently, did those consulting jobs help you find new interesting areas for research or were they just applications of your research?
We only did consulting that would be research at the same time. Actually, there are some firms that want proprietary research – so that they get the data, and the data can't get published. We don't do that. And so, usually, secrecy requirements like that have not been binding for us. Most of the

time, we can talk companies into providing information which we will then disguise. All we publish later on is stuff that has nothing to do with the company; it's just the outcomes of our experiments. As for who started our consulting jobs, well, sometimes it was upon the initiative of some company, sometimes it was us who pushed for it. In the case of the electric power research, the industry's interest in what we did was fueled by a series of workshops that we did for high-level management. We did about three of these, and had 20 people in them. That was in 1995. We then involved them in a demonstration experiment, with market and exchanges, all constrained by the physics of the grid. Of course, they knew what that meant. All we could really do was get them familiar with what an actual experiment is. They get an idea, and we show them the result. And some of them followed up on it. Southern Company, the holding which owns Southern Power, and Georgia Power had us do workshops. We gave them experience in markets. We started out with simple double auctions, did some stuff with options, and then did the electric power market design. Their idea was: look, deregulation is happening, let's get our top-end boys familiar with what it's all about. For them, it was better than taking some course in economics or finance. It gave them what they needed to know. They were one of the firms that actually fought deregulation. In a way, they were the smartest of all. They learnt enough about markets to make use of it at their advantage, at the same time holding on to the goodies that you get from regulation.

That's clever enough. But what about you?
For us, the consulting – and the research connected with it – has really been important. It's been a critical part of what we do. That's where we find answers to the questions of how what we found in the laboratory works out in the field.[45] We're just learning an incredible amount of how you take something that you've tested out in the lab, and then you take practitioners and interact with them, they have ideas, they have some things they like and some things that they don't like, and so, through that, they get involved in the design. One idea that they grab right on to was: wires are separate from energy. You rent the wires from one company, and you buy the energy that comes in from another company. Then, you need a lot of people out there experimenting with different menus for pricing – real time meters, switches just to cut appliances off in the middle of the day, etc. Who knows what combination of consumer preferences and technology is good. Nobody can do that. It's impossible. So you take what you think looks like the best technology now, make everybody buy it; but tomorrow, it is not nearly as good. It's important to realize that – and it is part of what Friedrich Hayek calls 'discovery'.[46]

The generation of new knowledge through social interaction.
Yes. And so you want to structure these markets in a way so that people can discover what they need to know and what you don't know. And you make it clear to industry: we don't know how to do stuff! If it doesn't come from the inside, it's not going to work. Also, people sometimes criticize that it's 'only' experiments what we do, it's not the real world, it's different out there. But what do they know about why it's different? Yes, there are differences, and we learn about them. General equilibrium models aren't the real world either, and the series on labor statistics isn't either. Tell me, what is the real world? I'd like to know!

Good question. . . Thank you, Vernon.

NOTES

1. Vernon L. Smith (2008).
2. Vernon L. Smith says that due to the (some) symptoms of Asperger's syndrome (a form of autism) that he suffers, he often times finds it difficult to communicate in large groups. If this is so, it is hardly noticeable for an outsider, though. In his memoir, he explains that while this syndrome sometimes alienated him, it also allowed him to concentrate especially well: 'When my mind is immersed in concentrated thought – mentalese, or composition mode – all my circuits seem to be sharply focused on that experiential world of mental creation, and I cannot switch out of it into something different without loss of those self-ordered connected trains of thought that make for coherence. I lose the emerged state of whole vision unity, and later, if I succeed in reestablishing that state of mental being, it reoccurs only after a considerable start-up cost in mental time and energy. Afterwards, I have a lingering sense of permanent loss in recovering an approximation to the original mental state.' See Vernon L. Smith (2008, pp. 27–8).
3. The interview was held on 4 and 5 August, 2007.
4. Paul A. Samuelson (1947).
5. Ludwig von Mises (1949).
6. Vernon L. Smith (1961).
7. IFREE was established in 1997, and it serves, as the mission statement says, 'to advance the understanding of exchange systems and the testing and application of market-based institutions, by funding basic research in economics through experimental methods, supporting the scholarly development of students and pre- and post-doctoral visitors, sponsoring innovative hands-on participatory learning in experimental economics in a variety of settings, and promoting extended discussion of experimental economic research applications to policy.' Vernon L. Smith invested his Nobel Prize money in IFREE.
8. He talks about classical liberalism, 'or its current libertarian incarnation, where my sympathies have slowly if naturally come to lie.' Smith (2005, p. 136).
9. Smith (2005, p. 136).
10. See Friedrich August von Hayek (1978).
11. Vernon L. Smith (2002/2003b, p. 553). And he continues: 'constructivism uses reason to deliberately create rules of action, and create human socioeconomic institutions that yield outcomes deemed preferable, given particular circumstances, to those produced by alternative arrangements. Although constructivism is one of the crowning achievements of the human intellect, it is important to remain sensitive to the fact that human

institutions and most decision making is not guided primarily, if at all, by constructivism. Emergent arrangements, even if initially constructivist in form, must have survival properties that take account of opportunity costs and environmental challenges invisible to our modeling efforts' (pp. 506–7).

12. Edward Hastings Chamberlin (1899–1967) was an American economist teaching at Harvard (1937–67). His most significant contribution was the theory of monopolistic or imperfect competition (see Edward H. Chamberlin, 1933).
13. Vernon L. Smith (1962).
14. Vernon L. Smith (1964).
15. Vernon L. Smith (1976a).
16. Vernon L. Smith (1976b).
17. V.M. Coppinger et al. (1980).
18. In first-price auctions, the first bidder pays his own bid to the seller; in second-price auctions, the winning bidder pays only the second highest bid.
19. Vernon L. Smith (1977).
20. See the interview with Douglass C. North in this book.
21. Linus Carl Pauling (1901–1994) was not only one of the most influential chemists of the twentieth century, working in the fields of quantum chemistry, molecular biology and orthomolecular medicine. He was also one of the few people who have been awarded more than one Nobel Prize (in chemistry, in 1954, and for peace, in 1962, for his campaign against above-ground nuclear testing), without having to share it with another recipient.
22. J. Robert Oppenheimer (1904–67) was an American theoretical physicist. He was the scientific director of the World War II effort to develop the first nuclear weapons at the secret Los Alamos National Laboratory in New Mexico. For this reason he is known as 'the father of the atomic bomb'.
23. Fritz Zwicky (1898–1974) was an American-based Swiss astronomer.
24. Paul A. Samuelson (1947), *Foundations of Economic Analysis*, Harvard University Press. The other book he stumbled on, as he mentions in his Nobel Autobiography, is Ludwig von Mises, *Human Action* (1949). (See www.nobel.se.)
25. Hollis B. Chenery (1918–94) was an economist well known for his contributions in development economics. See Hollis B. Chenery (1949).
26. Alvin Harvey Hansen (1887–1975), 'the American Keynes', was a professor of economics at Harvard. He played a role in the creation of the Council of Economic Advisers and the Social Security System of the US.
27. Wassily Leontief was awarded the Nobel Prize in 1973 'for the development of the input–output method and for its application to important economic problems'.
28. Gottfried Haberler (1900–95) was an Austrian economist who had immigrated to the US in 1936, and became famous working on international trade and on business cycles.
29. Edward Hastings Chamberlin (1899–1967) was an American economist teaching at Harvard (1937–67). His most significant contribution was the theory of monopolistic or imperfect competition. See Edward H. Chamberlin (1933).
30. http://nobelprize.org/nobel_prizes/economics/laureates/2002/press.html.
31. Eugen von Böhm-Bawerk (1851–1914), economist and politician, made crucial contributions to the development of Austrian economics, especially in capital theory. At the University of Vienna, he taught many students including Joseph Schumpeter, Ludwig von Mises. See, in particular, Eugen von Böhm-Bawerk (1891).
32. . . . and his ideas about spontaneous order and the self-coordination of markets.
33. Friedrich August von Hayek (1979, p. 17). The full quotation runs as follows: 'Fruitful social science must be *very* largely a study of what is *not*: a construction of hypothetical models of possible worlds which might exist if some of the alterable conditions were made different' (emphasis in the original). Hayek was awarded the Nobel Prize in 1974, together with the Swedish economist Gunnar Myrdal – both received it 'for their pioneering work in the theory of money and economic fluctuations and for their

penetrating analysis of the interdependence of economic, social and institutional phenomena'.

34.   This is about applying econometric methods to economic history. See the interview with Douglass C. North, one of the 'fathers of cliometrics', in this book.

35.   Vernon L. Smith (1962). The importance of this article is reflected by the fact that it is one of the two papers clearly emphasized in the advanced information provided by the Nobel committee. See www.nobel.se.

36.   Vernon L. Smith (1964).

37.   Vernon L. Smith (1965).

38.   Vernon L. Smith (1967).

39.   www.nobelprize.org/nobel_prizes/economics/laureates/2002/adv.html. The paper is: Vernon L. Smith (1976a).

40.   Charles R. Plott is a pioneer of experimental economics, currently teaching as a Professor of Economics and Political Science at the California Institute of Technology. His research covers the behavioral foundations of economics and political science; laboratory experimental methods; regulation, deregulation and policy design.

41.   James M. Buchanan, one of the founders of the Public Choice school, was awarded the Nobel Prize in 1986 'for his development of the contractual and constitutional bases for the theory of economic and political decision-making'.

42.   See, for example, Ross M. Miller et al. (1977).

43.   Daniel Kahnemann, currently a senior scholar and faculty member emeritus at Princeton University and at the Woodrow Wilson School of Public and International Affairs, received the Nobel Prize for his psychological work on prospect theory, in particular 'for having integrated insights from psychological research into economic science, especially concerning human judgment and decision-making under uncertainty'.

44.   Stephen J. Rassenti et al. (1982).

45.   For the power case, see, for example, Stephen J. Rassenti et al. (2002).

46.   Friedrich August von Hayek (1968/1978).

Edmund S. Phelps

*Columbia University,
New York, USA*

The Sveriges Riksbank Prize in Economic Sciences in Memory of Alfred Nobel 2006 'for his analysis of intertemporal tradeoffs in macroeconomic policy'.

INTRODUCTION

It's a beautiful warm summer day, and it's definitely nicer outside than inside the 'Center on Capitalism and Society', a number of rather charm-free office cubicles at The Earth Institute in Columbia's Hogan Hall, which Edmund S. Phelps presents with an ironic grin: 'Well, this is it.'[1] The Center has been created in 2004 with money from the Kauffman foundation.[2] Its purpose is

> to go beyond the mainstream models of markets to a serious study of capitalism, to the questions about its dynamism and its stability and how capitalism compares in these respects with its rivals, corporatism and market socialism. Such a study is imperative because a country needs to have a more thorough and reliable understanding . . . to make institutional choices. . .[3]

Interestingly, the Center has a rather 'Austrian' research agenda, and Phelps himself dryly affirms: 'Capitalism is Hayek country.'[4] But most of the Center's members can be said to be eclectic neo-Keynesians. Phelps himself is the embodiment of such a mixture, fully appreciating the self-regulating and knowledge-generating forces of market interaction on the one hand while not having excessive qualms about asking for some kind of state intervention on the other hand. Members of the Center include Amar Bhidé; Glenn Hubbard, formerly Chairman of the Council of Economic Advisers; Roman Frydman; Janusz Ordover, formerly chief economist for anti-trust in the Department of Justice; Jeffrey Sachs, Director of The Earth Institute; Robert Shiller; Joseph Stiglitz, Nobel Laureate of 2001; and Phelps himself as Director. The Center issues its own journal, by the name of *Capitalism and Society*.[5] The door to Phelps's office is always open; the noise level is not really zero, but moderate. Neon lamps artificially brighten up the place with their cold, no-nonsense light. A couple of bookshelves along the wall bear witness of the owner's own work – and of his various sources of inspiration.

But Phelps, right now, isn't inspired, he isn't even motivated, he is just tired. He remains charming as usual, but frankly, our conversation drags on. But it's not that he doesn't like to tell his story. It's also not that he needs time to warm up to his interviewer; we first met six years ago and have been friendly ever since. The reason is rather that he would like to take a nap and get over jet lag. Ever since his 'Nobelity', speaking engagements and interview requests have multiplied, and Ned Phelps is constantly on the road. Not that he can't stand traveling. He actually likes it very much – but in style. And that's not always guaranteed, even though, only ten months after the award, he already has managed to earn himself the reputation of being one of the most 'expensive' and 'difficult' Nobel Laureates. These absences take their toll on his research. 'Ever since I've received the Nobel Prize, I don't have so much time. I'm now really drawing on what I've done before. I don't like that', he complains. And then, after all, research in economics is not all that life is about. Phelps loves New York City life, the opera, concerts, theater. He is a trumpet player and also a gifted singer himself – and he often proves his talent at home, when he gives receptions and dinners at his apartment on the Upper East Side together with his Argentinean wife Viviana Montdor. He loves good food, he adores champagne and good wine: over the years, he has become an accomplished epicurean. He does and wants to enjoy life. Locking himself up in a sort of monk's cell atmosphere in order to be productive in research is something he did earlier in life but just wouldn't do any more. 'It's too big a price to pay', he affirms, serious for once. It is true that Phelps is proud of his own achievements, eager to preserve a good public image, and receptive to applause. For example, just two weeks before his prize was announced, he posted a new, extensive CV on his website, with helpful links and all relevant telephone numbers clearly marked. Maybe he just had an excellent intuition. Notwithstanding this, Ned Phelps shows an impressive degree of self-irony and laughs a lot. As a consequence, our conversation is not only instructive, but also tremendously fun to read.

Edmund Strother Phelps was born in Evanston, Illinois, in 1933 – at the height of the Great Depression. The family background was 'bourgeois', as he calls it. His father was in advertising, and his mother a nutritionist, and both had benefited from some economics education. He calls it a 'very practical background of economics', though. The financial and economic news was ever-present in dinner-time conversation. Both parents lost their jobs and got by only with help from their parents, until his father found a new job in New York. Young Edmund S. Phelps was more interested in music than anything else, playing the lead trumpet in various bands. Instead of pursuing a music career, he ended up going to Amherst College to get his undergraduate education. At first, he flirted with philosophy, but upon his father's request, he also took a course in economics – and that decided him to go for economics all the way. 'This was an extremely good fit for me', he says. 'It was a godsend.' And yet, philosophy had left its enduring trace in the encompassing depth of his thought. Reaching the end of his college years, Phelps went on to Yale for graduate studies. At Yale, very much a stronghold of Keynesianism, he was influenced by distinguished scholars such as William Fellner, Jacob Marschak, Tjalling Koopmans, Gérard Debreu, Robert Triffin, Henry Wallich, James Tobin and Thomas Schelling. James Tobin, his dissertation adviser, gave him the idea to write his thesis on the effect of demand and cost shocks on the correlation between changes in prices and output. It was a mathematically demanding paper, but conceptually, it was 'awfully problematic', as Phelps recalls[6] – which is probably the reason why no direct reference to it can be found anywhere. He received his Ph.D. from Yale in 1959 and then took off to the RAND Corporation in Santa Monica. After a year at the RAND Corporation, Phelps returned to Yale on behalf of the Cowles Foundation as an assistant and then associate professor, eventually, however, moving on to the MIT. In 1966, he spent a sabbatical at the London School of Economics (LSE) and at Cambridge. From 1966 to 1971, Phelps then assumed a professorship at the University of Pennsylvania. In 1969/70, he spent a year at the Center for Advanced Study in the Behavioral Sciences (CASBS) at Stanford University and got in touch with John Rawls. In 1971, for both professional and private reasons, he left Penn and moved back to New York, where he had found employment at Columbia

University. New York, to him, is 'the most exciting city in the US', and it is also close to the suburb of Hastings where he had grown up. 'So it seemed very natural to want to be back to the number one city', he says in our interview. So Columbia is where he's stayed until today, interrupted only by a short intra-city stint to New York University in 1978/79 – and of course by regular trips to various destinations in Europe. Ever since the 1980s, Phelps has increased his overseas collaboration with European universities and institutions, ranging from the Observatoire Français des Conjonctures Economiques (OFCE), the Banca d'Italia and the European Bank for Reconstruction and Development (EBRD), to the University of Rome Tor Vergata.

Edmund S. Phelps's first years in active research were the direct outcome of his training; they were dedicated to growth theory. One important paper, written in 1961 at the Cowles Foundation, adopting the intertemporal viewpoint, provided 'The golden rule of accumulation'.[7] He also published a book on economic growth.[8] Beyond that, a 1966 paper highlighted the role of managers in the diffusion of new technologies over the economy,[9] and another one, also from 1966, dealt with research and development and their relation to economic growth.[10]

Perhaps the most crucial period, however, began when Phelps left for the London School of Economics in 1966. This was the beginning of his famous 'micro–macro' years. Actually, most of Phelps's work ever since has been motivated by a profound uneasiness with the traditional 'schism' in economics, dividing the field up into microeconomics and macroeconomics. As he says in our interview, 'those Keynesian models where you turn the crank and you get what the GDP is going to be may be fascinating and they may even have some practical value, but I never felt very comfortable with them. I didn't think they had much foundation.' Ned Phelps set out to integrate the two by providing a micro-foundation of macroeconomics. This, however, meant not just that a simple bridge needed to be built. Since there were outright incompatibilities between the two fields, he had to reformulate a lot of microeconomic theory so that it could become a foundation for macroeconomics. The critical element that he introduced into microeconomics was uncertainty, imperfect information and imperfect knowledge.[11] The most famous result of this work, focusing generally on the link between employment, wage setting and inflation, was Phelps's challenging the traditional Phillips curve which claims that there is a trade-off between inflation and unemployment.[12] In the framework of his new micro-foundation of macroeconomics, Phelps now argued that inflation also depends on the expectations of firms and employees about price and wage increases – to the effect that, since there can be no permanent discrepancy between actual and expected inflation, there is also no long-run trade-off between inflation and unemployment.[13] This implies that Keynesian demand management can only have limited, mostly transitory effects. This was a result that Milton Friedman also reached simultaneously, but without providing a micro-foundation.[14] Phelps's model, presented in his famous (1968) paper on 'Money-wage dynamics and labor-market equilibrium', became known as the (vertical) 'expectations-augmented Phillips curve'. This was also the time of the first efficiency wage theories, of search unemployment, and so on, all of which were part of Phelps's important paradigm shift: while Neoclassic and Keynesian theory had so far dealt with unemployment as being a disequilibrium, the difference just being that Neoclassics were more optimistic about a return to equilibrium, Phelps showed that there can be unemployment in equilibrium. Phelps also introduced the notion of a 'natural rate of unemployment', again alongside Friedman. The Keynesian school viewed all this as a terrific blow – which it was – and reacted rather unpleasantly, as Phelps recalls.

But then, in a typical dialectic move of science, a new front opened as Robert Lucas entered the stage with his rational expectations approach. Phelps preferred to think of expectations as being adaptive. But Lucas proved Phelps's model along his own lines and on his own terms.[15] This directed the attention away from Phelps – which the latter regrets: 'It was only a simplified version of what I was doing. . . But it prolonged the debate, because it afforded the Keynesians with the illusion of a victory.' The rational expectations approach went too far for him as well, simply because people aren't fully rational – but nevertheless, his subsequent research aimed at strengthening the neo-Keynesian approach again while taking the rational expectations hypothesis into account. Together with John Taylor and Guillermo Calvo, Phelps thus started a research program building on his 1968 paper, now employing sticky wages and prices. In such a setting, monetary policy can be effective.[16] Finally, in the 1980s, Phelps began to question the explanatory value of all the three existing monetary theories of employment, that is according to the New Classical, the New Keynesian, and the Neo-Keynesian approaches. This started his 'structuralism' years, a phase of non-monetary modeling of employment determination and the underlying time patterns, beginning with the Fitoussi–Phelps book in 1988[17] and ultimately resulting in the book *Structural Slumps* in 1994.[18] The next topic, mainly in the next decade, was labor market participation and inclusion.[19]

Ever since the fall of the Iron Curtain, however, Phelps has directed much of his attention towards the more fundamental issue of capitalism. The question concerning what it is that allows for and fosters entrepreneurial activity, how the necessary institutions come into being, how knowledge is passed on – all these topics are close to his heart. And that's not surprising: they are the logical continuation of his endeavor to provide the micro-foundations, that is to dig deeper, to get at the core of things, to really understand the world. Even if it comes at the price of what may look like eclecticism.

As for his major sources of inspiration, Phelps is pretty outspoken: it was his 'bourgeois' background, with economics being very much a topic at home; it was his father's direct influence, urging him to take at least one class in economics at college; it was a good teacher (James Nelson) and an accessible, excellent textbook (Paul Samuelson's *Economics*); it was a brilliant environment at the Ivy-League university that he went to (Yale), with the philosophical undercurrent that William Fellner provided, as well as the role model and the latitude that his doctoral adviser James Tobin gave him; and it was the era, of course: a time where the Keynesian paradigm in economics, while still fresh and flourishing, had already showed its imperfections, and therefore there was much room for improvement. Topics were abundant. In that sense, Phelps has also been a puzzle-solver, in Robert M. Solow's wording[20] – but his curiosity and his ambitions have always been those of a system-builder. Summing up, it is fair to say that all three fundamental lines of inspiration were present in Ned Phelps's case, interacting systematically and with pretty equal weight. Sometimes just everything comes together to provide an interesting playground for an active, gifted mind.

INTERVIEW

Ned, you once said that you always had sort of a predisposition for becoming an economist. What makes you say that?
I may have had in mind that I grew up in a somewhat bourgeois setting, one oriented toward business. My father's father was a shoe manufacturer and had several shoe retail outlets in the Midwest. He was successful and made a fair amount of money. My mother came from a family with a good-size farm in southern Illinois. She went to a college in the region and was a trained nutritionist. My father's profession was advertising. He had majored in economics at the University of Illinois between 1920 and 1924. He must have been a pretty good student. He remembered so many things about economics that I had never heard of. He was always enthusiastic about that subject. So I had this very practical background in economics; it wasn't a background in science or in the arts.

But does that mean that you were discussing the economic situation and economic policy at home, at the dinner table? It must have been, given that you were born at the bottom of the Great Depression, and I understand the economic turmoil of these years had its effect on your parents' household, with both your mother and your father losing their jobs. When your father finally found a new job in 1939, your family settled in a New York suburb.

Oh yes, we sure we talked about the economy and Washington. The financial and economic news was ever-present in dinner-time conversation. Also, like many middle class people in those days, my parents were very concerned about people who didn't have much opportunity, and I kind of absorbed that.

I suppose this probably triggered a rising political awareness in you.

I remember that my parents always voted for the left, for the Democratic Party. They had some Republican friends, too, and I remember they had exchanges. So I saw that there was a right wing also, and I had a bit of a sense of what the differences were between them. Some who voted right wing didn't like high taxes and didn't like big government. I assumed that it was a superficial, self-interested thing; that there was nothing intellectual about it. The two sides were not talking macroeconomics. But I must have developed some curiosity about whether there were deeper differences between the left wing and the right wing.

What kind of job did you dream of?

At high school, I thought maybe I would go into business, to be the manager or the president of a company. I felt that I could run an organization. It's not that I was tremendously gregarious, or that I could instantly command a room or anything like that. But I did notice that in our musical groups, I tended to be the person that it revolved around. I was usually the lead trumpet. I was the guy who tended to make it work. Also, when I was in grades 10, 11 or 12, I didn't have much sense of what else I could do in my career. I didn't have any sense of economics. Remember, in the US in those times, it would have been unheard of to have a course of economics in high school.

In Germany, that still is more or less the case.

In France, they do have such classes. With the effect that students coming out of high school seem to think they know all about Adam Smith and Alfred Marshall. The Germans, I notice, seem to be just about burned out by the time they get to university. It's all about getting a degree and moving on. In my case, it was an intellectual adventure when I went to college.

You started out at Amherst College. Did you then know where you were going – intellectually speaking, or in terms of a career?
No. At first, I got seduced by Plato and Hume and the humanists, such as Montaigne, which we were required to read. I was stimulated and was fully expecting to become a philosophy major. My father may have seen this coming. In any case, he asked me a favor: to take one course in economics. I did. And I realized within a week or two that this was an extremely good fit for me. I couldn't explain why, and maybe to this day, I don't know why. But it was clear to me that in a philosophy course, out of 50 students, I could be among the three or four best. In economics, however, it was easy for me to be the best, certainly number one or two. I realized that I had an unusual talent for it. That counted for something. I mean, you like to be able to succeed when you study. And I also had a sense that with economics, I'd be able to get to the bottom of some of these political questions about left and right.

The fact that your father kind of pushed you in that direction, didn't that turn you away? Didn't you react in a rebellious way?
My father had hardly asked anything of me before so I didn't feel very pushed. Besides, the subject was just as interesting to me as philosophy had been. It came as a revelation to me that economics in the hands of Paul Samuelson, the author of the new textbook I was reading, could be so stimulating.[21] The lectures by James Nelson were also brilliant. Both of them were quite fun, too, and they were great comedians when they wanted to be. I concluded that this wasn't a second rate subject. This was probably as good as it gets. And there was a lot of stuff there to be thought about and to be made sense of. So no, I didn't have any resentment at all. It was a godsend.

And when you started out, did you find economics easy?
It was easy, from day one. But you asked about rebellion against one's parents. Remember, my mother was a nutritionist and my father was working in a bank in those days. I thought that I was now going to be on a higher plane. I was going to be the philosopher economist who would settle the issues of left versus right. So in a way, I did put some distance between myself and my parents.

When did you start thinking that economics could be a career for you?
It was not before I was well into my third year at college that I began to think about the relation of all this to a career, wondering whether it would be possible to make a living with this stuff. I think it was probably at the very end of the third year or perhaps at the beginning of my fourth year that Paul Samuelson was prevailed upon to come to Amherst and give a lecture and

meet some of the more promising seniors who were majoring in economics. He talked to me for about 20 minutes or so. He talked as if it was a given that I would be going to graduate school and that I'd find it interesting to go on to become a professional economist. So I thought, well, let's give this a try, I'll go to graduate school and I'll take each day as it comes and see whether I can find interesting challenges and some fun in the process.

I guess that if someone whom you admire treats you that way, expecting you to go on, it must be a tremendous motivation.
Yes, it was. I felt some pressure to live up to expectations.

So what made you go further was, for a good part, a top education and motivational support. What about the internal motivations, motivations that came out of the subject itself? You once joked that you went on and on with economics because you hoped that if you took just one more course you would finally understand it. [22]
It's true that I was trying to get to the bottom of the subject. But there was also my interest in left versus right – in the good economy, though that was somewhat unconscious.

You then went on to Yale on a fellowship. Who were your teachers? And how did they teach? What did your classes look like in those days? Was it very mathematical?
No, there wasn't a lot of math. I had one professor by the name of William Fellner. He came from Hungary. He had come from a business background. His father was the owner of a large brewery in Budapest. So Fellner was not only a highly intellectual person, smart, serious, cultivated; he also knew more than a little about business. He could actually talk about things from a realistic point of view that I had never heard before in a classroom.

Who else was there to impress and inspire you?
Another very influential teacher was James Tobin. [23] He taught me a ton of macroeconomics. I thought that the material was really clever and important. But I also thought it was maybe not fundamental enough. I appreciated the story, apocryphal I am sure, told in class by the instructor who was teaching the first year statistics course to graduate students, Robert Summers, father of Larry Summers, brother of Paul Samuelson and husband of Kenneth Arrow's sister Anita. [24] The story goes that a lecturer expounded the workings of a mathematical economic model, as if the economy was like a mechanical toy, upon which a student raised his hand and asked: 'But sir, where are the people in that model?' That student was so right. The Keynesian models where you turn the crank and

you get what the GDP is going to be may be fascinating and they may even have some practical value, but I never felt very comfortable with them. I didn't think they had much foundation. What I liked about Fellner was that he was very concerned with the foundations. You could see that he thought in terms of people and what their situations were, their beliefs, and their expectations. I soaked that up. Another very important influence was Thomas Schelling.[25] He was sixteen years younger than Willy Fellner. He had already had a practical career in Europe with the Marshall Plan, and in Washington, and now there he was, a still very young full professor at Yale. I just saw him recreate himself, in front of my very eyes. I saw him turn to issues of bargaining and transactions typically among small numbers of persons – what we now think of as game theory. But he didn't think of this as game theory yet. He was building this stuff from the ground up. I saw him create these little models of reciprocal fear of surprise attack.[26] It was bold, and I wondered whether I would ever be able to do something like that. Later, maybe two or three times in my career I did something as stimulating as that. But that doesn't matter. At any rate, Tom Schelling was a living example of what I thought it might be possible for me to do.

Specifically because he was already working on some kind of micro-foundations?
Yes. He was in fact interested in micro–micro. He was interested in thinking about the interactions of people at a very realistic level.

What was it that bothered you about macroeconomics the way it was?
There was no micro in it. There were no people, no beliefs, and no expectations. I saw Fellner and Schelling as having the people very much on their minds. So my research agenda was to get the people into growth economics. Growth economics was first. And then later I was concerned with getting the people into employment economics, along the lines that Fellner and Schelling would have said was about right.

Why was it so important to have micro within macro? I mean – microeconomic theory was out there, price theory had been fully established much earlier. It wasn't as if nobody had ever been thinking about human action and individual choices before in economics. Micro and macro, the two building blocks of economic theory, coexisted side by side, reflecting two different levels of abstraction. What was missing was a proper integration of the two. Why did you feel this was indispensable? Why is it important to understand the – non-mechanical, but interactive – process of aggregation by which you get from the micro level to the macro level?

It was not just about integrating two separate views that are like two ships in the night, not dependent on one another. The problem was that there actually was a real incompatibility between the two. And I wasn't the only person to see that there were contradictions. Standard microeconomics implies that there will be full employment, and that changes in that level of employment will depend upon things like changes in technology, changes in the capital stock and changes in the weather. But this is nothing at all of what Keynesian economics says determines employment. Keynesian economics delivers implications that are inconsistent with standard micro. It became clear that we cannot simply use the existing – neoclassical – microeconomics as the foundation of Keynesian macroeconomics. So – well, I was going to say that I had to invent a new microeconomics. But that's a little bit pretentious, and inaccurate. I had to make use of the little bit of knowledge that I had of microeconomics and start there and build up alternative microeconomic models that could easily be hooked up to macroeconomics. I'm not sure I can document it very well, but I have always felt that my year at the RAND Corporation[27] right after my dissertation in 1959/60 was helpful to me in this.

Why was that?
It was helpful in exposing me to a more realistic kind of macroeconomics than what I would otherwise have been aware of. RAND had a real-life mission of making sure that air force bases would always have spare parts on hand. In order to deal with that, I began to learn a little bit of probability theory and a little bit of modeling of stochastic processes. That was a leg up. And I also read my Tom Schelling. In the reciprocal fear of surprise attack, country A doesn't know what country B is up to, and country B can't observe what country A is up to. That kind of thing was very much on my mind. It connected with the fact that Fellner had communicated to me a deep sense of the radical uncertainty in which business people find themselves. They do not know what the probabilities are. So it's all nonsense to assume that we can predict anything. If at all, we have to use probabilities in a modified way. Summing up, it was thanks a bit to the RAND Corporation, a bit to Fellner, a bit to Schelling, that these things came together and helped me find my way.

In which year did you write your dissertation?
In 1959. In 1957/58, I was also at Yale, but I was getting nowhere. I was trying to find a good thesis topic, but I wasn't really successful at it.

Who was your adviser?
It was Tobin. But he had a sabbatical and spent a year in Switzerland. Which was good in a way, because I was on my own, shopping around for topics,

talking with Tom Schelling a little bit. And then I tried to work on one topic that Schelling had suggested but I didn't have the mathematical practice to know how I should have approached it. It wasn't mathematically difficult, but I just bit off more than I could chew. A year later, I had learned that lesson.

OK, back to your year at the RAND Corporation.
At RAND, I also learned a little bit of management science and operations research. It was fascinating, I was glad to have gone out there and met all sorts of interesting and stimulating and brilliant people. But after about six months, I knew that I had to get back into academia. Then, as luck would have it, I found myself right back at Yale. That was because the offer at Yale was a position at the Cowles Foundation,[28] which meant I'd have reduced teaching. So I took it, even though I wasn't very happy about being back in New Haven. It's a very boring place.

But intellectually, it wasn't boring.
Oh no. I was at Yale during its golden age.

And now you had a good degree of freedom there to think and not teach too much.
Yes, I did. No complaints.

How was interaction with your colleagues? Was that an environment that fostered your creativity? What directed the topics you were concentrating on?
In part because I was at the Cowles Foundation, it was terrifically easy – too easy – to interact with people. The consequence was that I wrote some co-authored papers that I shouldn't have been doing, but I did them. I probably had a tendency not to think too much about what my legacy was going to be in economics but rather about what I had to do to get from this page to the end of this paper. It was only after four years at Yale, one year of which was spent at MIT [1962/63], that I started to think more strategically. I had done very much in growth economics. I had written two papers that I think of as breakthroughs in growth economics, one on the role of managers in the diffusion of new technologies over the economy,[29] and another on research and development and their relation to economic growth.[30] As I was then moving toward my full professorship at the University of Pennsylvania,[31] for which I received the offer in 1965, I thought I could afford to have a shot at something more ambitious, and I began to work on the micro–macro thing. But it's very hard to get away from the papers that are already in the pipeline. It was only six months later when I had my own accumulated sabbatical in my last semester at Yale and I went overseas, to London, that I really got started.

Did you find a good work environment there?

Well, I went to see the Convenor of the London School of Economics. He asked me whether I was going to work a lot. I gave the wrong answer. I said: no. I should have said: of course I will be working my poor head off, that's what I do all the time. The effect was that he didn't give me an office. He gave me essentially a key to a locker in the library. This turned out to be great. If I had had an office, I would have talked with Richard Caves and Ronald Jones all day. And I would have gotten nothing done. With this locker, I was completely alone. Even if I wanted to talk I couldn't, because I was in room Q of the library and would have disturbed the others with my chit-chat. It was like being in a monk's cell.

How effective was that?

Very. I remember being at the opera one night to hear Wagner's *Parsifal*, with the great Jon Vickers in the title role. But there was a problem bothering me all day that I had not been able to solve and it was completely distracting me from the opera. There I was, in the front row of Covent Garden, the Royal Opera House, maybe 50 feet from Vickers, and I was not even listening, I was thinking only about that problem. But then, at the end of the first act, I realized what the solution was! I was able to concentrate on the music again after that. I'm just telling this story because it is an illustration that what I was doing was very consuming. I must have been almost impossible to live with.

You were probably told so.

No comment (*laughter*). But that was a difficult time. And then, that summer, I went on to Cambridge, England. I'd sit there in solitary confinement in an office provided to me by Richard Stone, head of the department of applied economics, later to win the Nobel Prize.[32] I'd sit there all day looking at the wall, trying to get through the next step in my work. The only bright moment would come when a young woman, I think her name was Rosie, would come in and give me my mail – if I had any. That was the high point of the day.

Sounds terrible. Did you need that monk's cell atmosphere in order to be productive?

Yes, I needed it. Now I am not sure that I would do something like that again. It's too big a price to pay. It's probably for this very reason more than any other that breakthroughs tend to be produced by young people. Now it would be very difficult for me to detach myself to that point, and to shut the world out and just do that. There were days back then when it was a bit difficult not to go crazy, you know. But I didn't.

In your memoir,[33] you show that you had sort of three different phases in your work, and in each one you had one major idea. Interestingly, you point out that new ideas came up every time you moved. Do you think there is a correlation?
Frankly, I can't tell whether I had new ideas because I changed places or whether the two just coincidentally happened at the same time. The causation is not clear. It is true that I always came to a new start after I moved. But I might have had a new idea anyway. You see, you work on something for six or seven years, and then you move on to a new topic – and I also was restless geographically, and after I had been in one place for a number of years, I moved on. At Columbia, I didn't work on just one thing, just because I didn't have the good fortune of moving any more. I did change (*laughter*).

Let's concentrate on a line of research that you started in Cambridge and completed at Penn. It dealt with the Phillips curve.[34] In those papers, you were challenging the alleged relationship between inflation and unemployment, arguing that inflation also depends on the expectations of firms and employees about price and wage increases.[35] Without coming up with as highly a formalized model, and particularly without integrating micro and macro the way you did, Milton Friedman[36] had a similar point.[37] How popular was it in those days to challenge the Phillips curve? Was the Phillips curve controversial at all? Was there a wave of rebellion against it? Or did you face a lot of criticism as you dethroned it?
Well, there is no question about it that while criticizing the Phillips curve I also had to take into account the grain of truth I thought it had. I couldn't really escape dealing with it in more detail. It wasn't controversial in academic circles, it was rather quickly accepted. I was one of the few who thought that it wasn't good enough and that we shouldn't let this stand as it was.

Did you have any interaction with Friedman on that issue?
No, none whatsoever. I thought that Milton Friedman's piece was a quick and dirty pass at the problem, one that really didn't deserve the vastness of attention that it got. What I tried to do was model the relation of unemployment to inflation, while at bottom, Friedman was more talking about labor force participation in relation to inflation, bringing in misperception about the real wage and consequent impact on the labor supply, or rather the labor supply curve. I took the labor supply curve as given throughout, however. I was talking about the relationship of the unemployment rate to these monetary disturbances.

What was the reaction in academia?
Yes, this was a big deal in the profession, a tremendous brouhaha. It sure was. When my two decisive papers came out in 1967 and 1968,[38] both of

them essentially in the summer, I was 34 and 35 years of age, and I was being attacked by the most senior and most admired figures in the profession. I was made fun of. Some of them still remained my friends at some gut level, but it was a very serious competition for academic status, and for the truth. It was a rivalry about who was to be regarded as the one who had understood this right. It was a huge topic in academia.

Who were the people you had the biggest fights with?
Jim Tobin and Bob Solow. They were dug in deeply in the Keynesian perspective, and so for them, it was a battle that they didn't want to lose. Paul Samuelson was more like a neutral bystander, a referee. He could go either way pretty happily.

How did this go on? It seems to me that your insights are so plausible and so hard to refute that people like Bob Solow might have given in at some point.
Well, there is a tendency of people to grow silent after they have made their case.[39] Right through the seventies, there was this bone of contention. And then, the entry of Robert Lucas[40] into the situation further complicated things. I have never been a rational expectations advocate, but like almost every economic theorist, I have dabbled in it from time to time. To some extent, the battle then became to be one between the Keynesians versus Lucas, and I was actually bypassed. I felt, however, that the battle should have been between me and the Keynesians! I didn't think that the Lucas variant was the important thing to focus on. Nor did I think that it had a great deal of utility. There is something there that was undeniably interesting, but it was only a simplified version of what I was doing. It was one of many possible simplifications. It was kind of inevitable because people do like simplicity. But it prolonged the debate, because it afforded the Keynesians with the illusion of a victory. They found Lucas' version absurd because expectations are in fact not rational, and so they thought they had won after all. But what about me? To get to the truth, you sometimes have got to be complicated.

Right in the middle of your work on the Phillips curve, in 1969, you went to the Center for the Advanced Study in the Behavioral Sciences (CASBS) at Stanford for a year. You met John Rawls[41] there. Did that encounter give you an impulse for something new?
I had met Amartya Sen[42] in New York when he was working at the United Nations. When I told him I was going out to the CASBS at Stanford, he said that John Rawls was going to be out there, too, and that I absolutely had to meet him. At that time, I wasn't quite aware of who John Rawls was. When I was a graduate student, I still had tried to pick up a little bit of philosophy. I used to go to the reading room of Sterling memorial

library in the morning. I would start with the letter A, and look at all the journals, and then go to the letter B, etc. It would take about three months until I reached the letter Z, and then I would start all over again. This means that I did know a little bit of philosophy in those days, but I wasn't reading systematically. And so ten years later, even though Rawls had in the meantime become a very important figure, I didn't know who he was. I glanced at one or two of his papers and realized this probably was something I should pay attention to. So I made a point of arriving at the Center a couple of days earlier than I might otherwise have done. I very quickly went to the Center and picked up my room ahead of most others. I saw that Rawls was there in one flight of offices. At the end, next to Rawls, there was a vacancy. I chose that office, next to him. We hit it off very well. We became good friends. He was significantly older than I was. I was 36, he was 48. Rawls had a very important influence on me.

Did he make you read parts or drafts of his Theory of Justice?
He didn't at first. But there was no doubt I was going to read some of it sooner or later. It was just that my own book was taking much, much, much longer than I had thought it would. I was kind of depressed about that. The book I was writing was later called *Inflation Policy and Unemployment Theory*.[43] It was a take-off on a whole series of books by Alvin Hansen. I had gotten a grant from the Brookings Institution to do it. I had been supposed to do it the previous year. I had gotten the money, but I had no book. When I got to CASBS, I had to start on that book even though that was not what I wanted to do with my year there. After ten or eleven months, I was still not quite done with it. The year had gone by, and I hadn't really taken as much advantage of the place as I had wanted and hoped to do. But I had a number of conversations with Rawls, and I listened to his talk very carefully. He listened to my talk, too. He liked me a lot. He told others in his field that 'Ned Phelps is different than the other economists'. I don't know what exactly he meant by that, but it was positive. At first, I didn't understand his book correctly. I even thought I had hit upon a better way of doing it. But then I realized that he wanted nothing to do with that way of doing it, and that the point of the whole book was to do it a different way. I didn't really master what he was doing until the book finally came out in January 1971.

Those papers that you later wrote about the structure of tax rates in a market economy, finding that the marginal tax rate on the top income from labor must be zero, were inspired by Rawls, weren't they?
Yes, absolutely. Those papers were an exploration of the implications of the Rawlsian maximin criterion. When I came back from the CASBS, I

cleaned up a few things around my desk, and I said to myself I was going to have a Rawlsian period now. The paper that you are referring to came out in 1973, and I wrote it in 1971/72.[44] It was one of the first papers I wrote of that kind. After my year in Stanford, I came back to Penn, but I was getting divorced and wanted to go and live in New York. I met Kelvin Lancaster on the train. He was the chairman of Columbia. That's how I came to Columbia in 1971. The deal was done very quickly.

Why New York?
Well, it's the most exciting city in the US. I had spent four years in the countryside in Massachusetts; I had spent four years in Connecticut, and then again another four and a half years after that; a year in Los Angeles; a year in Boston, visiting at MIT; a year in Palo Alto. . . And I had grown up right outside of New York. So it seemed very natural to want to be back to the number one city.

But it's a noisy city, full of distractions. And you said earlier that you needed a monkish atmosphere in order to be productive.
It's true. There were lots of nights when my wife, Viviana, and I would be up till midnight watching the last act of the opera at the Metropolitan, then, when we finally got home, I had to walk the dog, getting to sleep at one o'clock. There were days where I thought this was a hardship post, this New York City. Poor me (*laughter*). On the other hand, it's nice to have this excitement. I don't know that it's actually bad for my work. And it was good to get back to the financial capital of the country, and to see a lot of economists of various types.

Those were the seventies. What was your focus in the eighties? You've described those years as 'a period of synthesis'. The second part of that decade then was the beginning of your 'European years', with many trips to various places on the European continent.[45]
My non-monetary modeling of employment determination and the under-lying time patterns, beginning with the Fitoussi–Phelps book which germinated in 1986[46] and which ultimately resulted in my book *Structural Slumps* in 1994,[47] was for me a very satisfying period. I also liked very much what came out. There are parts of the book that are a mess which could be cleaned up now, but I'm not sure I'll ever get around to doing it. I understand now why it wasn't terribly well received by large elements of the economics profession. And that's because it is somewhat strange in that I suppose that some shock comes out of the blue, and nobody has ever conceived of that shock before, and now that the shock has arrived, it is permanent; nobody ever can imagine that a future will be any different.

And then later, some other damn thing comes along. I have expectations being correct after the shock, but each shock always comes completely out of the blue. It may be a little bit of a strain, but for practical purposes, it's useful, because that is probably the way that most policy economists actually think. I'm very happy about that book because I feel there are a lot of things I understand about the world economy that others won't understand until they get their heads into that book.

What exactly was it that people didn't like?
Some of the rational expectations people would probably say that it's true that each shock may have a different name on it, but then a good theory should be one that takes into account the stochastic properties of that process of shocks. I just don't have any interest in that point of view. That makes me an outsider to this little industry that wants to model everything as a known stochastic process. This is part of a huge war that has been going on between me, and on my side Roman Frydman, and some others from time to time, not a large group – and on the other side Robert Lucas, Robert Barro, Thomas Sargent, and a huge crowd of people. These fights have been a very big part of my career. I don't want to dramatize 'my struggle', but first there was the battle with the Keynesians, then the battle with the rational expectations crowd. It would be melodramatic, though, to say that this has been a huge drain on me. Also, I haven't been over-worked by the university system. There were times where I had a pretty large teaching load, but it's never been bone-crushing. There were many, many years where I had basically light teaching and a lot of support from the National Science Foundation. Right now, I have some very generous support by the Kauffmann Foundation. But still, these professional battles have taken a big chunk out of my time.

Were those fights inspiring or frustrating?
These two struggles with the Keynesians and rational expectationalists just consumed a lot of my research time over the years. The Frydman–Phelps conference volume attacking rational expectations,[48] for example, was to some extent an attempt to defend my earlier work in the late 1960s against later criticism by the rational expectations people that I was being pre-scientific.

That must have triggered something like a desire to move on again.
Oh, it did. It's been a nice thing to have this new phase that I've been in ever since my time at the EBRD in 1992/93, since the fall of the Berlin Wall and all that, taking up the subject of capitalism. The first thing that I worked on was inclusion, about how to integrate the disadvantaged into

the system. And then, as I was winding up my book *Rewarding Work*,[49] I realized that I was saying a lot of things about capitalism that nobody had said before: that it was actually fun to work in a capitalist economy. I'm not sure that one could have said this in the nineteenth century, but times have changed to some extent. After the book was out, I began to think more and more about this issue. Basically, what I am saying about capitalism is that it has dynamism. What I mean is not just that the GDP grows rapidly. GDP also grew rapidly under Lenin and Stalin. What I mean by dynamism is innovating in commercially successful directions. Discovering this field has been a kind of liberation for me. Speaking of meeting people on a train, I once was traveling back from California on a plane from John Wayne airport. The seat next to me was empty, and I was very relieved about it. But just before the door closed, somebody showed up, and that was Bob Shiller from Yale. He was pumping me about my work, and I distilled the whole thing, beginning with Aristotle. I just hoped he wouldn't steal it all, only one third of it. At one point he said: 'Gee, you're the only guy in the whole profession who is working on the core part of our subject'.

He was right!
It's on capitalism, dynamism, innovation, growth, and on what a good economy is, what the good life is. And it has been a tremendous liberation because I don't have to battle with Keynesians and the rational expectationalists any more. I'm just all by myself.

Won't there be new battles?
Of course, I will provoke people and they will attack me. So in the end, I will have to defend myself once more. But at least there won't be huge armies any more. Well, you never know. Maybe that's the way it will be.

This is also the core of what you're concentrating on at the 'Center on Capitalism and Society' that you're directing here at Columbia ever since 2001.
Right. We're still pretty small, though. It's very important that we have our annual conference, where we can show our face to the world, talk to each other and present our views. It's a very important operation, and there is nothing else out there. So we have to exist, it's very important.

Why is it so important? What do we need to find out about capitalism? What is it that we are failing to realize?
At bottom, all the discussions of political economy and economic policy have been conditioned by neoclassical economic theory. There are people

on the right who advocate a minimalist government and minimalist regulation; the *Wall Street Journal* would write about wealth accumulation of the economy as the be-all and end-all of the economy; others would talk about the GDP in worshipful terms. For me, all of this lacks appeal. This is not a very helpful way to look at what the economy actually is. And it is also not helpful in telling us the most important things we have to do in order to make the economy better. But the left wing also, for the most part, only looks at the economy in a very neoclassical way. People on the left are concerned with inequality, they are worried about unemployment. But the only role they see in jobs is just that it is cheaper for society to provide people with consumer goods in return for working than attempting to do that without any work at all. The left celebrates employment, but there is mainly nothing philosophical about it, it is simply about getting everybody working in order to grind out more consumer goods. And that gives the government more wherewithals with which to throw goods at disadvantaged people, that is, the elderly, the sick and the tired. I found that was a pretty uninspiring view of the economy, too. The typical left-wing piece would be John Maynard Keynes' famous essay 'Economic possibilities for our grandchildren'[50] in which he says that there will come a time when the horrors of the workplace will be a thing of the past because we won't need to work any more to have the incomes that will permit us to pursue the arts and all that . . . So we must do all we can to speed up economic growth so that we get a little quicker to this bliss level in which the commercial economy and the profit motive and all that fully serve their purpose. There is all sorts of absolutely crazy stuff out there that provides the core of conventional thinking in the area of political economy. I decided I had nothing to lose by attacking all that.

And how did you do that?
I developed the concept of what I called economic dynamism to understand its social benefits. This began in the years immediately after completing *Rewarding Work* – with interruptions. First, in the end of 1996, I got a phone call from Luigi Paganetto, the architect of the economics department in the new branch of the University of Rome, called Tor Vergata. He told me that he could get me appointed as the senior scientific adviser to a project on 'Italy in Europe'. I said I would do this, but only if I could write predominantly about dynamism. It was okay with him. So I had a little project going there at the University of Rome, with six or seven young people who would meet with me two or three times a year. I had to write a chapter on Italy every six months for three years. During this period, I began to form my thoughts about what was wrong with the Italian economy. I could see the lethargy, I could feel the stultification of

the workplace, I could see the emptiness in the faces of the young people as they wait to be age 35 to get married and to begin counting the days until they would reach retirement age 55. So I began to criticize Italy as suffering from a dearth of dynamism, and I tried to understand the origins of that. This of course also led me to think about France. At that time, Germany wasn't yet sputtering down the way it did later, and I wasn't so much aware of the problems in Germany at that time. I became well aware of it later, especially in October 2003, when I gave my first big blast of a paper on Europe at a CESifo[51] conference.

What about Germany?
Germany is actually my paradigm case of tragedy. Germany is a country in which things were going on in an unspectacular way until about 1860. And then, the land we now call Germany took off. Productivity began rising rapidly. There were all kinds of innovations going on, some of them very famous ones. It was an incredible golden age for Germany, and it was to some extent emblematic of what was happening over all of continental Europe and the UK, too. It was very much tied up with the rise of finance capitalism. This was a period in which Europe made the transition from a traditional economy with known stochastic processes to a system that is evolving and always transforming itself according to unknown processes in unpredictable ways. By the way, I made this the topic of my Nobel Prize Lecture.[52] Progress in economic theory in the twentieth century has consisted of small steps towards getting away from the economics of the traditional economy to the economics of a modern economy.

How comparable did you find Italy, France and Germany?
Well, as I tried to get at the roots of the problem, of course I found that the task wasn't easy because each one has its distinctive features. Generally speaking, I attacked the view that it's simply the welfare state and high tax rates. I took advantage of the fact that people said that we are making a theoretical error if we're holding constant private wealth when discussing the consequences of a decline of the after-tax wage owing to the tax burden of paying for the welfare state. I argued that after the fall of the after-tax wage caused by the higher tax rates to pay for the welfare state, private saving will fall in response, not just private consumption. So private wealth will go on falling and falling until finally it has come back to the same ratio of after-tax wage as the one it had before. At that point, however, you can't say that people aren't working because the after-tax wage is low. It's still higher than it was in the eighteenth century. So that doesn't make any sense. The only thing you can say is that the benefits themselves of the welfare state erode incentives to work and to be a good employee. But

then, how important is that? There are some countries such as Denmark and Sweden where they have pretty good sized welfare states, and they don't have high unemployment rates. So I felt fortified that I could make a case that the problem was not primarily the social model. What was more important was the economic model. I argued that what was wrong with the economic models on the continent was that the economies were not structured in such a way as to generate as much dynamism as some other economies possessed, such as the US and Canada, especially. That's where I am now.

What are you working on right now?
I'm seriously thinking about writing another book on the subject, even though I swore not to. It's just too draining, and there is too little reward for it. As I said, *Rewarding Work* wasn't very well received, and it didn't even get a review in the *New York Times*. It didn't sell very well either. And then there was a conference volume coming out of the 1998 conference at the Russell Sage Foundation.[53] I don't remember what the sales figures are exactly, but it's nothing. And that was hard work! We slaved over this for months. Then I put together my six reports for the Italian Science Foundation. I didn't want it to be a big deal.[54] It's almost hidden from view. Actually, I never had a bestseller. To be true, I never even tried. Actually, I had thought that my textbook *Political Economy*[55] might catch up. But that didn't happen.

What will be the topic of your next book if you do write it? Dynamism?
The working title that is on my mind is 'The Good Economy'. 'Dynamism' would be not bad either. Maybe there is some way of using that in the subtitle. 'How the West Found Dynamism and Lost It'? No? Well, something like that. I always spend a lot of time thinking about titles and subtitles. The problem is that ever since I've received the Nobel Prize, I don't have so much time. I'm now really drawing on what I've done before. I don't like that.

Thank you, Ned. Thank you, Professor.

NOTES

1. The interview was held on 1 August, 2007.
2. The Ewing Marion Kauffman Foundation was established in 1966 to support education and entrepreneurship for young people, particularly in the founder's home city of Kansas City and the surrounding area (www.kauffman.org).
3. www.earthinstitute.columbia.edu/ccs/people.html.
4. Edmund S. Phelps (2006/2007a).

5. See www.bepress.com/cas.
6. Edmund S. Phelps (1995).
7. Edmund S. Phelps (1961).
8. Edmund S. Phelps (1966a).
9. Edmund S. Phelps and Richard R. Nelson (1966).
10. Edmund S. Phelps (1966b).
11. As a corroboration of this point, but also for a more detailed evaluation of Phelps's contributions in general, it is worthwhile to read Philippe Aghion et al. (2001). The generation and diffusion of knowledge is a topic that occupies Phelps's mind until this day, entering also his more recent interest in capitalism.
12. Alban W. Phillips (1958).
13. Edmund S. Phelps (1967 and 1968). A third paper was an extension of the latter: Edmund S. Phelps (1970).
14. Milton Friedman (1968).
15. Robert E. Lucas (1972).
16. Edmund S. Phelps and John B. Taylor (1977).
17. Edmund S. Phelps and Jean-Paul Fitoussi (1988).
18. Edmund S. Phelps (1994).
19. Edmund S. Phelps (1997 and 2003).
20. See the interview with Robert M. Solow in this volume.
21. Paul A. Samuelson (1948). Now in its eighteenth edition, the book has in recent years (after 1985) been co-authored by William Nordhaus. The book has in total sold over 4-million copies.
22. Edmund S. Phelps (1995).
23. James Tobin (1918–2002) was awarded the Nobel Prize in 1981 'for his analysis of financial markets and their relations to expenditure decisions, employment, production and prices'.
24. Lawrence (Larry) Summers, himself an economist, was the President of Harvard University. He resigned in 2006 and is now one of Harvard's select university Professors.
25. Thomas Schelling received the Nobel Prize together with Robert Aumann in 2005 'for having enhanced our understanding of conflict and cooperation through game-theory analysis'.
26. Thomas Schelling (1959).
27. The RAND Corporation is a research institution created originally in 1946 by the United States Army Air Forces, under contract to the Douglas Aircraft Company. In 1948, it became an independent non-profit organization, sponsored initially by the Ford Foundation, to 'further promote scientific, educational, and charitable purposes, all for the public welfare and security of the United States of America'.
28. The Cowles Foundation is an economics research institute, founded in 1932 by the businessman Alfred Cowles under the name 'Cowles Commission for Research in Economics'. The Cowles Commission moved to the University of Chicago in 1939 and later on to Yale University in 1995, where it was renamed the 'Cowles Foundation'. The motto of the Cowles Foundation is 'Science is Measurement', and thus it has been dedicated to linking economics, mathematics and statistics.
29. Edmund S. Phelps and Richard R. Nelson (1966).
30. Edmund S. Phelps (1966b).
31. The appointment at Penn began a year later, in 1966. Edmund Phelps stayed there until 1971, when he moved on to Columbia University.
32. Richard Stone (1913–91) was awarded the Nobel Prize in 1984 'for having made fundamental contributions to the development of systems of national accounts and hence greatly improved the basis for empirical economic analysis'.
33. Edmund S. Phelps (1995).
34. Alban W. Phillips (1958). The paper ultimately implies that there is a trade-off between unemployment and inflation that policy makers can take advantage of.

35. Edmund S. Phelps (1967 and 1968a). A third paper was an extension of the latter: Edmund S. Phelps (1970). This conference volume is actually popularly dubbed 'the Phelps volume'. Phelps's model became known as the 'expectations-augmented Phillips curve'. This model focuses on the wage-setting behavior of firms in a labor market in which matching the unemployed with vacant jobs is a time-consuming process. It says that for a given unemployment rate a one percentage point increase in expected inflation leads to a one percentage point increase in actual inflation. So in the end, there is something like a 'vertical' Phillips curve, suggesting that there is no long-run trade-off between inflation and unemployment, as there can be no permanent discrepancy between actual and expected inflation.

36. Milton Friedman (1912–2006) was awarded the Nobel Prize in 1976 'for his achievements in the fields of consumption analysis, monetary history and theory, and for his demonstration of the complexity of stabilization policy'.

37. Milton Friedman (1968).

38. See note 35.

39. Actually, Robert M. Solow never agreed. In an interview with *The Region*, recorded in September 2002, he says: 'What replaced the initial Phillips curve was the Friedman–Phelps natural rate of unemployment long-run vertical Phillips curve. And I have never, from the very first day, thought that that was other than a flimsy theory supported by flimsy empirical analysis.' Available at http://minneapolisfed.org/publs/region/02-09/solow.cfm.

40. Robert Lucas was awarded the Nobel Prize in 1995 'for having developed and applied the hypothesis of rational expectations, and thereby having transformed macroeconomic analysis and deepened our understanding of economic policy'.

41. John Rawls is famous for his 'Theory of Justice' which he worked on while he was at Stanford (John Rawls, 1971).

42. Amartya Sen was awarded the Nobel Prize in 1998 'for his contributions to welfare economics'.

43. Edmund S. Phelps (1972a).

44. Edmund S. Phelps (1973a) (reprinted in E.S. Phelps (ed.), 1974).

45. Edmund S. Phelps (1995, p. 104).

46. Edmund S. Phelps and Jean-Paul Fitoussi (1988).

47. Edmund S. Phelps (1994).

48. That conference was held in 1981. Roman Frydman and Edmund S. Phelps (eds) (1983).

49. Edmund S. Phelps (1997).

50. John Maynard Keynes (1930).

51. CESifo (Center for Economic Studies/Institut für Wirtschaftsforschung) is an economic research institute in Munich (www.ifo.de).

52. Edmund S. Phelps (2006/2007a).

53. Edmund S. Phelps (ed.) (2003).

54. Edmund S. Phelps (2002).

55. Edmund S. Phelps (1985).

The questionnaires

PAUL A. SAMUELSON

1. *What was the most serious economic catastrophe so far?*
   The 1929–37 worldwide Great Depression.

2. *What has been the most promising economic development?*
   Improved macro knowledge and electorates' willingness to use it.

3. *What is the most important economic threat for the future?*
   Geopolitical new 'cold war' and chronic terrorisms.

4. *What is the worst economic policy error that you can remember?*
   Herbert Hoover and pre-1930 orthodox economists everywhere who resisted fiscal/central bank expansions of spending after 1929.

5. *What was the most enlightened concrete economic policy measure?*
   The Marshall Plan 1950–53.

6. *Please name a politician that you admire for his/her good hand in economic policy.*
   Franklin Delano Roosevelt.

7. *In your mind, what has been the most misleading theoretical approach in economics?*
   Libertarianism.

8. *What was the most important theoretical breakthrough?*
   Modern Finance Theory – micro and macro.

9. *If it was only for economic reasons, in which country would you like to live today?*
   Canada.

10. *If it was only for the intellectual challenge, in which times would you have liked to live?*
1930–70 as an adult.

11. *If you had to choose between efficiency and equality, which would you pick?*
Science's enhanced efficiency affords some inefficiency to enhance equality.

12. *If you had to choose between liberty and justice, which would you pick?*
The justice I'd espouse would target realized liberty.

13. *What is the absolute limit to taxation (give a maximum percentage of personal income)?*
Above 50% marginal tax rates are self-defeating.

14. *What is the absolute limit to state activity (give a maximum percentage of GDP)?*
There are no 'absolutes'. The UK and the US in World War II left only ½ of GDP for *private*[1] consumption.

15. *Who is your favorite economist today?*
Tobin/Okun brought back to life. Kenneth Arrow alive.

16. *Among the classics in economic theory, who is your favorite thinker?*
Adam Smith.

17. *Outside economics, which author has had the most influence on you?*
J. Willard Gibbs.

18. *Who are you most indebted to intellectually?*
E.B. Wilson and Alvin Hansen.

19. *Who was your major role model?*
Tobin and Keynes.

20. *Which piece of work in economics (book, article, speech) has impressed you most?*
Leon Walras, General Equilibrium.

21. *Can you remember your most striking intellectual 'epiphany'? Which was it?*
Unifying principles by Darwin and Maxwell.

22. *What qualities should economic researchers have?*
Knowledge of economic history.

23. *What do you consider to be your own most important contribution?*
Eclectic generalist: macro/micro, empirical.

24. *What would you name as your most painful failure in professional life?*
I was too slow in saying good-bye to deep depression economics.

25. *What do you consider to be your main personal character trait?*
Effort *not* to *stay* wrong.

26. *What do you think is your main personal flaw?*
Too intuitive; too wastefully disorganized.

27. *What is the character trait that you like most in your collaborators?*
Preoccupation with *new* truths.

28. *What is the character trait that you like most in your friends?*
Humorous friendliness.

29. *What does happiness mean for you?*
My intellectual preoccupations.

30. *What does fulfilment mean for you?*
Doing one's best; not home run records.

31. *What would be the most terrible economic misfortune in your eyes?*
A fascist–communist state.

32. *What, outside doing economics, is your favorite way to spend your time?*
Tennis, dog-petting, family laughter.

33. *What is your favorite dish?*
Skim milk.

KENNETH J. ARROW

1. *What was the most serious economic catastrophe so far?*
    In modern times, the Great Depression of 1929–40.

2. *What has been the most promising economic development?*
    In recent times, the information revolution.

3. *What is the most important economic threat for the future?*
    Apart from politico-military threats (the nuclear bomb), it is the growing scarcity of energy sources along with the implications of energy sources for global warming.

4. *What is the worst economic policy error that you can remember?*
    The governmental destruction of the economies of a number of African countries by bungling and kleptomaniac governments (latest example, Zimbabwe); but there are a lot of competitors.

5. *What was the most enlightened concrete economic policy measure?*
    The 'G. I. Bill of Rights', that is, the strong subsidy to World War II veterans in the United States to pursue higher education. This was the foundation for American technological progress.

6. *Please name a politician that you admire for his/her good hand in economic policy.*
    President Clinton and his Treasury Secretaries for their administration of the budget and of foreign economic crises.

7. *In your mind, what has been the most misleading theoretical approach in economics?*
    The Austrian a priori dogmatism (von Mises, especially; Hayek, to a lesser degree).

8. *What was the most important theoretical breakthrough?*
    In the last half of the twentieth century, asymmetric information.

9. *If it was only for economic reasons, in which country would you like to live today?*
    On purely economic accomplishments, Sweden.

10. *If it was only for the intellectual challenge, in which times would you have liked to live?*
    The present is good enough.

11. *If you had to choose between efficiency and equality, which would you pick?*
False dichotomy: either extreme is unsustainable.

12. *If you had to choose between liberty and justice, which would you pick?*
Same.

13. *What is the absolute limit to taxation (give a maximum percentage of personal income)?*
I don't think one can answer this question in the abstract. Certainly, if well managed, figures over 50% have been attained and been compatible with efficiency and growth.

14. *What is the absolute limit to state activity (give a maximum percentage of GDP)?*
Meaningless question; one can have great state control with little direct resource administration by the state and vice versa.

15. *Who is your favorite economist today?*
James Heckman.

16. *Among the classics in economic theory, who is your favorite thinker?*
Vilfredo Pareto (I mean 'most interesting', not 'best').

17. *Outside economics, which author has had the most influence on you?*
Fyodor Dostoevsky.

18. *Who are you most indebted to intellectually?*
Let me name several: John R. Hicks, Jacob Marschak, Tjalling Koopmans.

19. *Who was your major role model?*
I had none.

20. *Which piece of work in economics (book, article, speech) has impressed you most?*
Hicks's *Value and Capital*.

21. *Can you remember your most striking intellectual 'epiphany'? Which was it?*
I've had several, but I suppose understanding the social choice problem and seeing the Impossibility Theorem (which took me a few days) has to be number one.

22. *What qualities should economic researchers have?*
     I dislike methodological dogmatism. Good work can come in many forms.

23. *What do you consider to be your own most important contribution?*
     Two: social choice, asymmetric information as developed in the context of medical care (others were coming to the same end by different routes).

24. *What would you name as your most painful failure in professional life?*
     I have no painful failures; I have followed a large number of blind alleys, but I usually learned something in the process.

25. *What do you consider to be your main personal character trait?*
     Intense curiosity.

26. *What do you think is your main personal flaw?*
     An unwillingness to buckle down to work.

27. *What is the character trait that you like most in your collaborators?*
     Questioning me.

28. *What is the character trait that you like most in your friends?*
     Openness.

29. *What does happiness mean for you?*
     Cannot be answered.

30. *What does fulfilment mean for you?*
     Ditto.

31. *What would be the most terrible economic misfortune in your eyes?*
     A major depression.

32. *What, outside doing economics, is your favourite way to spend your time?*
     Literature, music.

33. *What is your favourite dish?*
     Roast duck.

ROBERT M. SOLOW

1. *What was the most serious economic catastrophe so far?*
   The Great Depression of the 1930s.

2. *What has been the most promising economic development?*
   Acceleration of productivity (over the long run).

3. *What is the most important economic threat for the future?*
   Population growth, especially in poor countries.

4. *What is the worst economic policy error that you can remember?*
   Thinking only of recent ones, perhaps the failure to finance the Vietnam War by taxation.

5. *What was the most enlightened concrete economic policy measure?*
   Social security (and Medicare) in the US, similarly elsewhere.

6. *Please name a politician that you admire for his/her good hand in economic policy.*
   John F. Kennedy (far from perfect, however).

7. *In your mind, what has been the most misleading theoretical approach in economics?*
   In recent years, 'real business cycle theory'.

8. *What was the most important theoretical breakthrough?*
   (a) The *concept* of general equilibrium
   (b) Imperfect competition

9. *If it was only for economic reasons, in which country would you like to live today?*
   Denmark.

10. *If it was only for the intellectual challenge, in which times would you have liked to live?*
    Hard to answer: maybe the 1930s.

11. *If you had to choose between efficiency and equality, which would you pick?*
    Equality.

12. *If you had to choose between liberty and justice, which would you pick?*
Liberty.

13. *What is the absolute limit to taxation (give a maximum percentage of personal income)?*
Differs by time and place; average rate maybe 50+ percent.

14. *What is the absolute limit to state activity (give a maximum percentage of GDP)?*
I will say one-half, but that is only a round number.

15. *Who is your favorite economist today?*
Paul A. Samuelson.

16. *Among the classics in economic theory, who is your favorite thinker?*
I do not have one.

17. *Outside economics, which author has had the most influence on you?*
Maybe Voltaire, maybe David Hume, maybe someone else.

18. *Who are you most indebted to intellectually?*
Wassily Leontief, Paul Samuelson, a high school English teacher.

19. *Who was your major role model?*
(a) My company commander in the war
(b) James Tobin

20. *Which piece of work in economics (book, article, speech) has impressed you most?*
Long ago, Samuelson's *Foundations of Economic Analysis*.

21. *Can you remember your most striking intellectual 'epiphany'? Which was it?*
'Seeing' the neoclassical growth model, while lying on the floor in our pediatrician's office.

22. *What qualities should economic researchers have?*
Honesty, modesty, clarity.

23. *What do you consider to be your own most important contribution?*
No doubt growth theory.

24. *What would you name as your most painful failure in professional life?*
No really good idea about the macroeconomics of the 'medium run'.

25. *What do you consider to be your main personal character trait?*
(a) Tendency to take things one at a time
(b) Tendency to see events as laughable

26. *What do you think is your main personal flaw?*
(a) Excessively critical
(b) Tendency to see events as laughable

27. *What is the character trait that you like most in your collaborators?*
Easy-going-ness, openness, reliability, sense of humor.

28. *What is the character trait that you like most in your friends?*
Easy-going-ness, openness, reliability, sense of humor.

29. *What does happiness mean for you?*
Too deep for me: but I have probably been happiest sailing a boat with my wife.

30. *What does fulfilment mean for you?*
Too deep for me: maybe getting some task done well, and then relaxing.

31. *What would be the most terrible economic misfortune in your eyes?*
For an individual, inability to support a family; for society, too many such individuals.

32. *What, outside doing economics, is your favorite way to spend your time?*
Reading, sailing, listening to music.

33. *What is your favorite dish?*
Roast cod.

VERNON L. SMITH

1. *What was the most serious economic catastrophe so far?*
The most impressionable one on me was the Great Depression. That's the first thing I remember in my life. Those were hard times.

2. *What has been the most promising economic development?*
    The incredible creation of wealth that is going on now, globally,
    thanks to the innovation coming from communication and computer
    technology, nanotechnology, biotech, . . .all those breakthroughs in
    science. The pace at which this kind of global specialization is taking
    place is just astonishing. It's creating a whole new world.

3. *What is the most important economic threat for the future?*
    Especially here in the United States, we might lose our capacity to
    innovate. And we might lose our freedom. Escalating interferences
    with our freedom are one of the late dangers of September 11, 2001.

4. *What is the worst economic policy error that you can remember?*
    The way the Carter administration mismanaged the oil crisis after the
    Arab embargo in the seventies. We should have bought petrol else-
    where, in Indonesia or Venezuela, changing international trade pat-
    terns – instead of rationing gasoline and fostering that public sense
    that we were running out of energy. And earlier, it was the failure in
    the Great Depression to have any understanding of how the mon-
    etary system should be flexible in operating. But that was a failure of
    knowledge, not a mistake in the proper sense. We've made progress
    in the meantime.

5. *What was the most enlightened concrete economic policy measure?*
    The Marshall Plan. That was a very successful operation. It was the
    right idea, and it was executed well enough to help Europe recover.

6. *Please name a politician that you admire for his/her good hand in eco-
    nomic policy.*
    In retrospect, my favorite American president was Dwight Eisenhower.
    His economic understanding wasn't very impressive at all. But basi-
    cally, he didn't do a whole lot. And that was good.

7. *In your mind, what has been the most misleading theoretical approach
    in economics?*
    The concept of preference or utility that is given. Once you push the
    explanation of some phenomenon back to this primitive assumption
    the conversation is over. Then, in two-person 'single play' games,
    cooperation is due to social preferences, and cannot be a conse-
    quence of social morality and reputational lifestyles in which some
    can accommodate cases of non-repeated interactions without defect-
    ing on opportunities to cooperate. Reducing cooperation to social

preferences in which I get utility for my as well as your payoff does not contribute to understanding.

8. *What was the most important theoretical breakthrough?*
In mathematical economics, it was auction theory and the underlying experimental economics, of course. It's all about taking theory seriously and testing it. We discovered a long time ago that institutions are important, but we didn't have the tools to analyze them properly.

9. *If it was only for economic reasons, in which country would you like to live today?*
In the United States, where else?

10. *If it was only for the intellectual challenge, in which times would you have liked to live?*
Oh, I like to live in the times in which I have lived, born in 1927. These eighty years so far have been good times for me. I have seen the best and also the depths of what humans can do to each other in society.

11. *If you had to choose between efficiency and equality, which would you pick?*
Well, to me, the important thing is not equality, but equity, that is, equality of opportunity. So I don't see any conflict, especially as I favor redistributing consumption, not income.

12. *If you had to choose between liberty and justice, which would you pick?*
I would hate to make that choice. As John Locke said, if there is no property, then there is no justice. And property has to do with the right to take actions, that is, liberty.

13. *What is the absolute limit to taxation (give a maximum percentage of personal income)?*
I would limit taxation primarily to consumption redistribution, providing opportunities for disadvantaged people, and to national defense and law enforcement. The tax rates could be a lot lower than today.

14. *What is the absolute limit to state activity (give a maximum percentage of GDP)?*
I don't know.

15. *Who is your favorite economist today?*
     Friedrich Hayek is probably the person that I most admire, largely
     because late in life, I discovered how relevant his comments were to
     experimental economics. I had to have a career in experimental eco-
     nomics before I could read and see. Many people read Hayek and have
     no idea what he is talking about. Among the Nobel Prize winners, my
     list would also include John Nash, William Vickrey, Ronald Coase,
     Douglass North and Robert Fogel. And Reinhard Selten, a wonder-
     ful man with an intense curiosity. He ranks second after Hayek.

16. *Among the classics in economic theory, who is your favorite thinker?*
     David Hume and Adam Smith.

17. *Outside economics, which author has had the most influence on you?*
     Richard Howey, at the University of Kansas. He was a specialist in
     economic thought, a fine scholar. He provided me with a model for
     inquiry: You acquire the tools that you need in order to master your
     subject. And some of them may be well outside economics.

18. *Who are you most indebted to intellectually?*
     Probably Paul Samuelson. He is a brilliant intellectual, in the old
     generation of economists. I've left all of that long and way behind.
     But still, it was his book that once sparked my interest in economics.

19. *Who was your major role model?*
     Richard Howey.

20. *Which piece of work in economics (book, article, speech) has impressed
     you most?*
     Hayek's 1945 paper on the 'Use of knowledge in society',[2] and its
     precursor, 'Knowledge and Economics',[3] where you can already see
     what he's struggling with and what he is trying to do. I also like his
     Law, Legislation, and Liberty[4], and the *Fatal Conceit*[5].

21. *Can you remember your most striking intellectual 'epiphany'? Which
     was it?*
     It was the recognition that markets work far better than you might
     think. Experiments show that. All that stuff about complete informa-
     tion is just useless. Hayek clearly understood this.

22. *What qualities should economic researchers have?*
     Curiosity.

23. *What do you consider to be your own most important contribution?*
The discovery of how effective market institutions are in aggregating dispersed information. I'm impressed though, by how little we know about where these institutions come from. That's a big gap in our understanding.

24. *What would you name as your most painful failure in professional life?*
I tried several times to model the Hayekian division of knowledge, that is, the dynamic adjustment process over time, whereby people learn, beginning with private information, discovering prices and allocations. I tried to come up with a formulation that would be testable – but it's just very hard because you lack equilibrium efficiency. For example, you can't just start out with budget constraints. They have no meaning if you haven't discovered prices yet.

25. *What do you consider to be your main personal character trait?*
I am capable of extreme, sustained concentration. ·

26. *What do you think is your main personal flaw?*
I don't like cocktail parties, and I get bored quickly. I'm not really a very social person.

27. *What is the character trait that you like most in your collaborators?*
Continuity of thought.

28. *What is the character trait that you like most in your friends?*
Integrity, dependability.

29. *What does happiness mean for you?*
It's pretty much what I'm doing. I'm happiest when I'm working on a problem, thinking about it, and writing. I like the feeling when I'm deepening my understanding and comprehension of things, when I'm putting something together myself. At any rate, happiness is more a state of the individual than of the environment. Not that you can be happy in a really disruptive and destructive environment, but often, people say they're unhappy and you can't really tell why.

30. *What does fulfilment mean for you?*
As above.

31. *What would be the most terrible economic misfortune in your eyes?*
–

32. *What, outside doing economics, is your favorite way to spend your time?*
    Fishing, jeeping – although I'm doing much less of that these days.

33. *What is your favorite dish?*
    Pasta and vegetables. I like Italian food.

EDMUND S. PHELPS

1. *What was the most serious economic catastrophe so far?*
   The Black Death plague (1347–50), the Irish potato famine (1845–49), and the Great Depression (1929–1937).

2. *What has been the most promising economic development?*
   Globalization.

3. *What is the most important economic threat for the future?*
   The big demographic problems that Europe is facing, and the US, to some lesser extent.

4. *What is the worst economic policy error that you can remember?*
   Russia's adoption of Communism after the Revolution, the rise of fascist political economy in Italy and Germany in the thirties, and China's Cultural Revolution.

5. *What was the most enlightened concrete economic policy measure?*
   –

6. *Please name a politician that you admire for his/her good hand in economic policy.*
   Ronald Reagan had some very important gifts and insights. Much earlier, Theodore Roosevelt made pioneering moves in the direction of regulation, and Franklin D. Roosevelt did important things for capitalism by means of investor and consumer protection. In Europe, Ludwig Erhard and Margaret Thatcher come to mind.

7. *In your mind, what has been the most misleading theoretical approach in economics?*
   So-called Keynesian economics in the period after World War II proved to be extremely misleading and misguided. Just like supply side economics, on which the jury is still out, it swept in to influence

without anybody having a chance to sit down and think about the merits and demerits.

8. *What was the most important theoretical breakthrough?*
Of course, Adam Smith brought about a breakthrough. It is impossible to exaggerate his importance. Also, in the 20th century, the theories of John Maynard Keynes and Friedrich Hayek.

9. *If it was only for economic reasons, in which country would you like to live today?*
The United States. I consider myself pretty fortunate to live here.

10. *If it was only for the intellectual challenge, in which times would you have liked to live?*
It would have been enormously exciting to have been in the prime of my career in the 1930s when all the new ideas sprang up, especially those by Keynes. Likewise, I would have been very turned on by what Hayek was beginning to say. But I was in at the beginning and the overthrow of Keynesianism, so I'm not complaining.

11. *If you had to choose between efficiency and equality, which would you pick?*
I don't like that question very much. If I had to choose between dynamism and equality, then, sure, I would chose dynamism. But efficiency smacks as some sort of static notion.

12. *If you had to choose between liberty and justice, which would you pick?*
That's a funny one. It's impossible to answer that.

13. *What is the absolute limit to taxation (give a maximum percentage of personal income)?*
That depends on what government does with the money. In the US, a lot of the money is spent very badly. In most of Europe, the public sector is run better, but there are all sorts of strange state activities.

14. *What is the absolute limit to state activity (give a maximum percentage of GDP)?*
See above.

15. *Who is your favorite economist today?*
My friends Amar Bhidé and Roman Frydman, here at Columbia. Beyond them, of course, my all-time favorite is Paul Samuelson.

16. *Among the classics in economic theory, who is your favorite thinker?*
     When I was young, I admired so much the mind of David Ricardo.
     I didn't like the prose style of Adam Smith very much, it's so
     tedious. I tended to like writers who sparkle a little bit more. So,
     over the years, Keynes and Hayek were the most interesting to
     read. They're goldmines. And Samuelson, I always enjoyed reading
     every paper that he ever wrote. He is the consummate neoclassical
     theorist.

17. *Outside economics, which author has had the most influence on you?*
     The literary and, more generally, humanistic thinkers that I read
     during my first year in college. For example, among the philosophers,
     David Hume and Henri Bergson. And also, Benvenuto Cellini, whose
     autobiography really shocked me.

18. *Who are you most indebted to intellectually?*
     Probably my teacher at Yale, William Fellner, a Hungarian who had
     come over in 1939. He was a walking repository of all 20th century
     knowledge. He had the biggest intellectual influence on me.

19. *Who was your major role model?*
     Could be James Tobin, could be Paul Samuelson. Some people say I
     write like Paul Samuelson.

20. *Which piece of work in economics (book, article, speech) has impressed
     you most?*
     One or two essays by Paul Samuelson that I happened to read in my
     junior years.

21. *Can you remember your most striking intellectual 'epiphany'? Which
     was it?*
     In my case, the awakening was not a solution, but the puzzle that
     comes before it. I didn't understand how microeconomics related to
     macro. That was why I went into economics.

22. *What qualities should economic researchers have?*
     Tremendous stubbornness and a decent level of energy.

23. *What do you consider to be your own most important contribution?*
     Building a connection between micro and macro.

24. *What would you name as your most painful failure in professional life?*
There are hunches that you can never turn into something publishable. For example, I've always wanted to tackle the Mezzogiorno problem in formal theoretical terms. But never did.

25. *What do you consider to be your main personal character trait?*
The good trait that I have is that I don't mind reaching for the stars, and I don't like the pain of making a fool out of myself, but it's only day's work, and I don't let it get to me too much.

26. *What do you think is your main personal flaw?*
Vanity. I fuss too much to try to make my work attractive and fetching, so that everybody will admire me for it, instead of just getting it out and moving on.

27. *What is the character trait that you like most in your collaborators?*
Diligence.

28. *What is the character trait that you like most in your friends?*
Tolerance.

29. *What does happiness mean for you?*
That's a colossal subject. I can only give a symbolic example. I remember once, my wife and I stayed in a hotel in St Paul de Vence, we didn't like the room, and Viviana was right back down at the desk complaining. They finally gave us this fantastic room with a wonderful view, we loved it so much. And we started dancing a little bit around the room, and our dog got up and wanted to dance with us, until it all dissolved into laughter.

30. *What does fulfilment mean for you?*
To do something with our lives. Achievement. That's very important. But beyond that, and more important, it's personal growth: the constant process of becoming better and better, of getting a deeper understanding of what you're doing, learning about life, learning to enjoy, learning to conduct yourself better.

31. *What would be the most terrible economic misfortune in your eyes?*
–

32. *What, outside doing economics, is your favorite way to spend your time?*
Listening to music, going to the movies.

33. *What is your favorite dish?*
For years, it was corned beef hash with an egg on top, put in a skillet with the top down, so that it gets all steamed. But Viviana, before we were married, was horrified by that. She said: Don't you know that in Argentina, only horses eat corned beef? So that was the end of the corned beef, I had to move on to more sophisticated dishes, and I grew heterodox, or let's say, diversified. Well, maybe it would be good pasta.

JAMES M. BUCHANAN

James M. Buchanan preferred not to fill in the questionnaire, commenting: 'I don't like these kinds of questions. They are irrelevant. You're forcing yourself to answer things you have no competence to answer, and no confidence either. There would be a presumptive arrogance underneath it.' Instead, however, he produced a list of the ten thinkers that most influenced him. The order is arbitrary. Here it is:

1. Frank Knight
2. Gustav Wicksell
3. Antonio de Viti de Marco
4. Kenneth Arrow
5. Rutledge Vining
6. Gordon Tullock
7. John von Neumann and Oskar Morgenstern
8. Friedrich August von Hayek
9. John Rawls
10. Adam Smith

NOTES

1. All highlights by the Nobel Laureate.
2. Friedrich August von Hayek (1945).
3. Friedrich August von Hayek (1937).
4. Friedrich August von Hayek (1979).
5. Friedrich August von Hayek (1989).

PART III

All those roads to wisdom: answers

Findings and insights

As a child, I was taught that curiosity was a sinful tendency to have. Not curiosity about things, of course, but about people. Curiosity about other people means that you are tempted to stick your nose into things that are none of your business. And to violate somebody else's private sphere is immoral. I still believe in this moral tenet that my parents have passed on to me. In this same vein, one of the Nobel Laureates that I have interviewed for this book, Robert M. Solow, says elsewhere that he is 'put off by peeks into the hearts and minds of people who should in some important sense be anonymous.'[1] But at the same time, it is not always easy to obey this rule of decency. For one, empathy makes one want to know more about others, and in many cases, one obviously should follow that instinct: reciprocity as the general law governing human interaction may require that one inquires.[2] But what is more, everybody learns from the example of others – beyond the classic pattern of elite formation that sociologists may be interested in and which Harriet Zuckerman describes as a process of accumulative advantage, that is as 'the spiraling of augmented achievements and rewards for individuals and a system of stratification that is sharply graded'.[3] In her view,

> the ascent into the ultra-elite follows an almost commonplace script. The future laureates begin their careers by working hard and long at their research. Consequently, they produce a good deal of it. This is generally judged as being superior quality by specialists in their field, with the result that they acquire a growing reputation in the wider community of scientists who depend on such judgments since they cannot assess the specialized work for themselves. Growing recognition tends to bring better facilities for research, better students and colleagues who are tuned in to the social networks through which scientific reputations are transmitted, and still more rewards. These in turn help the scientists to do more and better work.[4]

In order to learn from others and to follow them, one has to acquire knowledge about a little more than just the observable facts. A 'peek into hearts and minds' is exactly what is needed. The practical way out of the dilemma is simple, fortunately, if one exclusively relies on voluntary information. No investigative journalism here.

Preserving one's private sphere is only one very important concern.

Robert M. Solow's other concern is that knowing more about the individuals might distort the reception and perception of theories. There is undeniably such a risk. As the great Joseph Schumpeter said: 'Occasionally, it may be an interesting question to ask *why* a man says what he says; but whatever the answer, it does not tell us anything about whether what he says is true or false.'[5] Valid as this statement is, this indifferent void should be more than offset by some increased understanding, if only one goes about it in a respectful, sympathetic way. It may be useful to remember, for example, how John Stuart Mill suffered under the social conventions of his time. The *mores* of those days made it impossible for him to be seen in public together with Harriet Taylor, his soul mate. Society strongly objected to their affair – and made them feel it. And of course, living together with Harriet Taylor was excluded a fortiori, as long as her husband was alive. Divorce was not an option in those days. Mill suffered desperately from this social oppression. Knowing this does contribute more depth to one's understanding of why he wrote his famous book *On Liberty*[6] – and it allows one to see more clearly why his distinction between government coercion and societal pressures is not as clear-cut as one would find logical today. Without making his arguments less strong in any way, this kind of knowledge about Mill's personal background just helps to dissipate some of the fog.

While no insights of similar tragic scope and impact should be expected from the interviews in this book, it is certainly fair to say that the conversations have shed some very interesting light on the underlying motives, forces and influences that have moved the Nobel Laureates in the ways in which they have gone. There are multiple links running between the personal mentalities and research. It is indeed impossible to imagine that someone with a less independent mind than Gary S. Becker would have dared to swim so much against the mainstream of economics, for example. It is just as hard to imagine that someone with a less strong dislike of discriminatory state action than James M. Buchanan would have been able to come up with a theory endogenizing governments. These personal character traits have been decisive 'inner' influences on the direction that their respective fields of research have taken.

Character is part of what I have labeled 'personality' in the approach taken here to track down the factors that have determined a researcher's individual itinerary. That category also includes upbringing and more general family background. Yet, personality is but one influence. I have also set out to track down the impacts of 'history' and 'theory'. It should be remembered here that 'history' means the particular economic background of a country or the world at a given time, that is the economic problems and policy challenges that leave their marks in daily life and to which politicians need answers, sometimes directly seeking academic advice. The label 'theory' refers to the evolving 'state of the art' in economics, with its changing toolkits, its ongoing paradigmatic disputes, its ramifications and varying ideological fashions. Some people just set out to fill the glaring gaps in the existing body of theory.

In order to learn from the Nobel Laureates, one should now ask what unites or differentiates the interviewees in their paths. Of course, with a number of ten interviewees one cannot pretend to a 'representative' set. So no sort of 'laws' can be inferred from our observations. But there are interesting observations to consider and to dwell on.

MISSIONARY OR TECHNICIAN

It is easy to see that some Laureates have come to economics because they were immediately attracted by its questions – questions they felt an imperative urge to solve in order to improve the world. Those are the missionaries, and they usually have, as Joseph Schumpeter says, a 'vision'.[7] 'Economists should contribute to making people's lives better', says George A. Akerlof, for example. 'We have a duty to get it right.' Economists of his genre thus cannot avoid becoming policy advisers: 'The reason why I teach macroeconomics is that one thing the government can do and has responsibility for is to create the background market conditions in which people can live healthy, comfortable lives'.[8] He goes so far as to call the underlying intellectual approach 'libertarianism', I would call it liberal utilitarianism. Douglass C. North, too, says that he is 'still trying to save the world'.[9] Gary S. Becker talks about his youth referring to the emerging 'desire to do something for society'.[10] James M. Buchanan, too, says elsewhere that 'we have a moral obligation to think that we can constructively design and implement reform in social arrangements' but he is so humble as to admit: 'I cannot . . . move the world unaided, and it is morally arrogant of me to imagine myself in a position of power sufficient to enable me to act unilaterally.'[11] All of these have major mathematical skills as well, but that specific talent did not have a predominant role in directing them toward economics. Paul A. Samuelson was somewhere in between. Profoundly marked by the experience of the Great Depression, as he admits, he found that economics was 'quite attractive to somebody who is both interested in statistics, analysis, metrics, but also in people and policies'.[12]

On the other hand, there are born technicians, who possess the proper (mathematical) 'technique', as Schumpeter would say,[13] and who take a while to discover their interest in 'people and policies': those Laureates who have come to economics mainly through their mathematical talent. This is clearly the case of Kenneth J. Arrow who originally wanted to study mathematical statistics – for two reasons: first, because he had a striking talent for anything mathematical or logical, and couldn't resist the temptation. Because a temptation mathematical beauty truly is, and one that can easily divert from what the underlying problem is all about. As Arrow writes elsewhere, 'mathematics is certainly a source of aesthetic pleasure. Over and over we have the sense of symmetry, of elegance, of an abstract and pervasive unity of seemingly disparate parts. My mathematical skills and taste for abstraction led me to emphasize the aesthetic aspects of mathematics.'[14] The second, more prosaic reason is that Arrow wanted to provide himself with a good basis for a job. Traumatized by the Great Depression, 'all I wanted was security', he admits.[15] He enrolled in statistics and then switched to economics for his Ph.D. mainly in order to follow his teacher, Harold Hotelling, and to grasp the opportunity of a fellowship.

The more technical approach is true also for Reinhard Selten, who had taught himself mathematics from age 15 onward and always had his nose sticking in some kinds of calculations. He ultimately studied mathematics and even earned his Ph.D. degree in mathematics – but then turned to economics relatively late because he found that ultimately he 'was more attracted by social questions. Economics is good for that.'[16] Robert M. Solow had opted for economics because he wanted 'a rigorous social science', unlike sociology which he 'found a little soft'. 'The analytical aspect of economics already appealed to me'.[17]

Vernon L. Smith's story is similar. With his mathematical talent, he started out studying physics and electrical engineering at Cal Tech, where he was confronted with the social sciences more or less by accident. It was crucial that he stumbled over Paul Samuelson's new textbook, a textbook that was revolutionary in presenting the subject matter in mathematical terms: 'Samuelson's book indicated that economics was just physics'.[18] Ever since, he learned that economics is *not* like physics, but it stuck nevertheless. Paul Samuelson's textbook got many people with mathematical talent hooked; Vernon L. Smith is by far not the only one. Edmund S. Phelps remembers that 'it immediately came as a revelation that the textbook by Paul Samuelson was so brilliant'. Robert M. Solow calls Paul Samuelson's *Foundations of Economic Analysis*[19] the work in economics that has impressed him most throughout his career.[20]

The Keynesian revolution, together with the ensuing formalization of economics, has changed the profession enormously. Keynesianism got its foot in the door of economics after the Great Depression, when the world out there was looking for explanations and for possibilities to prevent another similar catastrophe in the future. John Maynard Keynes's path-breaking *General Theory of Employment, Interest and Money*[21] provided the mental framework, and his disciples provided the mathematics. It seems that the math was not just 'in the air'; it was badly needed in order to translate Keynes's approach into more coherent terms than his own words. This was the birth of mathematics as an indispensable logical tool in economics. Keynesian macroeconomics was thus appealing both to missionaries and technicians, but it soon became a selection mechanism in economics that was favorable only to those technicians who could cope with the mathematics. The ensuing debates between Keynesians, Neoclassics, New Keynesians and New Classics, the Neoclassical synthesis and so on – all that was carried out between mathematically high-performing, formal economists. Relative to that accidental trend, the others lost out. The more verbal economists were removed from the mainstream and found refuge only in the more exotic realms of economics: Austrian Economics, Institutional Economics, Constitutional Political Economy, Economic History, Epistemology, and so on.

Although Keynesianism must be understood within its historical context, and would likely not have come into being without the Great Depression, its main tenets are here to stay – that is the notion that markets may not spontaneously return to equilibrium, and that governments can use fiscal and monetary policy to fine-tune the economy. There seems to be a considerable amount of path dependence in economic theory. As John Maynard Keynes himself remarked, 'practical men, who believe themselves to be quite exempt from any intellectual influences, are usually the slaves of some defunct economist'[22] – and thus, even after the 2008 crisis, which should cast serious and long overdue doubts on the efficacy of fiscal and monetary policy, his legacy will probably prevail. It is too appealing for politics to drop it. Social learning is a long, tedious and pathological process, and maybe it only proceeds in circles.

Economics is thus nowadays almost unthinkable without mathematics. In our group of Nobel Laureates, James M. Buchanan and Douglass C. North, even though both have indubitable skills in mathematics and proved it in the past, now mostly refrain from using it. They do economics mainly verbally. In the interview, North even objects 'violently to the way economics is practiced today. It is abstract high level theory with formal mathematics. It's elegant. . . but it doesn't do anything. It doesn't solve problems.' When he said this, in the spring of 2008, he couldn't yet be aware just how much the further course of the – already ongoing – financial crisis would prove him right. The breakdown of the American banking system in October 2008 and its collateral damage in the rest of the world had been greatly promoted by modern finance theory, a branch of economics that had come up with an enormous amount of financial innovation. Unfortunately, this proved to be the kind of economics that excels in the brilliant use of sophisticated mathematical tools but loses fundamental risks out of sight, that is fundamental risks associated generally with human behavior. The real world differs from the textbooks, as the Nobel Laureate Myron Scholes had to admit at the 2008 General Meeting of the Mont Pèlerin Society in Tokyo.[23]

CHANCE AND OTHER TEMPTATIONS

There may be a humility bias in how much one ascribes to chance, or luck, looking back onto one's life – but it is probably true that the dice are just not thrown at age 16 or 17 in most cases. And the decisions that are made at such a young age are usually decisions under a lot of uncertainty, especially concerning one's own preferences, which one is still to discover. Thus it must be taken seriously when most people claim that they have more or less stumbled into economics. In Vernon Smith's case, it was chance exposure to economics at Cal Tech that turned him around. In Reinhard Selten's case, luck played a role anyway that cannot be overrated. And in particular, there was that crucial moment when he discovered a seminar in game theory for economists and enrolled in it even though he was in mathematics. Paul Samuelson says that he 'came to Chicago only because of location' and that it 'was an accident that I liked the subject. I had not even thought about economics in my high school years.' Robert M. Solow followed his wife's advice. Kenneth J. Arrow was successfully lured by help of a scholarship; and Edmund Phelps was already expecting to become a philosophy major when his father asked him 'to do him this one favor and take one course in economics'. He did, and it changed his life.

Interestingly, even for most 'missionaries', economics wasn't a clear and unequivocal choice before they saw it in class. Even James M. Buchanan embarked on economics due to a scholarship that was available; Gary S. Becker was forced to take an economics class at high school, found the class terrible but the subject interesting – but then lost interest again. It was sheer luck to have him back 'on track'. Douglass C. North was hesitating between economics, which he was strongly interested in but didn't have any good marks in, and photography, a field in which he had already worked quite successfully. From everything he says in this book and elsewhere, this was a serious temptation to ward off. Still today, he prides himself in being a remarkable photographer, and seems to have some regrets. George A. Akerlof is an exception here because, out of sheer rebellion, he refused to follow the usual family pattern, which would have led to a career in the natural sciences. 'When I went to college and was asked what I wanted to be one day, I remember saying that I wanted to be a professor of economics.'[24] He aimed high because, as he admits, didn't know anything else. He comes from a family with a broad academic background.

BOURGEOISIE OR NOT TO BE

This brings me to the next interesting aspect, that is the influence of the specific family background. In this respect, George A. Akerlof is an exception here, and the strength of that influence is obvious. No other family background in the group of our Nobel Laureates was so clearly intellectual. While Akerlof says that he simply couldn't imagine that studying economics could qualify him for anything but a being professor, the career of a professional economist was a bold step for all the others.

It was bold for those who came from a bourgeois setting, and even bolder for those from a more humble rural background. Edmund S. Phelps certainly hit the nail on the head when he once remarked in a conversation with me that it is not straightforward – not at all impossible, but difficult – to become an economist if one doesn't grow up in an at least somewhat bourgeois setting. Absent major crises that affect everybody, economic questions tend to subside into the fuzzy background of social life unless one lives in a context that brings with it some regular exposure. Phelps grew up in precisely what he calls a 'somewhat bourgeois setting', both parents being oriented towards business and coming from relatively wealthy backgrounds. Gary S. Becker's case is similar, his father being a pretty well-to-do businessman. The same is true for Douglass C. North, whose father was a successful insurance manager, and even for Paul A. Samuelson, whose father had his own drugstore and whose family had accumulated a relative degree of affluence and saw it gradually dissipating when the Florida land bubble burst in the 1920s. In Kenneth J. Arrow's case, the setting was bourgeois even though his family experienced poverty as a result of the Great Depression. It took his father, who had been working for a bank, five years to find a new job. Robert M. Solow's father was in the fur trade. In Reinhard Selten's case, his parents also didn't have much schooling, but his father was a talented businessman, starting a successful reading circle and employing some 20 people. This was a bourgeois setting, even though it was eventually destroyed by the Nazis – and yet, Selten says that 'it was pure luck that my life finally took an academic turn'.[25]

The situation was altogether different for Vernon L. Smith. Neither of his parents had an education beyond eighth grade. His father provided a work ethic and can-do knowledge, and his mother was active in political and social affairs in the community. Financial problems forced the family to practice autarky living on a farm for a couple of years. The situation of James M. Buchanan was quite similar. His family lived on a farm throughout his youth; his father had two years of university training ('and played football'). His mother, however, had been a school teacher. She had an excellent work ethic and a big intellectual appetite – and that of course left an imprint on the son.

FAMILY DISCUSSIONS

Even without much schooling, parents can provide their children with intellectual appetite and with a motivation for achievement. Discussions at the dinner table, or other regular family gatherings, are extremely important here – and it doesn't matter so much how high-powered or not the arguments are. What is crucial is that the awareness is there – awareness about the importance of certain topics relating to economics and economic policy, to anything that touches social questions, and of course the appetite to learn more about them. This is an experience that most Nobel Laureates share.[26] Vernon L. Smith was fascinated to find out at college that the topics that had been debated at the dinner table were actually 'things you could study, that it needn't be only a matter of opinion. You could actually base your opinions on analysis, on investigation, on some kind of understanding about how society and how the economy works'.[27] In the Buchanan household, discussions were more about politics – populist politics, that is. In George A. Akerlof's and Douglass C. North's cases, dinner conversations turned mainly around politics, too. More directly economic, in the Arrow household, much of the conversations turned around 'the question what was wrong with the system and what needed to be done' to get out of the Great Depression. The same was true many years later at the Phelps family's dinner table: 'the financial and economic news was ever-present in dinner time conversation'. Gary Becker reports that he had many discussions with his sister – and some arguments with his father. Only Paul A. Samuelson cannot remember much intellectual stimulation from his home environment, especially not from the time he was sent to live on a farm, away from his parents. Reinhard Selten's case is exceptional here. His parents probably avoided long-winded discussions about politics and economics due to the circumstances – mainly in order to avoid their children trouble. This was quite common in those bitter days.

WORLD VIEWS

World views also play a crucial role in instigating research. As Joseph Schumpeter wrote, world views, or ideologies, already enter the 'pre-analytic cognitive act' or 'vision' that 'supplies the raw material for the analytic effort'.[28] This later analytic effort, according to him, really begins

> when we have conceived our vision of the set of phenomena that caught our interest, no matter whether this set lies in virgin soil or in land that had been cultivated before. The first task is to verbalize the vision or to conceptualize it in such a way that its elements take their places, with names attached to them that facilitate recognition and manipulation, in a more or less orderly schema or picture. . . . Factual work and 'theoretical' work, in an endless relation of give and take, naturally testing one another and setting new tasks for each other, will eventually produce scientific models, the provisional joint products of their interaction with the surviving elements of the original vision, to which increasingly more rigorous standards of consistency and adequacy will be applied.[29]

But the very first step is entirely colored by a world view:

> Analytic work begins with material provided by our vision of things, and this vision is ideological almost by definition. It embodies the picture of things as we see them, and wherever there is any possible motive for wishing to see them in a given rather than another light, the way in which we see things can hardly be distinguished from the way in which we wish to see them.[30]

One might think that much of a person's world view is probably laid down during those dinner table conversations that have been a recurrent issue in the interviews. While this is true for what one might call the 'initial endowment', these may not persist as new influences come in later in life. Interestingly, in the case of our ten Nobel Laureates, the initial ideological endowments were mostly socialist. There is a saying according to which who, as a youngster, is not socialist, has no heart – and who still is a socialist in later years has no brain. There might be something to it. . . Vernon L. Smith comes from a socialist background; Gary S. Becker was a socialist, just like his father who, 'although he was a pretty successful businessman, strongly supported interventionist-type candidates'.[31] Douglass C. North was an outright Marxist; Kenneth J. Arrow regarded himself as a socialist ('not a communist'). James M. Buchanan doesn't make such a fine distinction. He came from a populist background, as already mentioned. Being discriminated against because he was not part of the establishment then turned him into a flaming communist. 'I would have signed up immediately to the Communist party had a recruiter come along', he says.[32] And when he got interested in economics, his peer group then lured him over to socialism. Edmund Phelps' parents were somewhat on the left, too. George A. Akerlof seems always to have been deeply liberal (and not libertarian, as he says, misleadingly); pretty much like Robert M. Solow. Paul A. Samuelson is tougher to categorize.

As predicted by the popular saying, however, those initial ideological endowments didn't last in most cases. It is hard, if not impossible, to remain a socialist when one begins to understand the workings of the market. In James M. Buchanan's case, it thus was studying economics at Chicago that turned him around. 'And in a hurry. We were about 30 people in Knight's course in price theory. Fifteen switched over completely within six to eight weeks, and 15 stayed exactly the way they were.' The same happened to Gary S. Becker who remembers that two things pulled him away from socialism, and with mighty force: Milton Friedman and economics.

> Studying economics, at the end of my sophomore year at Princeton, I remember I debated somebody about markets versus socialism. And I was on the market side. I had already shifted away from socialism. Entering Princeton, I was a socialist. Two years or so later, I was no longer a socialist. Three years later, I decided to go to Chicago. I still had an uneasy feeling. Even though I had the basic principles why I should lean in that direction, I still was missing the theory. I then got that at Chicago.[33]

When Douglass C. North got his first job at Seattle, he re-learned theory – and, as he says, this 'was the last step in my getting rid of Marxism. As I re-learned theory, I became a very rigid neoclassical, Chicago type economist.'[34]

TEACHERS MAKE A DIFFERENCE

As the Nobel Laureates went ahead with their schooling and academic training, they came across teachers and mentors that, in most cases, played a decisive role – in the sense that these mentors managed to entice their intellectual appetite even more, opened up interesting new fields for them, gave them good advice, and urged them ultimately to stay in academia. The role of teachers is as important as it is psychologically interesting. Teachers provide the intellectual socialization, as Harriet Zuckerman points out: 'the elite masters shape their apprentices and prepare them for elite status by inculcating and reinforcing in them not only cognitive substance and skills but the values, norms, self-images, and expectations that they take to be appropriate for this stratum in science'.[35] I am not able to go into much detail here, but I cannot resist the temptation to refer the reader to the works of the French philosopher René Girard in this context.[30] According to Girard's theory of 'mimetic desire', one borrows one's desires from others. The desire for a certain object – or field of research, in the present context – is always provoked by the desire of another person for this same object. Girard explains that in most cases, people desire something or engage in something because they think that this brings them closer to the person(s) from which they have inherited this desire. In some way, it is in fact the model which is sought.[37] Girard has demonstrated this – very plausible – theory by looking at the psychological patterns in novels, ranging from the writings of Marcel Proust to Fyodor Dostoevsky. While Girard's point is the potential for envy and hatred that results from this, something that doesn't have to be dealt with here, this pattern is interesting in our context as well because as such, it may also be at work in academic economics. Admiration and the ensuing imitation can be a strong incentive – and it pays: 'apprentices of elite scientists are less likely to be lost in the crowd'.[38]

While the impact of school teachers cannot seem to be considerable, the impact and the effect of admiration for outstanding academic teachers is clear from Gary S. Becker's experience with Milton Friedman at Chicago, for example. 'He was by far the greatest living teacher I have ever had', Becker says. At college in Princeton, Jacob Viner had been decisive in orienting Becker towards Chicago. But Becker was strong enough to defend his intellectual autonomy some years later, deciding to move on to Columbia University in New York City. James M. Buchanan was in Frank Knight's wake, and the works of Knut Wicksell came to widen his scope. Kenneth J. Arrow was attracted and molded in many ways by Harold Hotelling, but other famous people such as Abraham Wald, Arthur Burns, Wesley Clark Mitchell, John Hicks, Alfred Tarski and Tjalling Koopmans also left a mark and gave good advice. In Vernon L. Smith's case, Wassily Leontief and Gottfried Haberler left their mark, and especially Edward Chamberlin. Reinhard Selten was strongly influenced by a book he had read in younger years – John von Neumann and Oskar Morgenstern's *Theory of Games and Economic Behaviour*.[39] But apart from that, cooperation with Heinz Sauermann at Frankfurt University provided him with the understanding, ease and leeway in which he could evolve. Sauermann was crucial for Selten. Paul A. Samuelson, although he claims to have been very independent early on ('I didn't listen to my elders much'), refers to Aaron Director as an influence, and to 'famous people like Frank Knight, Jacob Viner, Paul Douglas, Henry Simons' as his mentors.

Robert M. Solow benefited greatly from Wassily Leontief and Paul Samuelson. Much later, George A. Akerlof had Robert M. Solow himself as an admired master and mentor, and Edmund Phelps got much inspiration from James Tobin, William Fellner and Thomas Schelling. Strikingly, these groups overlap a lot. Do they overlap because the world is small – or rather because, in order to be successful, you have to cluster with others? What is it about Chicago, Columbia, Princeton, Harvard and MIT that has drawn all these Nobel Laureates there? What about the Cowles Commission and the NBER? This is pretty much a chicken-and-egg problem. Do they all go there because these places are so good, or are these places so good because they all go there? This topic will have to be revisited.

Other than people and institutions, books may also prove highly influential. In that sense, books are teachers. This is clearly the case of the most influential textbook in economics of the past century, and its theoretical precursor: Paul A. Samuelson's *Economics* and his *Foundations*.[40] Edmund Phelps refers to that, Vernon Smith does, and many quote Samuelson as an inspiring teacher. A combination of good books and good teachers is of course the optimum.

HISTORY'S HEAVY FOOTPRINT

Great events leave great marks, on people and on theory. People get motivated by catastrophes to try to explain them, and theory changes correspondingly. A collateral of this is that all economic theory is necessarily historically bound, both in terms of the real-life events behind it and in terms of the trajectory of theory itself, as Joseph Schumpeter points out.[41] Looking back at the past century, it must be stated that there are only a couple of events from an economic point of view that qualify as having had this kind of importance. The first, and foremost, was the Great Depression. Paul A. Samuelson doesn't hesitate when asked what, in his mind, has been the most serious economic catastrophe so far: the Great Depression. Phelps, Solow, Arrow and Smith join in. The Great Depression, triggered probably essentially by bad monetary policy,[42] was a tragedy in many respects. It brought misery to the whole world, it began an era of erroneous anticapitalism, and it started the – soon to be excessive – rise of the welfare state with Franklin D. Roosevelt's legislations and New Deal programs that followed.[43] As Milton Friedman stresses elsewhere, instead of blaming the Great Depression on business and on capitalism, 'the lesson that should have been learned was that government let them down. That it was mismanagement of the monetary system that produced it and not a failure of the market system.'[44] Unfortunately, the same mistaken lesson seems to be learned again in 2008, after the burst of the real estate bubble in the US and the following breakdown of the banking system.

In the 1930s, the dire economic conditions, together with the effects of the Versailles Treaty, obviously made it easier in Germany for nationalistic – and eventually national socialist – thinking to spread. Germany counted 6 million people out of work, which was one tenth of the population and one third of the workforce. In the United States, where the Great Depression had originated with the stock market crash in 1929, unemployment rose to 25 percent of the workforce; profits dropped, poverty spread, and deflation began. Its effects were so serious that everybody who experienced it was puzzled and looked out for answers. 'The Great Depression was all around us. You saw all that unemployment in the streets; the papers and newsreels were full of it', remembers Kenneth J. Arrow, who was reluctant about going into academia due to this – security came first. Robert M. Solow remembers that 'the Depression had made a deep impression on me, and that did have some importance for my interest in the business cycle and unemployment'. Douglass C. North, even though he admits that he lived a life of comfort himself, acknowledges that one was surrounded by problems related to the Great Depression every day – and that made him, like others, ask questions. It was difficult to answer these questions within the established mainstream paradigm of economic theory. This made the Keynesian revolution, triggered by John Maynard Keynes's book *The General Theory of Employment, Interest, and Money*,[45] a true upheaval, the consequences of which are still felt today.

LONE WOLVES OR TRIBAL ANIMALS

What is the most promising strategy in academia? Can you survive as a lone wolf – or do you have to be a group animal? How much interaction is needed in order to be successful? Our interviews show that 'anything goes', as Paul Feyerabend would say.[46] Paul A. Samuelson certainly isn't a lone wolf. He has co-authored a lot, and much of his work – if not most of it – has been triggered by other people's papers that he felt an urge to straighten out. Kenneth J. Arrow has been more dependent on interaction in the sense that he often solved puzzles that others brought to him and confronted him with. James M. Buchanan co-authored a lot, and derived from it as much inspiration as despair, as it seems. I guess he would like to be a lone wolf but just doesn't happen to be one. George A. Akerlof also co-authored a lot, especially with his wife, Janet L. Yellen. Vernon L. Smith clearly isn't a lone wolf, although his Asperger's syndrome sometimes allegedly alienates him from the people around. Smith has always been co-authoring, and has worked out his experiments within groups. In the interview, he recognizes Charles Plott as one major source of inspiration, for example – Plott, who, as some say, should have received the Nobel Prize as well. Plott's work is mentioned expressly in the backgrounder for Smith's prize.

Reinhard Selten, however, denies that kind of disposition. 'I'm not so dependent on external inspiration', he says. 'I find stimulation wherever I am'.[47] Edmund S. Phelps likes company, but has written his major pieces in a monk-like atmosphere – something he says he needed but now finds too high a price to pay. And Douglass C. North is 'sure I have learnt a lot from other people. . . But in terms of where my ideas come from, I have been very much a loner'. This ties in with a study by Hendrik P. van Dalen that shows that 'most path-breaking publications are written alone, contrary to the trend in academia where co-authored papers have become the rule'.[48] Given this trend, those numbers may change with time. Co-authoring allows for more fruitful intellectual exchange, and it supposedly even saves time (there are exceptions which perhaps confirm the rule), and it will thus continue to spread. The logical result for the Nobel Prize may be that it will be given more and more to groups instead of individuals. This is a trend that actually seems to be already under way.

PUZZLE SOLVERS OR SYSTEM BUILDERS

Robert M. Solow, in his interview, introduces the distinction between 'puzzle solvers' – a notion which he borrowed from Thomas S. Kuhn, one of the most influential philosophers of science of the twentieth century[49] – and 'system builders'. These notions seem straightforward. Puzzle solvers go stepwise, they are humble, they are pragmatic, occasionally pedantic, they are somewhat eclectic, and they are not over-zealous. Too much zeal might mean pretension. 'You find something strange and not quite easy to understand, and then you try to get closer to understanding it.'[50] This 'piecemeal' approach – to borrow another famous notion, this time coined by the great philosopher Karl Popper[51] – is descriptive of researchers doing 'normal science', in Kuhnian terms. One might perhaps even view these people as 'arbitrageurs' in Israel Kirzner's sense of an alert (intellectual) entrepreneur,[52] providing better solutions for given problems, that is finding and filling the gaps in the existing body of theory, with the purpose of strengthening and enhancing the given paradigm. Obviously, Solow classifies himself amongst those 'puzzle solvers', just like Paul A. Samuelson, Kenneth J. Arrow, Edmund S. Phelps, George A. Akerlof, Reinhard Selten, Gary S. Becker and perhaps Vernon L. Smith also would.

People like James M. Buchanan and Douglass C. North are harder to classify in this respect. In their personal research itinerary, they have probably also been puzzle solvers initially. As new questions came up, they tackled them, one after the other – but their effective thrust, while doing this, was more powerfully directed toward creating a new, distinctive paradigm of their own. In Kuhnian terms, again, they experienced a 'scientific crisis', given that the existing paradigm in economic theory couldn't solve their foremost problems, and so they brought about a paradigm shift. However, the shift was not complete in the sense that the old paradigm – standard neoclassical economics – wasn't fully supplanted. In modern theory, a variety of approaches seem to coexist quite peacefully. Maybe the time for full-fledged 'scientific revolutions' is over, at least in economics. At any rate, people in this category can be viewed as rebellious 'innovators' in the sense of the Schumpeterian entrepreneur, providing new solutions for new problems, that is creating new paradigms and entailing a potentially substantial degree of 'creative destruction' as they move ahead.[53] James M. Buchanan started out with analyzing Public Debt, fully within the existing paradigm of economic theory, and ended up with Public Choice and Constitutional Economics. Douglass C. North began measuring history and ended up with 'New Institutional Economics'. Whether they originally intended it or not, these two Nobel Laureates did end up having built their systems and whole new paradigms.

In most cases, academic curiosity just carried people further and further in some direction. As they went forward, they didn't necessarily know where their journey would take them. Just as George A. Akerlof says, 'I'm not sure I'm taking an aim'.[54] What does that mean? Well, I guess the distinction between 'puzzle solvers' and 'system builders' is not so clear after all. Solving puzzles is the way all scientific endeavors start out. What differs is the scope of the puzzle that one is ready to tackle.

PUZZLER OR MASTER

As seen earlier, Friedrich August von Hayek distinguished between 'puzzlers' and 'masters of one's subject'.[55] This distinction refers less to the degree of zeal, as does the distinction between 'puzzle solvers' and 'system builders', but rather to mental capabilities. Hayek refers to the 'puzzler' as someone who, lacking perfect memory and all-encompassing erudition, has to rather painfully (re-)think through everything on his own – which however may make him more creative, allowing him to discover unconventional avenues that others may not see – and to the 'master of his subject' as someone who has excellent memory and therefore all-encompassing knowledge of a field, but lacks some, or all, originality. Of course, Hayek classifies himself in the first category. The psychological pattern behind Hayek's statement is the same relatively conceited one as in Solow's distinction, if I may say so rather bluntly: you accuse yourself of some deficiency, you make yourself look relatively small – only to show how great that really makes you if viewed from the right perspective. We therefore have to take this Hayekian distinction with a pinch of salt. But we can nevertheless try to guess who, amongst our Nobel Laureates, might fit into what category.

It is my vague intuition that Douglass C. North would probably set his foot into the 'puzzler' category, at least in describing his younger years; since he started both cliometrics and the New Institutional Economics mostly from scratch, coming from nowhere. Other candidates for this category perhaps also include James M. Buchanan, George A. Akerlof and Kenneth J. Arrow, just like Reinhard Selten who came from a relatively isolated research environment and had a very specific, concentrated intellectual approach. As for Paul A. Samuelson and Robert M. Solow, I would like to call them 'masters of their subject', because of the encompassing unfailing erudition that they have – without however denying them their originality. This is truly a tough one.

THE UNLIKELY SOURCES OF CRUCIAL IDEAS

It is interesting to compare how our ten Laureates managed to have their crucial ideas, those that the Nobel Committee later found prizeworthy. And again, Paul Feyerabend's dictum applies: 'Anything goes'. Crucial ideas are a gift; they tend to come from the most unlikely sources, at the most unlikely moments. As noted, James M. Buchanan owes his approach mainly to an old, dusty book he stumbled on by pure chance in the Chicago Library: Wicksell's *Finanztheoretische Untersuchungen*.[56] Vernon L. Smith owes his inspiration to a course taught by Edward Chamberlin, but the ensuing idea came later – without any announcement: 'In the middle of the night, in 1956 at Purdue, I wake up and I have this idea.'[57] Gary S. Becker remembers puzzling about a possible 'economics of marriage' while sitting in a hotel room all by himself. Edmund S. Phelps remembers how the surroundings didn't matter when he was thinking about a problem; even an opera wouldn't disturb him. Douglass C. North tells the story of how some serious criticism by a student prompted him to stay up all night drinking brandy and reflecting on the topic. George A. Akerlof, on the other hand, describes his 'Lemons' as the chance outcome of some other, more general research project on business cycles.

Kenneth J. Arrow remembers how painfully long it took him to jump off the starting block. Reading John R. Hicks' *Value and Capital*[58] was helpful, but in the end, the idea for his social choice paper, his dissertation came 'just like that'. And Paul A. Samuelson often just reacted to other people's influences. As he acknowledges, much of what he has been working on just came up as a topic because somebody else had written something that he felt an irresistible urge to straighten out. He says that his greatest achievement, the mathematization of economics, laid down in his *Foundations*, 'just grew out of actual lively topics that my teachers . . . weren't able to handle adequately'.[59]

WHAT FISH IN WHAT POND

Another important point is what area of research one chooses. From the point of view of clever self-marketing, it is of course more promising to place oneself in a new field, or even to create one from scratch: who would not prefer to be a big fish in a small pond rather than to be a small fish in a big pond? Ex post, this may seem straightforward. In order to prevail in science, one should try to come up with a truly pioneering idea, a fruitful idea that one can expand more and more and keep the creative monopoly on for at least a while. The problem with placing yourself outside the mainstream, however, is that the more fruitful your approach is, the more likely it is to become the new mainstream. What once was rebellion becomes tradition. Breaking free from the mainstream is a risky investment; becoming the mainstream is the reward. As Reinhard Selten says with regard to game theory, every time he broke free from some well-established approach, his method took some time to spread, and then 'the mainstream of economics was on my heels again'.[60] To differing degrees, most of the Nobel Laureates interviewed in this book have been rebels against the established mainstream at some point: Paul A. Samuelson and Robert M. Solow against the sterile neoclassical approach of their early days; Gary S. Becker against the narrow scope of economics; Vernon L. Smith against the black holes in general equilibrium theory; James M. Buchanan against the missing regard to the public sector and collective decision-making; Douglass C. North against the a-historic approach of economics; George A. Akerlof against the lack of consideration for sociological issues; and Edmund S. Phelps against the missing link between microeconomics and macroeconomics – a problem, by the way, the existence and importance of which Robert M. Solow denies outright: 'I do not think that the appeal to "microfoundations" amounted to much. Macroeconomic hypothesis had always been justified by some sort of appeal to microeconomic reasoning.'[61]

In Selten's case, his personal character traits predisposed him for swimming beyond the mainstream. As he admits, 'more than anything else, the effect was that I have always mistrusted majority opinion. I have always had to think independently. . . . I've never been swimming with the crowd.' The same is true for Gary S. Becker, who has always a strong urge for independence generally: 'I'm not someone who likes working in a crowded area.' And, if possible, it may be even more relevant for James M. Buchanan, who started out with strong personal convictions and an inherited horror of domination.

AMERICAN DOMINANCE AND EXCELLENCE

The interviews demonstrate, once more, how singularly rich and dynamic the American academic world has been so far. It doesn't come as a surprise that out of 62 Nobel Laureates in economics, 40 have American citizenship. Out of the ten Laureates interviewed in this book, all except one non-American, Reinhard Selten, and Douglass C. North, who stayed in the West, at Berkeley, have benefited during their professional training from the special cluster of knowledge at the famous US Ivy League universities on the East Coast, in New York, and in Chicago in the Midwest: it was Chicago and Harvard for Paul A. Samuelson; Chicago for James M. Buchanan; Princeton and Chicago for Gary S. Becker; Yale for Edmund S. Phelps and George A. Akerlof; (Cal Tech and) Harvard for Vernon L. Smith; Columbia for Kenneth J. Arrow. What is nowadays considered 'mainstream economics is pretty much an American invention, and has been sustained in its intellectual vigor by the American higher education system, specifically the rise of a large number of research universities in the postwar period',[62] explains the historian E. Roy Weintraub. This can be traced back to three major influences: brain gain, networks, size, good overall conditions, money and clever university management.

The situation had been different in the early twentieth century; economics was then still stronger in Europe. But that pattern was forever destroyed before and after the second World War. The American universities received a huge inflow of talent and knowledge in the person of Jews who had left their countries under the threat of extermination.[63] In New York, the 'New School' became a haven for refugees – and a tremendous center of new ideas.[64] Paul A. Samuelson describes what happened in Cambridge, Massachusetts, at that time: 'Harvard was in kind of a boom period because Adolf Hitler was so beastly and many refugees started out there.'[65] Those were years in which anti-Semitism was still very present even in the United States and at American universities in particular, as

Kenneth J. Arrow recalls: 'Anti-Semitism blocked the road to faculty appointments, not just student applications'.[66] And yet, this major tectonic shift in the geographic distribution of academic talent laid the ground work for the generation of new and growingly intense *networks*, on all sides. Specifically, Paul A. Samuelson explains: 'There was anti-Semitism in some degree everywhere, but less in Chicago than at Harvard or Princeton. As a result, this gave Chicago a certain monopoly advantage; they could get talent that the others didn't think they wanted.' Some of these mental walls were broken up as time went by, and at any rate, the new networks that were being knit in those days expanded rapidly. In those years and ever since, the University of Chicago has indeed accumulated talent in a very coherent manner, and it has paid off tremendously: Chicago has had 25 Nobel Laureates in economics so far,[67] including in that count even those that weren't employed at Chicago at the moment of their Nobel coronation – more than any other university in the United States or elsewhere. Almost a quarter of all Nobel Laureates have been members of the Chicago faculty, or offsprings. While Chicago is number one, Harvard, MIT and Columbia, however, follow closely on its heels.

Most American universities also benefit from the sheer *size* of their market – a market where supply caters not only to students and scholars from the home country, but from the entire world. On top of that, this market also happens to be a rather comfortable one generally. The all-over *conditions* are ideal for research. As Frey and Pommerehne point out,

> the country with the highest average per capita income offers the opportunities to provide scholars with particularly good research facilities. The American political and social system allows individual scholars to pursue their research in a liberal setting which compares favourably in a historical perspective. The beneficial preconditions have been used to create institutions . . . which provide the incentives for the production and publication of good research.[68]

Another influence is *money*, especially the presence of private money. Many of the outstanding academic institutions in the United States rely on private funding. Ivy League universities such as Harvard or Yale have huge endowments at their disposal. This has two consequences: they can invest heavily, and they exert active competition. Both activities have favorable consequences in any market, and they have been beneficial in the academic market as well. At the level of the individual universities, this entire background has led to a recruitment policy that differs fundamentally, still today, from 'old Europe'. In Europe, universities still follow a relatively holistic approach. This may be an inheritance from the deeply engrained *Humboldtian* ideal of universality. European universities therefore tend to recruit one scholar per field and to cover as many fields of economics as possible at one university. In contrast, American universities have never had qualms about specialization, building large, well-endowed departments in a smaller number of fields. This has simply turned out to be a very successful *strategy* – and that is a lesson that Europeans apparently still find hard to heed.

NOTIONS OF PROGRESS

Turning from the individual researchers to science as a whole again, that is to science as a social phenomenon, the aim is now to try to understand how progress in economic theory comes about and how individual scholars go about generating their particular ideas. In this context, it may be helpful to check how the laureates themselves think of 'progress'. Asking them this question is, however, of course to prepare the ground for an 'is-ought problem' of sorts: looking back, one is easily tempted to conclude that the specific path behind has necessarily been a path of scientific progress. After all, one has learnt something, that is one has added something to one's stock of knowledge. So there must have been progress. Of course progress doesn't mean that everybody thinks alike. Progress doesn't imply scientific consensus. As Paul A. Samuelson says elsewhere,[69] what has changed in economics over the last century is that economists are now able to delineate quickly the contours of their disagreements. Anyway, the temptation toward overconfidence is as pervasive as it is understandable: otherwise, one would all too easily admit that one has wasted one's time. But the problem with the notion of 'progress' and its underlying strong positive connotation is that everybody just moves ahead. One actually cannot even help moving ahead. Moving ahead, however, may lead into good or bad directions. And thus it might just all be a random walk.

James M. Buchanan is extremely humble in this respect: 'I don't know what progress really means. . . . . There are whole realms of discourse out there that we cannot reach, by definition. There are always going to be limits beyond which we cannot go. Knowing that they are there, you can always hope to move a little closer – but that's all.'[70] Robert M. Solow, however, indeed sees progress in economic theory. 'I think there is a line of progress. What matters is whether errors get corrected', he states, and pragmatically defines progress as the accumulation of solutions to given problems:

> You find something strange and not quite easy to understand, and then you try to get closer to understanding it. The accumulation of the solutions that you find is progress. Sometimes the right answer to a puzzle changes, because circum-stances change, or institutions change, or attitudes change. Very likely, we will never run out of puzzles to solve. As you can see, I have a very non-grandiose picture of progress in economics. It means more and more little things that

you are able to understand. And understand doesn't necessarily mean predict. Understanding is just kind of a confident belief that you could give a correct answer to the question what would happen if you changed some variable or other. What your understanding may lead to, may be this unpredictability.

And yet, he doesn't view progress as a pure random walk, as one might think. 'There tends to be a direction. The direction comes both internally and externally', that is from real world problems and from within the literature. The result, nowadays, is 'not that there are fewer questions, but there are now more difficult, more refined questions. Those are questions that turn on little things rather than big things.'[71] To paraphrase this: we are still confused, but at a higher level.

Somewhat in line with this, Edmund S. Phelps thinks that 'progress in economic theory in the twentieth century has consisted of small steps towards getting away from the economics of the traditional economy to the economics of a modern economy.'[72] Paul A. Samuelson just gives a concrete example: 'something like the Taylor rule[73] is progress'. Gary S. Becker also sees

> a lot of progress in economic theory . . . for example human capital theory, family economics, Public Choice theory, and informational economics. I could go on quoting things that have constituted progress in economic theory. And I think that will continue. . . . There are still a lot of things we don't understand about the world. . . and so therefore there will inevitably be progress in the next ten or 20 years. Inevitably, we will get better insights into human behaviour. We will build on the theories we have, and so they will obviously change over time. Theory is an evolving structure, and it will continue to evolve.[74]

George A. Akerlof, then, is perhaps over-optimistic when he states that 'in the last century, we made one major bit of progress. We explained how, if you get into a depression, you get out of it. . . . Today, we would know what to do. That is a major contribution. And that's due to Keynes, of course.' Viewed from the position the world is in by the end of the year 2008, this is, to say the least, questionable. Progress, in Akerlof's view, means that

> people will spring loose from the cognitive tradition and will try something different, mathematical economics, for example. As a result of this pattern of progress, we can now consider phenomena in ways in which we couldn't consider them before. . . . In order to get new solutions, you have to free yourself from the older, from all previous non-mathematical tradition.

Looking ahead, Akerlof recommends that we should 'enlarge our horizon', taking personal motivations into account, and social norms.[75] Kenneth J. Arrow agrees and demands that people take more into account 'the social nature of economics'.[76]

Thus, to recognize progress after the fact is necessarily a biased endeavor. The problem is that – coming back to the optimistic saying 'All roads lead to Rome' – one doesn't know exactly where Rome is.[77] Worse, one doesn't even know *what* Rome is. Sure enough, everybody hopes to get there and to find a 'there there', but what it consists of or what shape it ultimately takes, nobody has the remotest idea. This wider question concerning what truly constitutes progress as such in the economic sciences is even more intractable than the question about individual excellence. If lucky, Rome will be the yet unknown end of one's interactive journey of life. In an analogy to Hayek's famous phrase, academic life consists of competition to a large extent, and it is also very much a discovery procedure.[78] Does that which will be discovered automatically deserve the denomination 'progress'? Certainly not. It is probably wiser to use Joseph Schumpeter's completely value-free term, which is the 'filiation of economic ideas'. In his gigantic *History of Economic Analysis*, Schumpeter writes that

> scientific analysis is not simply a logically consistent process that starts with some primitive notions and then adds to the stock in a straight-line fashion. It is not simply progressive discovery of an objective reality – as is, for example, discovery in the basin of the Congo. Rather it is an incessant struggle with creations of our own and our predecessors' minds and it 'progresses', if at all, in a criss-cross fashion, not as logic, but as the impact of new ideas or observations or needs, and also as the bents and temperaments of new men, dictate.[79]

The 'filiation of scientific ideas', then, is a 'process by which men's efforts to understand economic phenomena produce, improve, and pull down analytic structures in an unending sequence'.[80] According to Thomas Kuhn, again, this can happen in two familiar ways: through normal 'puzzle-solving',[81] whereby little bits of knowledge are added to an already existing stock, or through scientific revolutions, which imply that the existing stock of knowledge may be overthrown as one paradigm is replaced by another.[82] This may, however, entail 'Kuhn losses', that is some phenomena that used to be successfully explained by the old paradigm may become an open question again with the new one.[83]

SUBSTITUTIVE, CUMULATIVE AND CIRCULAR PROGRESS

Even though it is a daunting task to normatively define progress as such, it is not impossible, in a more sober and humble approach, to logically distinguish different positive categories, or patterns of steps in the development of science. Following Ernst Helmstädter, one can differentiate between substitutive progress, cumulative progress and circular progress.[84] Substitutive progress means that some new insights replace earlier knowledge. This is the most revolutionary, the Kuhnian kind of progress Cumulative progress takes place when there is 'normal science' threading its slow, but steady puzzle-solving path. Scientific revolutions tend to be incompatible with cumulative progress; they may eradicate what has already been (l)earned ('Kuhn losses': see above). Helmstädter speaks of a particular form of cumulative progress when some scientific insights reach areas that were so far unknown. With respect to economics, as an example, Helmstädter refers to Gary Becker's advances into areas that were until then not the typical territory of economics. Less well-meaning people talk about his 'economic imperialism'. As George J. Stigler pointed out in his 1982 Nobel Memorial lecture, this kind of progress is relatively new. Until the age of Adam Smith, which really marks the beginning of economics as a science, scholars didn't even refer to each other.[85] As soon as cross-references became inevitable and more feasible, economics really got established as a field of science – and cumulative progress began to take place. Circular progress, finally, takes place when certain issues or patterns are reintroduced at some point, in a new dress and with fresh value added, however.

As Helmstädter claims, all three patterns are common to science, whatever the field. The respective relevance of the three patterns, however, varies greatly – and this reveals a lot about the character of progress in the social sciences such as economics, as compared to the natural sciences. As Helmstädter maintains, and I am inclined to endorse what he says, economics is predominantly a field characterized by circular progress. This may sound like a contradiction in terms, but it isn't. It just means that people regularly go back to old insights and to premises that they deem to be the basis of their thinking. There aren't that many. People are either optimists or pessimists about the market's tendency towards equilibrium. People are either optimists or pessimists about state intervention. People are either marginalists or not. People are either logical positivists or not. People are either rationalists or not. All these fundamental paradigms tend to come up in the theoretical debate time and again, each in a somewhat more original, more promising shape, based usually on more experience and on new methods. Progress, at any rate, is embodied in those changing shapes. This is how the neoclassical school followed the classical school, and how Keynesianism was made obsolete by Neo- and New Keynesianism.

Cumulative and substitutive progress are patterns that are much less the rule in economics than in the natural sciences. In economics, the streets are just not paved with cases like Gary S. Becker who venture out in neighboring fields. Cumulative progress is rare. And full-fledged substitution for its part has really taken place only in the field of methodology, with mathematization more or less crowding out the verbal, philosophical side of economics. If this deserves the citation 'substitution', I am less convinced that progress is the appropriate category. As Helmstädter writes, decreasing returns to scale are beginning to make themselves felt here. While I agree with this diagnosis, I am not sure it will be of much consequence. At any rate, if most progress in the field of economics – as opposed to progress in other fields – is circular, then it becomes relatively difficult to attribute it to individuals. And this is why peer-review processes are perhaps not the end of the story, but constitute a relatively acceptable approximation nevertheless.

SCIENCE VS. SCIENTISM

Following the Nobel Laureates, let me define progress in economic science pragmatically as some forward move compared to a most recent status quo that indeed allows a better understanding of the world. But again, what is it really that allows one to better understand the world? Is this all just about a world view, a paradigm, or is it so concrete as to envisage precise predictions? This amounts to the decisive question about whether or not one is now a positivist. As Bruce Caldwell writes in his brilliant intellectual Hayek biography, if progress in economics means that one understands more and more economic laws and law-like relations, in a positivistic sense, then

> improvements in empirical methods will allow ever more precise predictions to be made; theory change will involve the steady accumulation of a well-corroborated theory base; errant theories will be gradually but steadily falsified and eliminated; and as the findings of economic science become more widely accepted methodological debate across competing paradigms will wither away, as will, indeed the competing paradigms themselves.[86]

Looking back with an unromantic eye, none of these things have come about, however. As Hayek put it drastically in his Nobel Memorial Lecture, 'as a profession we have made a mess of things'.[87]

Hayek accuses the economics profession of *scientism*, that is of a

> propensity to imitate as closely as possible the procedures of the brilliantly successful physical sciences – an attempt which in our field may lead to outright error . . . since it involves a mechanical and uncritical application of habits of thought to fields different from those in which they have been formed.[88]

One problem that has arisen with Keynesian economics is the focus on quantitative methods, in an attempt to resemble the exact physical sciences as much as possible. All modelling nowadays is done in such a way that a problem can be treated mathematically and tested empirically. Hayek warns about the ensuing incentive effects on *economics*, which do not at all warrant progress:

> The correlation between aggregate demand and total employment, for instance, may only be approximate, but as it is the *only* one on which we have quantitative data, it is accepted as the only causal connection that counts. On this standard there may thus well exist better 'scientific' evidence for a false theory, which will be accepted because it is more 'scientific', than for a valid explanation, which is rejected because there is no sufficient quantitative evidence for it.[89]

And beyond that, the mere approach is misleading because the problem of the social sciences differs crucially from the physical sciences in that there is no clear, non-arbitrary distinction between what is exogenous and what is endogenous: the question in the social sciences is

> not how far man's picture of the external world fits the facts (as in the physical sciences), but how by his actions, determined by the views and concepts he possesses, man builds up another world of which the individual becomes a part. . . This is the field to which the social studies or the 'moral sciences' address themselves.[90]

And also, therefore, they 'have to deal with structures of *essential* complexity, that is, with structures whose characteristic properties can be exhibited only by models made up of relatively large numbers of variables.'[91]

Sure enough, with the almost secular trend toward mathematization[92] and the emerging of better statistical techniques, better data and better computers, the technical possibilities in economics have improved a great deal. As Hayek writes, 'the great strength of mathematics is that it enables us to describe abstract patterns which cannot be perceived by our senses, and to state the common properties of hierarchies or classes of patterns of a highly abstract character'.[93] Also, people simply don't squabble so much any more about what they mean. As George A. Akerlof points out, mathematics has provided the profession with 'a mutual language'.[94] And this enables people, potentially, to better describe the current situation and to track down correlations observable in the past. But predictions still systematically stand on rather shaky ground, which means that straightforward economic laws have not been established as yet. As Terence Hutchison has it, 'economists have constantly used, and are constantly using, trends, tendencies, patterns or temporary constancies, as the basis for predictions, because in fact, they have not available any genuine, relevant, non-trivial laws'.[95] Caldwell also quotes Roger Backhouse: 'Despite the immense effort, undreamed-of increases in computing power, and the development of vastly more sophisticated statistical techniques, econometrics has failed to produce the quantitative laws that many economists, at one time, believed it would'.[96]

Given this, Caldwell appropriately refers the reader back to Hayek, insisting that 'many of the phenomena that economists study are, in fact, examples of complex phenomena'.[97] The problem is in the subjectivity of the data of the social sciences. As Hayek says,

> the facts of the social sciences are merely opinions, views held by the people whose actions we study. They differ from the facts of the physical sciences in being beliefs or opinions held by particular people, beliefs which as such are our data, irrespective of whether they are true or false, and which, moreover, we cannot directly observe in the minds of the people but which we can recognize from what they do and say merely because we have ourselves a mind similar to theirs.[98]

Social phenomena are thus distinct from physical phenomena, which in turn can be 'described by relatively simple formulae'.[99] Social life never lends itself to such simple formulae.

It follows from this that when complex phenomena are dealt with, precise predictions will not be possible. As Caldwell explains, 'when we theorize about complex phenomena, usually the best that we are able to do is offer explanations of the principle by which the phenomena occur. Although this may enable us to predict broad patterns of behavior and, thereby, rule out certain outcomes, our ability to falsify theories is diminished.'[100] And, as Hayek himself once put it, 'what we can know in the field of economics is so much less than people aspire to'.[101] More precisely, 'the student of social phenomena cannot hope to know more than the types of elements from which his universe is made up'.[102] This means that 'economic theory is confined to describing kinds of patterns which will appear if certain general conditions are satisfied, but can rarely if ever derive from this knowledge any predictions of specific phenomena'.[103] So exact predictions are simply not feasible – whatever the database and however sophisticated the technical equipment.[104]

Progress in economic science then gets to mean something else, something more humble than in the traditional positivist approach. Progress can only mean that one produces new 'explanations of principle' and new 'pattern predictions', in Hayek's terms. Explanations of principle mean that one understands and therefore can explain the general principle by which something works, that is why and how it works the way it does. Pattern predictions are empirically testable as well, and they give a qualitative prediction (up or down, for example), instead of a quantitative one. Complex phenomena should teach everybody humility, along Robert M. Solow's humorous lines which parallel Oscar Wilde's famous description of a fox hunt,[105] saying that perhaps economics was just an example of 'the overeducated in pursuit of the unknowable'.[106] Solow's own modesty, however, doesn't lead him to question the use of mathematical models; it just makes him ask for more responsible, encompassing modeling. This, however, is more easily said than done. As John Maynard Keynes already cautioned, 'good economists are scarce, because the gift for using "vigilant observation" to choose good models, although it does not require a highly specialized intellectual technique, appears to be a very rare one'.[107]

Interestingly, Caldwell goes on to describe that 'a dominant research strategy in economics over the course of the twentieth century has been to provide models at varying levels of formality of what Karl Popper called situational analyses'.[108] Examples that easily come to mind are the economics of information, transaction cost economics and game theory. All of these fields start from snapshots of given situations, deriving theories from there. And they do so not just as a plausible default solution, but perfectly on purpose, as the interview with George A. Akerlof has shown. Akerlof speaks of the 'English garden' model of economic science, meaning that you 'look at the world out there, and from those detailed stories, you can then construct a more general theory'.[109] The problem with this is that those general theories are not necessarily worth much. As the explanatory value of these models is increased, they also become more punctual, and therefore less falsifiable – and therefore they cannot qualify as 'laws' in the positive sense. 'Either the models that we develop are less directly falsifiable, or . . . it is now a matter of methodological principle not to take falsifications seriously. This is an inevitable result when trying to model complex phenomena.'[110]

As Hayek formulates,

> a theory of essentially complex phenomena must refer to a large number of particular facts; and to derive a prediction from it, or to test it, we have to ascertain all these particular facts. Once we succeeded in this there should be no particular difficulty about deriving testable predictions – with the help of modern computers it should be easy enough to insert these data into the appropriate blanks of the theoretical formulae and to derive a prediction. The real difficulty, to the solution of which science has little to contribute, and which is sometimes indeed insoluble, consists in the ascertainment of the particular facts.[111]

In order to keep the theory falsifiable, according to the Popperian criterion, predictions can then not be any more precise than pattern predictions.

Of course, compared with the precise predictions we have learnt to expect in the physical sciences, this sort of mere pattern predictions is a second best with which one does not like to have to be content. Yet the danger of which I want to warn is precisely the belief that in order to have a claim to be accepted as scientific it is necessary to achieve more. This way ahead lies charlatanism, and worse. To act on the belief that we possess the knowledge and the power which enable us to shape the processes of society entirely to our liking, knowledge which in fact we do *not* possess, is likely to make us do much harm.[112]

This is true for politics – but also for economic science as such.

James M. Buchanan has also warned that 'we are human animals, and we are bound. There are whole realms of discourse out there that we cannot reach, by definition. There are always going to be limits beyond which we cannot go. Knowing that they are there, you can always hope to move a little closer – but that's all.'[113] But not everyone is so humble. And therefore Caldwell quite rightly laments the long-lasting damaging effects that positivism, triggered by the Keynesian answers to the Great Depression challenges, has had on economic science:

> Positivism in all its various guises fostered false hopes and permitted self-delusion. It misled economists into thinking that we can, and, indeed, that to be scientific we must, always improve the predictive adequacy of our theories. . . Our failure to recognize the limitations of economics has cast a long shadow over the discipline.[114]

The global financial breakdown that has hit the world in 2008 unfortunately demonstrates just how apt this analysis is. Without going much farther into this, suffice it to say that many factors have contributed to this crisis which was actually much more of a government failure than a market failure; policy was far from innocent. An over-generous social policy that operated through the real-estate market played a role, just as much as the easy money that the Federal Reserve pumped into the American economy to keep people spending. All these policies were acts of self-delusion. They all go back to this very 'belief that we possess the knowledge and the power which enable us to shape the processes of society entirely to our liking'. But modern economics, without realizing it, also carries some heavy burden of guilt.

Modern finance theory, especially portfolio theory, has exploded over the recent decades; researchers have paved the way for more and more sophisticated financial tools. The problem with those tools was not only that those who ended up using them were no longer capable of understanding them. The problem was also that the underlying models concentrated on risks and no longer took the fundamental uncertainty related with all human interaction into account.[115] Nobel Laureate Myron Scholes sums up that the crisis 'might have resulted from a) bad management, b) imperfect incentive compensation contracts, c) bad models, d) bad inputs to models, e) a lack of understanding of the aggregation problem, and f) a false sense fostered by government entities that the world was a safer place with less risk – or a combination of all of them.'[116] What he misses is that it was not only government that fostered this false sense. With its undeniable positivism and its blindness to underlying, fundamental uncertainty, financial theory did as well.

CAN MAINSTREAM ECONOMICS GO ASTRAY?

In this perspective, one cannot but state that mainstream economics has indeed gone astray. But does such a statement make any sense? Academia, or science, is basically a market for ideas.[117] Can a market go astray at all? This seems a priori possible, at least in a neoclassical framework allowing for something such as 'market failure'. It would be preposterous, however, to make such a claim if one remains within the 'discovery procedure' framework.

In this specific market, people within and without academia feed in their latest findings, submitting it to the judgment of their peers. What eventually survive in these markets are ideas, concepts or approaches that are promising enough for other scholars to pick them up. Can one be sure, or must one be worried whether only those ideas, concepts or approaches get picked up that really stand for progress? Is there, to use a notion coined by David Colander, 'an "invisible hand of truth" which guides the progression of science?'[118] Can everybody be happy as 'good Darwinians', as Robert M. Solow puts it?[119] No, and indeed one must be worried. It has been shown, for example, that even technical errors are commonplace in published papers; that intellectual effort also comes at a cost which is weighed against benefit; that interest-group behavior has some effect on research; and that ideology also plays a role in academic findings.[120] But all that doesn't mean that the market doesn't function. What is being traded on this market is just not necessarily the truth – but academic elegance, proofs of brilliance, a new language, and so on. While there are many criticisms that one may address to academia as a business or institution, with its own rather peculiar rules, incentives, reward systems and funding procedures,[121] the base line is still the same: it is basically a market that one is talking about.

The science-as-market parallel has been regularly used, but it has also been rejected at least just as often. The reason why I will be using it here is that, in accordance with Friedrich August von Hayek's idea of the 'division of knowledge' in society through markets, it will facilitate the understanding of the proper dynamics of science. As Hayek explains in *Economics and Knowledge*, the division of knowledge in an ordinary market for goods and/or services is a process tending toward an equilibrium, namely a process by which 'the spontaneous interaction of a number of people, each possessing only bits of knowledge, brings about a state of affairs in which prices correspond to costs, etc., and which could be brought about by deliberate direction only by somebody who possessed the combined knowledge of all those individuals.'[122] But how exactly does this take place? In *The Use of Knowledge in Society*, Hayek explains that this spontaneous process takes place through the price mechanism. 'We must look at the price system as such a mechanism for communicating information if we want to understand its real function.'[123] The reason is that as relative local scarcities change in a competitive market, relative prices change, too. Relative prices transmit the information about scarcity without the individual trader having to go out and measure global supply and demand – all he needs to do is look at the evolution of prices in the overall market. Hayek calls this 'a marvel'. As for the generation of knowledge, beyond the simple transmission, this takes place through competition. Through competition, external shocks which modify relative local scarcities will provoke differential reactions by supply and demand trying to find better solutions than before – reactions that are impossible to predict. This is the very source of evolutionary dynamics. Hayek thus frames competition as 'a procedure for the discovery of such facts as, without resort to it, would not be known to anyone'[124] and the results of which are 'unpredictable and on the whole different from those which anyone has, or could have, deliberately aimed at'.[125]

The generation of knowledge in the market for private goods thus takes place through competitive exchange. Goods are being traded between buyers and sellers for money, and information on scarcity is passed on between them and others in the form of relative prices. However, as Michael Polanyi writes, 'the coordinating functions of the market are but a special case of coordination by mutual adjustment'.[126] And thus, to draw a parallel that may seem daring at first sight, let me look now at the moral market. Here, what people 'trade' is good behavior toward each other, as Adam Smith describes in his *Theory of Moral Sentiments*.[127] As Adam's namesake Vernon Smith explains, everything is about gains from trade.

> Whether it is goods or favors that are exchanged, they bestow gains from trade that humans seek relentlessly in all social transactions. Thus, Adam Smith's single axiom, broadly interpreted . . . is sufficient to characterize a major portion of the human social and cultural enterprise. It explains why human nature appears to be simultaneously self-regarding and other-regarding.[128]

The beauty is that, just like self-interested behavior in the market for goods brings about the greatest good for all,[129] 'by acting according to the dictates of our moral faculties, we necessarily pursue the most effectual means for promoting the happiness of mankind'.[130]

Just as trade in goods only takes place when prices reflect scarcity correctly, that is when enough money is being paid for a given unit of a good, reciprocity in moral behavior implies that people treat each other equally, according to generally accepted norms. If reciprocity doesn't result, one of the two parties will usually walk away. Norms are the outcomes of behavioral interaction just as prices are the outcome of market exchange. Conversely, one can more or less observe relative norms, just as one can observe relative prices for goods, and these reveal something about the probability – or scarcity – of good moral behavior. The dynamic aspect is that as people interact in the moral market, new types of behavior may be tried. While the new knowledge that is being created in the market for goods refers to as yet undiscovered scarcities and potential solutions; the new knowledge generated through competitive interaction in the moral market refers to possibilities of dealing with each other.

Now let me try the same exercise with regard to the market for ideas, or scientific knowledge. What is being traded here is ideas, 'visions', approaches, techniques. Ideas are being exchanged against recognition in academia, provoking some checking comments at first, some refutations, and ultimately leading possibly to approval and emulation by others on a broad scale.[131] Success in science simply means that one's contribution survives and even spreads. Here, reciprocity means that a good piece of academic work that is being submitted to the community one way or another does receive its due amount of praise, general acceptance and emulation. How much recognition it gets is then encapsulated in the degree to which it becomes part of the dominant doctrine in the field. The relative degree of recognition of a new idea is, so to speak, its relative 'price'.[132] When the degree of recognition is high, a theory becomes '*monnaie courante*'. (The wording is of course not innocent.) Admittedly, this market parallel may seem a little bit of a conceptual stretch, but it is useful – even if the coordinating mechanism may perhaps not be entirely as powerful, precise and transparent as the price system in the market for goods and services. James M. Buchanan denies himself a promising avenue for further reflection when he criticizes it as outright 'improper, even metaphorically, to conceptualize scientists as "trading"'.[133]

While it is the relative price resulting in a global market that tells local sellers whether they should increase or decrease their production efforts, it is the relative degree of acceptance of a certain type of idea that gives an indication to a scientist whether to increase or decrease his effort, whether to pursue in some theoretical vein or not.[134] Connected with looking at academia this way is the implicit hope that Adam Smith's 'invisible hand' will come in to direct self-interested individual action towards a common effort that serves the advancement of scientific knowledge as a whole. When the social cooperation game is so structured that individual goals and social concerns are ultimately in harmony, then there could be hope that academic research goes the right way, and that it indeed generates new knowledge. The new knowledge that is being generated refers to new, promising avenues in research, as yet undiscovered 'holes' in an existing body of theory, or altogether new possible combinations of ideas. In this perspective, science can be pictured as a truly positive evolutionary process.

Whether competition in academia really turns out to be a 'good' evolutionary process, that is whether private and public interests are naturally aligned in such a way as to make the knowledge generation indeed socially desirable, is a question that Adam Smith may have answered positively. He did answer it in the affirmative with regard to the market for goods and services; with regard to the moral market, his approach was more positive than normative, but his general thrust was the same. His view of the 'simple system of natural liberty'[135] is generally an optimistic one. As modern Constitutional economics and game theory have shown, this outcome however does depend on the 'rules of the game', and these open themselves to collective choice. As Viktor Vanberg explains,

> market and science are games of competition. In both realms, the engine that drives the evolutionary invisible-hand process is the competing ambitions of reward-seeking agents. And in both realms, competition is . . . subject to rules that can be more or less suitable in channeling the participants' ambitions in socially productive directions.[136]

The only important caveat may be that, in science perhaps even more than in the market for goods and services, one may not be able to gauge *ex ante* what those 'socially productive directions' are. Where is Rome? Isn't the open competitive process needed precisely in order to find this out?

This is where Hayek's notion of pattern predictions may find application again. One may analyze the given rules under which academia operates and see whether some of them appear outright perverse. As Vanberg notes, science is not only directed by rules concerning the competition for recognition among peers, it is also affected by the necessary competition for resources. 'In order to be able to participate in the competition for recognition, scientists need to secure resources, and this introduces another level of competition that has its own rules.'[137] Vanberg guesses that a 'harmonious relation is by no means guaranteed'. And 'likewise, in the case of science, the ways in which research institutes, universities and professional associations assign positions, promotions, rewards and honors to their members will have an obvious effect on the ways in which scientists compete with each other.'[138] If these incentive structures direct behavior in obvious ways that cannot possibly be judged functional, then a modification of the rules may appear imperative in order to keep the social enterprise of research in line with a potential 'common good'.

If one wishes to argue that the market for economic research has gone astray in the sense that its over-mathematization and formalization has made economists close their eyes to relevant issues for all analysis of human interaction, to the detriment of the financial markets and the entire global economy, then one should be able to point out an incentive mechanism that might be responsible for that – or else it is impossible to properly argue that the market has gone astray. If the incentive mechanisms and selection principles look alright, that is if one accepts the basic principles that govern academia, then one has to accept its results. All that could legitimately be said is that one might have a preference for the market moving in some other direction.

The rules of the game, however, are themselves subject to a process of evolution. Some of the 'tangible' rules – especially as far as financial and organizational questions are concerned – are laid down by governments. They can be distortionary, and they will not spontaneously evolve; they will need to be corrected consciously. Most of the 'intangible' rules concerning peer-review processes and the like, however, have never been laid down by authority, but have sprung up in spontaneous interaction. They change over time, but of course there is no guarantee that they move in the 'right' direction. Some authors claim that here, 'the desire to raise their status by turning their discipline into a branch of applied mathematics . . . has lead economists to adopt selection principles that are counterproductive, both with regard to the outside reputation of their profession and with regard to its contribution to the growth of knowledge'.[139]

There is a host of studies concerning the reward system of science. The broadest, survey and interview-based study is the one by Harriet Zuckerman, which, however, extends over different fields. Zuckerman finds considerable evidence for the phenomenon of accumulation of advantage in the sense of a 'spiraling of augmented achievements and rewards for individuals and a system of stratification that is sharply graded',[140] and for a scientific equivalent to the Matthew effect according to which the rich get richer and the poor get poorer. In academia, the Matthew effect 'confers further authority and influence on those who are already influential and authoritative and brings further honors to those who have already been honored'.[141] 'Plainly, the reward system of science has its imperfections', writes Harriet Zuckerman. 'Rewards do not always accord with quality of contribution nor do they always serve to elicit continuing role performance of the highest quality.'[142] This is not to generally deny the quality of those who arrive at the top, but it is true that the system doesn't capture every work of quality. In many cases, breakthroughs come about *against* the odds of the reward system.

In a more recent study pretty much in the same vein, Henrik P. van Dalen has looked at Nobel economists in particular. He finds that 'economics is a young man's game', that is that most breakthrough achievements usually take place when the scientists are still in their twenties. He traces this back to typical character traits that eminent economists all share: 'The average Nobel laureate is equipped with the following blessings: talent, an independent or an outsider's mind, a love for risky projects, a nose for being at the right place at the right time, the gift to see fundamental problems and, last but not least, luck.'[143] This very much coincides with the findings from the ten interviews assembled here.

NOTES

1. Michael Szenberg (1992, p. 270).
2. See Adam Smith (1759/1982).
3. Harriet Zuckerman (1977, p. 249).
4. Harriet Zuckerman (1977, p. 145).
5. Joseph Schumpeter (1954, p. 11).
6. John Stuart Mill (1859/1974). See also Friedrich August von Hayek (1969b).
7. Joseph A. Schumpeter (1954, p. 41).
8. See the interview with George A. Akerlof in this volume.
9. See the interview with Douglass C. North in this volume.
10. See the interview with Gary S. Becker in this volume.
11. James M. Buchanan (1992, p. 100).
12. See the interview with Paul A. Samuelson in this volume.
13. Joseph A. Schumpeter (1954, p. 7).
14. Kenneth J. Arrow (1992, p. 49).
15. See the interview with Kenneth J. Arrow in this volume.
16. See the interview with Reinhard Selten in this volume.
17. See the interview with Robert M. Solow in this volume.
18. See the interview with Vernon L. Smith in this volume (Paul A. Samuelson, 1948).
19. Paul A. Samuelson (1947), *Foundations of Economic Analysis*, Harvard University Press.
20. See the questionnaire with Robert M. Solow in this volume.
21. John Maynard Keynes (1936).
22. John Maynard Keynes (1936, p. 383).
23. Myron Scholes had helped to create and run the LTCM hedge fund, together with Robert C. Merton and others. The heavily leveraged LTCM failed in 1998, after the Asian and Russian crises, one year after the Nobel nomination, causing a financial meltdown of its own.
24. See the interview with George A. Akerlof in this volume.
25. See the interview with Reinhard Selten in this volume.

26. This also explains why they did not necessarily start out with practical, applied problems. 'The best work of Samuelson, Stigler, Solow, Nash, or Debreu was inspired by a desire to improve the way we think the world works.' Hendrik P. van Dalen (1997, p. 13).
27. See the interview with Vernon L. Smith in this volume.
28. Schumpeter actually deplores the influence of what he also calls 'ideology'. He fears that, 'the more honest or naïve our vision is, the more dangerous is it to the eventual emergence of anything for which general validity can be claimed.' In Joseph A. Schumpeter (1954, pp. 42–3).
29. Joseph A. Schumpeter (1954, p. 42).
30. Joseph A. Schumpeter (1954, p. 42).
31. See the interview with Gary S. Becker in this volume.
32. See the interview with James M. Buchanan in this volume.
33. See the interview with Gary S. Becker in this volume.
34. See the interview with Douglass C. North in this volume.
35. Harriet Zuckerman (1977, p. 129).
36. I am indebted to Antoine Martin for drawing my attention to this.
37. 'L'élan vers l'objet est au fond élan vers le médiateur. . . l'hostilité apparente du médiateur, loin d'amoindrir le prestige de ce dernier, ne peut guère que l'accroître.' René Girard (1961, p. 24).
38. Harriet Zuckerman (1977, p. 135).
39. John von Neumann and Oskar Morgenstern (1944).
40. Paul A. Samuelson (1948 and 1947).
41. Joseph A. Schumpeter (1954, p. 4).
42. See Milton Friedman in Randall Parker (2002, p. 50).
43. See Amity Shlaes (2007).
44. Milton Friedman in Randall Parker (2002, pp. 50–51).
45. John Maynard Keynes (1936).
46. Paul Feyerabend (1970).
47. See the interview with Reinhard Selten in this volume.
48. Hendrik P. van Dalen (1997, p. 14).
49. See Thomas S. Kuhn (1962/1970, especially pp. 35–42).
50. See the interview with Robert M. Solow in this volume.
51. Karl R. Popper (1966, pp. 162–3).
52. See Israel Kirzner (1973, especially p. 48), and also (1979, especially pp. 130–31, 152).
53. See Joseph A. Schumpeter (1934).
54. See the interview with George A. Akerlof in this volume.
55. Friedrich August von Hayek (1978b, pp. 50–56).
56. Knut Wicksell (1896).
57. See the interview with Vernon L. Smith in this volume.
58. John R. Hicks (1939).
59. See the interview with Paul A. Samuelson in this volume.
60. See the interview with Reinhard Selten in this volume.
61. Robert M. Solow (1997).
62. E. Roy Weintraub (2007, p. 8).
63. 'By 30 June 1944, the staggering number of 279 649 persons from the Third Reich had found either temporary or permanent refuge in America. This emigration had distinctly intellectual character. . .' Helmut F. Pfanner (1983, p. 14). See Jean Medawar and David Pyke (2000). For figures see also Bruno S. Frey and Werner W. Pommerehne (1988, p. 103).
64. The social sciences division of The New School was founded as 'The University in Exile' in 1933. The New School, located at Greenwich Village, provides university services for adults – and has more than 9000 undergraduate and graduate students nowadays. 'Conceived by New School president Alvin Johnson, it rescued and employed European intellectuals and artists who had been dismissed from teaching

and government positions by the regimes of Hitler and Mussolini. More than 180 scholars and their families found refuge here, including Gestalt psychologist Max Wertheimer and economists Karl Brandt and Gerhard Colm. Nobel Prize winner Franco Modigliani was one of its first students.' (www.newschool.edu). In economic research, the Bernard Schwartz Center for Economic Policy Analysis, the economic policy research arm of the Department of Economics at the New School for Social Research, provides an extremely valuable resource on their website (www.cepa/ newschool.edu). See also Harald Hagemann and Claus-Dieter Krohn (eds) (1999).

65. See the interview with Paul A. Samuelson in this volume.
66. See the interview with Kenneth J. Arrow in this volume.
67. See www.uchicago.edu/about/accolades/nobel/.
68. Bruno S. Frey and Werner W. Pommerehne (1988, p. 108).
69. Paul A. Samuelson in Michael Szenberg (1992, p. 237).
70. See the interview with James M. Buchanan in this volume.
71. See the interview with Robert M. Solow in this volume.
72. See the interview with Edmund S. Phelps in this volume.
73. According to this rule, the central bank should change the nominal interest rate in response to divergences of actual GDP from potential GDP and divergences of actual rates of inflation from a target rate of inflation.
74. See the interview with Gary S. Becker in this volume.
75. See the interview with George A. Akerlof in this volume.
76. See the interview with Kenneth J. Arrow in this volume.
77. Talking about progress in economic science in an opinion piece for *Frankfurter Allgemeine Zeitung*, in 2006, I once quipped in the headline: 'where is up?' This is exactly what the non-directedness of progress is all about. (Karen Ilse Horn, 2006).
78. Friedrich August von Hayek (1968/1978).
79. Joseph A. Schumpeter (1954, p. 4).
80. Joseph A. Schumpeter (1954, p. 6).
81. Thomas S. Kuhn (1962/1970, pp. 35–42).
82. Thomas S. Kuhn (1962/1970, p. 92).
83. Thomas S. Kuhn (1962/1970, pp. 99–100).
84. Ernst Helmstädter (1999).
85. 'It was Smith who provided so broad and authoritative an account of the known economic doctrine that henceforth it was no longer permissible for any subsequent writer on economics to advance his own ideas while ignoring the state of general knowledge.' George J. Stigler (1982/83, p. 59).
86. Bruce Caldwell (2004, p. 373).
87. Friedrich August von Hayek (1975/1978/1989).
88. Friedrich August von Hayek (1952/1979, p. 24). See also Friedrich August von Hayek (1975/78/89, p. 3).
89. Friedrich August von Hayek (1975/1978/1989, p. 3).
90. Friedrich August von Hayek (1952/1979, p. 40).
91. Friedrich August von Hayek (1975/1978/1989, p. 4).
92. As David Colander sarcastically comments, 'while the economic models of the 1990s often contained a hearty dose of mathematics, the mathematics itself was almost never deep'. These are also the exact words of Robert M. Solow, by the way, in his 1997 Daedalus paper. The whole Colander paper is a satire of this Solow paper (David C. Colander, 2000a).
93. Friedrich August von Hayek (1964/1967, p. 24).
94. See the interview with George A. Akerlof in this volume.
95. Terence W. Hutchison (1977, p. 21).
96. Roger Backhouse (1997, p. 136).
97. Bruce Caldwell (2004, p. 372).
98. Friedrich August von Hayek (1952/79, p. 47).
99. Friedrich August von Hayek (1964/1967, p. 26).

100. Bruce Caldwell (2004, pp. 372–3). See Friedrich August von Hayek (1964/67, pp. 34–5).
101. Friedrich August von Hayek (1903, p. 258).
102. Friedrich August von Hayek (1952/1979, p. 73).
103. Friedrich August von Hayek (1964/1967, p. 35).
104. 'The kind of theory which I regard as the true explanation of unemployment is a theory of somewhat limited content because it allows us to make only very general predictions of the *kind* of events which we must expect in a given situation. But the effects on policy of the more ambitious constructions have not been very fortunate and I confess that I prefer true but imperfect knowledge, even if it leaves much indetermined and unpredictable, to a pretence of exact knowledge that is likely to be false. The credit which the apparent conformity with recognized scientific standards can gain for seemingly simple but false theories may, as the present instance shows, have grave consequences. In fact, in the case discussed, the very measures which the dominant "macro-economic" theory has recommended as a remedy for unemployment, namely the increase of aggregate demand, have become a cause of a very extensive misallocation of resources which is likely to make later large-scale unemployment inevitable.' Friedrich August von Hayek (1975/1978/1989, p. 5).
105. 'The unspeakable in pursuit of the inedible.' Quoted after Robert M. Solow (1997, p. 100).
106. Robert M. Solow (1997, p. 100).
107. Donald Moggridge (ed.)(1973, p. 297).
108. Bruce Caldwell (2004, p. 388).
109. See the interview with George A. Akerlof in this volume.
110. Bruce Caldwell (2004, p. 396). See Friedrich August von Hayek (1964/1967, pp. 28–9).
111. Friedrich August von Hayek (1975/1978/1989, pp. 6–7).
112. Friedrich August von Hayek (1975/1978/1989, p. 7). See also Friedrich August von Hayek (1952/1979, p. 95).
113. See the interview with James M. Buchanan in this volume.
114. Bruce Caldwell (2004, p. 400).
115. It may be useful in this context to reconsider Frank Knight's famous differentiation between risk and uncertainty (Frank H. Knight, 1921).
116. Myron Scholes (2008).
117. George J. Stigler has a pertinent description of this market: 'Those economists who seek to engage in research on the new ideas of the science – to refute or confirm or develop or displace them – are in a sense both buyers and sellers of new ideas. They seek to develop new ideas and persuade the science to accept them, but they also are following clues and promises and explorations in the current or preceding ideas of the science. It is very costly to enter this market: it takes a good deal of time and thought to explore a new idea far enough to discover its promise or its lack of promise. The history of economics, and I assume of every science, is strewn with costly errors.' (George J. Stigler, 1982/83, p. 59).
118. David C. Colander (1989).
119. 'Why is the line between mathematical economists and general economic theorists growing fuzzier and vaguer? As a good Darwinian I believe that this is no accident. I suspect it is because a large and growing fraction of what is interesting and valuable in the economic theory of the last twenty years (longer if we go back to Jevons, Marshall, Wicksteed, Walras, Pareto, Edgeworth, Barone, Bickerdike, Wicksell, etc.) has been produced by theorists who do at least some of their theorizing in mathematics. Survival in the literature is a test of fitness, if an imperfect one.' Robert M. Solow (1954, p. 373).
120. William G. Dewald et al. (1986), Richard W. Ault and Robert B. Eklund, Jr. (1987), Herbert G. Grubel and Lawrence A. Boland (1986).
121. George J. Stigler also points out that 'the institutional organization of economic

research is a potential influence upon the receptiveness of a science to new ideas'. (George Stigler, 1982/83, p. 69). See also David C. Colander (1989, pp. 145–6).

122. This, for Hayek, is the central question of all social sciences. Friedrich August von Hayek (1936/1980, pp. 50–51).
123. Friedrich August von Hayek (1945/1948/1980, p. 86).
124. Friedrich August von Hayek (1968/1978/1982, p. 179).
125. Friedrich August von Hayek (1968/1978/1982, p. 180).
126. Michael Polanyi (1962, p. 55).
127. Adam Smith (1759).
128. Vernon L. Smith (1998, p. 3).
129. 'It is not from the benevolence of the butcher, the brewer, or the baker, that we expect our dinner, but from their regard to their own interest. We address ourselves, not to their humanity but to their self-love, and never talk to them of our own necessities but of their advantages.' Adam Smith (1776, pp. 26–7).
130. Adam Smith (1759, p. 166).
131. Max Albert rejects the 'trading' aspect because in is view, there is no 'exchange between producers and customers, but the mutual recognition and checking between producers' (Max Albert, 2004, p. 128). This argument, however, is not very convincing. Albert seems to imply that researchers cooperate and compete in order to cater to a customer on the other market side, perhaps corporations, government or the general public. In my view, this is true only in exceptional cases. Most of the time, academia is a self-referential system. In the market for ideas, most readers/receivers are customers – and these customers happen to be producers as well. This is the reason why another argument of his, namely that 'production decisions are not governed by the evaluation of final consumers', also seems beside the point. (Max Albert, 2006, p. 25).
132. Philip Mirowski argues that 'the act of formal acknowledgement of published work does not look much like a price system' (Philip Mirowski, 2004, p. 60).
133. James M. Buchanan (2001, p. 158).
134. One may object that such an 'intangible price' may not adequately reflect the value of a new idea, since 'buyers' may need time to realize how promising it is. That is true, but this differs in nothing from the market for so-called 'experience goods' and services. In all markets, economic, moral, or academic, entrepreneurial action requires endurance.
135. Adam Smith (1776/1981, p. 687).
136. Viktor Vanberg (2008, p. 9).
137. Viktor Vanberg (2008, p. 18).
138. Viktor Vanberg (2008, p. 19).
139. Viktor Vanberg (2008, p. 22).
140. Harriet Zuckermann (1977, p. 249).
141. Harriet Zuckermann (1977, p. 249).
142. Harriet Zuckerman (1977, p. 254).
143. Hendrik P. van Dalen (1997, p. 16).

Conclusion

'There are many roads that lead to Rome.' This is how this present book started, and this is how it will end – in an act of humility and admiration. The interviews assembled in this book have shown an impressive variety of itineraries. What they all share is an independent mind, intense curiosity, a focus on relevant problems, and helpful networks.

The Nobel Laureates come from very different backgrounds, ranging from a poor life on a farm (James M. Buchanan) in Tennessee and life in a rather well-to-do family traveling all over the world (Douglass C. North). Most of them, but not all, shared an interest in political and economic questions with their families and thus had, as youngsters, some practicing ground at home. Most of them, but again, not all, started out wanting to improve the world, especially under the shocking experience of the Great Depression. Some sort of slipped into economics through their mathematical talent but then, in a second step, also discovered their 'missionary' tendencies. Some of them, but not all, were drawn to the Keynesian branch of macroeconomics. This was a logical, but not exclusive consequence of their mathematical talent given the historical background of their times.

Looking back, one is easily tempted into determinism: how could James M. Buchanan, with his pronounced sense for independence and non-discrimination, with his high degree of sensitivity for questions of dominance and injustice, possibly have chosen a different field? It is almost impossible to imagine him in growth theory, for example. How could Reinhard Selten, with his tremendous logical and mathematical talent, possibly have chosen anything but an extremely abstract, formal branch of economics? Well, as he himself says, many other paths would have been possible. Who knows. *Ex post*, everything seems straightforward, almost inescapable. All the steps in our individual career paths seem to follow logically from one another. And in some important sense, that is indeed the case. Personal character is a fundamental datum of extreme relevance, and it accounts for a lot. But there is also some path dependence in life, and luck. *Ex ante*, nothing is ever so neatly set out. Except for one person, George A. Akerlof, who already knew as a boy that becoming a professor of economics was his future, most Nobel Laureates attribute their career path to a tremendous load of chance as they came to the relevant crossroads. Most of them were exposed to other temptations in their younger years, either because of their broader intellectual curiosity or due to simple material needs, but then luckily for science and for the world, they ended up choosing economics.

In young age, everybody was socialist or at least had left-wing tendencies. Many, however, turned around towards free markets as soon as they took up their studies of economics: it seems difficult to escape the attraction of Adam Smith's 'Invisible Hand'. All of the Nobel Laureates, without exception, were strongly influenced by their teachers at university – those masters were role models in every respect. The colleges and universities, most of them along the Eastern Coast and the Midwest of the US, provided them with the necessary socialization as researchers and with the relevant networks, reaching out to institutions such as the Cowles Commission and the NBER. All of the Nobel Laureates clearly had the gift to ask relevant questions and ultimately to break free from the trodden paths of the economic mainstream, but they aren't all lone wolves. In science, some can bring in their talents in isolation, while others work better in groups. The world of academia, like the world in general, is open to all kinds of characters. Intellectual innovation may have many different sources. Or roads.

Turning from the micro-level, that is from the motivations that make for individual careers, to the macro-level, towards the miraculous process of the generation of excellence and progress in science, one can also be optimistic. Confused, perhaps, but at a higher level – and optimistic. For it seems that, yes, economics is making progress. Slowly, but surely. It is not following an entirely arbitrary path. Its path tends toward a moving target, and it is directed by a vast array of incentives, some of which may be dysfunctional, some of which will be with humankind a long time even though they deserve to get discarded. Theories are sometimes sticky. People get used to them. They are part of a generation's mental maps; it is difficult to imagine the world without them. But Hayek reminds one that 'man has been impelled to scientific inquiry by wonder and by need'.[1] And this, all Nobel Laureates interviewed in the present volume confirm, will go on, probably forever. This is a great source for optimism. I will therefore join Viktor Vanberg in his outlook:

> The principles of selection that prevail in research institutes and universities, the constraints that national rules and regulations define for scientific work, and conventions that come to prevail in professions such as economics may be dysfunctional, but man's ineradicable interest in knowing how the world around him works will be an incessant force that tends to select in favor of more informative theories, and stubborn reality will be an inescapable ultimate selector between conjectures that are compatible with the facts and those that are not. Globally and in the long run the capacity of markets to serve consumer

interests and the capacity of science to advance the growth of knowledge appear to be quite robust.[2]

And yet, Hayek's warning should be heard: 'It is high time, however, that we take our ignorance more seriously.'[3] Rome still needs to be discovered.

NOTES

1. Friedrich August von Hayek (1964/1967, p. 22).
2. Viktor Vanberg (2008, p. 22).
3. Friedrich August von Hayek (1964/1967, p. 39).

Bibliography

GENERAL BIBLIOGRAPHY (PARTS I AND III)

Albert, Max (2004), 'Methodologie und die Verfassung der Wissenschaft – eine institutionalistische Perspektive', in Martin Held, Gisela Kubon-Gilke and Richard Sturn (eds), *Ökonomik des Wissens. Jahrbuch Normative und Institutionelle Grundlagen der Ökonomik*, vol. 3, Marburg: Metropolis, pp. 127–50.

Albert, Max (2006), 'Product quality in scientific competition', Discussion Papers on Strategic Interaction 2006-6, Max Planck Institute of Economics.

Arrow, Kenneth J. (1951), *Social Choice and Individual Values*, New York: Wiley.

Arrow, Kenneth J. (1992), 'I know a hawk from a handsaw', in Michael Szenberg (ed.), *Eminent Economists: Their Life Philosophies*, Cambridge: Cambridge University Press.

Ault, Richard W. and Robert B. Eklund, Jr (1987), 'The problem of unnecessary originality in economics', *Southern Economic Journal*, **53**, 650–61.

Backhouse, Roger (1997), *Truth and Progress in Economic Knowledge*, Cheltenham, UK and Northampton, MA: Edward Elgar.

Banach, Wieslaw (2002), 'Hayek: an idea of self-organization and a critique of the constructivist utopia', *Studies in Logic, Grammar and Rhetoric*, **5**(18), 33–45.

Bernanke, Ben (1995), 'The macroeconomics of the Great Depression: a comparative approach', *Journal of Money, Credit, and Banking*, **27**(1), 1–28.

Blaug, Mark (1998), *Great Economists Since Keynes: An Introduction to the Lives and Works of One Hundred Modern Economists*, 2nd edn, Cheltenham, UK and Northampton, MA: Edward Elgar.

Brittan, Samuel (2003), 'The not so noble Nobel Prize', *The Financial Times*, 19 December.

Buchanan, James M. (1992), 'From the inside looking out', in Michael Szenberg (ed.), *Eminent Economists: Their Life Philosophies*, Cambridge: Cambridge University Press.

Buchanan, James M. (2001), 'The potential for tyranny in politics and science', in *Moral Science and Moral Order*, vol. 17 of *The Collected Works of James M. Buchanan*, Indianapolis: Liberty Fund.

Caldwell, Bruce (2004), *Hayek's Challenge. An Intellectual Biography of F.A. Hayek*, Chicago: University of Chicago Press.

Coase, Ronald (1937), 'The nature of the firm', *Economica*, **4**, 386–405.

Colander, David C. (1989), 'Research on the economics profession', *Journal of Economic Perspectives*, **3**, 137–48.

Colander, David C. (2000a), 'New millennium economics: how did it get this way, and what way is it?', *Journal of Economic Perspectives*, **14**(1), 121–32.

Colander, David C. (ed.) (2000b), *Complexity and the History of Economic Thought*, New York: Routledge.

Cole, Stephen (1979), 'Age and scientific performance', *American Journal of Sociology*, **84**, 985–77.

Cukierman, Alex, Sebastian Edwards and Guido Tabellini (1992), 'Seigniorage and political instability', *American Economic Review*, **82**(3), 537–55.

Dalen, Hendrik P. van (1997), 'The golden age of Nobel economists', Tinbergen Institute, Erasmus University Rotterdam, TI 97–120/1.

Davis, John B. (1994), *Keynes's Philosophical Development*, New York: Cambridge University Press.

De Vorkin, David H. (1990), 'Interviewing physicists and astronomers: methods of oral history', in John Roche (ed.), *Physicists Look Back: Studies in the History of Physics*, Bristol, New York: Adam Hilger, pp. 44–65.

Dewald, William G., Jerry G. Thursby and Richard G. Anderson (1986), 'Replication in empirical economics. The journal of money, credit and banking project', *American Economic Review*, **76**, 587–603.

Eucken, Walter (1950), *The Foundations of Economics. History and Theory in the Analysis of Economic Reality*, London: William Hodge and Company Limited.

Ferguson, Adam (1767), *Essay on the History of Civil Society*, London: T. Cadell.

Feyerabend, Paul (1970), 'Against method. Outline of an anarchistic theory of knowledge', *Minnesota Studies in the Philosophy of Science*, Analyses of Theories and Methods of Physics and Psychology, **4**, pp. 17–130.

Frey, Bruno S. and Werner W. Pommerehne (1988), 'The American domination among eminent Economists', *Scientometrics*, **14**, 97–110.

Fukuyama, Francis (1992), *The End of History and the Last Man*, New York: Free Press.

Girard, René (1961), *Mensonge Romantique et Vérité Romanesque*, Paris: Grasset.

Goldschmidt, Nils (2005a), 'Die Rolle Walter Euckens im Widerstand: Freiheit, Ordnung und Wahrhaftigkeit als Handlungsmaximen', in Nils Goldschmidt (ed.), *Wirtschaft, Politik und Freiheit. Freiburger Wirtschaftswissenschaftler und der Widerstand*, Tübingen: Mohr Siebeck, pp. 289–314.

Goldschmidt, Nils (ed.) (2005b), *Wirtschaft, Politik und Freiheit. Freiburger Wirtschaftswissenschaftler und der Widerstand*, Tübingen: Mohr Siebeck.

Goldschmidt, Nils and Michael Wohlgemuth (eds) (2008), *Grundtexte zur Freiburger Tradition der Ordnungsökonomik*, Tübingen: Mohr Siebeck.

Grele, Ronald J. et al. (1991), *Envelopes of Sound: The Art of Oral History*, New York: Praeger Publishers.

Grubel, Herbert G. and Lawrence A. Boland (1986), 'On the efficient use of mathematics in economics: some theory, facts and results of an opinion survey', *Kyklos*, **39**, 419–42.

Grüske, Karl-Dieter (ed.) (1994), *Die Nobelpreisträger der ökonomischen Wissenschaft, Vol. 3: 1989–1993*, Düsseldorf: Wirtschaft und Finanzen.

Grüske, Karl-Dieter (ed.) (1999), *Die Nobelpreisträger der ökonomischen Wissenschaft, Vol. 4: 1994–1998*, Düsseldorf: Wirtschaft und Finanzen.

Hagemann, Harald (ed.) (1997), *Zur deutschsprachigen wirtschaftswissenschaftlichen Emigration nach 1933*, Marburg: Metropolis.

Hagemann, Harald and Claus-Dieter Krohn (eds) (1999), *Biografisches Handbuch der deutschsprachigen wirtschaftswissenschaftlichen Emigration nach 1933*, Munich: K.G. Saur.

Hansen, W. Lee and Burton Weisbrod (1972), 'Towards a general theory of awards, or do economists need a hall of fame?', *Journal of Political Economy*, **80**, 422–31.

Hayek, Friedrich August von (1936/1980), 'Economics and knowledge', in his *Individualism and Economic Order*, Chicago: University of Chicago Press, pp. 33–56.

Hayek, Friedrich August von (1937/1980), 'Economics and knowledge', *Economica*, **IV**, 33–54.

Hayek, Friedrich August von (1943/1948), 'The facts of the social sciences', in his *Individualism and Economic Order*, Chicago: University of Chicago Press, pp. 57–76.

Hayek, Friedrich August von (1944), *The Road to Serfdom*, London: Routledge.

Hayek, Friedrich August von (1945/1948/1980), 'The use of knowledge in society', *American Economic Review*, **XXXV**(4), September, 519–30, and in his *Individualism and Economic Order*, Chicago: University of Chicago Press, pp. 92–106.

Hayek, Friedrich August von (1949), 'The intellectuals and socialism', *The University of Chicago Law Review*, pp. 417–33.

Hayek, Friedrich August von (1952/79), *The Counter-Revolution of Science. Studies on the Abuse of Reason*, 2nd edn, Indianapolis: Liberty Fund.

Hayek, Friedrich August von (1962/1967), 'Rules, perception, and intelligibility', in his *Studies in Philosophy, Politics, and Economics*, Chicago: University of Chicago Press, pp. 43–65.

Hayek, Friedrich August von (1964/1967), 'The theory of complex phenomena', in his *Studies in Philosophy, Politics, and Economics*, Chicago: University of Chicago Press, pp. 22–42.

Hayek, Friedrich August von (1968/1978a/1982), 'Competition as a discovery procedure', in his *New Studies in Philosophy, Politics, Economics, and the History of Ideas*, Chicago: University of Chicago Press, pp. 249–66.

Hayek, Friedrich August von (1968/1978b), 'The confusion of language in political thought', in his *New Studies in Philosophy, Politics, Economics, and the History of Ideas*, Chicago: University of Chicago Press, pp. 71–97.

Hayek, Friedrich August von (1969a), *Freiburger Studien*, Tübingen: Mohr Siebeck.

Hayek, Friedrich August von (1969b), *John Stuart Mill and Harriet Taylor. Their Friendship and Subsequent Marriage*, London: Routledge & Kegan Paul.

Hayek, Friedrich August von (1975/1978/1989), 'The pretence of knowledge', Nobel Memorial Lecture, in *American Economic Review*, **79**(6) (1989), pp. 3–7. Also in his *New Studies in Philosophy, Politics, Economics, and the History of Ideas*, Chicago: University of Chicago Press, pp. 23–34. Also available at Nobel Foundation, at www.nobel.se.

Hayek, Friedrich August von (1978a), 'The results of human action but not of human design', in his *New Studies in Philosophy, Politics, Economics, and the History of Ideas*, London: Routledge, pp. 96–105.

Hayek, Friedrich August von (1978b), 'Two types of mind', in his *New Studies in Philosophy, Politics, Economics, and the History of Ideas*, Chicago: University of Chicago Press, pp. 50–56.

Hayek, Friedrich August von (1979), *Law, Legislation and Liberty*, vol. 3, Chicago: University of Chicago Press.

Hayek, Friedrich August von (1982), *Law, Legislation and Liberty*, (3 volumes), Chicago: University of Chicago Press.

Hayek, Friedrich August von (1983), 'Nobel Prize winning economist', transcript of interview edited by Armen A. Alchian, UCLA, Charles E. Young Research Library, Dept of Special Collections, Oral History transcript no. 300/224.

Hayek, Friedrich August von (1989), *The Fatal Conceit: The Errors of Socialism*, Chicago: University of Chicago Press.

Held, Martin, Gisela Kubon-Gilke and Richard Sturn (eds) (2004), *Ökonomik des Wissens*, Jahrbuch Normative und Institutionelle Grundfragen der Ökonomik, vol. 3, Marburg: Metropolis.

Helmstädter, Ernst (1994), 'Die Geschichte der Nationalökonomie als Geschichte ihres Fortschritts. Eine Exposition zur Dogmengeschichte', in Otmar Issing (ed.), *Geschichte der Nationalökonomie*, 3rd edn, Munich: Vahlen, pp. 1–13.

Helmstädter, Ernst (1999), 'Zum Fortschritt der Wirtschaftswissenschaften: die Nobelpreise', in Karl-Dieter Grüske (ed.), *Die Nobelpreisträger der ökonomischen Wissenschaft, Vol. 4: 1994–1998*, Düsseldorf: Wirtschaft und Finanzen, pp. 62–76.

Hicks, John R. (1939), *Value and Capital: An Inquiry into Some Fundamental Principles of Economic Theory*, Oxford: Clarendon Press.

Horn, Karen Ilse (1997), *Moral und Wirtschaft*, Tübingen: Mohr Siebeck.

Horn, Karen Ilse (2006), 'Wo ist oben?', *Frankfurter Allgemeine Zeitung*, 10 October.

Hughes, Jeff (1997), 'Whigs, prigs, and politics: problems in the contemporary history of science', in Thomas Söderquist (ed.), *The Historiography of Contemporary Science and Technology*, Amsterdam: Harwood Academic Publishers, pp. 19–37.

Hutchison, Terence W. (1977), *Knowledge and Ignorance in Economics*, Chicago: University of Chicago Press.

Keynes, John Maynard (1936), *The General Theory of Employment, Interest, and Money*, London: Macmillan.

Kirzner, Israel (1973), *Competition and Entrepreneurship*, Chicago: University of Chicago Press.

Kirzner, Israel (1979), *Perception, Opportunity, and Profit*, Chicago: University of Chicago Press.

Klamer, Arjo (1984), *Conversations with Economists*, Totowa, NJ: Rowman & Allanheld.

Knight, Frank H. (1921), *Risk, Uncertainty, and Profit*, Boston, MA: Houghton Mifflin.

Kuhn, Thomas S. (1962/1970), *The Structure of Scientific Revolutions*, 2nd edn, Chicago: University of Chicago Press.

Lindbeck, Assar (1985), 'The prize in economic science in memory of Alfred Nobel', *Journal of Economic Literature*, **23**, 37–56.

Lindbeck, Assar (1999), 'The prize in economic sciences in memory of

Alfred Nobel 1969–2004', Nobel Foundation, available at www.nobel. se.

Lindbeck, Assar (2001), 'The Sveriges Riksbank (Bank of Sweden) Prize in economic sciences in memory of Alfred Nobel 1969–2000', in Agneta W. Levinovitz and Nils Ringertz (eds), *The Nobel Prize. The First 100 Years*, London and Singapore: Imperial College Press and World Scientific Publishing, pp. 197–217.

Medawar, Jean and David Pyke (2000), *Hitler's Gift. The True Story of the Scientists Expelled by the Nazi Regime*, London: Richard Cohen Books.

Menger, Carl (1871/1981), *Principles of Economics*, New York: New York University Press.

Merton, Robert K. (1968), 'The Matthew effect in science', *Science*, **159**, 56–63.

Merton, Robert K. (1973), *The Sociology of Science: Theoretical and Empirical Investigations*, Chicago: University of Chicago Press.

Mill, John Stuart (1859/1974), *On Liberty*, London: Penguin.

Mirowski, Philip (2004), *The Effortless Economy of Science*, Durham, NC: Duke University Press.

Moggridge, Donald (ed.) (1973), *The General Theory and After. Defense and Development. The Collected Works of John Maynard Keynes*, London: Macmillan.

Munzinger-Archiv/Internationales Biographisches Archiv, www.munzinger. de.

Neumann, John von and Oskar Morgenstern (1944), *The Theory of Games and Economic Behavior*, Princeton: Princeton University Press.

New School, website http://cepa.newschool.edu.

Nobel, Peter (2001), 'Alfred Bernhard Nobel and the Peace Prize', *International Review of the Red Cross*, **83**(842), 259–73.

Nobel Foundation, official website, www.nobel.se.

Parker, Randall E. (2002), *Reflections on the Great Depression*, Cheltenham, UK and Northampton, MA: Edward Elgar.

Perlman, Mark and Charles R. McCann, Jr (1998), *The Pillars of Economic Understanding: Ideas and Traditions*, Ann Arbor: University of Michigan Press.

Pfanner, Helmut F. (1983), *Exile in New York: German and Austrian Writers after 1933*, Detroit: Wayne State University Press.

Polanyi, Michael (1962), 'The republic of science', *Minerva*, **1**, 54–73.

Popper, Karl R. (1966), *The Open Society and Its Enemies*, vol. 1, London and New York: Routledge.

Recktenwald, Horst C. (ed.) (1989), *Die Nobelpreisträger der ökonomischen*

Wissenschaften, 1969–1988: Kritisches zum Werden neuer Tradition, vols 1 and 2, Düsseldorf: Wirtschaft und Finanzen.

Roux, Dominique (2002), *Nobel en Economie*, 2nd edn, Economica.

Samuelson, Paul A. (1947), *Foundations of Economic Analysis*, Cambridge, MA: Harvard University Press.

Samuelson, Paul A. (1948), *Economics*, New York: McGraw-Hill.

Samuelson, Paul A. (1992), 'My life philosophy', in Michael Szenberg (ed.), *Eminent Economists: Their Life Philosophies*, Cambridge: Cambridge University Press.

Samuelson, Paul A. (2006), 'The first fifteen Nobel Laureates in economics, and fifteen more Might-Have-Beens', mimeo.

Samuelson, Paul A. and William A. Barnett (eds) (2007), *Inside the Economist's Mind. Conversations with Eminent Economists*, Malden, MA: Blackwell Publishing.

Scholes, Myron (2008), 'The impact of information technology on freedom and communication', paper prepared for the 2008 Mont Pèlerin Society general meeting in Tokyo, Japan.

Schumpeter, Joseph A. (1934), *The Theory of Economic Development: An Inquiry into Profits, Capital, Credit, Interest and the Business Cycle*, Cambridge, MA: Harvard University Press.

Schumpeter, Joseph A. (1954), *The History of Economic Analysis*, New York: Oxford University Press.

Shlaes, Amity (2007), *The Forgotten Man. A New History of the Great Depression*, New York: HarperCollins.

Smith, Adam (1759/1982), *The Theory of Moral Sentiments*, Indianapolis: Liberty Fund.

Smith, Adam (1776/1981), *Inquiry into the Nature and Causes of the Wealth of Nations*, Indianapolis: Liberty Fund.

Smith, Vernon L. (1998), 'The two faces of Adam Smith', *Southern Economic Journal*, **65**, 1–19.

Solow, Robert M. (1954), 'The survival of mathematical economics', *Review of Economics and Statistics*, **36**(4).

Solow, Robert M. (1997), 'How did economics get that way and what way did it get?', *Daedalus*, **134**(4), 87–100.

Stein, Gertrude (1937), *Everybody's Autobiography*, Cambridge, MA: Exact Change.

Stigler, George J. (1970), 'Review of Robbins's "The Evolution of Economic Theory"', *Economica*, New Series, **37**(148), 425–6.

Stigler, Stephen M. (1980), 'Stigler's law of eponymy', *Transactions of the New York Academy of Sciences*, **39**, 147–58.

Stigler, George J. (1982), *The Economist as Preacher and Other Essays*, Chicago: University of Chicago Press.

Stigler, George J. (1982/83), 'The process and progress of economics', Nobel Memorial Lecture, Nobel Foundation, available at www.nobel. se and in *Journal of Political Economy*, **91**(4), 529–45.

Streissler, Erich, Gottfried Haberler and Friedrich A. Lutz (1969), *Roads to Freedom: Essays in Honour of Friedrich A. von Hayek*, London: Routledge.

Szenberg, Michael (1992), *Eminent Economists: Their Life Philosophies*, Cambridge: Cambridge University Press.

Thielicke, Helmut et al. (eds) (1979), *In der Stunde Null. Die Denkschrift des Freiburger Bonhoeffer-Kreises. Politische Gemeinschaftsordnung. Ein Versuch zur Selbstbesinnung des Christlichen Gewissens in den Politischen Nöten unserer Zeit*, Tübingen: Mohr Siebeck.

Vanberg, Viktor (2008), 'The "science-as-market" analogy: a constitutional economics perspective', paper prepared for the Special Session 'Evolution I' at the Annual Meeting of the European Public Choice Society, Jena, March.

Vane, Howard R. and Chris Mulhearn (2005), *The Nobel Memorial Laureates in Economics. An Introduction to their Careers and Main Published Works*, Cheltenham, UK and Northampton, MA: Edward Elgar.

Wahid, Abu N.M. (2002), *Frontiers of Economics. Nobel Laureates of the Twentieth Century*, Westport, CT: Greenwood Press.

Weintraub, E. Roy (2005), 'Autobiographical memory and the historiography of economics', *Journal of the History of Economic Thought*, **27**(2), 1–11.

Weintraub, E. Roy (2007), 'Economists talking with economists: an historian's perspective', in Paul A. Samuelson and W.A. Barnett (eds), *Inside the Economist's Mind*, Malden, MA: Blackwell Publishing, pp. 1–10.

Wicksell, Knut (1896), *Finanztheoretische Untersuchungen nebst Darstellung und Kritik des Steuerwesens Schwedens*, Jena: Fischer.

Zuckerman, Harriet (1977), *Scientific Elite: Nobel Laureates in the United States*, New York: Free Press.

INTERVIEW BIBLIOGRAPHY

Paul A. Samuelson

Cassel, Gustav (1923), *Theory of Social Economy*, London: Fisher Unwin.

Dorfman, Robert, Paul A. Samuelson and Robert M. Solow (1958), *Linear Programming and Economic Analysis*, New York: McGraw Hill.

Hayek, Friedrich August von (1944), *The Road to Serfdom*, London: Routledge.

Keynes, John Maynard (1936), *The General Theory of Employment, Interest, and Money*, London: Macmillan.

Lindbeck, Assar (1970), 'Paul Anthony Samuelson's Contributions to Economics', *Journal of Economic Perspectives*, **72**, 342–54.

Lindbeck, Assar (ed.) (1992), *Nobel Lectures, Economics 1969–1980*, Singapore: World Scientific Publishing.

Malthus, Thomas (1826), *An Essay on the Principle of Population: A View of its Past and Present Effects on Human Happiness*, London: John Murray.

Parker, Randall E. (2002), *Reflections on the Great Depression*, Cheltenham, UK and Northampton, MA: Edward Elgar.

Samuelson, Paul A. (1938), 'A note on the pure theory of consumer behavior', *Economica*, **5**, 61–71.

Samuelson, Paul A. (1939a), 'Interactions between the multiplier analysis and the principle of acceleration', *Review of Economic Statistics*, **21**, 75–8.

Samuelson, Paul A. (1939b), 'The gains from international trade', *Canadian Journal of Economics and Political Sciences*, **5**, 195–205.

Samuelson, Paul A. (1939c), 'A synthesis of the principle of acceleration and the multiplier', *Journal of Political Economy*, **47**, 786–97.

Samuelson, Paul A. (1947), *Foundations of Economic Analysis*, Cambridge, MA: Harvard University Press.

Samuelson, Paul A. (1948a), *Economics*, New York: McGraw Hill.

Samuelson, Paul A. (1948b), 'International trade and the equalisation of factor prices', *Economic Journal*, **58**, 163–84.

Samuelson, Paul A. (1948c), 'Consumer theory in terms of revealed preferences', *Economica*, **15**, 243–53.

Samuelson, Paul A. (1954), 'The pure theory of public expenditures', *Review of Economics and Statistics*, **36**, 350–56.

Samuelson, Paul A. (1958), 'An exact consumption-loan model of interest with or without the social contrivance of money', *Journal of Political Economy*, **66**, 467–82.

Samuelson, Paul A. (1966), *The Collected Scientific Papers of Paul A. Samuelson*, vols. 1 and 2, (ed. Joseph E. Stiglitz), Cambridge, MA: MIT Press.

Samuelson, Paul A. (1970/1972), 'Maximum principles in analytical economics', Nobel Memorial Lecture, Nobel Foundation, available at www.nobel.se and in *American Economic Review*, **62**(3), 249–62.

Samuelson, Paul A. (1970), 'Biography', in Assar Lindbeck (ed.) (1992), *Nobel Lectures, Economics 1969–1980*, Singapore: World Scientific Publishing, available at www.nobel.se.

Samuelson, Paul A. (1972), *The Collected Scientific Papers of Paul A. Samuelson*, vol. 3 (ed. Robert C. Merton), Cambridge, MA: MIT Press.

Samuelson, Paul A. (1977), *The Collected Scientific Papers of Paul A. Samuelson*, vol. 4 (eds Hiroaki Nagatani and Kate Crowley), Cambridge, MA: MIT Press.

Samuelson, Paul A. (1986), *The Collected Scientific Papers of Paul A. Samuelson*, vol. 5 (ed. Kate Crowley), Cambridge, MA: MIT Press.

Samuelson, Paul A. (2002), 'Is there life after Nobel coronation?', available at www.nobel.se.

Samuelson, Paul A. (2003), 'How I became an economist', available at www.nobel.se.

Samuelson, Paul A. (2004), 'Where Ricardo and Mill rebut and confirm arguments of mainstream economists supporting globalisation', *Journal of Economic Perspectives*, **18**(3), 135–46.

Samuelson, Paul A. and Robert M. Solow (1960), 'Analytical aspects of anti-inflation policy', *American Economic Review*, **50**, 177–94.

Say, Jean-Baptiste (1803), *A Treatise on Political Economy, or the Production, Distribution and Consumption of Wealth*, Philadelphia: Lippincott, Grambo & Co.

Skousen, Mark (1997), 'The perseverance of Paul Samuelson's "Economics"', *Journal of Economic Perspectives*, **11**, 137–52.

Smith, Adam (1776/1981), *Inquiry into the Nature and Causes of the Wealth of Nations*, Indianapolis: Liberty Fund.

Solow, Robert M. and Paul A. Samuelson (1953), 'Balanced growth under constant returns to scale', *Econometrica*, **21**, 412–24.

Stolper, Wolfgang F. and Paul A. Samuelson (1941), 'Protection and real wages', *Review of Economic Studies*, **9**, 58–73.

Taylor, John B. (1993), 'Discretion versus policy rules in practice', *Carnegie-Rochester Conference Series on Public Policy*, **39**, 195–214.

Kenneth J. Arrow

Arrow, Kenneth J. (1949), 'On the use of winds in flight planning', *Journal of Meteorology*, **6**, 150–59.

Arrow, Kenneth J. (1950), 'A difficulty in the concept of social welfare', *Journal of Political Economy*, **58**, 328–46.

Arrow, Kenneth J. (1951a), *Social Choice and Individual Values*, New York: Wiley.

Arrow, Kenneth J. (1951b), 'An extension of the basic theorems of classical welfare economics', in J. Neymann (ed.), *Proceedings of the Second Berkeley Symposium of Mathematical Statistics and Probability*, Berkeley: University of California Press, pp. 507–32.

Arrow, Kenneth J. (1953), 'Le rôle des valeurs boursières pour la répartition la meilleure des risques', *Proceedings of the colloque sur les fondements et applications de la théorie du risque en économétrie*, Paris: Centre National de la Recherche Scientifique, pp. 41–8.

Arrow, Kenneth J. (1962), 'The economic implications of learning by doing', *Review of Economic Studies*, **29**, 155–73.

Arrow, Kenneth J. (1963), 'Uncertainty and the welfare economics of medical care', *American Economic Review*, **53**, 941–73.

Arrow, Kenneth J. (1964), 'The role of securities in the optimal allocation of risk bearing', *Review of Economic Studies*, **31**, 91–6.

Arrow, Kenneth J. (1971), *Essays in the Theory of Optimal Risk Bearing*, Amsterdam: North Holland.

Arrow, Kenneth J. (1972/74), 'General economic equilibrium: purpose, analytical techniques, collective choice', Nobel Memorial Lecture. Nobel Foundation, available at www.nobel.se, and in *American Economic Review*, **64**, 253–72.

Arrow, Kenneth J. (1983), *Collected Papers of Kenneth J. Arrow, Vol. 1, Social Choice and Justice; Vol. 2, General Equilibrium*, Cambridge, MA: Harvard University Press.

Arrow, Kenneth J. (1984), *Collected Papers of Kenneth J. Arrow, Vol. 3, Individual Choice under Certainty and Uncertainty; Vol. 4, The Economics of Information*, Cambridge, MA: Harvard University Press.

Arrow, Kenneth J. (1985), *Collected Papers of Kenneth J. Arrow, Vol. 5, Production and Capital; Vol. 6, Applied Economics*, Cambridge, MA: Harvard University Press.

Arrow, Kenneth J. and Gérard Debreu (1954), 'Existence of equilibrium for a competitive economy', *Econometrica*, **20**, 265–90.

Arrow, Kenneth J. and Frank Hahn (1971), *General Competitive Analysis*, San Francisco: Holden Day.

Arrow, Kenneth J. and Leonid Hurwicz (1977), *Studies in Resource Allocation Processes*, New York: Cambridge University Press.

Arrow, Kenneth J., Theodore Harris and Jacob Marschak (1951), 'Optimal inventory policy', *Econometrica*, **19**, 250–72.

Arrow, Kenneth J., Samuel Karlin and Herbert E. Scarf (1958), *Studies in the Mathematical Theory of Inventory and Production*, Palo Alto: Stanford University Press.

Arrow, Kenneth J., Samuel Karlin and Patrick Suppes (eds) (1960), *Mathematical Methods in the Social Sciences*, Palo Alto: Stanford University Press.

Arrow, Kenneth J., Hollis B. Chenery, Bagicha S. Minhas and Robert M. Solow (1961), 'Capital–labor substitution and economic efficiency', *Review of Economics and Statistics*, **43**, 225–50.

Bergson, Abram (1938), 'A reformulation of certain aspects of welfare economics', *Quarterly Journal of Economics*, **52**, 310–34.

Black, Duncan (1948), 'On the rationale of group decision-making', *Journal of Political Economy*, **56**, 23–34.

Brennan, Geoffrey and James M. Buchanan (1984), 'Voter choice and the evaluation of political alternatives', *American Behavioral Scientist*, **28**, 185–201.

Brennan, Geoffrey and James M. Buchanan (1985/2000), *The Reason of Rules: Constitutional Political Economy, The Collective Works of James M. Buchanan*, Indianapolis: Liberty Fund, Vol. 10.

Buchanan, James M. (1954), 'Social choice, democracy, and free markets', *Journal of Political Economy*, **62**, 114–23.

Burns, Arthur F. (1946), 'On economic research and the Keynesian thinking of our times', 26th Annual Report, New York: National Bureau of Economic Research, p. 12.

Burns, Arthur F. and Wesley C. Mitchell (1946), *Measuring Business Cycles*, New York: NBER.

Condorcet, Marquis de (1785), *Essay on the Application of Analysis to the Probability of Majority Decisions*, Paris: Imprimerie Royale.

Feiwel, George R. (ed.) (1987a), *Arrow and the Foundations of the Theory of Economic Policy*, Basingstoke: Macmillan.

Feiwel, George R. (ed.) (1987b), *Arrow and the Ascent of Modern Economic Theory*, Basingstoke: Macmillan.

Hayek, Friedrich August von (1937), 'Economics and knowledge', *Economica*, **4**, 33–54.

Hayek, Friedrich August von (1945), 'The use of knowledge in society', *American Economic Review*, **35**, 519–30.

Hayek, Friedrich August von (1960), *The Constitution of Liberty*, Chicago: University of Chicago Press.

Hicks, John R. (1939), *Value and Capital: An Inquiry into Some Fundamental Principles of Economic Theory*, Oxford: Clarendon Press.

Hotelling, Harold (1929), 'Stability in competition', *Economic Journal*, **39**(153), 41–57.

Nansen, E.J. (1883), 'Methods of election', in *Transactions and Proceedings of the Royal Society of Victoria*, **XIX**, 197–240.

Shell, Karl and David Cass (1983), 'Do sunspots matter?', *Journal of Political Economy*, **91**(2), 193–227.

Weizsäcker, Carl Christian von (1972), 'Kenneth Arrow's contributions to economics', *Swedish Journal of Economics*, **74**(4), 488–502. Reprinted in Henry W. Spiegel and Warren J. Samuels (eds) (1984), *Contemporary Economists in Perspective*, vol. 1, Greenwich, CT: JAI Press.

Wohlgemuth, Michael (2002), 'Democracy and opinion falsification:

towards a new Austrian political economy', *Constitutional Political Economy*, **13**, 223–46.

James M. Buchanan

Aaron, Henry J. and Michael J. Boskin (1980), *The Economics of Taxation. Essays in Honor of Joseph Peckman*, Washington, DC: Brookings Institution Press.

Allen, Clark L., James M. Buchanan and Marshall R. Colberg (1954), *Prices, Income, and Public Policy: The ABCs of Economics*, New York: McGraw-Hill.

Arrow, Kenneth J. (1951), *Social Choice and Individual Values*, New York: Wiley.

Atkinson, Anthony B. (1987), 'James M. Buchanan's contributions to economics', *Scandinavian Journal of Economics*, **89**(1), 5–15.

Brennan, Geoffrey and James M. Buchanan (1980), *The Power to Tax: Analytical Foundations of a Fiscal Constitution*, New York: Cambridge University Press.

Brennan, Geoffrey and James M. Buchanan (1985), *The Reason of Rules: Constitutional Political Economy*, New York: Cambridge University Press.

Buchanan, James M. (1949), 'The pure theory of government finance: a suggested approach', *Journal of Political Economy*, **57**, 496–505.

Buchanan, James M. (1952), 'The pricing of highway services', *National Tax Journal*, **V**, 97–106.

Buchanan, James M. (1954a), 'Social choice, democracy, and free markets', *Journal of Political Economy*, **62**, 114–23.

Buchanan, James M. (1954b), 'Individual choice in voting and the market', *Journal of Political Economy*, **62**, 334–43.

Buchanan, James M. (1958), *Public Principles of Public Debt: A Defence and Restatement*, Homewood, IL: Irwin.

Buchanan, James M. (1959), 'Positive economics, welfare economics, and political economy', *Journal of Law and Economics*, **2**, 124–38.

Buchanan, James M. (1960), *Fiscal Theory and Political Economy: Selected Essays*, Chapel Hill: University of North Carolina Press.

Buchanan, James M. (1967), *Public Finance in Democratic Process: Financial Institutions and Individual Choice*, Chapel Hill: University of North Carolina Press.

Buchanan, James M. (1968), *The Demand and Supply of Public Goods*, Chicago: Rand McNally.

Buchanan, James M. (1969a), 'Is economics a science of choice?', in Erich Streissler (ed.), *Roads to Freedom – Essays in Honor of F.A. Hayek*, London: Routledge & Kegan Paul, pp. 47–64.

Buchanan, James M. (1969b), *Cost and Choice: An Inquiry in Economic Theory*, Chicago: Markham Publishing.

Buchanan, James M. (1970), *The Public Finances: An Introductory Textbook*, 3rd edn, Homewood, IL: Irwin.

Buchanan, James M. (1972), 'Rawls on justice as fairness', *Public Choice*, **13**, 123–8.

Buchanan, James M. (1975), *The Limits of Liberty: Between Anarchy and Leviathan*, Chicago: University of Chicago Press.

Buchanan, James M. (1976), 'The justice of natural liberty', *Journal of Legal Studies*, **5**, 1–16.

Buchanan, James M. (1978), *Freedom in Constitutional Contract: Perspective of a Political Economist*, College station: Texas A&M University Press.

Buchanan, James M. (1986/92), 'The constitution of economic policy', Nobel Memorial Lecture, in Karl-Göran Mäler (ed.), *Nobel Lectures, Economics 1981–1990*, Singapore: World Scientific Publishing, available at www.nobel.se and in *American Economic Review*, **77**(3), 243–50.

Buchanan, James M. (1986), *Liberty, Market, and State*, Brighton: Wheatsheaf.

Buchanan, James M. (1990), 'Europe's constitutional opportunity', in his *Europe's Constitutional Future*, London: The Institute of Economic Affairs, pp. 1–20.

Buchanan, James M. (1992a), *Better than Plowing, and other Personal Essays*, Chicago: University of Chicago Press.

Buchanan, James M. (1992b), 'From the inside looking out', in Michael Szenberg (ed.), *Eminent Economists*, Cambridge: Cambridge University Press, pp. 99–106.

Buchanan, James M. (2001), 'Notes on Nobelity', available at www.nobel.se.

Buchanan, James M. (2002), *The Collected Works of James M. Buchanan*, 20 volumes, Indianapolis: Liberty Fund.

Buchanan, James M. (2008), 'Let us understand Adam Smith', *Journal of the History of Economic Thought*, **30**(1).

Buchanan, James M. and Geoffrey Brennan (1980), 'Tax reform without tears: why must the rich be made to suffer?', in Henry J. Aaron and Michael J. Boskin (eds), *The Economics of Taxation*, Washington, DC: Brookings Institution Press, pp. 35–54.

Buchanan, James M. and Geoffrey Brennan (1985), *The Reason of Rules: Constitutional Political Economy*, Cambridge: Cambridge University Press.

Buchanan, James M. and Roger D. Congleton (1998), *Politics by Principle, Not Interest*, Cambridge: Cambridge University Press.

Buchanan, James M. and Gordon Tullock (1962), *The Calculus of Consent: Logical Foundations of Constitutional Democracy*, Ann Arbor: University of Michigan Press.

Buchanan, James M. and Richard E. Wagner (1977), *Democracy in Deficit: The Political Legacy of Lord Keynes*, New York: Academic Press.

Buchanan, James M. and Yong Yoon (2002), 'Globalization as framed by the two logics of trade', *The Independent Review*, **6**(3), 399–405.

Downs, Anthony (1957), *An Economic Theory of Democracy*, New York: Harper and Brothers.

Hansen, Alvin H. (1951), 'The Pigouvian effect', *Journal of Political Economy*, **59**, 535–6.

Hayek, Friedrich August von (1944), *The Road to Serfdom*, London: Routledge.

Hayek, Friedrich August von (1952), *The Counter-Revolution of Science. Studies on the Abuse of Reason*, 2nd edn, Indianapolis: Liberty Press.

Hayek, Friedrich August von (1976), *Law, Legislation and Liberty, Vol. 2: The Mirage of Social Justice*, London: Routledge & Kegan Paul.

Hayek, Friedrich August von (1978), *New Studies in Philosophy, Politics, Economics, and the History of Ideas*, Chicago: University of Chicago Press.

Hayek, Friedrich August von (1979), *Law, Legislation, and Liberty, Vol. 3: The Political Order of a Free People*, Chicago: University of Chicago Press.

Hobbes, Thomas (1651), *Leviathan, or The Matter, Forme and Power of a Common Wealth Ecclesiasticall and Civil*, modern reprint, London: Penguin Books.

Mises, Ludwig von (1949), *Human Action*, New Haven, CT: Yale University Press.

Patinkin, Don (1948), 'Price flexibility and full employment', *American Economic Review*, **38**, 543–64.

Polanyi, Michael (1951), *The Logic of Liberty*, Chicago: University of Chicago Press.

Rawls, John (1971), *A Theory of Justice*, Cambridge, MA: Harvard University Press.

Romer, Thomas (1988), 'On James Buchanan's contributions to public economics', *Journal of Economic Perspectives*, **2**, 165–79.

Samuelson, Paul A. (1956), 'Social indifference curves', *Quarterly Journal of Economics*, **70**, 1–22.

Samuelson, Paul A. (1977), 'Reaffirming the existence of "reasonable" Bergson–Samuelson social welfare functions', *Economica*, New Series, **44**(173), 81–8.

Schumpeter, Joseph A. (1942), *Capitalism, Socialism, and Democracy*, New York: Harper and Brothers.

Smith, Adam (1759/1982), *The Theory of Moral Sentiments*, Indianapolis: Liberty Fund.

Smith, Adam (1776/1981), *Inquiry into the Nature and Causes of the Wealth of Nations*, Indianapolis: Liberty Fund.

Tullock, Gordon (1959), 'Some problems of majority voting', *Journal of Political Economy*, **67**, 571–9.

Viti de Marco, Antonio de (1936), *First Principles of Public Finances*, Jonathan Cape London/New York: Harcourt Brace & Co.

Whately, Richard (1831), *Introductory Lectures on Political Economy*, London: B. Fellowes.

Wicksell, Knut (1896), *Finanztheoretische Untersuchungen nebst Darstellung und Kritik des Steuerwesens Schwedens*, Jena: Fischer.

Wicksell, Knut (1958), 'A new principle of just taxation', in Richard A. Musgrave and Alan T. Peacock (eds), *Classics in the Theory of Public Finance*, pp. 72–118, translated by James M. Buchanan and Elizabeth Henderson, London: Macmillan.

Robert M. Solow

Blinder, Alan S. (1989), 'In honor of Robert M. Solow: Nobel Laureate in 1987', *Journal of Economic Perspectives*, **3**, 99–105.

Blinder, Alan S. and Robert M. Solow (1973), 'Does fiscal policy matter?', *Journal of Public Economics*, **2**, 319–37.

Domar, Evsey (1946), 'Capital expansion, rate of growth and employment', *Econometrica*, **14**, 137–47.

Dorfman, Robert, Paul A. Samuelson and Robert M. Solow (1958), *Linear Programming and Economic Analysis*, New York: McGraw Hill.

Harrod, Roy (1939), 'Essay in dynamic theory', *Economic Journal*, **49**, 14–33.

Harrod, Roy (1948), *Towards a Dynamic Economics: Some Recent Developments of Economic Theory and Their Application to Policy*, London: Macmillan.

Hayek, Friedrich August von (1978), 'Two types of mind', in his *New Studies in Philosophy, Politics, Economics, and the History of Ideas*, Chicago: University of Chicago Press, pp. 50–56.

Hicks, John R. (1939), *Value and Capital: An Inquiry into Some Fundamental Principles of Economic Theory*, Oxford: Clarendon Press.

Kuhn, Thomas S. (1962/1970), *The Structure of Scientific Revolutions*, 2nd edn, Chicago: University of Chicago Press.

Leontief, Wassily (1941), *The Structure of American Economy, 1919–1929*, Cambridge, MA: Harvard University Press.

Lucas, Robert Jr (1988), 'On the mechanics of economic development', *Journal of Monetary Economics*, **22**, 3–42.

Matthews, R.C.O. (1988), 'The work of Robert M. Solow', *Scandinavian Journal of Economics*, **90**(1), 13–16.

Prescott, Edward C. (1988), 'Robert M. Solow's neoclassical growth model', *Scandinavian Journal of Economics*, **90**(1), 7–12.

Romer, Paul M. (1986), 'Increasing returns and long-run growth', *Journal of Political Economy*, **94**, 1002–37.

Romer, Paul M. (1990), 'Endogenous technological change', *Journal of Political Economy*, **98**, 71–102.

Samuelson, Paul A. (1989), 'Robert Solow: an affectionate portrait', *Journal of Economic Perspectives*, **3**, 91–7.

Samuelson, Paul A. and Robert M. Solow (1960), 'Analytical aspects of anti-inflation policy', *American Economic Review*, **50**, 177–94.

Solow, Robert M. (1954), 'The survival of mathematical economics', *Review of Economics and Statistics*, **36**(4), 372–4.

Solow, Robert M. (1956), 'A contribution to the theory of economic growth', *Quarterly Journal of Economics*, **70**, 65–94.

Solow, Robert M. (1957), 'Technical change and the aggregate production function', *Review of Economics and Statistics*, **39**, 312–20.

Solow, Robert M. (1958), 'A skeptical note on the constancy of relative shares', *American Economic Review*, **48**, 618–31.

Solow, Robert M. (1960), 'Investment and technical progress', in Kenneth J. Arrow, Samuel Karlin and Patrick Suppes (eds), *Mathematical Methods in the Social Sciences*, Stanford: Stanford University Press, pp. 89–104.

Solow, Robert M. (1962), 'Substitution and fixed proportions in the theory of capital', *Review of Economics and Statistics*, **29**, 207–18.

Solow, Robert M. (1963), *Capital Theory and the Rate of Return*, Amsterdam: North-Holland.

Solow, Robert M. (1972), 'Congestion, density, and the use of land in transportation', *Swedish Journal of Economics*, **74**, 161–73.

Solow, Robert M. (1974), 'The economics of resources or the resources of economics', *American Economic Review*, **64**, 1–14.

Solow, Robert M. (1979), 'Another possible source of wage stickiness', *Journal of Macroeconomics*, **1**, 79–82.

Solow, Robert M. (1980), 'On theories of unemployment', *American Economic Review*, **70**, 1–11.

Solow, Robert M. (1985), 'Insiders and outsiders in wage determination', *Scandinavian Journal of Economics*, **87**(2), 411–28.

Solow, Robert M. (1987/1992/2005), 'Nobel autobiography', in Karl-Göran Mäler (ed.), *Nobel Lectures, Economics 1981–1990*, Singapore: World Scientific Publishing, available at www.nobel.se.

Solow, Robert M. (1987/1988), 'Growth theory and after', Nobel Memorial Lecture, Nobel Foundation, available at www.nobel.se and in *American Economic Review*, **78**, 307–17.

Solow, Robert M. (1990), *The Labour Market as a Social Institution*, Oxford: Basil Blackwell.

Solow, Robert M. (1997), 'How did economics get that way and what way did it get?', *Daedalus*, **134**(4), 87–100.

Solow, Robert M. (2000), *Growth Theory: An Exposition*, 2nd edn, Oxford: Oxford University Press.

Solow, Robert M. (2002), Interview in *The Region*, available at http://minneapolisfed.org/pubs/region/02–09/solow.cfm.

Solow, Robert M. and Joseph E. Stiglitz (1968), 'Output, employment, and wages in the short run', *Quarterly Journal of Economics*, **82**, 537–60.

Swan, Trevor (1956), 'Economic growth. Seminar and notes on growth', *Economic Record*, **78**, 381–7.

Thünen, Johann Heinrich von (1826), *Der isolirte Staat in Beziehung auf Landwirthschaft und National-Oekonomie*, Hamburg: Perthes.

Gary S. Becker

Becker, Gary S. (1952), 'A note on multi-country trade', *American Economic Review*, **42**, 558–68.

Becker, Gary S. (1957), *The Economics of Discrimination*, Chicago: University of Chicago Press.

Becker, Gary S. (1958), 'Competition and democracy', *Journal of Law and Economics*, **1**, 105–9.

Becker, Gary S. (ed.) (1960a), *Demographic and Economic Change in Developed Countries*, Princeton: Princeton University Press.

Becker, Gary S. (1960b), 'An economic analysis of fertility', in Gary S. Becker (ed.), *Demographic and Economic Change in Developed Countries*, Princeton: Princeton University Press, pp. 209–31.

Becker, Gary S. (1962), 'Investment in human capital: a theoretical analysis', *Journal of Political Economy*, **70**, 9–49.

Becker, Gary S. (1964), *Human Capital. A Theoretical and Empirical Analysis with Special Reference to Education*, New York: Columbia University Press.

Becker, Gary S. (1965), 'A theory of the allocation of time', *Economic Journal*, **75**(299), 493–517.

Becker, Gary S. (1968), 'Crime and punishment: an economic approach', *Journal of Political Economy*, **76**, 169–217.

Becker, Gary S. and H. Gregg Lewis (1973), 'On the interaction between the quantity and quality of children', *Journal of Political Economy*, **81**(2), 279–88.

Becker, Gary S. (1973), 'A theory of marriage: part I', *Journal of Political Economy*, **81**(4), 813–46.

Becker, Gary S. (1974), 'A theory of marriage: part II', *Journal of Political Economy*, **82**(2), 11–26.

Becker, Gary S. (1976), *The Economic Approach to Family Behaviour*, Chicago: University of Chicago Press.

Becker, Gary S. (1981), *A Treatise on the Family*, Chicago: University of Chicago Press.

Becker, Gary S. (1983), 'A theory of competition among pressure groups for political influence', *Quarterly Journal of Economics*, **98**, 371–400.

Becker, Gary S. (1985), 'Public policies, pressure groups, and dead weight costs', *Journal of Public Economics*, **28**, 329–47.

Becker, Gary S. (1992), 'Autobiography', in Tore Frängsmyr (ed.), *Les Prix Nobel, The Nobel Prizes 1993*, Stockholm: Nobel Foundation, available at www.nobel.se.

Becker, Gary S. and William Baumol (1952), 'The classical monetary theory: the outcome of the discussion', *Economica*, **19**, 355–76.

Becker, Gary S. and Guity Nashat Becker (1996), *The Economics of Life*, New York: McGraw-Hill.

Becker, Gary S. and William M. Landes (eds) (1974), *Essays in the Economics of Crime and Punishment*, New York: Columbia University Press.

Becker, Gary S. and Kevin M. Murphy (1986), 'A theory of rational addiction', *Journal of Political Economy*, **96**, 675–700.

Becker, Gary S. and George Stigler (1974), 'Law enforcement, malfeasance, and compensation of enforcers', *Journal of Legal Studies*, **3**, 1–18.

Becker, Gary S. (1992/1993), 'The economic way of looking at behaviour', Nobel Memorial Lecture, available at www.nobel.se and in *Journal of Political Economy*, **101**(3), 385–409.

Domar, Evsey (1992), 'How I tried to become an economist', in Michael Szenberg (ed.), *Eminent Economists their Life Philosophies*, Cambridge: Cambridge University Press.

Febrero, Ramon and Pedro Schwartz (1995), *The Essence of Becker*, Stanford: Hoover Institution Press.

Friedman, Milton (1953a), 'The case for flexible exchange rates', in his *Essays in Positive Economics*, Chicago: University of Chicago Press, pp. 157–203.

Friedman, Milton (1953b), 'The methodology of positive economics', in his *Essays in Positive Economics*, Chicago: University of Chicago Press, pp. 3–43.

Friedman, Milton and Gary S. Becker (1957), 'A statistical illusion in judging Keynesian models', *Journal of Political Economy*, **65**(1), 64–75.

Fuchs, Victor R. (1994), 'Gary S. Becker: ideas about facts', *Journal of Economic Perspectives*, **8**, 183–92.

Grossman, Michael (1972), *The Demand for Health: A Theoretical and Empirical Investigation*, New York: Columbia University Press.

Hayek, Friedrich August von (1944), *The Road to Serfdom*, London: Routledge.

Hayek, Friedrich August von (1960), *The Constitution of Liberty*, Chicago: University of Chicago Press.

Hayek, Friedrich August von (1978), 'Two types of mind', in his *New Studies in Philosophy, Politics, Economics, and the History of Ideas*, Chicago: University of Chicago Press, pp. 50–56.

Knight, Frank H. and Thornton W. Merriam (1945), *Economic Order and Religion*, New York: Harper and Brothers.

Lazear, Edward P. (1999/2000), 'Economic imperialism', *Journal of Economics*, **115**, 99–146, also available as a Working Paper, Stanford University, Hoover Institution and Graduate School of Business, at http://faculty-gsb.stanford.edu/lazear/personal/pdfs/economic%20 imperialism.pdf.

Levitt, Steven D. (2006), 'Honoring Gary Becker: capital ideas', Chicago Graduate School of Business, April, available at www.chicagogsb.edu/ capideas/apr06/intro.aspx.

Nobel Foundation (1992), 'Presentation speech', in Torsten Persson (ed.) (1997), *Nobel Lectures, Economics 1991–1995*, Singapore: World Scientific Publishing, available at www.nobel.se.

Pies, Ingo and Martin Leschke (eds) (1998), *Gary Beckers ökonomischer Imperialismus*, Tübingen: Mohr Siebeck.

Rosen, Sherwin (1993), 'Risks and rewards: Gary Becker's contributions to economics', *Scandinavian Journal of Economics*, **95**(1), 25–36.

Samuelson, Paul (1948), *Economics*, New York: McGraw Hill.

Sandmo, Anders (1993), 'Gary Becker's contributions to economics', *Scandinavian Journal of Economics*, **95**(11), 7–23.

Shackelton, J.R. (1981), 'Gary S. Becker: the economist as empire-builder', in J.R. Shackleton and Gareth Locksley (eds), *Twelve Contemporary Economists*, London: Macmillan.

Stigler, George and Gary S. Becker (1977), 'De gustibus non est disputandum', *American Economic Review*, **67**, 76–90.

Douglass C. North

Coase, Ronald H. (1960), 'The problem of social cost', *Journal of Law and Economics*, **3**, 1–44.

David, Paul (1985), 'Clio and the economics of QUERTY', *American Economic Review Papers and Proceedings*, **75**(2), 332–7.

Davis, Lance E. and Douglass C. North (1971), *Institutional Change and American Economic Growth 1607–1860*, Cambridge: Cambridge University Press.

Goldin, Claudia (1995), 'Cliometrics and the Nobel', *Journal of Economic Perspectives*, **9**, 191–208.

Hayek, Friedrich August von (1945), 'The use of knowledge in society', *American Economic Review*, **35**, 519–30.

McCloskey, Donald N. (1994), 'Fogel and North: statics and dynamics in historical economics', *Scandinavian Journal of Economics*, **96**(2), 161–6.

Miller, Roger LeRoy and Douglass C. North (1971), *The Economics of Public Issues*, New York: Harper & Row. New edition: Roger LeRoy Miller, Daniel K. Benjamin and Douglass C. North (2007), *The Economics of Public Issues*, 15th edn, Boston, MA: Addison-Wesley.

Miller, Roger LeRoy, Daniel K. Benjamin and Douglass C. North (2007), *The Economics of Public Issues*, 15th edn, Boston, MA: Addison-Wesley.

Myhrman, J. and Barry R. Weingast (1994), 'Douglass C. North's contributions to economics and economic history', *Scandinavian Journal of Economics*, **96**(2), 185–93.

North, Douglass C. (1958), 'Ocean freight rates and economic development', *Journal of Economic History*, **18**(4), 537–55.

North, Douglass C. (1960), 'The United States balance of payments 1790–1860, Trends in the American economy in the nineteenth century', 24th Conference on Income and Wealth, NBER, Princeton: Princeton University Press.

North, Douglass C. (1961), *The Economic Growth of the United States, 1790–1860*, Englewood Cliffs, NJ: Prentice Hall.

North, Douglass C. (1966), *Growth and Welfare in the American Past: A New Economic History*, Englewood Cliffs, NJ: Prentice Hall.

North, Douglass C. (1968), 'Sources of productivity change in ocean shipping 1600–1850', *Journal of Political Economy*, **76**(5), 953–70.

North, Douglass C. (1977), 'The first economic revolution', *The Economic History Review*, New Series, **30**(2), 229–41.

North, Douglass C. (1978), 'Structure and performance: the task of economic history', *Journal of Economic Literature*, **16**(3), 963–78.

North, Douglass C. (1981), *Structure and Change in Economic History*, New York: W.W. Norton.

North, Douglass C. (1983), 'The second economic revolution in the United States', Proceedings on the Industrial Revolution and Technological Change, Washington University at St Louis (WUStL).

North, Douglass C. (1990), *Institutions, Institutional Change, and Economic Performance*, Cambridge: Cambridge University Press.

North, Douglass C. (1991), 'Institutions', *Journal of Economic Perspectives*, **5**, 97–112.

North, Douglass C. (1993/1994), 'Economic performance through time', Nobel Memorial Lecture, available at www.nobel.se and in *American Economic Review*, **84**, pp. 359–68.

North, Douglass C. (1993/2005/1994), 'Autobiography', in Tore Frängsmyr (ed.) *Les Prix Nobel, The Nobel Prizes 1993*, Stockholm: Nobel Foundation, available at www.nobel.se.

North, Douglass C. (1994), 'Institutions and credible commitment', *Journal of Institutional and Theoretical Economics*, **149**, S. 11–23.

North, Douglass C. (1995), 'The paradox of the West', in Richard W. Davis (ed.), *Origins of Modern Freedom in the West*, Stanford: Stanford University Press, pp. 7–34.

North, Douglass C. and Robert P. Thomas (1971), 'The rise and fall of the manorial system: a theoretical model', *Journal of Economic History*, **31**(4), 777–803.

North, Douglass C. and Robert P. Thomas (1973), *The Rise of the Western World: A New Economic History*, Cambridge: Cambridge University Press.

North, Douglass C. and Barry R. Weingast (1989), 'Constitutions and commitment: the evolution of institutions governing public choice in seventeenth-century England', *Journal of Economic History*, **49**(4), 803–32.

North, Douglass C., Barry Weingast and John Wallace (2006), 'A conceptual framework for interpreting recorded human history', NBER Working Paper 12795.

Reinhard Selten

Cournot, Antoine Augustin (1838), *Recherches sur les Principes Mathématiques de la Théorie des Richesses*, Paris: Hachette.

Damme, Eric van and Jörgen W. Weibull (1995), 'Equilibrium in strategic interaction: the contributions of John C. Harsanyi, John F. Nash and Reinhard Selten', *Scandinavian Journal of Economics*, **97**(1), 15–40.

Gul, Faruk (1997), 'A Nobel Prize for game theorists: the contributions of Harsanyi, Nash, and Selten', *Journal of Economic Perspectives*, **11**, 159–74.

Harsanyi, John C. and Reinhard Selten (1988), *A General Theory of Equilibrium Selection in Games*, Cambridge, MA: MIT Press.

Neumann, John von and Oskar Morgenstern (1944), *The Theory of Games and Economic Behavior*, Princeton: Princeton University Press.

Perlman, Mark and Morgan Marietta (1994), 'Die Nobelpreise der ökonomischen Wissenschaft in den Jahren 1994–1998', in Karl-Heinz Grüske (ed.), *Die Nobelpreisträger der ökonomischen Wissenschaft, Vol. 3: 1989–1993*, Düsseldorf: Wirtschaft und Finanzen, pp. 20–61.

Royal Swedish Academy of Sciences (1995), 'The Nobel Prize in Economics 1994', *Scandinavian Journal of Economics*, **97**(1), 1–7.

Sauermann, Heinz and Reinhard Selten (1959), 'Ein Oligopolexperiment', *Zeitschrift für die gesamte Staatswissenschaft*, **115**, 427–71.

Selten, Reinhard (1961), *Bewertung von n-Personenspielen*, Frankfurt: Universität Frankfurt.

Selten, Reinhard (1965), 'Spieltheoretische Behandlung eines Oligopolmodells mit Nachfrageträgheit', *Zeitschrift für die gesamte Staatswissenschaft*, **121**, 301–24 and 667–89.

Selten, Reinhard (1970), *Preispolitik der Mehrproduktenunternehmung in der Statischen Theorie*, Berlin/Heidelberg/New York: Springer.

Selten, Reinhard (1975), 'Reexamination of the perfectness concept for equilibrium points in extensive games', *International Journal of Game Theory*, **4**, 25–55.

Selten, Reinhard (1978), 'The chain store paradox', *Theory and Decision*, **9**, 127–59.

Selten, Reinhard (1988), *Models of Strategic Rationality*, Theory and Decision Library, Series C: *Game Theory, Mathematical Programming and Operations Research*, Dordrecht: Kluwer.

Selten, Reinhard (1990), 'Bounded rationality', *Journal of Institutional and Theoretical Economics*, **146**, 649–58.

Selten, Reinhard (1994/5), 'Autobiography', in Tore Frängsmyr (ed.), *Les Prix Nobel, The Nobel Prizes 1994*, Stockholm: Nobel Foundation, available at www.nobel.se.

Selten, Reinhard (1998), 'Aspiration adaptation theory', *Journal of Mathematical Psychology*, **42**, 191–214.

Selten, Reinhard (1999), *Game Theory and Economic Behaviour: Selected Essays*, 2 volumes, Cheltenham, UK and Northampton, MA: Edward Elgar.

Selten, Reinhard (2001), 'Die konzeptionellen Grundlagen der Spieltheorie einst und jetzt', Bonn Graduate School of Economics, Discussion Paper 2/2001.

Selten, Reinhard and Peter Hammerstein (1994), 'Game theory and evolutionary biology', in Robert J. Aumann and Sergiu Hart (eds), *Handbook of Game Theory*, vol. 2, Amsterdam: Elsevier Science, pp. 929–93.

Selten, Reinhard and Heinz Sauermann (1962), 'Anspruchsanpassungs-theorie der Unternehmung', *Zeitschrift für die gesamte Staatswissen-schaft*, **118**, 577–97.

Selten, Reinhard and R. Stoecker (1986), 'End behaviour in sequences of finite prisoners' dilemma supergames', *Journal of Economic Behavior and Organization*, **7**(1), 47–70.

Simon, Herbert (1947), *Administrative Behaviour*, New York: Macmillan.

Simon, Herbert (1957), *Models of Man*, New York: Wiley.

George A. Akerlof

Adams, William and Janet L. Yellen (1976), 'Commodity bundling and the burden of monopoly', *Quarterly Journal of Economics*, **90**(3), 475–98.

Akerlof, George A. (1967), 'Stability, marginal products, putty and clay', in Karl Shell (ed.), *The Theory of Optimal Economic Growth*, Cambridge, MA: MIT Press, pp. 281–94.

Akerlof, George A. (1970), 'The market for 'lemons': quality uncertainty and the market mechanism', *Quarterly Journal of Economics*, **84**, 488–500.

Akerlof, George A. (1976), 'The economics of caste and of the rat race and other woeful tales', *Quarterly Journal of Economics*, **90**, 599–617.

Akerlof, George A. (1980), 'A theory of social customs of which unem-ployment may be one consequence', *Quarterly Journal of Economics*, **94**, 749–75.

Akerlof, George A. (1982), 'Labour contracts as partial gift exchange', *Quarterly Journal of Economics*, **97**, 543–69.

Akerlof, George A. (1984), *An Economic Theorist's Book of Tales*, Cambridge: Cambridge University Press.

Akerlof, George A. (2001/2002a), 'Behavioral macroeconomics and mac-roeconomic behavior', Nobel Memorial Lecture, Nobel Foundation, available at www.nobel.se and in *American Economic Review*, **92**, 411–33.

Akerlof, George A. (2001/2002b), 'Autobiography', in Tore Frängsmyr (ed.), *Les Prix Nobel, The Nobel Prizes 2001*, Stockholm: Nobel Foundation, available at www.nobel.se.

Akerlof, George A. (2003), 'Writing the "the market for lemons": a per-sonal and interpretive essay', available at www.nobel.se.

Akerlof, George A. and Rachel E. Kranton (2002), 'Identity and school-ing: some lessons for the economics of education', *Journal of Economic Literature*, **40**, 1167–201.

Akerlof, George A. and Rachel E. Kranton (2005), 'Identity and the economics of organizations', *Journal of Economic Perspectives*, **19**(1), 9–32.

Akerlof, George A. and Janet L. Yellen (1985), 'A near rational model of the business cycle with wage and price inertia', *Quarterly Journal of Economics*, **100**, 823–88.

Akerlof, George A. and Janet L. Yellen (1986), *Efficiency Wage Models of the Labor Market*, Cambridge: Cambridge University Press.

Akerlof, George A., William T. Dickens and George L. Perry (1996a), 'The macroeconomics of low inflation', *Brookings Papers on Economic Activity*, **1**, 1–59.

Akerlof, George A., William T. Dickens and George L. Perry (2000), 'Near-rational wage and price setting and the long-run Phillips curve', *Brookings Papers on Economic Activity*, **1**, 1–44.

Akerlof, George A., Janet L. Yellen and Michael Katz (1996b), 'An analysis of out-of-wedlock childbearing in the United States', *Quarterly Journal of Economics*, **111**(2), 277–317.

Akerlof, George, Andrew K. Rose, Janet L. Yellen and Helga Hessenius (1991), 'East Germany in from the cold: the economic aftermath of currency union', *Brookings Papers on Economic Activity*, **1**, 1–105.

Arrow, Kenneth J. (1971), *Essays in the Theory of Optimal Risk Bearing*, Amsterdam: North Holland.

Boaz, David (1998), *Libertarianism*, New York: Free Press.

Caldwell, Bruce (2004), *Hayek's Challenge. An Intellectual Biography of F.A. Hayek*, Chicago: University of Chicago Press.

Edgeworth, Francis Ysidro (1889), 'The mathematical theory of political economy: review of Léon Walras, Eléments d'économie politique pure', *Nature*, **40**, September, pp. 434–6.

Galbraith, John Kenneth (1954), *The Great Crash 1929*, New York: Houghton Mifflin.

Gossen, Hermann Heinrich (1854), *Entwicklung der Gesetze des menschlichen Verkehrs und der daraus fliessenden Regeln für menschliches Handeln*, Braunschweig: Vieweg.

Hayek, Friedrich August von (1937), 'Economics and knowledge', *Economica*, **4**, 33–54.

Hayek, Friedrich August von (1945), 'The use of knowledge in society', *American Economic Review*, **35**, 519–30. Reprinted in his *Individualism and Economic Order*, Chicago: University of Chicago Press, pp. 77–91.

Hayek, Friedrich August von (1968/1978), 'Competition as a discovery procedure', in his *New Studies in Philosophy, Politics, Economics and the History of Ideas*, London: Routledge, pp. 179–90.

Löfgren, Karl-Gustaf, Thomas Persson and Jörgen W. Weibull (2002), 'Markets with asymmetric information: the contributions of George

Akerlof, Michael Spence and Joseph Stiglitz', *Scandinavian Journal of Economics*, **104**(2), 195–211.

Shlaes, Amity (2007), *The Forgotten Man: A New History of the Great Depression*, New York: HarperCollins.

Solow, Robert M. (1960), 'Investment and technological progress', in Kenneth J. Arrow, Samuel Karlin and Patrick Suppes (eds), *Mathematical Methods in the Social Sciences 1959*, Palo Alto: Stanford University Press, pp. 89–104.

Solow, Robert M. (1962), 'Substitution and fixed proportions in the theory of capital', *Review of Economics and Statistics*, **29**, 207–18.

Stigler, George J. (1961), 'The economics of information', *Journal of Political Economy*, **69**, 213–25.

Stiglitz, Joseph E. (1994), *Wither Socialism?*, Cambridge, MA: MIT Press.

Vernon L. Smith

Bergstrom, Theodore C. (2003), 'Vernon Smith's insomnia and the dawn of economics as experimental science', *Scandinavian Journal of Economics*, **105**(2), 181–205.

Binmore, Ken and Paul Klemperer (2005), 'The biggest auction ever: the sale of the British 3G Telecom licenses', *Economic Journal*, **112**, C74–C96.

Böhm-Bawerk, Eugen von (1891), *The Positive Theory of Capital*, London: Macmillan.

Chamberlin, Edward H. (1933), *The Theory of Monopolistic Competition*, Cambridge, MA: Harvard University Press.

Chenery, Hollis B. (1949), 'Engineering production functions', *Quarterly Journal of Economics*, **63**, 507–32.

Coppinger, Vicki M., Vernon L. Smith and Jon A. Titus (1980), 'Incentives and behaviour in English, Dutch, and sealed-bid auctions', *Economic Enquiry*, **18**, 1–18.

Hayek, Friedrich August von (1968/1978), 'Competition as a discovery procedure', in his *New Studies in Philosophy, Politics, Economics and the History of Ideas*, London: Routledge, pp. 179–90.

Hayek, Friedrich August von (1978), 'Two types of mind', in his *New Studies in Philosophy, Politics, Economics and the History of Ideas*, Chicago: University of Chicago Press, pp. 50–56.

Hayek, Friedrich August von (1979), *Law, Legislation, and Liberty*, Chicago: University of Chicago Press.

Miller, Ross M., Charles R. Plott and Vernon L. Smith (1977), 'Intertemporal competitive equilibrium: an empirical study of speculation', *Quarterly Journal of Economics*, **91**, 599–624.

Mises, Ludwig von (1949), *Human Action*, New Haven, CT: Yale University Press.

Plott, Charles R. and Vernon L. Smith (1978), 'An experimental examination of two exchange institutions', *Review of Economic Studies*, **45**, 133–53.

Rassenti, Stephen J., Vernon L. Smith and Robert L. Bulfin (1982), 'A combinatorial auction mechanism for airport time slot allocation', *Bell Journal of Economics*, **13**, 402–17.

Rassenti, Stephen J., Vernon L. Smith and Bart J. Wilson (2002), 'Using experiments to inform the privatization/deregulation movement in electricity', *The Cato Journal*, **21**, 515–44.

Samuelson, Paul A. (1947), *Foundations of Economic Analysis*, Cambridge, MA: Harvard University Press.

Smith, Vernon L. (1959), 'The theory of investment and production', *Quarterly Journal of Economics*, **73**, 61–87.

Smith, Vernon L. (1961), *Investment and Production*, Cambridge, MA: Harvard University Press.

Smith, Vernon L. (1962), 'An experimental study of competitive market behaviour', *Journal of Political Economy*, **70**, 111–37.

Smith, Vernon L. (1964), 'Effect of market organization on economic behaviour', *Quarterly Journal of Economics*, **87**, 181–203.

Smith, Vernon L. (1965), 'Experimental auction markets and the Walrasian hypothesis', *Journal of Political Economy*, **73**, 387–93.

Smith, Vernon L. (1967), 'Experimental studies of discrimination versus competition in sealed-bid auction markets', *Journal of Business*, **40**, 56–84.

Smith, Vernon L. (1968), 'Economics of production from natural resources', *American Economic Review*, **58**, 409–31.

Smith, Vernon L. (1971), *Economics of Natural and Environmental Economics*, New York: Gordon & Breach.

Smith, Vernon L. (1975), 'Economics of the primitive hunter culture with application to Pleistocene extinction and the rise of agriculture', *Journal of Political Economy*, **83**, 727–55.

Smith, Vernon L. (1976a), 'Experimental economics: induced value theory', *American Economic Review*, **66**, 274–9.

Smith, Vernon L. (1976b), 'Bidding and auctioning institutions: experimental results', in Yakov Amihud (ed.), *Bidding and Auctioning for Procurement and Allocation*, New York: New York University Press, pp. 43–64.

Smith, Vernon L. (1977), 'The principle of unanimity and voluntary consent in social choice', *Journal of Political Economy*, **85**(6), 1125–39.

Smith, Vernon L. (ed.) (1979), *Research in Experimental Economics*, vol. 1, Greenwich, CT: JAI Press.

Smith, Vernon L. (1980), 'Experiments with a decentralized mechanism for public goods decisions', *American Economic Review*, **70**, 584–99.

Smith, Vernon L. (ed.) (1982), *Research in Experimental Economics*, vol. 2, Greenwich, CT: JAI Press.

Smith, Vernon L. (ed.) (1985), *Research in Experimental Economics*, vol. 3, Greenwich, CT: JAI Press.

Smith, Vernon L. (1991a), *Papers in Experimental Economics*, Cambridge: Cambridge University Press.

Smith, Vernon L. (1991b), 'Rational choice: the contrast between economics and psychology', *Journal of Political Economy*, **99**(4), 877–97.

Smith, Vernon L. (1998a), 'Behavioral foundations of reciprocity. Experimental economics and evolutionary psychology', *Economic Inquiry*, **36**(3), 335–52.

Smith, Vernon L. (1998b), 'Do the rich get richer and the poor poorer? Experimental tests of a model of power', *American Economic Review*, **88**(4), 970–83.

Smith, Vernon L. (2002), 'The experimental economist', interview with Nick Gillespie and Michael W. Lynch for 'Reason Online', available at www.reason.com/news/show/32546.html.

Smith, Vernon L. (2002/2003a), 'Autobiography', in Tore Frängsmyr (ed.), *Les Prix Nobel. The Nobel Prizes 2002*, Stockholm: Nobel Foundation 2003, available at www.nobel.se.

Smith, Vernon L. (2002/2003b), 'Constructivist and ecological rationality in economics', Nobel Memorial Lecture, Nobel Foundation, available at www.nobel.se, and in *American Economic Review*, **93**, 465–508.

Smith, Vernon L. (2005), 'Hayek and experimental economics', *The Review of Austrian Economics*, **18**(2), 135–44.

Smith, Vernon L. (2007), 'Sustaining cooperation in trust games', *Economic Journal*, **117**, 991–1007.

Smith, Vernon L. (2008), *Discovery. A Memoir*, Bloomington, IN: Authorhouse.

Smith, Vernon L. and Arlington W. Williams (1981), 'On nonbinding price controls in a competitive market', *American Economic Review*, **71**, 467–74.

A very useful website with all the details about Vernon L. Smith's papers and a great number of downloadables is http://econpapers.repec.org/RAS/psm12.htm.

Edmund S. Phelps

Aghion, Philippe, Roman Frydman, Joseph Stiglitz and Michael Woodford (2001), 'Edmund S. Phelps and modern macroeconomics', in Philippe Aghion, Roman Frydman, Joseph Stiglitz and Michael Woodford (eds),

Knowledge, Information, and Expectations in Modern Macroeconomics: In Honor of Edmund S. Phelps, Princeton: Princeton University Press, pp. 3–22, also available online at http://press.princeton.edu/chapters/i2_7521.pdf.

Friedman, Milton (1968), 'The role of monetary policy', *American Economic Review*, **58**, 1–17.

Frydman, Roman and Edmund S. Phelps (eds) (1983), *Individual Forecasting and Aggregate Outcomes: 'Rational Expectations' Examined*, New York: Cambridge University Press.

Heertje, Arnold (ed.) (1999), *The Makers of Modern Economics*, Cheltenham, UK and Northampton, MA: Edward Elgar.

Keynes, John Maynard (1930), 'Economic possibilities for our grandchildren', in John Maynard Keynes (1963), *Essays in Persuasion*, New York: W.W. Norton, pp. 358–73.

Keynes, John Maynard (1963), *Essays in Persuasion*, New York: W.W. Norton.

Lucas, Robert E. (1972), 'Expectations and the neutrality of money', *Journal of Economic Theory*, **4**, 103–24.

Ordover, Janusz A. and Edmund S. Phelps (1975), 'Linear taxation of wealth and wages for intergenerational lifetime justice: some steady-state cases', *American Economic Review*, **65**, 660–673.

Ordover, Janusz A. and Edmund S. Phelps (1979), 'On the concept of optimal taxation in the overlapping-generations model of economic growth', *Journal of Public Economics*, **12**, 1–26.

Phelps, Edmund S. (1961), 'The golden rule of accumulation: a fable for growthmen', *American Economic Review*, **51**, 638–43.

Phelps, Edmund S. (1962), 'The accumulation of risky capital: a sequential utility analysis', *Econometrica*, **30**, 729–43.

Phelps, Edmund S. (1965a), 'Second essay on the golden rule of accumulation', *American Economic Review*, **55**, 793–814.

Phelps, Edmund S. (1965b), *Fiscal Neutrality Toward Economic Growth*, New York: McGraw-Hill.

Phelps, Edmund S. (1966a), *Golden Rules of Economic Growth*, New York: W.W. Norton.

Phelps, Edmund S. (1966b), 'Models of technical progress and the golden rule of research', *Review of Economic Studies*, **33**, 133–45.

Phelps, Edmund S. (1967), 'Phillips curves, expectations of inflation and optimal unemployment over time', *Economica*, **34**, 254–81.

Phelps, Edmund S. (1968a), 'Money-wage dynamics and labor-market equilibrium', *Journal of Political Economy*, **76**, 678–711.

Phelps, Edmund S. (1968b), 'Population increase', *Canadian Journal of Economics*, **35**, 497–518.

Phelps, Edmund S. (1969), 'The new microeconomics in inflation and employment theory', *American Economic Review, Papers and Proceedings*, **59**, 147–60

Phelps, Edmund S. (1970), 'Money-wage dynamics and labor-market equilibrium', revised version, in Edmund S. Phelps et al. (eds), *Microeconomic Foundations of Employment and Inflation Theory*, New York: W.W. Norton, pp. 124–66.

Phelps, Edmund S. (1972a), *Inflation Policy and Unemployment Theory*, New York: W.W. Norton.

Phelps, Edmund S. (1972b), 'The statistical theory of racism and sexism', *American Economic Review*, **62**, 659–61.

Phelps, Edmund S. (1973a), 'Taxation of wage income for economic justice', *Quarterly Journal of Economics*, **87**, 331–54.

Phelps, Edmund S. (1973b), 'Inflation in the theory of public finance', *Swedish Journal of Economics*, **75**, 67–82.

Phelps, Edmund S. (ed.) (1974), *Economic Justice*, Harmondsworth: Penguin.

Phelps, Edmund S. (1978a), 'Disinflation without recession: adaptive guideposts and monetary policy', *Weltwirtschaftliches Archiv*, **100**, 239–65.

Phelps, Edmund S. (1978b), 'Inflation planning reconsidered', *Economica*, **45**, 109–23.

Phelps, Edmund S. (1979), *Studies in Macroeconomic Theory, Vol. 1: Employment and Inflation*, New York: Academic Press.

Phelps, Edmund S. (1980), *Studies in Macroeconomic Theory, Vol. 2: Redistribution and Growth*, New York: Academic Press.

Phelps, Edmund S. (1983), 'The trouble with rational expectations and the problem of inflation stabilization', in Roman Frydman and Edmund S. Phelps (eds), *Individual Forecasting and Aggregate Outcomes: 'Rational Expectations' Examined*, Cambridge: Cambridge University Press, pp. 31–41.

Phelps, Edmund S. (1985), *Political Economy: An Introductory Text*, New York: W.W. Norton.

Phelps, Edmund S. (1994), *Structural Slumps: The Modern Equilibrium Theory of Employment, Interest, and Assets*, Cambridge, MA: Harvard University Press.

Phelps, Edmund S. (1995), 'A life in economics', in Arnold Heertje (ed.), *The Makers of Modern Economics*, vol. II, Cheltenham, UK, and Northampton, MA: Edward Elgar, pp. 90–113.

Phelps, Edmund S. (1997), *Rewarding Work: How to Restore Participation and Self-Support to Free Enterprise*, Cambridge, MA: Harvard University Press.

Phelps, Edmund S. (2000), 'Lessons in natural-rate dynamics', *Oxford Economic Papers*, **52**(1), 51–71.

Phelps, Edmund S. (2002), *Enterprise and Inclusion in the Italian Economy*, Boston, MA: Kluwer Academic Publishers.

Phelps, Edmund S. (ed.) (2003), *Designing Inclusion: Tools to Raise Low-end Pay and Employment in Private Enterprise*, Cambridge: Cambridge University Press.

Phelps, Edmund S. (2006), 'The genius of capitalism', *The Wall Street Journal of Europe*, 10 October, p. 12.

Phelps, Edmund S. (2006/2007a), 'Macroeconomics for a modern economy', Nobel Memorial Lecture, Nobel Foundation, available at www.nobel.se and in *American Economic Review*, **97**(3), 543–61.

Phelps, Edmund S. (2006/2007b), 'Autobiography', in Karl Grandin (ed.), *Les Prix Nobel, The Nobel Prizes 2006*, Stockholm: 2007, Nobel Foundation, available at www.nobel.se.

Phelps, Edmund S. and Jean-Paul Fitoussi (1988), *The Slump in Europe: Open Economy Theory Reconstructed*, Oxford: Basil Blackwell.

Phelps, Edmund S. and Richard R. Nelson (1966), 'Investments in humans, technological diffusion and economic growth', *American Economic Review, Papers and Proceedings*, **56**(1–2), 69–82.

Phelps, Edmund S. and Alberto Petrucci (2005), 'Capital subsidies versus labor subsidies: a trade-off between capital and employment?', *Journal of Money, Credit and Banking*, **37**(5), 907–22.

Phelps, Edmund S. and Robert A. Pollak (1968), 'On second-best national saving and game-equilibrium growth', *Review of Economic Studies*, **35**, 185–99.

Phelps, Edmund S. and John G. Riley (1978), 'Rawlsian growth: dynamic programming of capital wealth for intergeneration "Maximin" justice', *Review of Economic Studies*, **45**, 103–20.

Phelps, Edmund S. and Karl Shell (1970), 'Public debt, taxation and capital intensiveness', *Journal of Economic Theory*, **1**, 330–46.

Phelps, Edmund S. and John B. Taylor (1977), 'Stabilizing powers of monetary policy under rational expectations', *Journal of Political Economy*, **85**, 163–90.

Phelps, Edmund S. and Sidney G. Winter (1970), 'Optimal price policy under atomistic competition', in Edmund S. Phelps et al. (eds), *Microeconomic Foundations of Employment and Inflation Theory*, New York: W.W. Norton, pp. 309–37.

Phelps, Edmund S., Armen A. Alchian, Charles C. Holt et al. (eds) (1970), *Microeconomic Foundations of Employment and Inflation Theory*, New York: W.W. Norton.

Phillips, Alban W. (1958), 'The relation between unemployment and the rate of change of money wage rates in the United Kingdom 1861–1957', *Economica*, **25**, 283–9.

Rawls, John (1971), *A Theory of Justice*, Cambridge, MA: Belknap Press.

Samuelson, Paul A. (1948), *Economics*, New York: McGraw Hill.

Schelling, Thomas (1959), 'The reciprocal fear of surprise attack', RAND Corporation Paper 1342.

Index